Praise for *Backyard Garden Witc*

T0265840

"Laurel Woodward has done it again! Another beautiful boo
into pure magic. If you loved her book *Kitchen Witchery*, I promise you will to
yard Garden Witchery just as much." —**Raina Starr, host and producer of *Desperate House Witches* podcast**

"*Backyard Garden Witchery* is a delightful journey through an enchanted garden. Half love letter to the natural world, half tutorial for the novice or intermediate gardener, this book is an excellent resource for the budding green witch. *Backyard Garden Witchery* is chock full of information and ideas to inspire your own magickal garden. It features exercises and meditations for connecting to the spirits of the land, fauna, flora, and fungi around you. If you are longing to get your hands into the soil, this book is an excellent support for your journey into magickal gardening." —**Irene Glasse, author of *Blackfeather Mystery School: The Magpie Training***

"I was delighted to delve into Laurel Woodward's *Backyard Garden Witchery*, as someone who is looking to improve my gardening, loves to cook, and nerd out on botany—this book is a lovely collection of recipes, spells, and folklore that will keep you reading and re-reading throughout your life! A perfect book for any kitchen witch, green witch, gardener, or foodie!" —**Dean Jones, podcaster and food writer for *The Well-Seasoned Librarian* podcast**

"Whether you are a city dweller struggling to grow in your apartment, a beginning gardener and witch, or an experienced plant lover and practitioner, *Backyard Garden Witchery* will give you endless creative ways to reconnect and reinvent your relationship with nature. In this magical, poetic, and comprehensive guide on how you can craft and enjoy a garden in any environment, Laurel Woodward will inspire you to connect with the flow of energy in your own backyard like you never have before! This approachable, impressive, and artistic work will help anyone deepen their relationship with nature spirits in new, exciting, and engaging ways and deserves a permanent spot on every green witch's bookshelf!" —**Julia Halina Hadas, author of *WitchCraft Cocktails* and *Moon, Magic, Mixology***

BACKYARD GARDEN WITCHERY

About the Author

Laurel Woodward (Portland, OR) has been a witch for twenty years and is also a tarot reader. She has written for magazines and e-zines on the subjects of healthy living, organic gardening, sustainable living, and the magick of tapping into creative energy. She is the author of *Kitchen Witchery: Unlocking the Magick in Everyday Ingredients.*

LAUREL WOODWARD

BACKYARD
GARDEN
WITCHERY

Creating *Magickal* Space
Outside Your Door

Llewellyn Publications
Woodbury, Minnesota

Backyard Garden Witchery: Creating Magickal Space Outside Your Door © 2022 by Laurel Woodward. All rights reserved. No part of this book may be used or reproduced in any manner whatsoever, including internet usage, without written permission from Llewellyn Publications, except in the case of brief quotations embodied in critical articles and reviews.

FIRST EDITION
First Printing, 2022

Book design by Christine Ha
Cover design by Kevin R. Brown
Interior art on pages 27 & 28 by the Llewellyn Art Department

Llewellyn is a registered trademark of Llewellyn Worldwide Ltd.

Library of Congress Cataloging-in-Publication Data
Names: Woodward, Laurel, author.
Title: Backyard garden witchery : creating magickal space outside your door
   / Laurel Woodward.
Description: First edition. | Woodbury, MN : Llewellyn Worldwide, Ltd, 2022.
   | Includes bibliographical references and index. | Summary: "Covers not
   only the ins and outs of dirt types, zones, and sun exposure, but also
   the energy of plants, regions, and land spirits. Includes a compendium
   of plants and their magical and medicinal uses"-- Provided by publisher.
Identifiers: LCCN 2022011879 (print) | LCCN 2022011880 (ebook) | ISBN
   9780738770703 | ISBN 9780738770963 (ebook)
Subjects: LCSH: Gardening—Miscellanea. | Magic. | Witchcraft.
Classification: LCC BF1623.G37 W67 2022 (print) | LCC BF1623.G37 (ebook)
   | DDC 133.4/3—dc23/eng/20220401
LC record available at https://lccn.loc.gov/2022011879
LC ebook record available at https://lccn.loc.gov/2022011880

Llewellyn Worldwide Ltd. does not participate in, endorse, or have any authority or responsibility concerning private business transactions between our authors and the public.
   All mail addressed to the author is forwarded, but the publisher cannot, unless specifically instructed by the author, give out an address or phone number.
   Any internet references contained in this work are current at publication time, but the publisher cannot guarantee that a specific location will continue to be maintained. Please refer to the publisher's website for links to authors' websites and other sources.

Llewellyn Publications
A Division of Llewellyn Worldwide Ltd.
2143 Wooddale Drive
Woodbury, MN 55125-2989
www.llewellyn.com

Printed in the United States of America

Also by Laurel Woodward

Kitchen Witchery: Unlocking the Magick in Everyday Ingredients

Contents

Exercises, Spells, and Recipes

Kitchen Witchery Recipes

Garden Witchery

Disclaimer

Never use a plant unless you are 100 percent sure of its identity. Misidentifying a plant may result in injury, illness, and even death. Not all plants are friendly, and some are very poisonous. Experimenting with these plants can be dangerous. Some are dangerous in large doses or with extended use. Others may be harmful to pregnant women, children, or people with certain medical conditions. All should be treated with respect.

This book is not intended to provide medical advice or to take the place of medical advice and treatment from your personal physician. Readers are advised to consult their doctors or other qualified healthcare professionals regarding the treatment of their medical problems. Neither the publisher nor the author take any responsibility for any possible consequences from any treatment, action, or application of medicine, supplement, herb, or preparation to any person reading or following the information in this book.

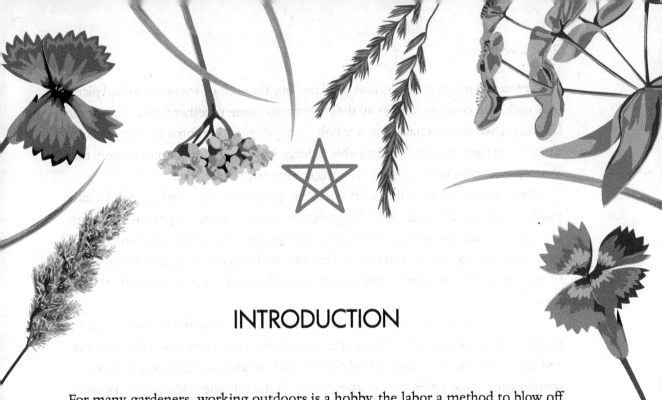

INTRODUCTION

For many gardeners, working outdoors is a hobby, the labor a method to blow off steam, ground out anxiety, and tone muscles on the quest to create something beautiful. And while it is all those things, for someone who practices an earth-based spirituality, the act of minding a garden is a vehicle to put spirituality into action. To observe the sprouting of a seed, the unfurrowing of a leaf, the opening of a newly discovered blossom fosters an awareness of life under the turning of the sun and the moon. The knowledge initiates communion with the earth and all its beings, large and small. It creates a dialog that enforces our awareness of our place in the great thrumming web of life and inspires an awareness of the natural year that syncs our own rhythms to the shifting seasons.

Caring for a garden connects us to the traditions of our individual ancestors and the practices they performed for thousands of years, as it reaches back through time to grant knowledge that is being lost. Tending a garden as your plants grow, to flower, fruit, and seed, is a way to forge a connection with nature that allows us to become grounded in the turning of the seasons as we bear witness to the land waking, becoming fruitful, and falling dormant again. It was this connection that inspired our calendar, founded our celebrations and observances, and kept ancient peoples alive.

A garden is not just a collection of plants but the sum of every individual plant, tree, rock, and creature, and as all these elements come together into a captivating landscape, we witness nature as a whole, a moving, awing force we recognize as deity. It is in these moments we are able to forge a spiritual connection to nature that elevates gardening from a chore to a joyous, expansive experience.

There is nothing quite like working in the garden as you mind a patch of land you have taken under your care. The garden becomes a magickal gateway transporting the gardener into a therapeutic zone that soothes the mind and nourishes the soul. Step through and you step out of routine and into the amazing natural world to work with the earth under the majestic blue sky, cool water at the ready to help something grow.

Your land is teeming with energy to heal, restore, and manifest just waiting to be focused. Draw a breath, close your eyes, open your senses, and you will feel it, raw and wild. We come to nature to feed our sense of wonder, to cultivate a deeper connection with the something more that resides in the otherness around us. Through day-to-day interaction you too can transform your yard into a place of healing, peace, and power, for nothing is sacred unless you make it so.

Creating a sacred outdoors space is a hands-on approach to putting nature back into your earth-based practice. When you deem part of your yard sacred space, it becomes a healing area you can visit on a daily basis simply by stepping into it, a personal sanctuary where you can step out of your busy life so that your mind can grow still and you may feel the presence of the gods.

My garden is my church, my everyday sanctuary where I commune with the wild gods. When I step through the door and come face-to-face with nature, it is a full-on sensory experience that pulls my thoughts from their brooding and sets them in the moment. Every sense becomes engaged as I emerge: the light fills my eyes with the vibrant colors all around; the scented breeze ruffles my hair and strokes my skin; birdsong fills my ears, dozens of voices united in one song that sings to my soul. The engagement creates a total shift as my mood lightens and my perception opens. It conjures up pure joy, and my chest unclenches so that I can draw a deep breath and smile as the power calls to me, a great swelling force that flows through all things, from the small energies underfoot, nestled in the rocks and hiding in the trees, to the genius loci dwelling in the very earth itself. There is great power in the knowledge that the land is alive, a keeper of an ancient wild magick that runs just beyond sight, but for those who pay attention, it can be felt and sometimes even smelled and tasted. It is in these moments when my energy soars, my perception opens, and I become a witness to the synchronicities at work all around me, that I am truly alive. Not just a cog in the wheel but a resonating, expanding, contributing, and oh so vibrant part of the fabric of the universe.

While the garden is a place of work, it is also a place of quiet contemplation, a place to rest and recharge, and a place to come to spirit. There is a restorative, energizing, inspiring magick in just being in the space. You will often find me quietly sitting on one of my garden benches, watching the shifting lights and shadows, and listening to the leaves stirring in the wind.

As I write this, it is September, the time I am most aware of the turning of the wheel as the season shifts from summer to fall. The nights begin to come quicker as the sun sets noticeably earlier. The cool morning air is charged with an exhilarating promise that change is coming. Now the vegetable garden is at its height of production. The tomato and zucchini plants are heavy with a multitude of fruit and are still flowering. There are newly opened blossoms on squash and pumpkin vines even as fat acorn and butternut squash line the ground. Just this morning, the round pumpkins nesting in the grass began to turn from green to orange. Ears of corn are growing plump on corn stalks that have begun to dry. They stir in the breeze and make a soft rustling sound as the wind comes up. A few bright sunflowers still stand tall, but most are downcast, ripe with seeds. A chickadee perches on top of the nearest and works to free a seed from the flower's face. Beyond the vegetable garden, a flock of birds feasts on ripe elderberries that fall in a shower as the birds dart from branch to branch. The air carries the calls of robins, towhees, crows, and a lone meadowlark. A woodpecker begins to rap on the maple just behind me, and I turn to see the last of the blackberries have grown ripe and are dropping to the ground in dark splats. Just beyond, pink and white blossoms cover hollyhock spires while bright red berries stud hawthorn branches and bittersweet vines. Bees crowd the maroon, pink, red, white, and yellow dahlia and cosmos flowers, while the bumblebees prefer the lavender and salvia blossoms.

A cool breeze stirs my hair. It swoops by, setting the maple's branches to shiver and rustle. Already the leaves of the box elder have begun to turn. A dozen yellow leaves pull free and fall in a bright shower. Fall will soon be here. All around me I can feel the shift. The air itself is charged with it. I can feel it on my skin, an energy with an electric buzz that whispers the promise of the coming change. Soon it will be Mabon, the fall equinox and the second harvest festival, marking the moment that the hours of light and the hours of darkness become equal. It won't be long before the nights grow long and dark and the world becomes cold. But right this moment, it is heaven in the garden.

For me, gardening isn't a hobby. It is a passion. I am constantly reading and learning from other gardeners' experiences, and when I first moved to the Pacific Northwest, I enrolled in Oregon State University's Master Gardener program to better understand the complexities and challenges of this new grow zone. I spend a large chunk of my time working the dirt, tending the living things, propagating plants from cuttings, saving seeds, and reaping the harvest. My garden provides me with produce, herbs, and flowers for food and my magickal practice. Growing plants is good for the body, mind, and soul. It feels good to be outside with your hands dirty with earth, a witness to the lives of the creatures sharing your space. It's an uplifting experience to watch something you helped grow become a strong plant and reward you in return with bright cheery flowers, herbs to cook with and empower your magick with, and fruit to eat. The joyful satisfaction at picking vegetables that you grew from seed and preparing and sharing them with your family creates a bond with your land that grows each time you spend time with it.

It is my hope that within these pages you find the inspiration to embrace the magick of gardening.

Part 1
The Magick Garden

Chapter 1

THE RESTORATIVE POWER OF NATURE

It is widely believed by researchers that spending time in nature restores the body, mind, and spirit.[1] We take comfort from immersing our senses in the natural world. Step into nature and life's complications fade. Walk beneath the open sky and the mind opens to the sensations of the warmth of the sun, the gusts of the bracing wind, or the refreshing scent and coolness of the rain. The spring of the soil underfoot promises the peace of sanctuary. The chatter of a squirrel overhead inspires curiosity. A moment of rest in the shade of a tree allows the body to relax as thoughts untangle and the soul becomes light and free.

Our brains evolved in nature. The scent of the woods, the sound of the wind in the trees, and the sensation of the lovely fresh air all work together to ground us in

....

1. A. Armstrong et al., "Why Society Needs Nature: Lessons from Research during Covid-19," Natural Resources Wales, Forest Research, Natural England, NatureScot, and the Environment Agency, 2021, https://www.forestresearch.gov.uk/documents/8053/Why_Society_Needs_Nature_4FUC2GT.PDF; Madhuleena Roy Chowdhury, "The Positive Effects of Nature on Your Mental Well-Being," *Positive Psychology* (blog), February 19, 2021, https://positivepsychology.com/positive-effects-of-nature/.

the moment. The song of birds calling around us lightens the heart. When we spend time in the natural world, life slows and worries are forgotten, but as human life became more and more modern, our relationship with nature became disconnected. According to the United Nations Department of Economic and Social Affairs, "Today, 55% of the world's population lives in urban areas."[2] Instead of working in a field beneath the sky, we drive to work or take mass transit. Instead of growing our food, we buy it at a market. As our cities became great stretches of asphalt and cement, our connection to nature became more tenuous than ever. We feel this separation in our deepest selves, and with a sense of urgency, we seek out natural areas to hike, camp, and practice forest bathing so that we might escape our modern lives and foster a mindful connection with the natural world.

Experiencing nature through our senses immerses us in an experience that opens a bridge to the natural world and allows us to understand that we are a part of something so much bigger. It takes us out of our small, overstressed lives and exposes us to a realness of something that is so much more. Being in nature brings our senses alive. And now research has begun to link our association with nature as positive therapy for a healthy mind, body, and spirit.[3] We now know a dose of green space, hiking through a forest, picnicking in a park, or meditating on a beach helps alleviate worry, anxiety, and depression. In an article for the Yale School of the Environment, Jim Robbins writes, "These studies have shown that time in nature—as long as people feel safe—is an antidote for stress: It can lower blood pressure and stress hormone levels, reduce nervous system arousal, enhance immune system function, increase self-esteem, reduce anxiety, and improve mood."[4] But the nature experience doesn't require a pilgrimage. It only takes a shift in perception to see that it is

2. United Nations Department of Economic and Social Affairs, "68% of the World Population Projected to Live in Urban Areas by 2050, Says UN," May 16, 2018, https://www.un.org/development/desa/en/news/population/2018-revision-of-world-urbanization-prospects.html.

3. Richard Louv, *Last Child in the Woods: Saving Our Children from Nature-Deficit Disorder* (Chapel Hill, NC: Algonquin Books, 2008), 3.

4. Jim Robbins, "Ecopsychology: How Immersion in Nature Benefits Your Health," *Yale Environment 360*, Yale School of the Environment, January 9, 2020, https://e360.yale.edu/features/ecopsychology-how-immersion-in-nature-benefits-your-health.

waiting just outside the window. The very land we inhabit thrums with life force. Your yard is teeming with potential to become your very own personal sanctuary. With a bit of effort, it can become a sacred place where you can build a relationship with the green world around you, where your inner self and spirituality can grow. By introducing garden elements into the space, whether an expansive lawn bordered with flowers or a woodland setting dappled in shade, you can create a sanctuary to fortify your sense of well-being and establish an emotional connection with nature that grounds you in the seasons.

When we work with the earth, we reinforce our link to her as we become witness to the vastness and power of nature around us. The act of gardening becomes a vehicle to restore wellness as it brings us to spirit. It allows us to rediscover awe and reclaim our relationship with the world as a whole. And studies are proving that the act of working with the earth under the blue sky and helping something grow is very therapeutic. Time spent outdoors boosts mental acuity, creativity, and intelligence.[5] A 2007 study in the journal *Neuroscience* found that exposure to *Mycobacterium vaccae*, a bacterium found in dirt, boosts the levels of serotonin circulating in the systems of mice.[6] Serotonin is the neurotransmitter that affects sleep cycles, mood, and memory. Low levels of serotonin are linked to aggression, anxiety, and depression. Many gardeners already know that running their naked finger through the soil not only makes their spirits soar but grounds them in the shifting of the seasons. Now science is saying that by digging in the dirt and breathing deep the scent of rich soil, we dose ourselves like taking antidepressant pills.[7]

While working outside makes us feel alive, there is another great gratifying magick in gardening. I feel it each time I admire a new flower, harvest a tomato, or

. . . .

5. Richard Louv, *The Nature Principle: Reconnecting with Life in a Virtual Age* (Chapel Hill, NC: Algonquin Books, 2011), 27.

6. C. A. Lowry et al., "Identification of an Immune-Responsive Mesolimbocortical Serotonergic System: Potential Role in Regulation of Emotional Behavior," *Neuroscience* 146, no. 2 (May 2007): 756–72. doi:10.1016/j.neuroscience.2007.01.067.

7. Pagan Kennedy, "How to Get High on Soil," *Atlantic*, January 31, 2012, https://www.theatlantic.com/health/archive/2012/01/how-to-get-high-on-soil/251935/; Catharine Paddock, "Soil Bacteria Work in Similar Way to Antidepressants," Medical News Today, April 2, 2007, https://www.medicalnewstoday.com/articles/66840#1.

clip an herb, knowing I am the cocreator of something beautiful, something that teems with life force and holds the power to manifest abundance, and I too become restored. You become a part of the magick each time you witness a seed that you planted peek through the soil as it becomes a young sprout. The experience fills the heart with a childlike joy, lifting mood and elevating spirit to know the tiny new life was fostered by your very own efforts. The joy prompts an acknowledgment. "I see you. Welcome! Grow well and strong." It is pure positive energy, a great reclaiming of power as we reclaim that ability to heal the earth, even if it is our one small plot.

For thousands of years humans have been cultivating plants, influencing and altering their evolution. We formed a bond with plants that directly affects our well-being. Yet a disturbing trend has come to light, something botanists Elisabeth Schussler and James Wandersee termed "plant blindness," or "the inability to see or notice the plants in one's own environment."[8] As technology takes up more of our lives, we are not just losing the ability to identify individual plants; we are losing our relationship with them, and some people are even losing their ability to see them. Yet it is our relationship with plants that keeps us healthy. "Plants communicate directly with our immune system and unconscious" mind, writes biologist Clemens G. Arvay.[9] By getting outside and creating our own natural places and spending time with the flora and fauna in them, we are able to establish a personal connection to nature, one in which we become aware of the changing seasons, and as we step out of ourselves, we find we become *more*.

. . . .

8. Christine Ro, "Why 'Plant Blindness' Matters—And What You Can Do About It," BBC Future, April 28, 2009, https://www.bbc.com/future/article/20190425-plant-blindness-what-we-lose-with-nature-deficit-disorder.

9. Clemens G. Arvay, *The Biophilia Effect: A Scientific and Spiritual Exploration of the Healing Bond Between Humans and Nature* (Boulder, CO: Sounds True, 2018), 5–6.

Exercise
Appreciate the Beauty of Nature

Immersing our senses in nature has a profound effect upon our mood and our sense of self. When we turn off our thoughts, step out of the busyness of our lives, and focus our attention on nature's beauty, a magickal thing happens as our mood lightens, the heart swells with gratitude, and thoughts become happy. When you slip into a present and receptive state, the perception of the smallest things, such as the details of a flower, the dance of a bee, and the flitting of a butterfly, all hold the power to fill the heart with joy and the mind with wonder. Nature is beautiful. When we allow ourselves to observe this beauty, we ourselves are affected.

Step out into your yard without any electronic devices. Go to a wild but comfortable place in your yard where you can be alone. This can be under a tree, beside a flower bed, or even on a step as long as you can view nature from your position. Sit down and relax.

When you are comfortable, close your eyes and tune your senses in to listen to the sounds around you. Listen to the wind rushing through the trees, listen to the voices of the birds. Move your attention to your skin. Is it being warmed by the sun or cooled by the wind? Take a moment to notice how it feels.

Open your eyes and know that the land is alive. As light fills your eyes, be present with the moment, listening, looking, drinking in the sights and sounds and the way you feel to be right there in the moment. Mindfully observe the life around you. Breathe deeply and allow the moment to swell with the beauty and majesty of nature. Surrender yourself to the moment. Allow your heart to swell with happiness and appreciation. Let it fill you with mesmerizing wonder, and as your heart opens, smile. Be thankful for the moment. Allow gratitude to fill your center and smile.

Return to repeat this exercise as often as you are able.

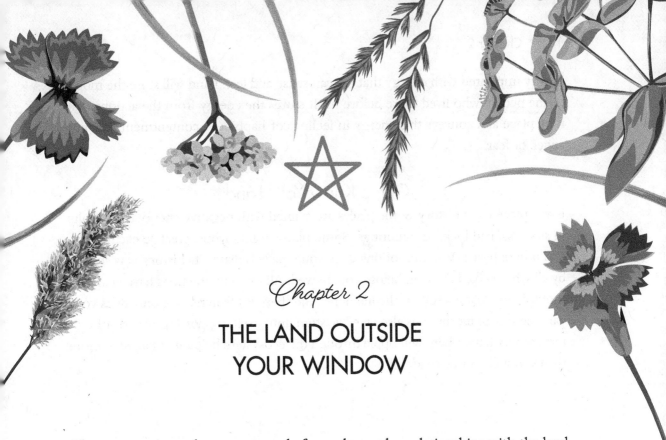

Chapter 2

THE LAND OUTSIDE
YOUR WINDOW

There was a time when most people formed complex relationships with the land they inhabited. They were aware of their land and the happenings taking place on it and formed a deep attachment with it. Each piece of land had its own sense of place that became a part of a person's identity.[10] Working the land contributed meaning to who you were and what you did, as it granted stability and ultimately enhanced well-being. Today, for many of us, the focus has shifted to harried work and school schedules, and many have lost touch with the natural world. The land has gone ignored. Instead, we have filled our lives with busy, hollow, artificial experiences lacking in authenticity that leave us yearning for more. But the land is alive. It thrums with energy to heal, renew, and create, each plot with its own personality, and not all are friendly. You have probably experienced this. Have you ever gone somewhere and wanted to turn right around and leave? Have you ever walked into a tranquil space where you instantly felt relaxed? That is because each plot of land has a long

....
10. Louv, *The Nature Principle*, 120.

history imprinted with energy that we can sense and feel. Land will store the mood of the people who lived there before us. It stores the energy from the actions that took place and conveys this energy in feelings of happiness, contentment, anxiety, anger, or fear.

Get to Know Your Land

Every place has a history. Some places are stained with negative energy that results in sickness, bad luck, or hauntings. Some places hold joyous, creative excitement, and others peace. What emotions does your space radiate? Its history was shaped by all who walked the land before you arrived. All these interactions have changed, molded, and taken a toll on the life here. And there is life here. Not only does your yard teem with life, but it is also an ecosystem unto itself, supporting all sorts of critters. Your behavior here will ripple through the ecosystem helping or harming more than you will ever be aware of.

Exercise
Solitary Walk

In this exercise, you will take a solitary walk to acquaint yourself with your land.

You will need:
- ★ notebook
- ★ pen
- ★ quiet mindful attention

Leave your phone inside and take only a notebook and a pen. Begin with a few deep breaths as you quiet your spirit and allow your perception to sharpen. When you are fully present, go outside and begin walking the boundary of your area.

Give the walk your full attention. Make note of what you see, hear, and smell and how it makes you feel. Allow yourself to react to what you encounter. If you meet a beautiful flower, call out a greeting. "Oh hello, beauty. I see you." If you come across something disturbing, give voice to your emotional response, then let the feeling go as you note down the experience.

Natural areas are homes to presences and powers that we are often unaware of. If you feel one, introduce yourself. Try to make a friend. They could become an important ally, guardian, or teacher in your spiritual practice. Pay attention to any feelings that come up and write them in your notebook.

Be on the lookout for areas that resonate power. Every stretch of land generates a reaction, some stronger than others. It may be the awe of a captivating view, the sense of tranquility of an open glade, a sensually scented curving pathway, or a secreted nook veiled in dappled shade. As you walk your yard, pause to stand quietly in each area and open your senses by drawing your attention in to what you can see, hear, smell, and feel. If you come across an area that speaks to you and holds your interest more than the other areas, treat this as your power place. Name the area. When we name something, we add to and help shape its power. Place something to mark the area to signify that it is different, or *more*, than the surrounding space. You may want to mark the area with a bench to establish that this is your sitting place to observe, think, and meditate or place a statue or an altar to signify the specialness of the area.

Grounding

When you have finished your walk, review your notes. If you encountered any feelings of anger, fear, or worry, you might want to perform a meditation to heal and clear the area. If you are not familiar with using basic meditation techniques to move and direct energy, you will want to get comfortable performing a meditation to ground energy before you attempt a healing.

The act of grounding refers to entering a meditative state to connect with the energy of the earth to release excess energy, neutralize chaotic energy, or balance our body's energy. Through grounding, one can also draw earth energy up to fuel an action, heal, or restore. With the mastery of this next exercise, you will learn to form an energetic connection with the earth, sense the subtle energies present, move them, and direct them.

Exercise
Meditation to Ground

Turn off your electronic devices and settle comfortably in a quiet place where you will not be disturbed. (Every meditation exercise requires a complete disconnect, as meditation is the act of stilling the mind to gain power over distraction.) If you are able to, kick off your shoes and place your bare feet against the earth. With your back straight, sit on the ground, sit in a chair, or stand. Assume the position that feels right to you, a position in which you can rest comfortably for an extended period of time. Slowly draw in a deep, even breath to the count of three. Focus on your breath. Follow it as it enters your body. Notice how your chest expands and rises. Notice how your body feels. Don't allow other thoughts to distract you. Keep your mind solely focused on what it feels like in this moment. When your lungs are fully expanded, hold the breath for the count of three. Then slowly release it, exhaling out to the count of three. This is the meditative breath, the mindful or "conscious breath."

Do it again. Inhale. Focus on your breath as you draw air into your lungs. Notice as your chest expands. Allow the muscles in your head, face, neck, and shoulders to relax. If you are holding any tension, release it as you exhale. If a thought interferes, just notice it and let it go as you gently move your attention back to your breath. Soon you will notice a deep sense of relaxation fill your limbs as your awareness begins to sharpen and expand.

When you have reached a meditative state, move your focus down to where your body meets the floor. If you are sitting cross-legged, this will most likely be the base of your spine. If you are sitting in a chair or standing, this will be your feet. Visualize roots or tendrils slowly unfurling from this place. See your roots extending as they reach down to meet and sink beneath the soil. Send your tendrils down through the cool, nourishing, secure soil. Feel your roots travel down until they meet a simmering pool of earth energy that is waiting beneath the surface. Visualize the energy as a lovely cool light that pools around your roots. Inhale, and as you draw in your breath, draw the energy up your roots, like a straw. See the energy flowing up through your roots, glowing as it flows up into your body. Inhale and draw the cool, healing energy up with your breath until it floods up your spine to fill your core. Breathe and pull the energy, drawing it up into your chest, then your throat, until it spills out the top of your head. See it spill down over your aura to sink back into the earth again. Breathe and run the energy loop, allowing it to nourish and refresh your body and spirit.

If you feel anxious, aggressive, or simply negative, you can run this exercise in reverse to "ground" the excessive energy you've absorbed. Your spine, feet, and head are not the only expulsion points. You can also send energy out or pull it in through your hands. To ground through your palms, sit cross-legged on the floor or in a chair with your hands resting parallel to each other and facing the ground. Close your eyes and visualize roots slowly extending from the base of your spine or your feet. Send them down through the soil until they meet a pool of energy. Begin running the energy by drawing it up your roots as you draw in your breath. Inhale and draw the energy up your spine to fill your center. Visualize the energy concentrating at your center, which could be in your chest or lower in your belly. Let it pool in the area that feels right to you. When you have a pool of glowing energy at your center, release it with your breath by moving the energy as you exhale, pushing it down into your arms, into your hands, and through your palms to pour out into the ground. This is a handy visualization to employ after spellwork if you are left feeling light-headed or scattered and need to release any leftover energy.

Healing the Land

Look at the area that needs healing and make a list of things you can do to restore it. Begin by clearing away the clutter. This could be as easy as picking up trash or more intensive like hauling away refuse. Look at the health of the plants in the area. Cut out and remove any that are dead. Cut out and dispose of any plants that are diseased.

Look at the ground. If there are any holes, you should fill them in and rake them over. Clean up what needs to be cleared away to instigate new energy flow. When the area has been cleared, you can do a healing.

Spell
Water Blessing to Cleanse and Heal

You will need:
* ⋆ clean water from a natural source (rainwater, spring water, or well water)
* ⋆ bowl or bucket

Rinse the bowl or bucket and fill it with the water you are going to bless. Take the water and go out to the site and communicate your intentions. Tell the area what you would like to accomplish. Ask permission to begin. Then begin your meditation.

Settle into a comfortable position where you can work easily with the water. You can perform this meditation sitting on the ground with the water in front of you or holding it in your lap. If it is more comfortable, you may wish to sit in a chair or even standing with the water in front of you. Choose the position that feels right to you and draw yourself up so that your back is straight. If you are sitting in a chair or standing, you will want to plant your feet firmly on the earth.

To begin, tell the space,

> *I am sorry. Please let me help you release the harm.*
> *Release the pain. Release the past.*
> *I offer you love in its place. Together we will start anew.*
> *With your permission, I commence this healing.*

Draw a few deep breaths as you let go of the concept of time. Slowly draw in a deep, even breath to the count of three. Focus on your breath. Follow it as it enters your body. Notice how your chest expands and rises. Notice how your body feels. Don't allow other thoughts to distract you. Keep your mind solely focused on what it feels like right there in that moment. When your lungs are fully expanded, hold the breath for the count of three. Then slowly release it, exhaling out to the count of three.

Do it again. Inhale. Focus on your breath as you draw air into your lungs. Notice as your chest expands. Allow the muscles in your head, face, neck, and shoulders to relax. If you are holding any tension, release it as you exhale. If a thought interferes, just notice it and let it go as you gently move your attention back to your breath.

When you have reached a meditative state, as your limbs relax and your awareness begins to sharpen and expand, move your focus down to your feet. Visualize your roots or tendrils slowly extending from your feet. See them as they travel down out of your feet to meet and sink beneath the soil. Send your tendrils down through the cool, nourishing, secure soil. Feel them reach down until they find a simmering pool of earth energy that is waiting beneath the surface. Visualize the energy as a lovely cool light that pools around your tendrils. Inhale, and as you draw in your breath, draw the energy up your tendrils, like a straw. See the energy flowing up through your tendrils, glowing as it flows up into your feet, up your legs, and up your spine to fill your center. Let your heart fill with gratitude. When you are ready, reach your hands out over the water and direct the earth energy to flow down your arms, out through your palms to spill into the bucket or bowl.

If you have trouble getting the energy to flow, you can use your breath to push it. Draw a deep breath and use your exhalation to push the energy where you want it to go. Breathe and run the energy until it has flooded the water with nourishing earth energy. See the energy change the water so that it glows and shimmers with all the colors of the rainbow. Bless the water by saying,

> *By the healing energy of the earth, you are now blessed.*
> *By the earth, you are blessed.*
> *You are blessed.*

When you feel the water is ready, move your attention to the space that needs healing and say something like, "Accept this gift of healing."

Pour out the water on the space you are healing and say,

> *Allow this water to wash away all the anger and the fear.*
> *With this water, all that is negative clears away.*
> *By the energy of the earth, you are blessed.*

Forgive the past and release it.
Let love reside in its place.
Allow yourself to be healed.
Be healed.
Be healed.

When you are ready to end the meditation, announce,

By the healing, nurturing energy of the earth, you are healed.

Chapter 3

WORKING WITH
WHAT YOU HAVE

Location, location, location. A lot of your gardening success will depend on whether or not the location of your garden provides the basic necessities for what is going to live in it. Two of the most basic needs to consider are the availability of water and sunlight. During dry or hot months, most gardens require regular supplemental waterings. Be sure the site you are considering has easy access to water.

The next thing on your checklist is to determine the amount of sunlight exposure the area gets. Each location of your yard has its own specific conditions that create a microclimate based on the amount and length of sun and shade exposure the area receives. Each and every plant has its own specific sunlight requirement. A woodland plant needs to be planted under the shelter of trees and will burn if planted in an area with too much sun exposure. Most garden flowers and vegetable plants require at least six hours of bright, full sun exposure to flower and fruit.

Determine Your Available Sunlight Exposure Zones

What do you have to work with? Each area of your garden will have different amounts of sun and shade throughout the day. By mapping out where the sunlight falls in your yard and how many hours it shines there, you will discover what areas are considered to have full sun exposure, partial sun exposure, and dappled or full shade. Sunlight intensity is determined by whether the sun is direct or filtered. Morning sun is not as hot or intense as afternoon sun exposure. Dappled sun is a term to describe sunlight that is filtered through an object that casts a shadow, like the leaves on a tree.

Full Sun: At least six hours of direct sunlight, with most of them being between 11 a.m. and 4 p.m.

Partial Sun: Three to six hours of direct sun, often morning sun.

Full Shade: Less than three hours of sunlight.

Dappled Sun: Sunlight that is filtered through tree leaves, arbors, bush branches, or tall fence slats.

Exercise
Make a Sun Map

You will need:
* 12 colored pencils
* map of your plot

Either sketch out your yard or print out a photo of your plot from Google Maps. Next, figure out your compass points and mark them on the map. The sun rises in the east and travels across the sky to set in the west, which means in the Northern Hemisphere, areas with a southern exposure will get more sun than ones with a morning or northern exposure. Next, mark the place each tree stands in your yard. Your trees are most likely to be the oldest residents of your yard. An older tree is a warehouse of knowledge and can act as guardian and ally in your quest to create sanctuary, but it will also create shade, and if all your trees are on the south side of your property line, then anytime they are in full leaf, they will be creating a shaded yard.

Take a day to observe the hours of daylight your yard actually gets. Plan to go out every 2 hours throughout the day to note which areas of your yard are in sun and which are in shadow. Make a color key on your map to represent the hour. Designate 6 colors for shade and 6 colors for sun and assign each a time period. Beginning in the morning, take the map out and mark the areas that are sunlit and the areas that are shaded. Two hours later, use the next pair of colored pencils to mark the sunny areas and also the shady places. Repeat this process every 2 hours and at the end of the day, you will have a map detailing how much sun each part of your yard gets.

If you are mapping in the winter or spring, take note of the trees, as many deciduous trees will not have their leaves.

Consider the Dirt

The type of soil in your garden and the health of it are the key factors to growing healthy plants. A plant needs to carry air from the atmosphere down to its root tips to respire. It moves water and oxygen through the air pockets around the roots. This process is impeded if the soil is too heavy. On the other hand, if the soil is too sandy, it will not hold enough water for a plant to absorb.

Take up a handful and look at your soil. Is it sand, loam, or clay? Soil type refers to the coarseness of the soil, or the combination of particles of sand, silt, and clay. The optimal soil is composed of a balance of the three so that both air and water can pass through easily. Soils with too much sand drain too fast and are subject to drought, while soils high in clay lock in water and air.

Exercise
Dirt Testing

Perform this simple test to see what kind of soil you have.

You will need:
- ⋆ clean, empty jar with a lid
- ⋆ clean water
- ⋆ soil sample

Fill the jar ⅓ full with the soil. Add water until the jar is filled halfway. Seal the jar with the lid and shake it vigorously. Then set the jar aside overnight. The next morning, without disturbing your jar, examine it to determine your soil type.

Sand: Clear water with the soil settled at the bottom.

Loam: Slightly cloudy water with bits of matter suspended in it floating above the settled soil.

Clay: Murky water with a visible layer of sediment at the bottom of the jar.

While every gardener hopes for rich, sandy loam filled with earthworms and castings, it usually requires a bit of work to achieve. My lot is on a gently sloping hill. At the top, the soil is rich and loamy and alive with earthworms, sow bugs, beetles, and centipedes. The bottom of my lot is composed of very heavy clay. Like me you may have different types of soil in different parts of your yard. Mark your soil types on your sun map so that you have a record of what areas of your yard have the best soil to work with.

Hardiness Zones and Growing Seasons

Every US gardening catalog and gardening manual refers to hardiness zones. By applying this information, gardeners can judge whether a plant or plant group will survive the climate in their area. By applying the information provided by zone maps, a gardener gains a much higher success rate. To find your hardiness zone, use the following chart. Find out your area's lowest temperatures and use the corresponding information to find your zone. Before you plant, be sure to read about the plants you want to grow. If they are not hardy to your zone, then think twice before spending money on them, or understand that you will need to dig them up and bring them in to overwinter.

Zone	Average Annual Minimum Temperature	Length of Growing Season
1a	-60 to -55 degrees F	30 days
1b	-55 to -50 degrees F	
2a	-50 to -45 degrees F	90 days
2b	-45 to -40 degrees F	
3a	-40 to -35 degrees F	120 days
3b	-35 to -30 degrees F	
4a	-30 to -25 degrees F	125 days
4b	-25 to -20 degrees F	
5a	-20 to -15 degrees F	165 days
5b	-15 to -10 degrees F	
6a	-10 to -5 degrees F	180 days
6b	-5 to 0 degrees F	
7a	0 to 5 degrees F	180 days
7b	5 to 10 degrees F	

Zone	Average Annual Minimum Temperature	Length of Growing Season
8a	10 to 15 degrees F	245 days
8b	15 to 20 degrees F	
9a	20 to 25 degrees F	265 days
9b	25 to 30 degrees F	
10a	30 to 35 degrees F	335 days
10b	35 to 40 degrees F	
11a	40 to 45 degrees F	365 days
11b	45 to 50 degrees F	
12a	50 to 55 degrees F	365 days
12b	55 to 60 degrees F	
13a	60 to 65 degrees F	365 days
13b	65 to 70 degrees F	

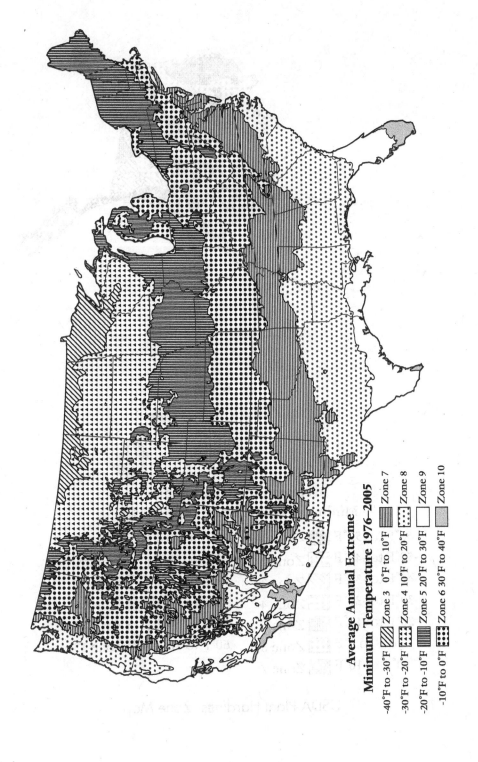

Average Annual Extreme
Minimum Temperature 1976–2005

-40°F to -30°F   Zone 3   0°F to 10°F   Zone 7

-30°F to -20°F   Zone 4   10°F to 20°F   Zone 8

-20°F to -10°F   Zone 5   20°F to 30°F   Zone 9

-10°F to 0°F   Zone 6   30°F to 40°F   Zone 10

USDA Plant Hardiness Zone Map

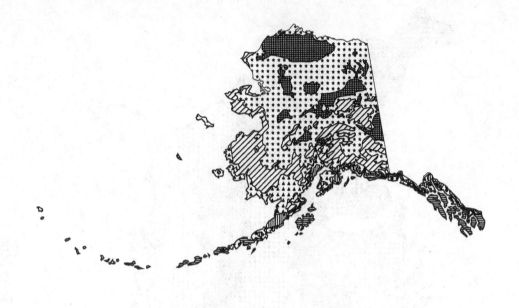

Average Annual Extreme
Minimum Temperature 1976–2005

-60°F to -50°F	Zone 1	10°F to 20°F	Zone 8
-50°F to -40°F	Zone 2	20°F to 30°F	Zone 9
-40°F to -30°F	Zone 3	30°F to 40°F	Zone 10
-30°F to -20°F	Zone 4	40°F to 50°F	Zone 11
-20°F to -10°F	Zone 5	50°F to 60°F	Zone 12
-10°F to 0°F	Zone 6	60°F to 70°F	Zone 13
0°F to 10°F	Zone 7		

USDA Plant Hardiness Zone Map

Know the Length of Your Growing Season

A growing season is the period of the year that is suited for plants to grow successfully. Some areas have a short-season climate that makes it impossible to grow warm-season crops. Some plants are quick to mature, while others require a long growing season. Knowing the length of your growing season will help you determine what kinds of plants to include in your garden.

Knowing the length of your growing season is especially important when you grow plants from seed. Crops like radish, spinach, lettuce, and peas are quick to mature and do not require a lengthy growing season. Long-season tender crops like cantaloupe, cucumber, eggplant, okra, peppers, and watermelon will not grow as successfully in an area without a long growing season.

Most seed packets list the number of days the seeds need to germinate and reach maturity. While plants grow well here in Oregon, the growing season isn't terribly long. The nights are too cool for most warm weather flower and vegetable seeds to germinate until summer. To get a jump on the season, I extend it by starting seeds inside. Even so, some crops like cantaloupe and watermelon will sprout but refuse to grow.

You will save on money, effort, and aggravation if you figure out your growing season and stick to plants that will live vigorously within it.

Chapter 4

MEET THE OTHER RESIDENTS

Your garden plan is going to affect everyone who shares your space, so before you begin any changes, get familiar with the life that is going on in the space. Sit down in a comfortable viewing spot and note what creatures visit. If your yard is a healthy biome, it will be home to many residents. As I got to know my yard, I discovered I had two resident robin families, a blue jay family, and a female skunk who had made her home under the shed. As summer warmed, flocks of bushtits, nuthatches, and chickadees and a group of squirrels were frequent visitors, while a large raccoon occasionally kept watch from the maple tree. At night a chorus of frogs filled the summer night with song. In mid-June I was greeted with a thrilling sight when momma skunk ushered five frisky babies to the porch to eat from the cat's dish. It was a delight to bear witness to all the life in the yard.

As we design our sacred places, we need to be humane gardeners, aware of the other lives our actions will impact. Try to embrace the existing elements and add them to your schemes. Every plant, animal, stone, bird, bee, and flower can add to the wonder of a setting if only we take the time to consider the role of each. As you begin to interact with nature, you will come to realize how precious her denizens are. It is wrong not to acknowledge the other creatures sharing the space.

Gardening is much easier and much more rewarding if you let nature guide your actions. If you create space for wildlife, its presence will add to the charm and function of your garden. A bank of wildflowers will draw nectar-feeding pollinators as well as insects to feed on the bugs you don't want. A birdbath or bird feeder will attract birds to grace your garden, while a pond will provide water for all and attract frogs and toads, small hunters who will patrol for bugs and slugs.

Opening the Senses to Nature

There is a reason the Pagan, the druid, and the witch all venerate nature. There is also a reason why nature-based systems of worship still persist. Energy abounds in nature. Being outdoors acts as a catalyst to open the senses. One merely has to step outside to make the connection. Let your spirit quiet. Hug a tree. Open yourself to its gentle grounding energy. Sit with your back to its trunk and meditate. Your practice will become sacred as you cultivate relationships with the inhabitants of your yard. Starhawk writes in *The Earth Path*, "A Witch must not only be familiar with the mystic planes of existence beyond the physical realm; she should also be familiar with the trees and plants and birds and animals of her own backyard, be able to name them, know their uses and habits and what part each plays in the whole."[11]

As you develop a relationship with your garden, you will foster a deeper relationship with nature. Even a small garden will forge a sense of solitude and sanctuary if you spend time with it to become witness to the life systems unfolding under your nose. When you work with nature and do not try to dominate her, the experience becomes joyous as you discover that the process not only changes your yard but changes you as well. Your knowledge will deepen, and your spirituality will grow as you witness the intricacies of your garden's web of life as it goes through the changing seasons of the year.

. . . .

11. Starhawk, *The Earth Path: Grounding Your Spirit in the Rhythms of Nature* (San Francisco, CA: HarperCollins, 2004), 7.

Exercise
Silent Observation

This small ritual allows you to reconnect with nature by coming to awareness of the interconnectedness of the natural world. This is an introduction to the other creatures that call your yard home. A nature observation is the practice of tuning in to use our senses, to quietly watch and listen, so that we may learn and appreciate the natural environment that already lives in our yard. As we observe the life of the plants, trees, insects, birds, and animals, we expand the way we think of and engage with them.

You will need:
* notebook
* pen
* timer

This is time set aside and free of any modern distraction, so leave your phone inside. Gather up your notebook, pen, and timer and go outside. Choose a place you wish to connect with. It should be a comfortable, convenient place you can easily return to again and again. Next, settle into a comfortable position and set your timer for 15 minutes. By setting the timer, you are pledging not to think of how much time has passed and instead to allow a full disconnect as the timer keeps track.

Draw a deep breath and let your spirit quiet. Draw your attention to where you are right there in that very moment as you breathe and allow your perception to sharpen. Be present as you silently observe. Breathe. Look around. What do you see? When something attracts your attention, note it down. Note it in detail. What do you hear? What do you smell? Make note of what is taking place around you and who is sharing the moment. Make note of how it makes you feel.

As you return to the spot over and over, you will begin to feel a connectedness and familiarity with the spot. The area around will take on new meaning and put the rest of your life into a larger context. By taking time out to tune in to nature, you will begin to notice and attune to natural patterns, cycles, and seasonal changes. Becoming aware of nature and forging a relationship with her is an integral part of natural witchcraft, and it all starts by unplugging and going outside.

Meet Your Trees

Trees are complex beings that support multitudes of life systems in the environment in which they live. They are the longest-living species on Earth, some living more than five thousand years. A tree can create the identity of a place, bridging the past, present, and the future. Trees provide food and shelter for wildlife. They stabilize the soil, store carbon, and replenish oxygen.

A tree adds form and color to a garden. Trees add a sense of permanence and become a part of the history of a place, adding to the continuity and giving a sense of permanence. Trees help create the identity of a place and act as an anchor of theme and style. A tree can hide an eyesore or form a boundary. Trees provide shade and shelter. They provide habitat for birds, animals, and pollinators. Some trees produce fruit or nuts that will provide a source of food for you or the birds and animals that share your space.

Trees evolved long before we did. Some have stood sentry on Earth for thousands of years, yet we are only just beginning to understand the way they interact with their environment and the depth of their perception. Recent studies are revealing that trees are sentient beings leading complex lives we can only imagine.[12] They are "sophisticated organisms that live in families, support their sick neighbors, and have the capacity to make decisions, and fight off predators," describes Peter Wohlleben, best-selling author of *The Hidden Life of Trees*, in an interview. He elaborates, "Trees send chemical signals through the air when they are attacked by insects. Nearby trees receive these messages and have time to prepare their defenses. … Plants process information just as animals do, but for the most part they do this much more slowly."[13]

Trees can add a lot of value to a garden. They help control flooding and clean the air. In a year, a single tree produces 260 pounds of oxygen as it absorbs 10 pounds

12. František Baluška and Stefano Mancuso, "Plant Neurobiology: From Stimulus Perception to Adaptive Behavior of Plants, via Integrated Chemical and Electrical Signaling." *Plant Signaling and Behavior* 4, no. 6 (June 2009): 475–76, doi:10.4161/psb.4.6.8870; Eric D. Brenner et al., "Plant Neurobiology: An Integrated View of Plant Signaling," *Trends in Plant Science* 11, no. 8 (August 2006): 413–19, doi:10.1016/j.tplants.2006.06.009.

13. Richard Schiffman, "Are Trees Sentient Beings? Certainly, Says German Forester," *Yale Environment 360*, Yale School of Environment, November 16, 2016, https://e360.yale.edu/features/are_trees_sentient_peter_wohlleben.

of pollutants.[14] Get to know the trees in your yard. Try to identify each one and research their history and lore. You might be surprised by what you discover. As you spend more time with your trees, you will begin to understand that each tree has its own personality. Some trees are welcoming and some are not. Some trees are very generous, while others are standoffish.

Trees are beautiful. Just being around them is calming. Trees house life-giving energy. Choose a tree and lean against its trunk or bask in its shade and you may sense it. The Celts felt this presence of power and named it *shunnache*.[15] To them forests and groves were places of sacred power. Preindustrial societies viewed trees as being inhabited by unseen beings from dryads to devas. Interact with a tree and you may become aware of it on another level. You can hug it, meditate with it, and even call on it to enrich your spiritual practice.

Exercise
Tree Gazing

If you are fortunate to have a large tree in your yard or even adjacent to your lot so that it adds to the backdrop of your garden, you can get to know it through the practice of tree gazing.

Tree gazing is the practice of reclining under a tree, quieting your mind, and gazing up into its branches as you observe what is happening there. By quietly observing, you can bond with the tree and form a connection to it and the activities going on in its branches. If practiced regularly, tree gazing works to fortify your sense of well-being and establish an emotional connection with nature that grounds you in the seasons.

....

14. "State Forest Carbon Incentives and Policies," National Conference of State Legislatures, September 22, 2021, https://www.ncsl.org/research/environment-and-natural-resources/state-forest-carbon-incentives-and-policies.aspx.

15. Jan Johnsen, *Heaven Is a Garden* (Pittsburgh, PA: St. Lynn's Press, 2014), 44.

You will need:
* notebook
* pen
* recliner or blanket that you can spread on the ground

To begin, notice a tree and approach it. Say hello. Note the day and time at the top of your notebook page and make note of how the tree is in the present season. Look at the tree and allow yourself to appreciate its beauty. Notice the bark. Is it light or dark, rough or smooth? Notice the leaves. What color, size, and shape are they? Do you know what kind of tree this is? If so, make note of it.

Set aside your journal and position the recliner or the blanket under the tree in a good spot that allows you to gaze comfortably up into the tree's branches. Be present and notice everything. Watch who is visiting and what they are doing. Look at the patterns of light and watch as they shift between the leaves. Gaze up at the tree and smile as you send it gratitude for existing. Let your chest open as you immerse yourself in the experience.

When you are ready to sit up, take your journal and note what you saw, heard, smelled, and felt. Repeat this observation as often as you are able, noting how the tree and the birds, animals, and insects in its branches change throughout the seasons. Reread your previous observations to gain understanding of the life of the tree and how it supports the wildlife in your yard.

Trees and Their Magickal Attributes

Each tree has its own magickal energy. Here is a simplified reference list:

Acacia: Protection, psychic powers, spirituality, and success

Alder: Charm, courage, divination, healing, and protection

Almond: Abundance, beauty, blessing, communication, health, love, money, and wisdom

Apple: Fertility, garden magick, healing, love, and youth

Apricot: Attraction, beauty, and love

Ash: Confidence, courage, communication, faery magick, prosperity, protection, and sea magick

Aspen: Anti-theft, divination, eloquence, healing, and protection

Bay: Curse-breaking, luck, psychic development, protection, strength, victory, and vitality

Bayberry: Business success, wealth, and well-being

Beech: Creativity, healing, intuition, love, positive welcoming energy, wisdom, and wishes

Birch: Beginnings, fertility, healing, protection, and purification

Box Elder: Abundance, love, luck, and wealth

Buckeye: Luck, money, and protection

Cedar: Communication, divination, healing, protection, purification, and summoning

Cherry: Beauty, fertility, love, protection, and wisdom

Chestnut: Abundance, fertility, harmony, love, protection, and vision

Chinaberry: Change, good luck, and transitions

Coconut Palm: Beauty, clear thinking, moon magick, healing, protection, and purification

Crepe Myrtle: Calmness, creativity, love, stability, and strength

Cypress: Comfort, healing, longevity, loss, protection, and truth

Date Palm: Abundance, fertility, potency, spirituality, and wishes

Dogwood: Empathy, love, protection, and wishes

Elder: Blessings, exorcism, faery magick, healing, protection, and seduction

Elm: Fertility, focus, healing, love, protection, rebirth, spirituality, and summoning

Eucalyptus: Healing, health, protection, success, and visions

Fig: Divination, fertility, love, and strength

Fir: Abundance, enlightenment, fertility, love, protection, strength, and wisdom

Grapefruit: Cleansing, communication, joy, and vitality

Hawthorn: Cleansing, faery magick, healing, protection, and wishes

Hazel: Fertility, finding, healing, luck, knowledge, protection, wisdom, and wishes

Hemlock: Cleansing, healing, perseverance, strength, and transformations

Holly: Death and rebirth, dream magick, luck, protection, and success

Juniper: Anti-theft, comfort, exorcism, love, protection, and visions

Lemon: Brightening, clarity, friendship, healing, love, and purification

Lime: Cleansing, healing, love, protection, and purification

Linden: Calmness, love, protection, purification, and rest

Magnolia: Fidelity, love, peace, protection, and psychic abilities

Mandarin Orange: Attraction, fertility, hospitality, love, and marriage

Mango: Dream magick, fertility, love, and uplifting energy

Maple: Divination, longevity, love, luck, and wealth

Mimosa: Cleansing, counter-magick, prophetic dreams, protection

Mulberry: Communication, divination, fertility, inventiveness, knowledge, and wind magick

Myrtle: Attraction, fertility, love, prosperity, and youth

Nectarine: Abundance, happiness, health, and love

Oak: Faery magick, fertility, healing, luck, money, protection, stability, and success

Olive: Fertility, healing, love, lust, peace, potency, prosperity, and protection

Orange: Clarity, divination, fertility, health, happiness, love, luck, money, and weddings

Peach: Abundance, fertility, happiness, health, love, luck, and wishes

Pear: Energy, enthusiasm, longevity, love, lust, and strength

Pecan: Abundance, employment, inspiration, health, money, and prosperity

Persimmon: Abundance, changing sex, healing, love, prosperity, and self-realization

Peruvian Pepper Tree: Cleansing, health, protection, and travel

Pine: Banishing, fertility, health, prosperity, purification, and spiritual awakening

Pistachio: Antidote, energy, health, longevity, love, and sight

Plum: Abundance, good luck, happiness, healing, love, and youth

Pomegranate: Beauty, creativity, death, divination, fertility, health, luck, and wealth

Rowan: Astral work, divination, protection, psychic abilities, strength, and success

Sassafras: Anger, health, and money

Sequoia Redwood: Healing, longevity, strength, and wisdom

Spruce: Healing, protection, purification, and wisdom

Sycamore: Communication, divination, harmony, love, longevity, prosperity, and strength

Tangerine: Beauty, creativity, energy, hospitality, joy, love, strength, and vitality

Walnut: Communication, fertility, healing, love, mental powers, protection, and wishes

Willow: Divination, enchantments, healing, love, moon magick, and protection

Yew: Crossroads, eternal love, longevity, rebirth, summoning, transitions, and visions

Get to Know Your Weeds

Chances are you have a multitude of plants already growing in your yard. Before you discount that small, unknown plant, see if you can identify it. You might discover a treasure. Ralph Waldo Emerson once wrote that a weed is "a plant whose virtues have not yet been discovered."[16] Another common definition is any plant that grows where you don't want it. Many plants we call weeds are actually herbs that were brought to this land by settlers who prized them and planted them in gardens. These plants escaped to naturalize in the countryside, and some became invasive.

Invasive plants are different for every microclimate. What is common in your area may not thrive in my zone. Dandelion, burdock, bittersweet, purple nettle, and broadleaf plantain grow voluntarily in the corners of my yard. The delicate herb Robert with its little pink flowers has become a favorite. Though this innocuous plant seems to grow everywhere here in the Pacific Northwest, it is new to me. A bit of research has made it familiar. Herb Robert is a relative of the garden geranium. It has a diminutive flower that the bees adore and feathery parsnip-flavored leaves. It was a medicinal herb made into teas that were used as a mouth rinse to treat sore throats and toothache.[17] This little plant holds a healing, uplifting energy. I often include it in both my edible and magickal herbal blends for cheer and comfort.

Other plants, like Armenian blackberry, English holly, ivy, and my personal bane, wild clematis, are troublesome and must be continuously removed to prevent them from taking over. While an afternoon's efforts make headway to control the ivy, blackberry, and holly sprouts, this claim cannot be made for wild clematis (*Clematis vitalba*), better known as old man's beard and traveler's joy. It spreads aggressively across the ground and over fences and trees to blanket everything in its path much like kudzu. I am constantly pulling it out by the wheelbarrow load only to have it crop up again and again. Here in Oregon it is classified as a noxious weed and considered a bane to natural areas, where it often blankets everything, causing even trees to collapse.

. . . .

16. Ralph Waldo Emerson, *Fortune of the Republic and Other American Addresses* (Boston, MA: Houghton Mifflin, 1889), 16.

17. Betsy Strauch, "Herb to Know: Herb Robert," *Mother Earth News*, April 1, 1997, https://www .motherearthliving.com/plant-profile/an-herb-to-know-27.

After an afternoon of ripping out a patch of the tenacious weed, I sat back wondering why any traveler would purposely bring such a plant to another continent. After a bit of research, I discovered the woody vines were once used to make baskets and ropes and are very effective in binding magick, and wild clematis essence is used as a Bach flower essence to treat the detached and dreamy by anchoring them to the moment.[18] *Clematis vitalba* is a component in the homeopathic remedy Rescue Remedy, used to help treat agitation, shock, and fear, and the leaf extract is used in some antidandruff shampoos.[19] The information caused me to see this plant in a new light. Oh, I still spend hours pulling it out of my hedges, but now I also burn the dried leaves when the need arises to unravel difficult issues and find my way to a solution. The vines work well in binding rituals, while the fluffy seed cotton can be stuffed into poppets to boost binding energy.

Get familiar with the residents of your yard. Some might be useful in your practice. You have no idea what gems are waiting for you to discover unless you look. But be aware of the fact that plants that grow well in your area will multiply, so keep a watchful eye on what is going on in your yard. One year I ended up with an unintended bumper crop of sunflowers. Another year it was thistles. If you don't want a yard full next season, clip off the flowers before they seed. See part 2 for a list of weeds and their magickal uses.

If you have any doubt about the identity of a plant, don't experiment with it. *Never* use a plant unless you are 100 percent sure of its identity. Misidentifying a plant may result in injury, illness, and even death. Not all plants are friendly. Some are very poisonous, and experimenting with these plants can be dangerous. Some are dangerous in large doses or with extended use. Others may be harmful to pregnant women, children, or people with certain types of medical conditions. All should be treated with respect.

. . . .

18. "Bach Flower—Clematis (Clematis Vitalba)," Bach Flower Reference Guide, accessed September 1, 2021, https://www.bachflower.org/clematis.htm.

19. "Rescue Remedy & Rescue Remedy Spray," Original Bach Flower Remedies, accessed September 1, 2021, http://www.bachflower.com/rescue-remedy-information/.

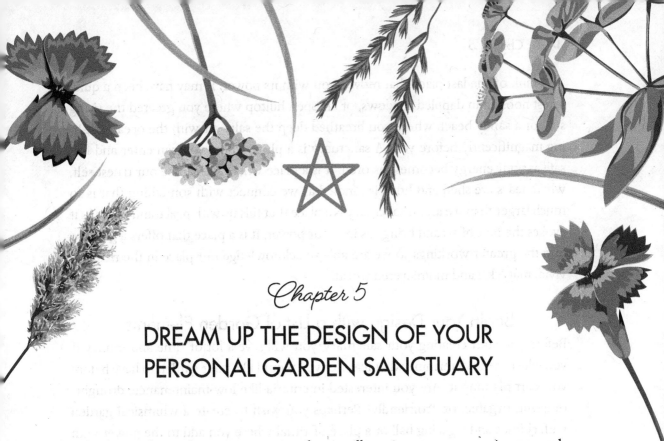

Chapter 5

DREAM UP THE DESIGN OF YOUR PERSONAL GARDEN SANCTUARY

Ask what makes a place a sanctuary and you will receive answers as unique as each individual. Sanctuary is something different for everyone because we each are moved by different sights, scents, and sounds. By understanding this, we can incorporate elements into our garden designs to create the space that moves us the most. You might wish to create an ordered space to meditate with a shaded natural place to sit and breathe or a serene water garden full of life and sound. Perhaps a symbol like a spiraling labyrinth, a stone circle, or a garden cairn helps you forge a connection with the wild energies and brings you to spirit.

A personal sanctuary garden offers a place of wellness, a place to calm the psyche, a place to ground and find balance, a place to pause and find our breath. It is in these places we tend our inner landscapes with a mere visit. In the sanctuary garden, life slows so the mind may come to awareness as the heart opens, allowing us to find wonder in the amazing details of a tiny flower. Spirit is set soaring with the movement of the wind stirring through tall grasses, the high trilling notes of a bird's song, or the wonder of a butterfly drifting on the breeze.

Think of the last place that moved you with its power. It may have been a quiet forest nook lit in dappled shadows, or an open hilltop where you greeted the rising sun, or a sandy beach where you breathed deep the salty air with the ocean crashing magnificently before you. A sanctuary is a place where you can enter and feel safe as your energy becomes restored. It is a place where we can be our truest self, where fears are shed and hope is kindled as we connect with something that is so much larger than we are. A sanctuary is a place that fills us with peace and cheer as it evokes the best of us and brings us into our power. It is a place that offers a glimpse into the greater workings so we are able to acknowledge our place in the rich and vivid, magickal and multilayered world.

Begin Your Design with a List of Garden Elements

Before you start creating your sanctuary, you will save a lot of time and money if you take time to determine what features you would like your garden to have before you start planting it. Are you interested in criteria like low-maintenance, drought-resistant, organic, or ecofriendly? Perhaps you wish to create a whimsical garden with chimes and a gazing ball or a place of ritual where you add to the power with offerings. Your garden design could include natural elements to create a wild place for contemplation or be as simple as a plant-filled patio space to do yoga.

Sometimes it is the actions performed in the space that define it. A space designed for solitude will have very different features than a comfortable outdoor area for social gatherings. Consider what you are going to use this space for and what you will need in it to do it comfortably. Will you need room to stretch out beneath the sky, or do you wish to include elements like a table, an altar, or a fire pit in your plans? Whatever the case, decide what you want to create and write it down. This declaration will be the main directive in creating your garden. A statement like "I want a water garden filled with lilies, koi, and frogs" will take you in a completely different direction than "I want a forest setting with wildflowers and organic berries." So decide what kind of garden you are going to create and next make a list of features you would like to incorporate.

The idea of sacred space is unique to us all, as we each respond to stimuli differently. What moves me might not evoke a response in you. You might be inspired by a faery woodland meadow set with swaying grasses and wildflowers, or perhaps you respond to the comfort of a gazebo strung with fairy lights, or a ritual area with an altar and a fire pit. Think about the last time you were moved in a natural setting. What elements triggered your response? How did it make you feel? Perhaps you recalled a favorite spot from your childhood. Maybe your idyllic place was your grandmother's vegetable garden. Go back to your memory and fill in as many details as you can remember. Try to remember if there was something sharing the space with you that triggered an emotional response or if there was a unique scent or sound. When you have a detailed image fixed in your mind, write down the elements you remember. Try to describe how they moved you. Look at your notes and see if there is a way to duplicate these powerful elements into your new garden space.

When you choose to create sanctuary, you acknowledge the intent to create a transformative space, a personal refuge of your own making that acts as a portal into another world where spirit is acknowledged and personal practices are strengthened. By filling it with elements that stir your senses and speak to your own inner landscapes, you empower a place to nourish your soul. It becomes a refuge where you can step out of the busyness of life and into a slower reality, rich in sensory input, where your rhythms sync with those of the natural world.

Garden Features

Use features to introduce a personal element into your garden scheme. A wind chime or a gazing ball can give an area a mystical quality, while a water feature will add movement and sound as it nourishes life around it. You might wish to set a focal point with a garden sculpture to invoke reverence, joy, or even playfulness. Whimsical figures like a garden gnome or a gargoyle create a different response than a smiling Buddha or a beautiful goddess.

Choose one or two elements and work them into your garden plan. Try to start simple. Here is a reference list of possible features to help you get started.

Altar: A place that is set aside to honor deity or receive offerings or that acts as a focal point for rituals.

Arbor: An entrance, threshold, or portal to delineate separate space.

Bird Feeder or Birdbath: Hospitality and appreciation of wildlife.

Bench or Chair: Hospitality and rest. A place you are welcome to return to.

Boundary: A fence, hedge, lattice, or wall that divides an area and creates safety, containment, and privacy.

Cairn: A stack of stones used to mark an area, house a genius loci, or place an intention. Add a stone with each visit to add power to a place or desire.

Fire Pit: An open-air space to safely contain an outdoor fire. In the garden a fire pit represents comfort, safety, warmth and ceremony. There is a comfort in gathering around a fire. It serves as a hypnotic focal point and can be a place to celebrate, socialize, or worship.

Fountain: A mechanism to simulate the flow of water. Fountains represent abundance, eternity, and the continuous flow of energy. A gurgling fountain introduces a mystical element that stimulates feelings of happiness, peace, and relaxation. Fountains are associated with wishes and water magick.

Gate: A border crossing between one area and another. Gates mark the boundary between one place and another. They both contain and protect, and they designate the change from public to private.

Gazebo: A protective outdoor structure often designed for lounging, gatherings, and outdoor dining. A gazebo can also be designated as a place of ritual used to house deity.

Gazing Ball: A glass globe that reflects the garden and the sky. It is associated with good luck, happiness, and prosperity. They were once used to ward off evil spirits.

Labyrinth: A curving pathway that leads to the center, providing a walk to come to knowledge, find comfort, or heal and restore. One of the oldest labyrinths is inside Chartres Cathedral in France.

Lanterns or Solar Lights: Lanterns symbolize safety, guidance, and light. A garden lantern is a source of light used to illuminate an area or mark a pathway. A lantern can be made of many things: it could be as simple as a mason jar with sand in the bottom and a candle or strings of fairy lights. Luminaries add ambiance as they bring light to gardens, decks, and gazebos.

Line of Sight: A view across a long space that focuses on a point at the far end to draw the eye and give a sense of distance. This works well in an enclosed space with a bench, arch, or gate at the far end. This gives the garden a sense of flow to draw someone into the space and make them feel interested and welcome.

Pathway: A garden path is a safe and easy trail taken though the garden. By staying on a path, we are promised a safe return. A path symbolizes our pace and process. To take a path sometimes means to find enlightenment.

Pond: A garden pond symbolizes life and tranquility. Water brings life to the garden as it acts as a water source for wildlife.

Reflecting Pool: In meditation one gazes at the surface of the water or finds the reflection of the moon in the water to come to knowledge. A pool connects the sky above with the earth below.

Wind Chime: In 1100 BC in China, the wind chime was hung in doorways and windows to promote peace and deter bad luck from entering.[20] Chimes are associated with protection, east, the element of air, ideas, and inspiration. Wind chimes can signal imminent danger, scare away wayward spirits, or announce a spirit is present.

. . . .

20. "Wind Chime," Encyclopedia.com, accessed September 1, 2021, https://www.encyclopedia .com/manufacturing/news-wires-white-papers-and-books/wind-chime.

Including Sacred Symbols

There are many sacred symbols, each with a rich history and layers of meanings. Incorporating a sacred symbol into our garden space is a way to fix an intention for the space. If we hang an image of something that holds a personal meaning for us, then simply catching sight of it sends our thoughts in a certain direction and signals spirit to become receptive. Including a sacred symbol can be as easy as hanging a ceramic image or laying out bricks or stones in a certain shape. A symbol can be set in a mosaic of shells, stones, or even bones.

Here is a short reference list of sacred symbols for you to consider.

Ankh: An Egyptian symbol of life often depicted by a cross with a looped top.

Circle: A symbol of containment and protection used to designate a boundary between spaces, realities, or worlds. Stonehenge is one of the world's most famous stone circles.

Elemental Symbols: The elements of earth, air, fire, and water correspond with the cardinal directions north, east, south, and west. Earth is represented by an upside-down triangle with a line through the bottom. Air is represented by an upright triangle with a line through the top. Fire is represented by an upright triangle symbol. Water is represented by an upside-down triangle.

Equal-Armed Cross: An ancient symbol representing the four seasons of the year, the four directions, and balance.

Green Man: The image of a man's head sprouting with foliage representing the environment, death and rebirth, the fertility of nature, and the mortality of man. He is associated with the Celtic god of springtime, Esus, and Cernunnos, the horned Celtic nature god of the forest. The Green Man motif usually features a face with foliage sprouting from the face or mouth representing cycles of growth and the rebirth of plant life. He is one of the oldest existing Pagan symbols, and yet his many variations can be found carved high in the columns of medieval churches across Europe.

Moon: The moon is the symbol of feminine divinity and can be depicted by any moon phase.

Pentagram: A five-pointed star often enclosed in a circle. The pentagram is a protective symbol.

Spiral: A coiled line that represents a journey, migration, and change. Incorporate a spiral to your garden design to enhance spiritual development and inspire creativity.

Sun: Depicted as both a stylized sun and a solid dot within a circle. The sun is a symbol of male divinity and God power.

Triquetra: A popular Celtic knotwork also known as the trinity knot design composed of three interlaced arcs. A protective symbol sometimes used to depict both the trinity and the Triple Goddess.

Triple Moon: An image of the moon's three phases: waxing, full, and waning. The triple moon is also known as the Triple Goddess symbol because it represents Divine Feminine power as the three faces of the Goddess as Maiden, Mother, and Crone.

Triskele or Triple Spiral: One of the oldest Celtic symbols associated with the Triple Goddess, the cycles of life (birth, death, and rebirth), and the trio of land, sea, and sky. The triskele also symbolizes durability, stability, and strength, as well as the three worlds (celestial, physical, and spiritual) and the balance of body, mind, and soul.

Craft an Intention to Match Your Desire

Now that you have an idea about what kind of garden you want to create, it's time to put it into words and tell the universe. Every magickal act begins with an intention. An intention is a short, concise statement formulated to narrow your focus into exactly what you wish to manifest. Think about what it is you hope to achieve. What are you working toward? Your answer is your intention. Decide what you want and simplify your desire into a clear, concise statement as though you have already created it.

To manifest an idea into reality, you need to treat it as though it has already come to fruition. This moves your intention from being held at a place in the future to the present where it will arrive. Instead of wishing for something, give thanks for it! Visualize your perfect garden. Hold your desire in your heart and speak it to the universe with conviction. Words have power. Believe that if you ask, it will be given.

Nature is a great provider. If you work with her to cocreate your garden space, instead of choosing to battle her, it will become a place of power. Open your garden notebook to a blank page and write your intention at the top. Then as you visit the space, speak your intention to it, giving thanks for what is going to manifest. Try something like one of these:

* ★ I step into a space that feeds my soul and inspires my well-being.
* ★ I craft this space to restore peace and nourish my soul.
* ★ This garden is a magickal realm brimming with energy to foster my spiritual growth and grant communion with wild gods.
* ★ This is a place of protection where I may be my truest self.

Exercise
Dream Your Garden into Being

You will need:
* ★ your garden notebook
* ★ pen or pencil

Go out to the place you have chosen for your garden and settle into a comfortable position. Close your eyes and visualize the elements you would like to bring to your garden space. Envision the sanctuary you wish to create. See it in your mind's eye as though it already exists. Place each item visual where you would like it to be. Bring in as many senses as possible. If you are incorporating a water feature into the area, hear the water as you visualize it and see its movement. If you are placing a garden bench, sit with it as you breathe and consider how it makes you feel to be with it there. Visualize the garden as you wish it to be, and use your visualization to decide if the space feels right. If not, adjust your ideas to fit the space until they feel true.

When you have built the space in your mind, it's time to sketch it out. Turn to the page with your garden intention at the top and draw a sketch of the area, incorporating as many details as you are able to. When you have finished, sit with your design and consider how each element makes you feel. Adjust or change points that need fixing. When it feels right to you, let your spirit fill with gratitude, then voice your intention for the space.

Chapter 6

THE SPIRIT OF THE LAND

The Romans believed that there was an individual spark of divine nature dwelling in every person, activity, object, and place.[21] This spirit of place was held to be a guardian spirit they referred to as the *genius loci* or the *lares* of the crossroads. Small towers were built at the crossroads and offerings were left for the spirits.[22] To the Norse, the guardian spirits of the land were the *landvættir,* or "land wights."[23] These living, sentient beings were not quite of this world but tied to a spot.[24] A life force, able to stir hearts and minds, composed of the awareness of all the trees of a forest focused into one voice, all the power of a waterfall, or all the stones of a mountain working

· · · · · · · · · · · · · · · · · ·

21. Joshua J. Mark, "Roman Household Spirits: Manes, Panes and Lares," World History Encyclopedia, October 28, 2019, https://www.ancient.eu/article/34/roman-household-spirits-manes-panes-and-lares/.

22. Georges Dumezil, *Archaic Roman Religion*, vol. 1 (Baltimore, MD: Johns Hopkins University Press, 1996), 342–43.

23. "Landvættir," Encyclopedia.com, accessed September 1, 2021, https://www.encyclopedia.com/environment/encyclopedias-almanacs-transcripts-and-maps/landvaettir.

24. H. R. Ellis Davidson, *Myths and Symbols in Pagan Europe: Early Scandinavian and Celtic Religions* (Syracuse, NY: Syracuse University Press, 1988), 103–4.

together to preserve the safety and fertility of the area. You could feel this presence when you entered an old grove or visited a spring or a well. In *Demons and Spirits of the Land: Ancestral Lore and Practices*, Claude Lecouteux writes, "They guided our ancestors to respect their environment and to be careful because they knew they were not alone and had accounts to pay to those who were called—and are still called, here and there—the Invisible Folk and the Underground Folk."[25]

In many places these voices have fallen silent. But if you invite them, they may allow you to feel their presence. Open your senses and cast out, and you might find one next time you are in a large woodland, walking across a forgotten field, hiking a woodland path, or even crossing a small corner of your yard.

Next time you are outside, close your eyes and ground. Draw a breath as you tune in. Then introduce yourself. Ask if there is anyone who would like to speak with you, and most importantly, take note of what turns up. As you formulate your garden plan, present your intention and ask the spirit to bless your act of conscious creation.

In many places the spirits have been neglected for so long they need to be encouraged to return. You can do this by offering attention, holding conversations, and leaving offerings. Offer them some power by asking their permission before you begin any work. Then offer your thanks when you have completed your project.

The Custom of Offering

An offering is a token of thanks acknowledging the attention of your allies and the work that is in process. It is customary to leave an offering after a petition or a harvest to show your gratitude and respect for the plant, the earth, and the energies present.

Offerings can be in the form of a song or a prayer. An offering can be a gift of food or water. It might be an act of maintenance or the gift of a special token that means something to you or the energy present, such as a special stone, flower, or shell. When making an outdoor offering, consider what you are asking and of whom you are asking it, and then leave an offering that is appropriate. Plant energies appreciate a handful of ash, compost, some crushed eggshells, or a bucket of rain or river

· · · · · · · · · · · · · · · · ·

25. Claude Lecouteux, *Demons and Spirits of the Land: Ancestral Lore and Practices* (Rochester, VT: Inner Traditions, 1995), 182.

water. Faery energies appreciate a bouquet of flowers, a bit of sweet-scented resin like frankincense or myrrh, honey, or a dish of beer, milk, or cream. A thimble of wine and a gift of a buckeye or a handful of acorns will gain faery favor, especially if the acorns were gathered under a full moon's light. Spirit animals like the crow and rat enjoy an egg, a piece of meat, or a small shiny treasure. The fox, wolf, and bear also appreciate an offering of meat. If you are working with a water energy, leave a beautiful shell. If you are working with dragon energy, leave a coin or a gem. Squirrels and birds enjoy nuts and seeds.

Offerings should always be of the best quality, such as the first of the cream out of the carton or the first or nicest loaf of bread made that day. To make an offering, present the token and acknowledge the space. Whisper a greeting. When we feed a space energy, it becomes a sacred space. Quietly spend some time in silent observation. When you have finished, it is important to not leave any trash. We are stewards of nature. Remove cans, bottles, paper, wrappers, candles, or any other debris. Dispose of offering remains that linger. Collect the remains and bury them, add them to the compost pile, or throw them out.

Another valuable offering is one of time. Whenever we spend time in our gardens, we feed the connection with our attention and work. Natural areas also benefit from our attention. You might choose to dedicate some of your time to a natural area and visit weekly to pick up trash.

The Stone Cairn

Cairns can be found on mountaintops, beside rivers, at the start of trailheads, and at burial sites on every continent. These carefully arranged man-made mounds of stone have been used since the prehistoric age to mark spots around the globe.[26] Cairns were built to mark a place or boundary or to commemorate an action or event. A cairn stands at the boundary of Norway and Sweden. There is another marking the boundary of Durham and Northumberland in the United Kingdom, and a well-known cairn marks the summit in Graubunden, Switzerland.

. . . .

26. Tori Chalmers, "What Are Rock Cairns and How Should They Be Used?" Culture Trip, June 20, 2018, https://theculturetrip.com/europe/united-kingdom/scotland/articles/what-are-rock-cairns-and-how-should-they-be-used/.

The word *cairn* comes from the Gaelic *càrn*, and it is said that before a battle, Highlanders would each toss a stone into a pile. Those who survived the battle returned and removed a stone. The stones that remained were built into a cairn to honor those who died. The Scottish Gaelic blessing *Cuiridh mi clach air do chàrn* translates to "I'll put a stone on your cairn," or "I will remember you."[27]

Exercise
Building a Stone Cairn

You can build a cairn to mark a power spot in your garden and add to the energy every time you visit by adding a stone. A cairn can house the spirit of the land so that you may have a place where you can meet and speak and leave offerings.

This project begins with a walking meditation. Meditation is not restricted to sitting. Meditation can be done while you are standing under your shower, mindfully listening to the water's flow and rejoicing in the feeling of it on your skin. It can be done while you are running, feet rhythmically striking the ground, and lungs and heart pumping, and it can be done while walking through nature, immersing yourself in the sounds and sights as you connect with the wild energies present. All it takes is being present with a mind that is engaged and focused on the moment.

You will need:
* place and time you can walk uninterrupted
* something to carry your stones in (a backpack, bucket, or a wagon depending on the size of the stones you are planning to gather)
* clear and present mind

Choose a place where you can walk around and pick up stones. When you arrive at your starting point, turn off all electronic devices. Get whatever you are going to

....
27. Tori Chalmers, "What Are Rock Cairns and How Should They Be Used?" Culture Trip, June 20, 2018, https://theculturetrip.com/europe/united-kingdom/scotland/articles/what-are-rock-cairns-and-how-should-they-be-used/.

carry the rocks in and let go of all your plans and worries. The goal here is to step out of one reality into another.

Draw a deep breath and close your eyes. Bring your focus to your center and let your mind fall quiet. If you are not sure where your center is, spend a moment focusing on the area behind your breastbone. You may feel a tug to slide your attention to a spot lower in your belly, and that is fine too. When you have found it, draw your attention in, and focus on your center. Visualize it glowing with light. Spend a few breaths with it. Soon you will experience a shift as your senses fill and swell with the moment. As the moment grows sharp, draw a breath and open your eyes. Allow your perception to expand and spread to what is right in front of you. Open your mind to your senses. Focus on what you can feel, see, smell, and hear.

Begin your walk. Be intensely present. Notice everything. Keep track of what shows up. When we open to the signs and symbols we encounter, they speak to our intuitive nature, stimulating our intuition and allowing what we "know" but do not recognize to rise to our conscious mind, thereby creating radiant glimpses of insight and divine inspiration. Take note of everything. When you see a stone that catches your interest, pick it up. Do this until you have mindfully gathered at least nine stackable stones.

When you get home, go to the place you have chosen to spend time in. Come to center. Bring your intent sharply into focus. It doesn't matter if you are creating a sacred space for the genius loci of your land to reside in, creating a faery house, or simply marking the spot as a power site. Whatever your intention, call it up sharply and hold it firmly as you mindfully stack the stones into a cairn.

Next call out an invitation. You might say something along these lines:

> I call out to the spirits of the land
> and invite you to take up residence here.
> Let this be a sacred site,
> a place where we can meet and commune.
> A place where I might return,
> to share my gratitude,
> as I return with a grateful heart,
> thankful for all that I have,

all that I am,
and all the potential I have to be.
Thanks be to thee.

Hold gratitude in your heart and set out an offering. This can be any earth-centered item that won't harm the environment or your backyard wildlife. The offering can be elaborate, such as a small home-baked cake. It might be the pouring out of a portion of mead, wine, or beer or simply the gift of an interesting stone, a shell, a pinecone, a flower, or a handful of seeds or nuts.

Over the next few days, go out and spend time with your cairn. Every time we give an energy our attention, we feed the relationship. Allow your spirit to quiet as you treat the space with honor. When the spirit moves you, add a stone to the cairn to add to its power. Leave tokens in offering and keep it well cared for. Treat it as a place of power and include it in your magickal practice.

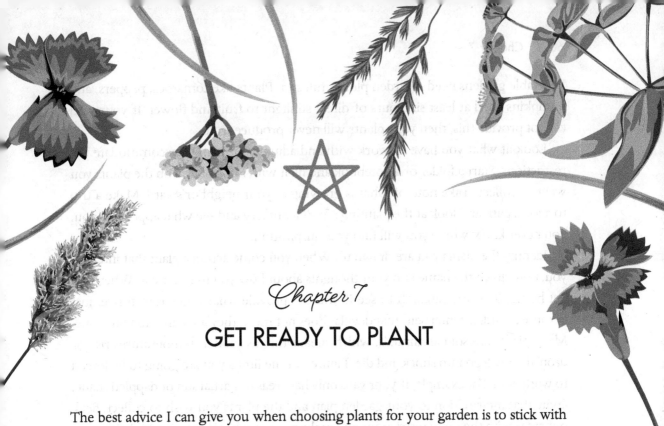

Chapter 7

GET READY TO PLANT

The best advice I can give you when choosing plants for your garden is to stick with plants that will be happy in your hardiness zone. When I first moved to Oregon, I brought my Meyer lemon and mandarin orange and planted them in a nice sunny spot. Unfortunately, that winter was one of the harshest in recent history, and even though I'd wrapped them in frost protection and dug them out of the snow every morning, they were both dead by the end of February. It was laborious and heartbreaking, and it all could have been avoided if I'd stuck to plants hardy to my climate zone.

Each plant has its own set of requirements that must be met in order for it to thrive. Some require sun. Some need shade. Some plants flourish in dry conditions, while others must have their feet wet. Before making your purchase, I advise reviewing the information you discovered about your zone and the sunlight availability in chapter 3 and checking it against the needs of the plants you wish to buy. Arming yourself with this knowledge will prevent a lot of wasted effort and money.

You will save yourself a lot of frustration if you stick to growing plants that will flourish in the microclimate of your yard. You can plant an avocado tree, but it will not grow and fruit if it can't tolerate the temperatures of your microclimate.

Vegetable gardens need a garden plot in full sun. Plants like tomatoes, peppers, and pumpkins need at least six hours of direct sunlight to fruit and flower. If your yard cannot provide this, then your plants will never produce fruit.

Look at what you have to work with and adjust your plan to accommodate the restrictions. Start a folder or a notebook and fill it with information on the plants you want to collect. Take note of what is growing in your neighbor's yard. Make a trip to a local park and look at the plantings. Visit a nursery and see what appeals to you. You never know where you will find your inspiration.

Identify the plants you are drawn to. When you come across a plant that interests you, note down the name and your thoughts about how you might use it. When you get home, do some research to see if you can provide what it needs to thrive. Just because a garden center sells mandevillas does not mean they are hardy to your zone. Many plants are sold as annuals, which means that as soon as temperatures rise or drop, they will go into shock and die. Figure out the limits you are going to be forced to work with. For example, if your yard only has areas of partial sun or dappled shade, apply that information to your garden plan and the plants you wish to collect. Seek out areas with the same restrictions and make note of what is growing in them.

Take a walk around your neighborhood and see what is growing in the well-established gardens and parks. Shortly after moving to Oregon, I realized that all of my years of accumulated knowledge didn't quite translate to the conditions of the temperate rainforest climate. To learn more about gardening in the local micro-climate, I enrolled in Oregon State University's Master Gardener program. There I learned enough to adapt my thinking, and instead of learning through trial and error, I experienced astonishing success. Half the battle for a successful garden is choosing plants that want to live in your garden.

Consecrate the Site Before Breaking Ground

Sacred space is an expression of what is dear to us. It is a place to create, a place to restore, a place where we may embark on a spiritual quest and commune with deity. Any natural place can be deemed sacred, even your own garden. By bringing positive intentions to honor the land and the time you will spend here, you initiate a relationship in which you respond and acknowledge that it is a sacred space. The act of consecrating the site of your new garden space will help transform it into a sanctuary. When you deem a place sacred, you create a safe place where just showing up initiates a connection and evokes an emotional response that nurtures spirituality. When you consider something special and treat it with respect, it becomes *more*.

By consecrating the site, you will change the way you perceive and interact with it. When you approach something as sacred, you open your awareness and shift your response, giving it power to energize, inspire, heal, and fill your inner well of peace. It is this shift that creates the ability to exit the busyness of our lives and shed our constraints as we step into sanctuary.

Exercise
Ritual to Consecrate the Land

By performing a consecrating ritual, you elevate an everyday relationship, shifting focus and changing the response, making it possible to step out of one view of reality into another. The garden as sacred space offers a forum with nature as the central focus to foster both a relationship with the earth and an awareness of the shifting of seasons and the tides of the year.

You will need:
* offering or libation

Come to center. When you are ready, say,

> I call out to the spirits of the land.
> I come to you now with a grateful heart,
> thankful for all that is here and all the potential of what may be.
> I ask your blessing on the work begun and the work to come.
> May this be a place to feed the soul, a sacred site,
> where we come together to heal and create.
> A place where we coauthor beauty and harmony,
> peace and love, for all things bright and beautiful.
> May this ground be a place of sanctuary.

Pour out or set out an offering. You might choose to pour out a libation or dust the area with cold ash from a ritual fire.

May this now and forever be a sacred space.

Over the next few days, go out and spend time visiting it. Spend time in meditation. Treat the space with honor. Do not neglect it. Treat it as a place of power and include it in your magickal practice.

Preparing the Garden Bed

If you are planting a new garden bed, you will need to clear it, dig it, and amend it. An easy way to do all three in one go is to start at one end and dig out a trench that is roughly two feet wide and eight inches deep. Remove all the weeds, roots, and rocks as you dig. Place the soil in a wheelbarrow to give you room to start. When you have cleared the trench to the depth of seven or eight inches, spread a layer of organic matter three inches deep over the bottom. Then, moving to the next two-foot section, dig out a second trench to a depth of seven or eight inches, and as you dig, shovel the dirt over the organic matter in the first trench until it is filled just over halfway. When you reach this point, pause your work on the second trench and return to the first trench to turn the soil over. Take the shovel and dig the dirt into the organic matter. When you have finished, return to the second trench and finish digging it out to the depth of seven or eight inches, moving the soil to fill in the first trench. Add organic matter to the second trench and dig it in the same way you did in the first trench before you move to the next portion. Continue to do this until you have dug the entire bed. Last, use the dirt in the wheelbarrow to fill in the very last section.

After you have your bed dug and amended, avoid walking on it. Every time you put pressure on the soil, you compress it and undo all the hard work you just put into it.

Amend the Soil Before You Plant

A generous addition of organic matter will correct most soil conditions. A healthy plant needs three things: sunlight, water, and rich healthy soil. Soil needs to provide all the nutrients and trace minerals a plant needs to live and grow. Soil supports life.

Your soil is the foundation of your garden's health. If your soil is poor, your plants are not going to thrive. By improving the nutrient content and soil structure before you plant, you will start your garden off with the best possible advantages.

To amend the soil means adding material to your soil to improve it. Organic matter, such as decayed leaves, composted food scraps, and yard clippings, is a standard amendment applied by spreading three inches over soil and then digging it into the top six inches to make it available to the growing roots. All soil types improve with an application of organic matter. Not only does organic matter boost soil nutrients, but it also improves soil structure. An application of organic matter allows sandy soils to improve water- and nutrient-holding capacity, and when mixed into clay soils, an application of organic matter increases drainage, aeration, and permeability so that growing roots can spread more easily and grow deeper.

Keep in mind that your thoughts also affect the energy structure of the soil. Use your intent to influence the future of your garden. As you dig and spread and turn the soil, state your intention of enriching the ground and nurturing the plants so the energy of your mind and your body becomes a part of the amendment. Concentrate as you work and soon you will feel a wonderful ethereal feeling of being a part of the web, as you connect to something so much larger than yourself as it comes over you. This awareness is part of the magick of gardening. Smile and breathe the feeling deep.

Here is a list of everyday garden amendments:

Leaves: Leaves are loaded with nutrients and quickly break down into leaf mold to provide an accessible source of carbon. Run them through a mower to shred and store in a pile, pit, or bin until they have broken down. Use the leaf mold to amend your soil or to mulch around your plants.

Coffee Grounds: Coffee grounds contain nutrients that feed soil organisms, enrich the soil, and improve soil structure to boost drainage and aeration. Add them to your garden compost to enrich the soil and decrease weed growth.

Kitchen Scraps: According to the United States Environmental Protection Agency, 63.1 million tons of food scraps ended up in the trash in 2018.[28] Potato peels, onion skins, carrot tops, and banana peels all contain nutrients to feed a garden. And if you keep a small plastic bucket with a lid by the sink, it makes saving kitchen scraps a snap. During any meal prep, toss all your fruit and vegetable scraps into the bucket, and then at the end of the day, dump it into your compost bin.

Eggshells: Eggshells are a source of calcium. Save your eggshells and toss them into your compost, or dry the shells and grind them to add a dose directly to the soil.

Wood Ash: Wood ash is an excellent source of lime, potassium, and calcium. It also provides trace elements that plants need to thrive. Crops like asparagus, chives, garlic, leeks, and lettuce and stone-fruit trees appreciate a dose of wood ash. But wood ash can raise pH levels to make soil less acidic, so use it sparingly. Either lightly scatter it over the soil or add it to compost and let it sit. Avoid using wood ash around acid-loving plants like azaleas, blueberries, camellias, holly, parsley, potatoes, rhododendrons, or strawberries.

Urea: Urea, also known as carbamide, is a colorless crystalline compound that is a product of the metabolic breakdown of proteins from mammalian bile, blood, milk, sweat, and urine.[29] Urea provides a concentrated dose of nitrogen to help plants produce lush leaf growth. It is available in granules and pellets that can be broadcasted over the soil, or you can make your own. According to a study from a Finnish university, "human urine and wood ash make a reasonably potent

. . . .

28. United States Environmental Protection Agency, "National Overview: Facts and Figures on Materials, Wastes and Recycling," accessed September 1, 2021, https://www.epa.gov/facts-and-figures-about-materials-waste-and-recycling/national-overview-facts-and-figures-materials.

29. *Encyclopaedia Britannica Online,* s.v. "urea," accessed September 1, 2021, https://www.britannica.com/science/urea.

tomato fertilizer, boosting plant growth and fruit yield dramatically over untreated plants and nearly keeping pace with conventional fertilizer."[30]

Keep a Written Record

Much of a gardener's wisdom is garnered through experience. Start by recording what, when, and where. Write down the name of each plant, packet of seeds, or six-pack of seedlings you plant. Note the date of planting and location. You might make a sketch of your garden layout. As your plant collection grows, individuals are sometimes forgotten. You might record where your plant came from and its state before planting. As your garden matures, keep notes on the plant's progress. Note when and how it flowers, the bloom time, and fruit production. By tracking individual plants, you forge a connection with them as your knowledge of their life cycle grows.

Record any signs of stress and try to remedy them. If aphids or slugs attack your plants, respond. Spray the aphids with a soap shield solution. Deal with the slugs by picking them off by hand or setting out a dish of beer to trap them in. If you notice spots on leaves or notice some are turning yellow or beginning to drop, do some research and test out remedies. And write it all down. It's easy to think, "Oh, I'll remember..." Until you don't and the eureka moment or the elevating bit of knowledge is lost. And those moments add up until you're grasping at wisps trying to dredge up details that could have been easily jotted down.

Also keep track of seasonal change. Note significant weather events like periods of heat and drought or first freezes and the results of these conditions. Like the gardeners of old, we are at the mercy of changing climate conditions. September 2020 was a month of historic wildfires. A great cloud of smoke blanketed Portland, turning the sky an ominous shade of orange. Business stopped, life stalled, and even the trash collection service was canceled as we all hid inside our homes watching the world outside change. As the fires edged closer, reports of evacuated neighborhoods buzzed on the airwaves. Air quality grew worse until it became hazardous. Days passed and the

. . . .

30. John Matson, "P Is for Plants: Human Urine Plus Ash Equals Tomato Fertilizer, Study Says," *Scientific American*, September 4, 2009, https://blogs.scientificamerican.com /news-blog/p-is-for-plants-human-urine-plus-as-2009-09-04/.

smoke remained. When I put on a mask and ventured out to take out the trash, it was like stepping out into a strange world. Not only were the neighboring houses still, the birds and squirrels were also silent. In the garden the dahlias drooped. Many of the leaves looked withered. I began to worry about the lasting effects. In the weeks that followed, life returned to normal. When I was able to resume gardening, I discovered that not only had the lettuce bed bolted and gone to seed, but the pumpkin vines and the dahlias were covered in fungus.

Keep your journal close. Take time to add to your notes. As you note your interactions, you will be able to determine what worked and what did not. The more you record, the better you will know your garden. Tracking each success and failure will give you a blueprint to replicate or avoid making the same mistake. Use your journal during the resting months as a reference for the garden plan as you dream a future garden into reality.

Chapter 8

NATURAL AND ETHICAL GARDENING PRACTICES

We are stewards of the earth. Part of being a good steward means not damaging functioning ecosystems as we modify or regenerate a landscape. Your actions affect all who live in your space, now and in the future. It is important to value the functioning ecosystems present and all their living beings. The earth is a living scape webbed with intricate relationships between all who live upon her. Your decisions matter. When we do something that damages the ecosystem, we potentially harm the soil, water, and air quality.

Before modifying or changing a space, first ask if the actions are going to cause any harm to the existing systems. As you work toward your goal, cocreating with nature, the methods you employ will color your experience. Aim for designs that are sustainable and environmentally friendly. Consider your product choices, and whenever possible, choose to use biological resources. Keep notes of all your progress and setbacks. A written record acts as a guide to help the gardener duplicate successes and avoid repeating mistakes.

Plant Native Species

Look at planting native species. You will discover that because native species are biologically adapted to live in your yard, they have a natural resistance to the local insect and fungus attacks and can thrive with less work from you. By planting local species, you will encourage more wildlife, as it is these plants that naturally feed and shelter the local birds, native bees, butterflies, moths, and bats that share your plot.

Adopt Practices That Help Build the Soil Food Web

The cornerstone of a healthy garden is healthy living soil. Scoop up a shovelful and look at it. You should see signs of life. While healthy soil is made up of particles of sand, silt, clay, and minerals, it also contains a whole host of living microorganisms. Soil microbiology professor Ann-Marie Fortuna explains, "A 'biological universe' exists in a gram of soil," including "micro-organisms (bacteria, fungi, archaea and algae) and soil animals (protozoa, nematodes, mites, springtails, spiders, insects, and earthworms)."[31] This complex microscopic population called soil biota is an entire biological universe of decomposers who work together to convert plant and animal remains into the dark, rich, life-sustaining organic matter we gardeners know as humus. As the biota work together consuming organic matter, they break down nutrients, extract chemicals, and make them available to plants. And plants reciprocate by exuding roughly 40 percent of the sugars they produce through photosynthesis back into the soil to feed the bacteria and fungi, whose numbers then grow as a result.[32]

When we feed the soil compost and other amendments, we encourage the helpful soil biota. When the biota thrives, the soil food web functions smoothly, and our plants flourish. Just as when a soil sterilizer is applied, it harms the soil food web. By definition, if you sterilize soil, no organisms will remain within it. The safety of chemical herbicides has been in question for years, but there is no question that herbicides and pesticides are harmful to the rich soil biota and the beneficial insects, birds, and other animals that call our gardens home.

. . . .

31. Ann-Marie Fortune, "The Soil Biota," *Nature*, 2012, https://www.nature.com /scitable/knowledge/library/the-soil-biota-84078125/.

32. Elaine Ingham, "How It Works!" Soil Food Web School, accessed September 1, 2021, https:// www.soilfoodweb.com/how-it-works/.

Exercise
Start a Compost Pile

Start composting. Composting is a way to recycle nutrients and energy and put them back into the soil. Whether you save kitchen scraps in a small plastic bucket with a lid by the sink or fill a backyard bin full of leaves, composting is the best investment you can make in your quest for a healthy garden. A backyard bin or pit is made by collecting leaves, kitchen scraps, and garden waste then setting them aside to let the decomposers (microorganisms, fungi, worms, insects, etc.) break down the raw materials into a nutrient-rich material. Healthy compost has four ingredients: browns, greens, moisture, and oxygen.

Browns: Browns introduce carbon. These include leaves, straw, hay, pine needles, shredded paper, cardboard, and wood shavings or sawdust. Browns should make up the bulk of your compost.

Greens: Greens introduce nitrogen. These include fruit and vegetable scraps, coffee grounds, eggshells, and grass clippings.

Moisture: Because the compost pile needs to be kept moist during dry weather, a convenient source of water should be available. If the pile is dry, add water and mix thoroughly. If the pile is wet and muddy, let it air out.

Oxygen: Use your muscles to turn the pile periodically with a shovel or a pitchfork to incorporate oxygen. The microorganisms that turn food and garden waste into compost require oxygen, and they get a boost every time air is trapped in the spaces within the pile.

As you focus your energy, hold an intention of what you want the compost to become and how it will boost the health of your soil and feed your plant.

Select a dry, shady spot near a water source for your compost pile or bin. Use a ratio of three parts brown to one part green as you layer your compost heap or bin. Keep it moist. Add water to dry materials as they are added, but do not create standing water—this will stall the decomposing process. Cover the top of the compost with a lid or tarp to retain the moisture. The compost is ready when it becomes brown and crumbly.

Compost improves soil structure and its ability to retain the nutrients, moisture, and oxygen plants need. It boosts the vital nutrients that help plants grow and keep them healthy.

Plastics

Limit your use of plastics, and when you are confronted with using them, treat them well so you may use them again and again. Repurposing things like plastic nursery pots and cardboard egg cartons gives the gardener tools for other uses. A saved nursery pot is the perfect pot to propagate cuttings in or transplant seedlings into. In winter before a freeze, I get out my old plastic nursery pots and use them like a cloche, upending them over my garden dahlias to shelter the bulbs under the soil and protect them from freezing.

Weed and Pest Control

If there is one mindful thing you could do to put your garden first, it would be to choose to dig up or pull your weeds instead of choosing to spray a chemical. So much damage is inflicted every year by household gardeners because they rely on soil sterilizers instead of digging out or pulling the weeds. Make a conscious choice to engage with the land by using your muscles instead of relying on an outside source. Invest in a shovel, hoe, or digging stick and dig the weeds out.

Use mulch to suppress weed growth. Mulch acts as a physical barrier to block out sunlight. A layer of mulch also acts to improve the soil's ability to retain moisture. And if you find you must spray, limit the consequences by choosing a natural herbicide. Experiment with some homemade options.

Avoid any recipe that calls for salt. Salt inhibits a plant's ability to use water, which causes dehydration and eventually death. Salt will make your soil infertile, and after it has been introduced, the only way to get rid of it is by leaching it out or by removing the treated soil and replacing it with fresh soil. So please never salt the earth.

If you do use salt as a protective aid for outdoor rituals, try replacing it with ground eggshells instead. Eggshell powder, also known as cascarilla powder, is a protective powder that has been used down through the ages to set barriers of protection against negativity, hexes, and malicious spirits. Strew a circle of cascarilla powder to form a circle. The powder boosts soil health by adding calcium. You can purchase cascarilla powder or save your eggshells and dry and crush them to make your own. Any colored egg will do.

Choosing a Natural Spray When You Must Spray

Sometimes a gardener needs to wage a war to save their plants. When insects invade or fungus infects, it becomes necessary to employ a chemical to control the problem. It is good practice to use the least toxic approach that will do the job effectively. Many garden remedies can be made at home with ingredients you already have in your kitchen.

Recipe
Beer Slug Trap

If you notice that something is devouring your plants overnight, chances are you have a snail or slug problem. While one or two snails is a lovely sight in the garden, if they amass, you could end up with an army of hungry mouths with the power to consume your entire flower collection right down to the soil. You could go out with a flashlight and pick them off by hand, or you could set out a dish of beer. Snails and slugs love the yeasty smell and will choose it over your dahlias.

You will need:
* bowl or clean empty tuna can
* beer

Choose a bowl or a rinsed tuna can and set it near the plant that is being eaten. Just before dark, fill the bowl with beer so that it is about ⅓ full. The attacking slugs or snails will creep into the dish and drown in the beer.

Recipe
Soap Shield

Mix up a batch of soap shield when aphids attack. Soap shield spray uses a mild liquid soap like dish soap or castile soap to cause soft-bodied insects like aphids, mites, and whiteflies to dehydrate.

> **You will need:**
> * spray bottle
> * water
> * 2 Tablespoons mild liquid soap like dish soap or castile soap
> * marker

Fill a spray bottle halfway with water. Add the mild liquid soap and gently swirl the bottle to incorporate the soap into the water as you focus on the intention. Fill the rest of the way with water and fix on the nozzle. Write your intention on the spray bottle and use the solution to spray your infected plants. Spray in the cool of the morning or evening to treat all affected areas. Avoid using it during the hot part of the day. It may take several treatments to get rid of an infestation.

Recipe
Neem Oil Fungus Spray

Spraying is almost always inevitable when a garden fungus strikes. A treatment with neem oil is a remedy for powdery mildew, leaf scab, and tomato blight. Neem oil is extracted from the leaves of the neem tree and is a natural insecticide certified for use in organic gardens. It can be used on aphids, spider mites, or ants to end an invasion. Neem oil is nontoxic to beneficial insects like bees and butterflies (just don't spray them with it).

You will need:

* ★ marker
* ★ 1 spray bottle
* ★ warm water
* ★ 1 Tablespoon neem oil
* ★ ½ teaspoon baking soda
* ★ 1 teaspoon mild liquid soap like dish soap or castile soap

Write your intention on the spray bottle. Fill the bottle halfway with water and add the other ingredients. Gently swirl the bottle to incorporate the oil and soap into the water as you focus on the intention. Fill with water and fix on the nozzle. Generously spray all affected areas.

Recipe

Garlic Spray for Apple Scab

You will need:

* ★ 6 cloves garlic, minced
* ★ warm water
* ★ 1 spray bottle
* ★ marker
* ★ 1 teaspoon mild liquid soap like dish soap or castile soap

In a food processor, whiz the garlic with 1 cup of warm water until the mixture is liquefied. Write your intention on the spray bottle with a maker. Fill the bottle with the liquefied garlic mixture and add the soap. Gently swirl to incorporate the mixture as you focus on the intention. Fill the spray bottle the rest of the way with water and fix on the nozzle. Generously spray all affected areas.

Nurture Local Wildlife

Many different birds, animals, and insects share our garden spaces. I cherish their presence and am often amazed by the things I discover observing their routines. This year a creature, I thought probably a mouse or maybe a squirrel, planted its own row of vegetables next to one of my flowerbeds. When I noticed the row, which consisted of a Swiss chard, a pumpkin, and a sunflower, I watered it and staked the sunflower. Then I waited and watched to see who was gardening with me. I never discovered who planted the garden, but I did see momma skunk help herself to the pumpkin.

The wild creatures that share our world will enrich our lives and bring wonder if we allow them to. Unfortunately, their lives, which are already perilous, are being threatened even more. Forests and meadows, once wild places, are being converted at an alarming rate into fields to farm and housing tracts in place of the natural habitats.[33] In my town alone, farmland and forests are being cleared at a shocking rate to make way for a project of forty thousand new homes—which is terrible planning because when it is finished and populated, it will create chaos, as the town was not planned for such growth, and the single-lane roads are already gridlocked.

Our world is changing. As civilization encroaches on more and more of the wild areas, the natural inhabitants are forced out as the land is cleared and lumbered and sprayed. In 2017, 2018, and 2019 insect decline made the top news.[34] In 2019 a report

. . . .

33. Christina Nunez, "Deforestation Explained," *National Geographic*, February 7, 2019, https://www.nationalgeographic.com/environment/article/deforestation/; Joel Berger et al., "Disassembled Food Webs and Messy Projections: Modern Ungulate Communities in the Face of Unabating Human Population Growth," *Frontiers in Ecology and Evolution* 8, no. 128 (2020), doi:10.3389/fevo.2020.00128.

34. Asher Jones, "Q&A: Global Insect Declines Due to Death by a Thousand Cuts," The Scientist, January 15, 2021, https://www.the-scientist.com/news-opinion/global-insect-declines-due-to-death-by-a-thousand-cuts-68360; Karen Schik, "Why Insects Matter and What You Can Do about Their Decline," Friends of the Mississippi River, January 29, 2021, https://fmr.org/conservation-updates/why-insects-matter-and-what-you-can-do-about-their-decline.

found a million plant and animal species to be at imminent risk of extinction.[35] The perilous drop in insect numbers sparked global concerns.[36]

The awareness of the fragility of natural habitats stirred the desire for a more conscientious approach to gardening. For many the news was an awakening as people around the world realized their every action echoed through the ecosystems of their yards and they had the power to help heal the earth one yard at a time.[37] By encouraging the biodiversity of their gardens, they helped increase insect numbers, which fed the smaller animals like fish, frogs, lizards, salamanders, voles, mice, birds, and bats and encouraged growth in their populations as well.

As gardeners, we have the power to embrace the life of our gardens and become a sort of guardian to all its residents. Through small actions we can boost their numbers and improve the health of our land's ecosystems. By avoiding or reducing pesticide use, by not planting seeds or seedlings that were treated with neonicotinoid pesticides, and by limiting the use of outdoor lights, we can help our yards be healthy habitats.

Our planting choices also matter. Many hybrid flowers sold today as bedding plants are sterile and contain little or no pollen.[38] Instead of choosing new cultivars, seek out old-fashioned and heirloom varieties. Choose simple, open-face flowers over double-flower varieties that have less or impossible-to-reach nectar. Feed the bees by growing flowers with flat surfaces to land on like cosmos and zinnias.

Creating a haven for wildlife also creates a haven for us. When a gardener stops fighting nature and embraces the garden's biodiversity, life swells. Bees and butterflies visit the garden's flowers. Small vertebrates return to where the food is.

. . . .

35. Eduardo Brondizio et al., "Global Assessment Report on Biodiversity and Ecosystem Services" (Bonn, Germany: IPBES, 2019), 24, https://zenodo.org/record/3553579#.YctWNS2ZPUI.

36. Douglas Main, "Why Insect Populations Are Plummeting—and Why It Matters," *National Geographic*, February 14, 2019, https://www.nationalgeographic.com/animals/article/why-insect-populations-are-plummeting-and-why-it-matters/.

37. Douglas W. Tallamy, "Bring Biodiversity Back to Your Garden to Help Save the Planet," *The Independent*, February 29, 2020, https://www.independent.co.uk/property/gardening/rewilding-gardening-biodiversity-insects-native-species-a9356941.html.

38. Justin Wheeler, "Picking Plants for Pollinators: The Cultivar Conundrum," Xerces Society, November 21, 2017, https://xerces.org/blog/cultivar-conundrum.

Backyard birds move in to raise their families in the bird-friendly zone. The interaction also changes us. The surprise sighting of a toad, the delight of a visiting butterfly, or the fascination of watching a bee busily rub itself in the pollen of a flower reawakens a childlike joy and fortifies our relationship with nature. When gardeners and wildlife share the same space, both are rewarded. See part 2 for a list of favorite food plants for a wildlife garden.

Plant Native Species to Sustain Bees and Butterflies

The plight of pollinators is a news-grabbing global crisis. The monarch butterfly and the honeybee are dying out in record numbers. Movements have been organized to plant milkweed to feed hungry caterpillars and ban harmful, bee-killing sprays. And while this is all well and good, your local pollinators are facing the same fate.

Get to know your local pollinators and what they need to feed on and reproduce. Rewild areas to host local pollinators. By not spraying or mowing, a bed of wildflowers or a grassy field becomes a place for caterpillars to live, eat, and complete their life cycles. Let native grasses grow. Grow native vines on walls and fences to create habitat. Seek out packs of native wildflower seeds. Plant the seeds in the spring or fall, sowing them directly into the soil.

Native plants are suited to grow in your zone. Many need little help to thrive. Plant a variety of local wildflowers in a mass to draw wildlife to your garden. Florida researchers found that insects are attracted to landscapes where flowering plants of the same species are grouped together to create blocks of color.[39] White flowers attract moths and bats. Red flowers attract hummingbirds. Blue and purple flowers attract bees. Yellow and purple flowers attract butterflies.

Check out the National Wildlife Federation's native plant finder at nwf.org /NativePlantFinder/Plants for a list of native plants and the caterpillars they host by zip code.

. . . .

39. Elizabeth Y. Braatz et al., "Bloom Evenness Modulates the Influence of Bloom Abundance on Insect Community Structure in Suburban Gardens," *PeerJ* 9 (April 2021): e11132, doi:10.7717/peerj.11132.

Turn Your Lawn into a Wildflower Meadow

The lawn into meadows movement provides space for wildlife by creating no-mow zones. It is estimated that in the United States lawns comprise 40 to 50 million acres of outdoor urban space.[40] A lot of time and resources are spent each year on maintaining these spaces, even though many are largely ignored. The lawn often takes up the largest portion of a yard. Shrink your lawn by turning a portion of it into a meadow.

Your lawn is home to moths and butterflies that shelter in the leaves and grass. By allowing it to transition into a meadow, you are creating a refuge where they will be able to complete their life cycles. You might want to start small. Choose an out-of-the-way section with full to partial sun exposure. Start by removing the sod and digging the topsoil to prepare the area for the native plants. Scratch the dirt with a rake and then scatter local wildflower seeds. Press them firmly into the soil and water the area well. Soon the flowers will grow to create a lovely wildflower meadow area.

Make or Buy a Bee Hotel for Native Solitary Bees

While solitary bees won't make you honey, they are docile, helpful workers that pollinate more effectively than the honeybee. By providing a place for them to live and lay their eggs, you will increase their numbers in your garden. A bee hotel is a shelter made of wooden tubes. All you need to do is hang it up and provide a small mud pit for the bees to use to stop up the end of the tube they choose. Keep the shelter dry and bring it in at winter to protect it from the weather. Store the bee hotel in a dry cool place like an outdoor shed. When the weather warms, hang the bee house outside again.

Many native bees nest below the ground in tunnels or cavities and need an area of exposed dirt to build their homes in. If you spot a small mound of dirt with a hole in it, you might already have a bee in residence.

. . . .

40. Tik Root, "Ditching Grass Could Help Your Backyard Thrive," *Washington Post*, June 30, 2021, https://www.washingtonpost.com/climate-solutions/2021/06/30/climate-friendly-backyard/.

Feed the Birds

Birds are a delight to watch and listen to. They bring enjoyment and fascination. Setting up a feeding station or hanging a hummingbird feeder is a simple way to invite birds to spend time in your garden.

Fill hummingbird feeders with a solution of boiled water and sugar (4 parts water and 1 part sugar). Keep your feeders clean. Hummingbird feeders should be washed out at least every 5 days to prevent mold growth and sugar fermentation. Take your feeder down and dump out any remaining sugar water. Scrub it with hot water and a bottle brush. Don't use dish soap—it is harmful. Refill it with a fresh sugar water solution and hang it up again.

Hang a suet feeder to attract insect-eating birds. Choose sunflower seeds and high-quality seed mixes to feed songbirds. Birdseed feeders also need to be changed weekly. Throw out leftover seed and refill to keep the food fresh. Keep an eye out for moldy seeds. They are deadly. Throw them out the second you spot them. Seed feeders should be scrubbed down monthly. Dirty feeders spread salmonella. Take your feeder down and scrub it with warm soapy water. Rinse and then soak each feeder in a diluted bleach solution (9 parts water and 1 part bleach) for at least 10 minutes. Rinse it thoroughly and let it air dry before refilling.

Provide Water

Water brings life to a garden. Add a water feature and life will show up. Place a birdbath where you can observe it from afar so that you can enjoy watching your visitors without disturbing them. Add a pond to provide drinking water and habitat. The birds and bees will use it to get a drink while frogs and dragonflies will move right in. It doesn't have to be large or costly. You can use anything that holds water—even a bucket will work. Choose an area that gets partial sun exposure and dig a hole large enough to hold your container. Place the container into the hole and bury it so that the rim is flush with the earth. Fill it with water. Create a ledge next to it by placing a log or a stack of rocks to allow easy access in and out of the water. Plant grasses and low-growing plants at its edge to provide habitat and give animals like small frogs shelter.

Let the water sit for a few days for the chlorine to dissipate before adding native water plants. Control mosquitoes by installing a pump to circulate the water or stocking it with small fish.

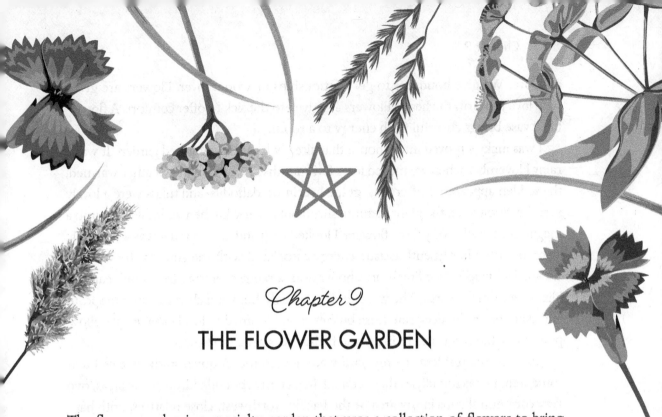

Chapter 9

THE FLOWER GARDEN

The flower garden is a specialty garden that uses a collection of flowers to bring beauty, color, and fragrance to a space. In a flower garden flowers are collected and planted according to a gardener's own style. Planting a flower garden can be as simple as scratching the soil to expose the dirt and casting seeds where they will make contact with the soil and germinate, but the flowers' placement can be elaborately mapped by height and color and even by bloom time. No matter how a flower garden is planted, flowers hold a magick all their own.

If you bought plants from a nursery, before you plant them, set out the pots where you think they should go and step back and look at how they go together visually. Make some adjustments and then plant. Try to plant in bunches of color instead of single spots of it. Try arranging the color in drifts to carry the eye through the garden. If you have a single showy plant, try using it as a focal point and planting around it to complement it.

Flowers are beautiful. Tending a colorful, fragrant flowerbed is work that feeds the soul. Flowers add instant color to a garden. They provide essential foods for many small mammals, birds, bees, and butterflies. Flowers hold the power to connect us to different emotions. Their very presence conveys happiness, contentment, and love. We give bouquets to gel relationships or woo a lover. Flowers are given with love to warm the heart. Flowers are given to the sick to offer comfort. A flower-filled vase brings cheerful fresh energy to a room.

I was lucky. I moved into a house that already had an established garden. It was a rainy November when we moved in. A few months later, when the weather warmed, the sudden appearance of crocus, grape hyacinths, daffodils, and tulips were a lovely surprise. Soon after, the giant, demure shrub outside my kitchen window burst into a magnificent display of yellow flowers. I looked it up and discovered it was a forsythia, a shrub with a hardy, enthusiastic energy associated with the sun. As the weather warmed, bluebells, bleeding hearts, hollyhocks, a range of hostas, iris, lamb's ear, and lilies rose from the earth. The warmer days brought hops and clematis vines to sprout and clamber up the deck rail. Rose bushes soon bloomed in lovely shades of yellow, pink, and white, and later hibiscus and hydrangeas began to flower.

Many of the residents of my yard were new to me. A quick study revealed that some were not as friendly as they seemed. In fact, my rhododendron and azaleas, two very common shrubs in my area of the Pacific Northwest, close relatives, both have toxic compounds in the leaves and flowers that if ingested can cause life-threatening blood pressure and heart issues. The nectar is so toxic it poisons honey if enough pollen is collected. This honey is commonly referred to as "mad honey." Again, I say emphatically, know the plant you work with!

While there is danger in working green magick, there also is great satisfaction when you make a plant ally and forge a relationship with an energy you helped grow. It fosters a familiarity with the energy you are working with as you add to your well of knowledge. And remember, knowledge is power.

See the compendium of plants in part 2 for a list of flowers and their magickal uses.

Botanical Symbolism

Each flower has its own personality, and each has evolved a symbolic meaning that has been reflected down through the ages in literature, art, and song. Jennifer Meagher, senior collections cataloguer at the Met Museum, writes, "Botanical symbolism has its origin in the literature of antiquity, where plants are often used in metaphors for virtue and vice. In classical mythology, human beings are transformed into plants as a reward or punishment, such as in the story of Narcissus, the vain youth who fell in love with his own reflection and transformed into a flower."[41] Crocus, a Greek youth accidentally killed by Hermes; Hyacinth, a youth accidentally killed by Apollo; and Daphne, who was transformed into the laurel tree rather than be taken as Apollo's lover, are more examples.

In Victorian-era England, France, and America, when showing affection was frowned upon, a communication system dubbed the language of flowers evolved: flowers were used to deliver messages that couldn't be spoken. Lists were made and definitions shifted until 1809, when Joseph von Hammer-Purgstall published *Dictionnaire du langage des fleurs*, the first published list on the language of flowers. Other versions soon followed until almost every home had one, though often the definitions would still shift. A beautiful 1884 volume illustrated by Kate Greenaway is available online at the Internet Archive.[42]

The magick of flowers goes deeper than mere symbolism, for each flower has its own magickal and mystical properties. In the past, flowers were carried in pockets, worn as amulets, hung over doorways, and stuffed into pillows and poppets. They were dried and boiled and turned into formulas and potions.

Flowers are lovely when cut from the garden. They are eye-catching when placed in a vase and used as a centerpiece. Wearing flowers in your hair or braided into a crown not only adds to your beauty and makes you feel special, but it also raises spirits and heightens celebrations. A gift of flowers can cheer a friend. Flowers are versatile and can be pinned to a collar, placed in a bouquet, and even floated in a bath to utilize their magickal energy. Many garden flowers are edible and can be used to decorate baked goods, added to salads, and brewed into infusions that are drunk as tea or added to bathwater. But again, I warn you to know the plant you are working with. Not all flowers are harmless. In fact, some garden favorites are deadly. Do your research before ingesting or using any ingredient on your skin.

. . . .

41. Jennifer Meagher, "Botanical Imagery in European Painting," Met Museum, August 2007, https://www.metmuseum.org/toah/hd/bota/hd_bota.htm.

42. Kate Greenaway, *Language of Flowers* (London: George Routledge and Sons, 1884), https://archive.org/details/languageofflower00gree/page/n7/mode/2up.

A Quick Brushup on the Basics

In this chapter, I've provided a few spells to help you incorporate flowers into your magickal practice. Before sharing the spells, I've included an explanation of some of the magickal terms and actions used in the magickal rituals should they be unfamiliar.

Exercise
Come to Center

The act of coming to center is the process of letting the mind quiet while drawing attention in. To do this, fix your attention on what you can sense. Focus your thoughts on your breath, the rise and fall of your chest, the feeling of your skin, the taste in your mouth, and the sounds you can hear.

By drawing in your focus, you draw scattered thoughts into a single sharp focus that consists only of you there in that single moment. And as perception shifts, it expands and sharpens into a wondrously exhilarating experience of being right there, awake and alive, and oh so aware of being there in your own skin.

Get into the meditative position you are most comfortable with and draw a deep breath. Close your eyes and bring your focus to the area behind your breastbone. This area is known as your center. You may feel this spot lower in your belly and that's fine too. Focus on your center as you breathe. Draw in a slow, deep meditative breath, to the count of three, hold and pause to the count of three, and breathe out to the count of three. Breathe, and as your breath moves through your body, visualize a light glowing brightly within your center. If you need to, you can add the sense of touch by pressing your hand over the area as you follow your breath. Breathe deeply as you hold your focus on the glow. Breathe and feel the energy expand with each breath. See it grow as it glows brighter. As you sit with your center, you will begin to experience a shift in perception as the moment grows sharp. Allow the feeling to intensify as you become intensely aware of the exhilarating way it feels to be there, in that moment, within your skin.

Exercise
Set a Catchphrase for a Positive Outcome

A catchphrase for a positive outcome is a line that asks that whatever manifests from your working be for the best of all. Words are powerful. It's easy to ask for what you want, but it's not always easy to see how what we ask for will affect our lives. Sometimes the changes we ask for bring events and feelings that are not what we expected. Including a brief stipulation such as "may the outcome be for the best of all" or "for the highest good" after each request will help to prevent unseen consequences.

Exercise
Prepare Your Ritual Space

This instruction sets the mood for the ritual. The area should be cleaned. All items needed for the ritual should be gathered, brought to the space, and set within reach. Turn on any music you are going to use. Set the lighting. Light a stick of incense. All this preparation works to help trigger a magickal mindset and get you ready for spellwork.

Exercise
Take a Ritual Bath

The ritual bath is an ancient practice that uses the energy of water to submerge the body to clear the mind, energy field, and spirit. Often the entire body and head are submerged. Other times the body is submerged and water is scooped up with a hand and poured over the head. A ritual bath is a bath taken with the intention to cleanse, heal, or prepare the body, mind, and spirit for spellwork.

Come to a ritual bath mindfully. The tub should be clean and ready for use. Salt, oils, and herbs are often used to infuse the water. Get in, lie back in the water, and relax, letting go of all negativity and worry. When you take a ritual bath, tune in to your higher self. If you feel the need, dunk yourself completely under until you feel free and your body, mind, aura, and spirit are clear. When you step from the tub, leave all the negativity behind to disappear down the drain. You may blot yourself dry with a clean towel and go to your sacred space.

If you don't have a bathtub, you can take a ritual bath by using a shower or a large bowl. Fill a bowl with water and empower it, just as you would a bath by adding salt, oil, and/or herbs, and stir with your hand. Pour the water over you, starting with the crown of your head, then work your way downward.

Exercise
Make a Batch of Moon Water

Moon water is water that has been blessed and charged in the light of the full moon. If you plan on drinking it, use artesian water or spring water. Pour the water into a clear jar and seal it with a lid. Set it on a moonlit windowsill to charge in the moonlight.

If you are using the moon water for magickal work, you may want to choose water from a living source, as each has a unique essence. Here is a list with correspondences for empowering your work:

Artesian Water: Good health, knowledge, and wishes

Morning Dew: Beauty, faery magick, glamour, and luck

Rainwater: Abundance, communication, fertility, and inspiration

River Water: Banishing, opportunity, protection, renewal, and setting things in motion

Seawater: Healing, manifesting, renewal, power, and strength

Spring Water: Health, healing, renewal, and acquiring knowledge

Fill a bowl with whichever water you chose, speak your intention to it, and set it on a moonlit windowsill. If you have an outdoor place where it will not be disturbed, you may set it outside under the light of the moon, but you will want to cover it. Retrieve the moon water before sunrise.

The Flower Spells

Flowers brim with positive energy to attract happiness, love, and beauty. Remember, you are always the most beautiful when you radiate your best self.

Spell
I Set My Desire upon the Wind

For this spell you need a windy moment to send out a call for a new love or set a whisper into the mind of someone you already know.

You will need:
* your favorite scented essential oil
* small dish
* red ink pen
* small piece of paper
* dried lavender and rose petals
* windy moment

Pour out a few drops of the oil into the dish. Dip in your finger and anoint your pulse points. Come to center. Take the pen and paper into your lap and think about the love you want to summon. Dip the pen into the oil and compose a short message that you will send out to the universe. It should be clear and concise. Write it on the page and crumble the dried flowers over it. Take the paper and fold it toward you. Carry the folded paper to a spot at an open window, a balcony, or someplace outdoors where the wind will catch the flower bits when you open it. When the wind picks up, whisper what you have written and to whom it is intended, then open the paper and blow the flower bits out onto the wind. As the wind gusts, send your intention off with the flowers.

Spell
Spell to Draw the Love of the One You Desire

You will need:
- ★ 2 handfuls of a mixture of dried rose, jasmine, and violet flowers
- ★ drain strainer that fits the tub
- ★ bit of sweet almond oil
- ★ frankincense, rose, vanilla, or ylang-ylang essential oil
- ★ small white or red candle
- ★ carving tool, such as a thorn from the rose
- ★ matches
- ★ small piece of rose quartz to carry in your pocket
- ★ dish of moon water (see page 84)

Prepare your ritual space. Gather and set out all the things you need before you take a ritual bath.

Fill the tub with water. Take half of the flowers and float them on the water. When you let the water out, be sure to put the strainer in the drain to make cleanup easier and keep the flower bits from clogging the pipes.

Pour a small amount of almond oil into your palm. Add a few drops of essential oil and anoint yourself. Start with your throat, then your breastbone. Rub the oil into your skin and get into the tub. Soak while you visualize being with the one you desire. See them smiling at you, reaching for you, kissing you. When you are ready, completely submerge yourself. Get out of the tub and return to your ritual place.

Take the remaining flowers and crush them into small bits and pieces to use as candle dressing. Use your hand, a mortar and pestle, or a rolling pin. Do not grind the flowers into powder, only small bits. As you work the blossoms, say,

Flowers of love, with your power charge this working.

Take the candle and carve a heart and the initials of the one you desire into it. Dress the candle with oil and roll it in the crushed flower bits. Come to center, draw a breath, and light the candle. Take the stone in your dominant hand and speak your desires to it. Dip your fingers in the moon water and run them over the stone. Lift the stone to your lips and blow across it. Hold it in your dominant hand and meditate as you visualize the love you desire. Meditate until the candle burns down. Tuck the rose quartz into your left pocket or into the left side of your bra to hold your intention and remind yourself to be your best self. When you go to bed, place the stone underneath your pillow so that it influences your dreams while you sleep.

Spell

Petition the Goddess of Love

Myrtle is sacred to the goddesses of love Aphrodite and Venus and the fertility goddess Demeter. Ask for divine assistance by making a bouquet from rose and myrtle.

You will need:
* several cut roses
* several sprigs of myrtle
* ribbon to bind the base

Arrange the flowers and myrtle sprigs to form an attractive bouquet. With clear, focused intent, bind the stems with ribbon, wrapping it around the ends to secure the bunch. Knot the ribbon. Hold the bouquet in your lap as you visualize the love you desire. When you have finished, place the bouquet on your altar as a gift to the goddess.

Spell
New Love Spell

For the seeds for this spell, some good choices are aster for eternal love, daisy for a love that is loyal, gloxinia to inspire love at first sight, carnation (red for admiration, white for a love that is pure, or pink for a love that will never be forgotten), forget-me-not for true love, and yarrow for love everlasting.

You will need:
* pink candle
* 1 piece of natural paper
* handful of flower seeds
* 1 eggshell
* 1 garden trowel

Gather your ingredients, prepare your space, and take a ritual bath. Return to your spell place and light your candle. Meditate until you have come to center. Set the paper before the candle and place the seeds upon the paper. Say,

> Tiny seeds, holder of life,
> before I sow, a task I charge thee.
> As you grow, reach out your power,
> a subtle energy that grows with each hour.

Crumble the eggshell over the seeds.

> A love to bring blessing into my life.
> A love that is pure without any strife.
> Someone known or someone new,
> in their heart grows a love for me that is true.
> As I say, so mote it be.

Carry the paper with the seeds outside to a place suited for their growth. Dig a small hole with your garden trowel and place the seeds in the hole. Cover with dirt and mind the seeds to help them grow, knowing that as they grow, so shall your love prospects.

Spell
See Me, Hear Me Glamour

Use this spell when you need to boost your charisma and transform into a radiant, glowing beacon of love energy. Work this before a party or a get-together and make note of how people respond to you when you turn on the charm.

You will need:
* pink candle
* handful of jasmine blossoms or rose petals
* scoop of shea butter or a small dish filled with a spoonful of carrier oil like sweet almond or apricot oil
* rose and jasmine essential oils, or vanilla and ylang-ylang essential oils
* pinch of silver glitter

If you are able, work this spell in front of a mirror. Just before you get ready for your outing, run a bath. Light the candle. Drop in a handful of jasmine blossoms or rose petals and get in. Relax and let go of all the other distractions so that it is only you, and the bathwater, and the glorious feeling of soaking. Breathe deep and smile as loving energy fills your heart. Feel it flow through your core, energizing you as well as bringing you peace. Breathe deep, and with your breath, feel the energy swell. It fills your senses as it radiates from your skin to fill the whole room with loving energy. When you are ready, step out of the tub. Blot yourself dry and face the mirror. Take a scoop of shea butter into your palm and drip 2 drops of each essential oil over it. Work the butter between your palms until it becomes liquid. (Shea butter melts at body temperature no matter how cold it is in the room.) Run the butter up over your forearms and massage into your skin as you say,

I embrace the energy of the goddess of love and am empowered.

Coat the backs of your hands. Take another scoop of shea butter into your palm. Add 2 drops of each essential oil and the glitter and work the butter again between your palms. (If you are using a carrier oil, add 2 Tablespoons to a small dish along with 5 drops of each oil. Add the silver glitter and start here.) Use your finger to mix it and trace your coated finger over your stomach to draw a heart. Your finger should be coated with enough glittery oil to leave a shimmering trail. Say,

> *I am empowered.*

Lift the finger to your heart and press it to your skin as you say,

> *I radiate the love of the goddess.*
> *See me shine for I am loved.*

Look at your reflection and smile before you dip your finger into the oil, touch your lips, and say,

> *Hear me and warm to my voice.*
> *Know that I am beautiful. For I am love.*

See yourself glowing, radiating with the energy of the goddess. Breathe deep and smile as you get ready for your party, meeting, or date knowing that you embody the goddess herself. Do your hair. Wear something special. When you get there, smile. Touch the hand or arm of the person you are talking to and radiate love energy. Boost the power by silently repeating this phrase in your mind:

> *I am loved. I am beautiful. I am love.*

Spell

Apple Blossom Compulsion Spell

While this spell won't force someone to love you, it will get you into their thoughts and dreams. Before you work this spell, you will need to make two items. First, you will need a small heart-shaped sachet. Choose some fabric. Fold it in half and cut out a small heart to make a pillow. You will want it to be about 2 inches across so you can wear it in your left pocket or tucked into your bra. Stitch the pieces together, leaving a small opening so that you are able to stuff a small braid of hair and a small gemstone into it. Second, you need a batch of moon water, water from a living source (rainwater, river, or spring water) that has been left to charge in the light of the full moon. To make the moonlight stronger, you can set a mirror under the bowl.

You will need:
* strands of your hair
* hair of the one you desire
* length of red string
* candle
* small dish of moon water
* small knife, rose thorn, or carving tool
* small dish of honey
* handful of dried apple blossoms (jasmine flowers can be substituted)
* candle dish
* matches
* small heart-shaped sachet with one of the seams still open
* small rose quartz or piece of coral
* needle
* thread
* pair of scissors

Tie both sets of hair together at one end with the string and then braid the string and hair together into a small braid. Secure the end with the string. Take the candle in your dominant hand and tell it what you want it to do. Dip the finger of your other hand in the moon water and trace a heart on the body of the candle. Lift the candle to your lips and breathe the name of the one you desire onto it. Take your carving tool and carve a heart into the candle. Inside the heart carve the first initial of the one you desire, a plus sign, and your first initial. Dip your fingers in the moon water and run them over the carving. Dip your fingers in the honey and smear it over the candle as you tell it what you want it to do. Roll the candle in half of the apple blossoms, and then set the candle in the candle dish and light it. Gaze at the flame and come to center.

When you are ready, pick up the braid, lift it to your lips, and tell it what you want it to do. Blow your breath across it. Then stuff it into the heart-shaped sachet you made. Next, take the gemstone do the same, programming it with your breath before you stuff it in with the braid. Add the remaining apple blossoms and use the needle and thread to sew the heart closed, sealing the hair, stone, and flowers inside. With each small stitch, as your needle dips and raises, whisper what you want the charm to do. When you have finished, knot the thread and clip it. Set the needle aside and take the sachet in your dominant hand. Lift it to your lips and tell it what it is going to do. Breathe out over the charm and then tuck it into the left cup of your bra or into your left pocket. When you aren't wearing it, keep it tucked away in a safe place.

Spell
Right Decision Spell

Have you been brooding over a big decision? Use this helpful spell when you must make a choice between different paths.

You will need:
* notebook paper (1 page for each option with the choice written across the top)
* blue pen
* black pen
* yellow candle
* sweet almond oil
* small dish of blossoms plucked from a California lilac or a butterfly bush
* handful of nasturtium flowers
* matches

Lay the pages and the pens out before you. Anoint the candle with sweet almond oil as you focus on making the best decision. Place the nasturtiums in the dish with the blossoms. Light the candle and then take the dish of flowers and bruise them between your fingers. Draw a deep breath and rub them over your forehead. Then strew them over the burning candle. Gaze at the candle's flame. When you reach a meditative state, say,

> Powers that be, grant this request, the gift of clear sight.
> I ask to be blessed to see with crystal clear understanding
> the result of each choice I might make and to understand
> the cost of each and the path I would take.
> Thanks be to thee for your guidance.

Draw a deep breath and look over the heading on the top of each page as you listen for any input. Take the blue pen and list each positive point. Use the black pen to list each possible negative result. Do this as long as you are able.

When you have finished, reread what you have written. Then fold each page in half twice and meditate on the options. When you are ready, say,

> By your guidance, let me see the path that is best.

Take the pages out and reread them whenever you have a quiet moment. Add both positive and negative points as they come up. Be open. Don't favor one decision more than another. Instead, take time to open your awareness and listen. Write down any information that comes through. By the end of the week, you should be able to make your decision.

Chapter 10

THE COTTAGE WITCH'S GARDEN

While many gardens are filled with plants grown solely for their beauty or scent, a witch's cottage garden contains plants cultivated for their magickal and medicinal powers. If you choose well, you will find it is this type of garden that fuels your magickal practice and brings out your inner witchiness. Start your collection. Do your research. Long for knowledge and hold it tight. Apply what you learn as often as you are able. Spend time daily outside. Work within the requirements of the zone you live in. Experiment and keep a written record. Honor nature. Open your perception to the turning of the wheel and let the magick of the universe fill you with wonder. And most of all, allow yourself to enjoy the experience.

Working with plants is a magickal act that allows the gardener to reclaim the wisdom of ages past. Connect with nature under the endless sky, opening your heart to the restorative peace of digging your hands in the earth, aware of the world around you as the season shifts, and you witness that the change in light and weather invokes a deep-rooted response and awakens spirituality. Ritual takes on a life of its own as our awareness of the powers that be advances.

You will discover that while some will grow like weeds in your yard, other must be coaxed in indoors pots, but it is these small plants vibrating with potential, collected and cared for, nurtured and researched, and grown for no other purpose but to empower your spellcraft, that will stimulate and fuel your magickal practice. It is through this interaction, through the practice of the green craft, we grow our power and, with its knowledge, nurture our inner life and come to deity.

Start with Something to Inspire Your Magickal Nature

When I first started on this path, it was the work that I did in the garden that most inspired my magickal practice. I turned my backyard into a garden and learned to identify each plant growing there. I studied the history and lore and started making note of the different energies, and when it was time to branch out, I discovered a local nursery that sold specimens of rue, wormwood, mugwort, and cinquefoil, plants that made me feel magickally motivated. I would stop on my way home from work and discover a new specimen, and each discovery woke a part of my spirituality that felt both liberating and a little bit forbidden. Soon toadflax, morning glories, moonflowers, hollyhocks, rosemary, periwinkle, and poppies were added. It was such a wonderful feeling to discover a new ally brimming with magickal energy to take home and work with.

My garden was a magickal place where I spent most of my free time, working, meditating, and simply observing. Quiet and solitary, I worked through a secret study that became profoundly empowering. A discovery of knowledge that sparked my curiosity, freed my thoughts, woke my spirit, and expanded my consciousness. It led me to find others, four lovely women, and we became a group of five, a company of strengths as we each came from different walks of life, brought together and bound by our love of gardening. Gardening brought us together, but knowledge fused us into a circle of friends, a liberating relationship that gently fueled our own individual and completely unique spiritual advancement. We began an open exchange of herbal lore and gardening tips and then began to experiment with group meditations and tarot readings. Our friendship gelled into a collaborative psychic circle. We would meet and test ideas with no judgment, each coming from a place of open curiosity and kindness. It was liberating. It was empowering. With exposure to their ideas and viewpoints, my spirituality grew as my knowledge and awareness expanded. No longer was I a product of my programming. I'd come awake, alive in a world that became fascinating and the possibilities limitless.

As the seasons shifted, our gardens would rise, bloom, and fade. Each resonating with a different sort of energy that was both observable and tangible, each reflecting a bit of the personal gardener's own psyche. Just as we each were different, our labors produced different results. Your garden is a reflection of your ideals and perspective. When you come upon an obstacle, look around at other gardens in your community to see what is going on in them. You may discover a different approach that will be successful. Talk to other gardeners in your community so that you may learn from their successes and their setbacks. Use your community resources. Visit your local nursery. Join a local gardening group to expand your knowledge and your connections.

See part 2 for a list of plants for a witch's garden and their magickal uses.

The Art of Strewing Herbs

The practice of strewing herbs is an ancient practice to freshen the air and keep away vermin. Herbs were also strewn to instigate positive energy flow and honor the spirits. Richard Folkard writes, "In olden times on Feast days places of worship were significantly strewed with bitter herbs."[43] In June during the Roman Catholic procession of the Corpus Domini, along "the entire route of the procession at Rome, the ground is thickly strewn with Bay and other fragrant leaves."[44] To strew herbs, fresh or dried herbs are crumbled and scattered about and left to impart their lovely scent and their cleansing, repelling, or drawing powers. Through strewing, we can reconnect with an ancient practice and awaken memories of a past we have forgotten. Strew rose petals over a table to create a romantic atmosphere. Before a garden party, strew mint or lavender down the walkway or across a patio to elevate mood and create ambiance. Strew herbs to freshen the air in a stale room and instigate energy flow. Strew herbs in a sickroom to make it fresh again.

. . . .

43. Richard Folkard, *Plant Lore, Legends, and Lyrics* (London: Sampson Low, Marston, Searle, and Rivington, 1884), 57.

44. Folkard, *Plant Lore, Legends, and Lyrics*, 32.

Here are a few strewing blends to try:

Agrimony, Peppermint, and Rue: Use to end mischief and break a hex.

Chamomile, Hyssop, Lavender, and Rue: Strew to guard and protect and give feelings of comfort.

Meadowsweet, Mint, and Vervain: Use for a house blessing to instill harmony and draw happiness.

Rosemary, Sage, and Rue: Strew these to cleanse and clear and keep negativity away.

Rose Petals, Thyme, and Yarrow: Try this blend to heal past hurts and soothe aggravation.

Sprinkle the mixture across the floors and leave overnight. When you wake the next morning, sweep up the herbal bits and carry them out your door. Dump the bits on the other side of your property line.

The Magick of Herbs

Since the dawn of time, herbs have been valued for their medicinal and magickal properties. Stories attribute herbal knowledge as being given to man by angels, Nephilim, faeries, and even the gods themselves. Evidence from prehistoric burial sites supports the claim that Paleolithic peoples had knowledge of herbal medicine 60,000 years ago.[45] When a potion maker created a brew that proved effective, he noted the process and passed it down, making it possible for us to take that knowledge and apply it today.

For each plant, flower, shrub, and tree contain a unique magickal signature, an enormous potential stored within that, when aligned with intent, not only enhances a magickal working but causes the results to be more predictable. Knowledge is power. When you learn and understand the behavior of an herb, you gain the ability to predict a magickal response. To empower your work, do your research. Get to know the

. . . .

45. Yvette Brazier, "What Was Medicine Like in Prehistoric Times?" Medical News Today, November 2, 2018, https://www.medicalnewstoday.com/articles/323556.

herbs and flowers you are working with. And remember, just because something is common does not make it safe. Many common plants irritate the skin, and others are toxic.

As you write your recipe, learn as much as you can about every ingredient. Begin with your intent. Write it out as clearly and concisely as you can. Then align like with like. Keep in mind it's all about energy. And keep a written record. Your notes will act as a guide to help you identify what worked and what didn't. Make note of the date, the time of brewing, what aspect the moon was in, and each ingredient. And later, as events unfold, record the results in as much detail as you can. It is this data that enables the spellcaster to evolve.

As you create your brew, craft it with mindfulness and precision. Measure your ingredients. Be neat. And always use clean, dry jars with tight-fitting lids. Remember, any introduced water will encourage mold growth and spoil your herbal blend. Gather your ingredients and add each mindfully as you empower it with the power of the spoken word. Employ a statement or chant as you work to raise the energy. Then boost the power of your intent by writing it on a label and fixing it to the jar.

Homemade Teas

Herbal teas are simple to make. They offer support and comfort to improve your health and well-being. Most "teas" are created by infusing, decocting, or making a tincture of dried leaves, roots, twigs, bark, and flowers.

Infusion

An infusion is prepared by adding 1 to 2 teaspoons of dried herb (or 3 to 6 teaspoons of fresh herb) to a cup of boiling water and allowing it to steep before straining out the plant material. When you make a cup of tea, you are using the infusion method.

Some preparations fare better with a cold infusion, in which the plant matter is added to cold water and left to sit outside in the cold, in the refrigerator, or on a moonlit windowsill for an extended period of time. Moon tea and cold-pressed coffee are both examples of a cold infusion.

Some infusions are made with oil instead of water. The plant matter is covered with a carrier oil and left to macerate or sit for several weeks before the plant matter is strained out and the oil rebottled in clean jars with tight-fitting lids.

Decoction

This is usually the method to brew dense matter like roots, bark, and seeds. A decoction is prepared by placing 2 to 4 teaspoons of plant matter in a pan with 1 cup of water. The mixture is brought to a gentle boil. The heat is then reduced, and the pan is covered and left to simmer for a determined amount of time before being allowed to cool. The plant matter is strained out and the leftover liquid, or decoction, is ready for use.

Tincture

A tincture is an herb extraction by alcohol. The alcohol dissolves the active properties of the plant matter and acts as a preservative allowing the tincture to retain its effectiveness for a much longer time. Fill a canning jar ⅓ full of finely chopped fresh or dried leaves, flowers, roots, barks, or berries. Cover with a high-proof alcohol, filling the jar to the top. For best results use a high-quality, clear, and low-flavor alcohol like vodka. Seal with a tight-fitting lid and store in a cool place out of direct sunlight. Shake your tincture several times a week, checking to make sure the herb is still completely submerged and the alcohol level is still at the top. Do not allow the herb exposure to air. Add alcohol if needed to avoid oxidation. After 4 weeks, strain the tincture through a cheesecloth into a brown glass bottle and label it.

Some Sample Recipes

Here are some sample magickal infusions for you to try using flowers and herbs that you can grow in your own cottage garden.

Recipe
Cup of Comfort Blend

This blend infuses the loving energy of rose with the soothing energy of chamomile and lavender. Brew up a mug and sip when you need to soothe your spirit or just unwind from a hectic day.

You will need:
* dried rose petals
* dried chamomile flowers
* dried lavender buds

Mix the dried flowers together in equal parts and store in a tightly sealed container. To make a cup of tea, use 1 teaspoon of herbal mixture to every 1 cup of water. Boil the water. Measure the herbal mix into a heat-resistant teapot or bowl and pour hot water over it. Steep for 4 to 5 minutes and strain. Pour the liquid into a mug. Sweeten with honey if desired. Breathe deeply as you sip and relax.

Recipe
Cup of Cheer

This brew has an uplifting energy to lift your spirits when you are feeling blue.

You will need:
* dried lavender buds
* dried skullcap
* dried rosemary leaves

Mix the dried flowers and herbs together in equal parts and store in a tightly sealed container. To make a cup of tea, use 1 teaspoon to every 1 cup of water. Boil the water. Measure the herbal mix into a heat-resistant teapot or bowl and pour hot water over it. Steep for 5 minutes, then strain into a mug. Breathe deeply, smile, and sip this tea to instill a dose of happiness.

Recipe
Hawthorn Heart Charger

The leaves, flowers, and fruit of the hawthorn are used to cheer and strengthen the heart.

You will need:
* 1 Tablespoon hawthorn leaves and flowers
* 1 Tablespoon rose petals
* ½ cinnamon stick

Bring 1 cup of water to a boil. Put the leaves, flowers, and cinnamon stick into a heat-resistant teapot or bowl and pour hot water over them. Allow the blend to steep for 15 minutes. Strain out the herbs. Pour the tea into a teacup and sip to enhance heart health, improve outlook, and warm the spirit.

Recipe
Reenergize Brew

Become yourself again with this invigorating, restorative brew.

You will need:
* 1 Tablespoon chopped dandelion root
* 1 Tablespoon St. John's wort
* 2 Tablespoons dried nettle

Measure 2 cups of water into a pan. Add the herbs and roots and bring to a boil. Reduce to a simmer, cover with a lid, and simmer for 7 to 10 minutes. Remove the pan from the heat. Strain the liquid into a mug and stir in a spoonful of honey. Sip to restore and revive.

Recipe
Headache-No-More Tea

End stress headaches and muscle tension with a cup of this nerve soother.

You will need:
* ⋆ dried feverfew flowers
* ⋆ chopped lemongrass

Measure out the herbs in equal amounts and mix them together. Store the blend in a tightly sealed container. To make a cup of tea, use 1 teaspoon to every 1 cup of water. Boil the water. Measure the herbal mixture into a heat-resistant teapot or bowl and pour hot water over it. Steep for 10 minutes, then strain into a mug. Breathe deeply, relax, and sip.

Recipe
Pleasant Dreams Brew

You will need:
* ⋆ dried California poppy
* ⋆ dried passionflower
* ⋆ dried skullcap

Mix the dried flowers and herbs together in equal parts and store in a tightly sealed container. To make a cup of tea, use 1 teaspoon to every 1 cup of water. Boil the water. Measure the flower mix into a heat-resistant teapot or bowl and pour hot water over it. Allow it to steep for 7 minutes. Strain out the herb. Pour the liquid into a teacup and sip for an effective nerve tonic that relaxes the mind and body and induces pleasant dreams.

Recipe
Keep Calm and Carry On

This relaxing brew will help you keep your calm during a stressful day.

You will need:
* ★ 2 Tablespoons dried lemon balm
* ★ 1 hops cone, crumbled into pieces
* ★ 1 Tablespoon dried catnip
* ★ 1 Tablespoon dried skullcap
* ★ 1 Tablespoon dried raspberry leaves

Mix the dried herbs and flowers together and store in a tightly sealed container. To make a cup of tea, use 1 teaspoon to every 1 cup of water. Boil the water. Measure the flower mix into a heat-resistant teapot or bowl and pour hot water over it. Allow it to steep for 4 minutes. Strain out the herb. Pour the liquid into a teacup, relax, and sip.

Recipe
Horehound Lozenges

Employ the age-old tradition of folk medicine and mix up a batch of horehound lozenges, a hard candy with a unique and pleasant flavor hinting of licorice and root beer.

You will need:
* ★ cookie sheet
* ★ 1 Tablespoon butter, plus more for greasing the cookie sheet
* ★ 1 cup fresh horehound leaves and flowers
* ★ large saucepan
* ★ water

- ★ 3 cups brown sugar
- ★ 1 teaspoon cream of tartar
- ★ sugar to dust
- ★ candy thermometer

Generously coat the cookie sheet with butter. Wash the horehound and place it in a saucepan. Cover with 3 cups of water. Bring to a boil. Turn off the heat and let the herbs steep for 20 minutes. Stain out the herb, keeping the liquid. Measure 2½ cups of liquid back into the saucepan. Stir in the sugar and cream of tartar. Bring the liquid to a boil. Stir in the butter and continue to heat until liquid reaches 300 degrees Fahrenheit on a candy thermometer (hard crack stage).

Pour the liquid into the buttered cookie sheet and let it cool. Just before it sets up, score the candy into squares with a knife to make it easier to break apart. When cool and set, break the candy into pieces and dust them with sugar to keep them from sticking together. Store the candy in an airtight container.

Magickal Washes

Boost your cleansing power with magical infusions. Make a magickal washwater by adding an herbal infusion to your cleaning water. Use it to rid a dwelling of residual energy from the past occupant, cleanse a room of unwanted spirits, or dispel residual energy after a fight or an argument. Choose one room and begin by clearing out the clutter. Look around your space. Put things away. If you come across something you do not have a use for, then get rid of it. This is the act of space clearing, or the act of releasing the old and stifled to allow the flow of fresh energy into the space you've made. After you've deemed what is going, sort it into piles for trash, recycling, and the donation center and get rid of it. When you return, it's time to clean.

Decide what you want to accomplish, and with a clear intent, choose an herb to empower your washwater. Make an infusion by adding 1 to 2 teaspoons of dried herb (or 3 to 6 teaspoons of fresh herb) to a cup of boiling water and allowing it to steep before straining out the plant material. Add the infusion to your washwater, and clean. When you have finished cleaning, dispose of leftover washwater by pouring it out away from your property line.

While magickal cleaning can be performed anytime, you can power up your actions by performing your cleaning spell on a Saturday. Saturdays are ruled by Saturn, who will infuse work for health and restoration, and his energy supports clearing out the old and removing obstacles to make way for new energies.

Recipe
Infusion to Instill Harmony

Anger builds more anger. Instead of tiptoeing around it, remove the residual resentment with this brew.

You will need:
* borage flowers
* bachelor's buttons
* periwinkles
* a sprig of rosemary

Bring 2 cups of water to a boil. Remove the pan from heat. Add the flowers to the water and steep for 10 minutes. Strain out the plant matter and add the infusion to your washwater. Breathe out any tension you may be holding. Let go of all your resentment and clean. Smile as you wash down the kitchen table, then the counters, and the floor. Sing as you wash away resentments and restore harmony and family love. Dump leftover water into the street.

Recipe
Infusion to Deflect Jealousy

Jealousy has been the root for one of the oldest hexes throughout history: the evil eye, a curse transferred by a jealous glance or malicious gaze that has the power to bring about illness, bad luck, and injury.

If you fall victim to a hostile run-in, brew up this infusion to deflect the negative thoughtform before your luck turns or your health is compromised.

You will need:
* ⋆ 2 Tablespoons fennel
* ⋆ 2 Tablespoons hyssop

Bring 2 cups of water to a boil. Put the herbs into a heat-resistant bowl and pour hot water over them. Allow the herbs to steep for 10 minutes. Strain the herb out and add the liquid to your washwater. Wash down the room where the offense took place. If a neighbor caused the harm, add the infusion to your washwater and wash down your porch or your car. If a coworker caused it, use the infusion to wash your work area. You can even add it to your bathwater and soak to deflect the negativity from your person.

Recipe
Infusion to Clear Away Obstacles

Both bay and coltsfoot encourage energy flow. Use this infusion to open channels and clear away blockages. Add it to washwater to clear out the energy of your space when it becomes stagnant.

You will need:
* ⋆ 2 Tablespoons bay leaves
* ⋆ 2 Tablespoons coltsfoot

Bring 2 cups of water to a boil. Put the herbs into a heat-resistant bowl and pour hot water over them. Allow the herbs to steep for 10 minutes. Strain out the herbal matter and add the liquid to your washwater. Use the washwater to wash down your workspace, your door and threshold, or your front porch to clear away obstacles and encourage opportunity.

Recipe
Infusion to Get Rid of a Persistent Memory

Brew up this regret-clearing brew and add it to your washwater to clear away nagging memories and put the past to rest. Use it to clean up an area after a difficult roommate has moved out or after a relationship has ended.

You will need:
* 2 Tablespoons hyssop
* 1 Tablespoon bay leaves
* 1 Tablespoon coltsfoot

Bring 2 cups of water to a boil. Put the herbs into a heat-resistant bowl and pour hot water over them. Allow the liquid to steep for 10 minutes. Strain the herbs out and add the liquid to your washwater. As you clean, do some breathing exercises. Exhale out your hurt and regret and inhale peace. Dump the leftover washwater out into the street. You can also add 1 cup of the infusion to your bathwater and dunk yourself under to rinse away hurt and resentment. Scoop a portion of the water up from the tub as it drains and throw it out on the street.

Recipe
Infusion for Protection for Your Home

Rue has the power to not only rid an area of malevolent energy but return it to its sender! Combine rue with hyssop and juniper and you get a potion to safeguard against mischief.

You will need:
* 2 Tablespoons rue
* 2 Tablespoons hyssop
* 1 Tablespoon crushed juniper berries

Bring 2 cups of water to a boil. Put the herbs into a heat-resistant bowl and pour hot water over them. Allow it to steep for 10 minutes. Strain the herbs out and add the liquid to a bucket of washwater. Use it to rinse your front step, door, entryway, or anywhere you deem the protection is most needed.

Recipe
Infusion for Protection for Possessions

You will need:
* handful of aspen leaves
* 1 Tablespoon crushed juniper berries

Bring 2 cups of water to a boil. Put the leaves and berries into a heat-resistant bowl and pour hot water over them. Allow the plant material to steep for 10 minutes. Strain and use the liquid to wash down any item or place, or even add it to your bathwater when you fear you have caught the attention of a thief.

Recipe
Cinquefoil Curse Removal Infusion

You will need:
* 3 Tablespoons cinquefoil

Bring 2 cups of water to a boil. Put the herb into a heat-resistant bowl and pour the hot water over it. Steep for 9 minutes. Strain and pour the liquid into your bathwater and soak to rid yourself of a curse, stop a string of accidents, or end a run of bad luck.

Homegrown Herbal Smoke-Cleansing Wands

The ritual burning of fragrant herbs and herbal resins has been practiced by almost every culture down through the ages from the burning of offertories on the altars of the ancient gods, the smoking sage bowls of Indigenous peoples, and the burning of bukhoor, to the more modern practice of lighting a smoking incense stick. There is something spiritual about the aromatic smoke that shifts our perspective and connects us with the Divine. The fragrant smoke is a great visual in meditation to carry prayers to the heavens or form a bridge to unseen worlds while the power of scent is a powerful trigger to shift realities or slip into a centered awareness.

Smoke-cleansing sticks can be burned to clear away negative thoughts, hostile emotions, and the residual energies left from others. Cleanse after an argument to rid a space of hostile emotions. Cleanse an area when a roommate moves out or when you move into a new house to remove residual energy left behind. Cleanse your space to get rid of stale energy and restore flow when you begin a new project or take an old one back up again. Burning sage clears out spiritual impurities. Smoke-cleanse yourself when you need to step out of an old mindset into a new one or you need help releasing an emotion that is holding you back.

Spell

Make a Basic Smoke-Cleansing Wand

Many store-bought smoke-cleansing sticks are made from bundled white sage (*Salvia apiana*), a traditional smudging herb used for thousands of years by North American Indigenous peoples. White sage grows in bushy clumps across the Southwest. Recently, big business has moved in to harvest wild plants, and because there are little to no regulations, white sage is being overharvested and the natural habitat destroyed. If you live in zones 8 through 10, you can grow white sage, but garden sage (*Salvia officinalis*) makes a lovely smoke-cleansing wand also.

You will need:
* ⋆ sage, cedar, or another herb of your choice
* ⋆ cotton string, thread, or yarn

Gather a bundle of the fresh herbs, cut to the length that you want. Align the twigs so they each face the same direction and hold the bottom of the stems together tightly. Take your string and tightly wind the string around the bottom of the bundle, making sure that it is tight. As the herbs dry, the bundle will shrink and the string will become looser. After you have wound the string around the bottom a few times, wind it up and around until the string is within 1 to 2 inches from the top. Then wind the string around back down to the stem again and tie it off. Hang your wands out to dry for a 1 to 2 weeks

Here are some herbs to choose from and their correspondences:

Cedar: Healing, protection, purification, enhancing communication, and summoning

Eucalyptus: Protection, boosting success, and inspiring visions

Juniper: Comfort, protection, and exorcism

Lavender: Instilling calmness and promoting happiness

Mugwort: Enhancing psychic sight and deflecting malevolent thoughts

Sage: Cleansing, purifying, warding, and sharpening awareness

Sweetgrass: Cleansing, balancing, and purification

Spell

Smoke-Cleansing Wand to End Gossip

The flower stalk of the lamb's ear plant is known as lamb's tongue. It holds a protective energy to negate hostile influences.

You will need:
* stalk of lamb's tongue
* sprig of sage almost the same length as the lamb's tongue
* stalk of lavender
* cotton string, thread, or yarn

Gather the bundle of the fresh herbs, aligning them so they each face the same direction. Tightly hold the stems together. Take your string and wind it tightly around the bottom of the bundle, making sure that it is secure. After you have wound the string around the bottom a few times, wind it up and around until the string is within 1 to 2 inches from the top. Then wind it around back down to the stem again and tie it off. Hang your wand out to dry for 1 to 2 weeks.

To use the wand, hold a match to the end until it lights. Let it catch, then blow the flame out. Wave the wand so that the smoke wafts around the area you would like to cleanse. Use it in binding and defensive magick to stop gossip or end communication with someone.

Empower Your Spellwork with Homegrown Herbs

Imagine the convenience of walking out through your door and clipping a sprig from an herb that you nurtured to use as an ingredient for a magickal potion. Imagine the potency. Some herbs are quite powerful and the reaction immediate: the scent of lemon instantly lifts the spirit, lavender calms the mind, and chamomile triggers restfulness. Those herbs elicit immediate reactions, but there are many others with subtle energies, each causing a reaction, setting things in motion, some so subtle you don't even realize you are reacting. Combining herbs and rituals creates a sensory experience that deepens thought and emotions to strengthen our magickal abilities. These blends burn well on charcoal disks, but feel free to use an incense heater or a tea candle oil burner as an alternative.

Recipe
Wealth-Drawing Incense Powder

You will need equal parts of:
* dried galangal root
* dried ginger root
* cedar twigs
* dried patchouli leaves

Chop and grind the roots, twigs, and leaves into small bits. Store the mixture in a tightly sealed jar. Burn a pinch at a time on a charcoal disk to draw wealth.

Recipe
Love-Drawing Incense Powder

You will need:
* small spoonful of powdered sandalwood
* handful of dried jasmine flowers
* handful of dried rose petals
* ½ spoonful of powdered orris root

Grind the ingredients together and store in a tightly sealed jar. Burn a pinch on a charcoal disk to empower love magick. Roll oiled candles in the powder to empower love spells.

Recipe
Energy-Clearing Incense Powder

You will need equal parts of:
* dried rue
* dried vervain
* dried white sage

Grind the ingredients together and store in a tightly sealed jar. Burn a pinch on a charcoal disk to clear away stagnant or negative energy and raise the vibration of a room.

Recipe
Protection Incense Powder

You will need:
- ★ small spoonful of powdered frankincense
- ★ handful of dried bay leaves
- ★ handful of dried rue
- ★ small spoonful of powdered dried orris root

Grind the ingredients together and store in a tightly sealed jar. Burn a pinch on charcoal disk to calm the spirit. Roll candles in the powder to empower protection magick.

Spell
Show Me Spell

Need to see the truth of a situation? Work this spell to reveal a person's true intentions. Note that mugwort tea should not be used during pregnancy.

You will need:
- ★ 1 cup mugwort tea
- ★ small hand mirror
- ★ clean cloth
- ★ mortar and pestle, or a bowl and a smooth stone
- ★ pinch of ground cloves
- ★ pinch of dried sage
- ★ white or yellow candle
- ★ cedarwood or sandalwood essential oil
- ★ pen
- ★ slip of paper

* small personal belonging of the person you are going to focus on (some hair or nail clippings, a note they wrote, a small personal item, or a photo of them)
* matches

Sip the tea and think of what you would like to discover. Splash some of the tea over the mirror and dry it with the cloth. Mindfully grind the cloves and the sage together as you ask them to add their energy to your working. Anoint the candle with oil and roll it in the ground herbs. Write the person's full name on a small piece of paper and set the paper on the mirror. The mirror should be large enough that a portion of its surface is not obscured. Set the personal item on the paper. Then set the candle on the mirror and light it. Sit comfortably where you can fix your attention on the surface of the mirror. Meditate on what you would like to know as you send your thoughts into it. Power it with your breath. Exhale as you visualize sending your breath through the mirror, energizing it to reveal the answer you seek. Gaze upon its surface and say,

Mirror, mirror glowing bright.
Reveal to me the truth this night.
Is (he/she/they or name) just or is (he/she/they) conniving?
What are (his/her/their) motives? What is (he/she/they) hiding?
All glamour falls away to reveal what is lying underneath.
Bare now and honest for me to see,
the truth is revealed by my will, so shall it be.
Lean close and breathe across the surface of the mirror.
All that is concealed is now revealed.

Gaze upon the mirror and be open for any messages. They could be in the form of a feeling, a vision, a word or phrase that comes to mind, or a realization that comes through.

Spell
Traveler's Good Luck Bag

You will need:
- ⋆ olive oil
- ⋆ nutmeg essential oil
- ⋆ white or orange candle
- ⋆ matches
- ⋆ piece of turquoise
- ⋆ comfrey leaf
- ⋆ small cloth bag
- ⋆ 9 whole cloves
- ⋆ 9 juniper berries

Pour a bit of olive oil into a small dish. Add 9 drops of nutmeg oil and use the mixture to anoint your candle. Light the candle and come to center. Take the turquoise in your dominant hand. Visualize it being filled with light until it glows. Dip your finger in the dish of oil and anoint the stone. Lean to blow across it, then say,

Stone of blue, stone of luck, add your power to this charm.
Let this journey be joyful as your power keeps me free from harm.

Wrap the stone in the comfrey leaf and tuck it into the pouch. Take the cloves into your dominant hand, blow across them, and say,

Herb of spice with power true,
add your energy to empower this charm.

Drop them into the bag and say,

By your power and your protection,
this journey will be a safe and pleasant one.

Drop in the juniper berries as you repeat the phrase.

When you have added all the ingredients, hold the charm bag up to your lips and blow across it before you say,

With this charm, good luck is mine.

Tuck the bag into your left pocket while you are traveling.

Herbal Protection Power

Mankind has been turning to herbs for their powers to protect for thousands of years. Herbs are ground into incense, tied into bundles, and braided into wands. Herbs are brewed into infusions and potions. They are burnt, hung, and tucked into sachets and poppets.

Carry a sprig of rue in your pocket when you must face a jealous rival to avoid carrying their negativity back home with you. Stuff a mojo bag with agrimony and a handful of rue and wear to send back the evil eye. To end gossip, brew up an infusion of a rue. Spit into it forcibly three times. Then carry the liquid out into your yard and toss it out toward the troublemaker to neutralize the hostility and end the unwanted attention. Or stuff a pouch with agrimony, rue, and a burdock root for a protective amulet to deflect a curse and send the ill will back to the one who conjured it. Brew up a mugwort infusion and soak your feet after you return home from an unpleasant encounter to counter the negative exchange. Or simply drop a sprig of lemon verbena into a cold drink and sip it to counter negative thoughts or avoid old habits. If your luck changes, you become ill, or you are the victim of a series of accidents and suspect you've been hexed, brew up an infusion of cinquefoil, feverfew, or hyssop and pour it into your bathwater. Add a handful of sea salt and centaury flowers and soak to counter the spell.

Spell
European Witch Bottle

The witch bottle was both a form of counter-magick and a protection device that was buried at the entrance of the home, hidden in the chimney, or somewhere in the structure of a home to protect against magickal attacks and repel those with evil intentions. Antique witch bottles have been found with pins, nails, shards of glass, broken razor blades, stones, feathers, ash, hair, and urine sealed inside. The nails were often bent to "kill" them, which moved them from one reality to another to give them more power on the spiritual plane.[46]

You will need:
* white, red, or black candle
* olive oil
* matches
* bottle with a lid
* combination of sharp things such as broken glass, pins, needles, or nails
* rosemary, rue, or wormwood
* seeds from a box elder or other maple
* salt
* urine, vinegar, or wine

Anoint the candle with the oil and light it. Come to center.

Take the bottle and begin to fill it with the sharp objects as you tell each of them what you want them to do. Something like this:

Pins and needles, nails and glass,
I charge you to repel those with ill wishes,
catch the harm and hold it fast.

. . . .

46. Brian Hoggard, *Magical House Protection* (New York: Berghahn Books, 2019), 29–30.

Add the rosemary, rue, wormwood, or a combination of the three to neutralize malevolent energy and return a hex to the sender. You might charge each with a personal task:

> *Rosemary and rue, I call you by name:*
> *empower this charm,*
> *to bind all that is harmful,*
> *the power reclaimed.*
>
> *Protect this home and all who reside here,*
> *so that all are safe and may abide without fear.*

Add the seeds from a box elder or other maple and say,

> *Tree of power, tree of might, by your seeds a bind is cast.*
> *What was sent remains within this charm bound fast.*

Add the salt and tell it to neutralize or cleanse. And last, add the liquid. Some of your urine or saliva will do. If you'd rather not use those, you could pour in some vinegar or red wine. Then cap the jar and seal it by dripping candle wax over the top. When you are finished, charge the bottle. Lean over and blow across it as you say,

> *Bottle, you have been enchanted to ward and protect.*
> *Halt all magickal attacks and turn away all those with evil intent.*

Bury it near the entrance of your home or hide it where it will not be disturbed. The goal is to place it somewhere where it will be left alone and remain intact, so be careful where you place it.

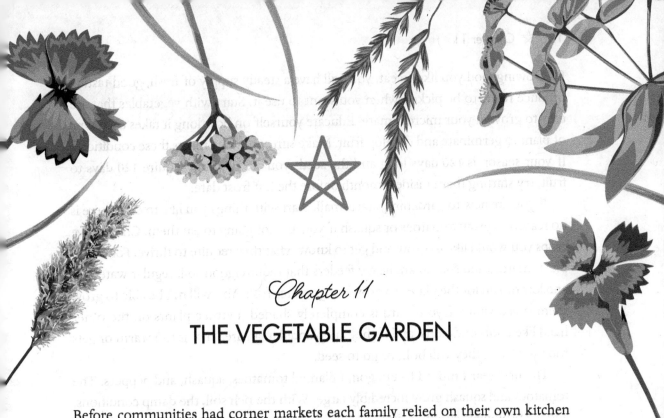

Chapter 11

THE VEGETABLE GARDEN

Before communities had corner markets each family relied on their own kitchen garden to provide herbs, vegetables, and fruit for the family table. Then as lifestyles changed, so did the family garden. Today most homes have a manicured grass lawn that stretches over most of the yard serving no purpose other than being ornamental. In fact it is estimated that lawns cover 50 million acres in the United States, a great waste of land and water usage that is often ignored by the homeowner, who often pays for someone else to mow and care for it.[47] But just as victory gardens rose in times of war, today's concerns with our food systems and the uncertainty of supply and quality are spurring a resurgence of interest in self-sufficiency, and more and more family lawns are being shrunk to make way for a kitchen garden.

The kitchen garden provides security as well as sustenance. It also gives control over the quality of the food we are eating, as it reconnects us to our food and the knowledge of how it was grown, knowledge that carries history and heritage.

. . . .

47. Mary Talbot, "More Sustainable (and Beautiful) Alternatives to a Grass Lawn," Natural Resources Defense Council, September 30, 2016, https://www.nrdc.org/stories/more-sustainable-and-beautiful-alternatives-grass-lawn.

By growing food you like to eat, you will have a steady supply of fresh, good-tasting produce ready to be picked when you want to use it. Start with vegetables that are easy to grow in your microclimate. Educate yourself on how long it takes each type of plant to germinate and develop fruit. Make sure your area meets these conditions. If your season is 120 days long and the seeds you are planting require 120 days to fruit, try starting them inside a month before the last frost date.

If you are new to gardening, start small. Start with things you like to eat. There is no reason to grow tomatoes or squash if you are not going to eat them. Choose five crops you would like to grow and get to know what they require to thrive. For example, tomatoes and squash are heavy feeders that require good soil, regular watering, and lots of sun for the plants to grow and produce fruit. You will not be able to grow them successfully if your yard is completely shaded. Lettuce plants on the other hand like cool conditions, and if they are planted in an area that is too warm or gets too much sun, they will bolt, or go to seed.

The first year I moved to Oregon, I planted tomatoes, squash, and peppers. The tomatoes and squash grew incredibly large. With the rich soil, the damp conditions, and the prolonged summer sunlight hours, quick-growing crops do exceedingly well here. However, the soil is cold for long periods of time, even in summer, and the nights get so cool that warm-weather crops like peppers and watermelon are nearly impossible to grow. I've been experimenting with different cultivars. This spring I had success growing peppers in my greenhouse. I still have not been able to grow a watermelon any bigger than a tennis ball. Will I keep trying? Probably. Watermelon is my husband's favorite summer fruit, and I have been told there are short-season cultivars that will produce here. Now I only need to find one.

The Importance of Location

One of the most important decisions for your vegetable garden is where to put your garden bed. The first thing to consider is the amount of sun exposure. Vegetable plants require full, direct sun to produce fruit. Choose a site with eight or more hours of direct sunlight.

You will also need easy access to a source of water. Vegetable plants need to be watered regularly so the soil does not dry out while the plant is flowering and fruiting.

Next, consider space. Some vegetable plants grow bushy, while others are sprawlers that will creep across an entire lawn or garden bed. One of the most important steps in planning a vegetable garden is to allot the amount of space each plant needs as it matures. While beans and peas can be grown vertically, plants like squash, peppers, and tomatoes need to be spaced apart, and creeping plants like pumpkin and butternut need their own patch or to be planted at the garden's edge so they can grow out over the lawn or a walkway.

The Right Time to Plant the Garden Bed

The soil is ready to plant when it is dry enough to work and warm enough for seeds to germinate or support seedlings that have been transplanted without the danger of shock. Tender crops like cucumbers, tomatoes, eggplant, and squash will die if temperatures fall too low. On the other hand, cold-season crops like spinach will germinate poorly when temperatures get too warm. You can significantly raise soil temperature by covering it with plastic. Remove the plastic before planting, or if you are experiencing a prolonged cool period, leave the plastic and plant through holes in it. Likewise, you can shelter an area with shade cloth to provide cooling shade for cool-weather plants when temperatures warm.

Soil moisture is also a concern. If you live in an area with spring rains, avoid working soil that is too wet, as it will compact and ruin the soil's structure. You can do a test by digging a small hole and taking a handful of soil into your hand. Squeeze it hard and open your palm. The perfect soil should crumble apart. If the soil clumps together and looks like a ball of clay, it is too wet. Do not work it until it dries out, or you will end up with a bed full of hard dirt clods. Likewise, if the soil is too dry, you need to water it well several days before planting.

Tap into the Energy of Garden-Fresh Produce

There is an amazing store of energy in the foods we eat. Not only does it supply our bodies with nutrients and calories, but it also contains magickal energy that, when prepared with intent, can maximize mealtime in a magickal way.

Kitchen witchery is the act of setting an intention, aligning it with the energy in food items, and charging the food with action—the action of measuring, mixing, stirring, and cooking to transform a substance into a meal, all while focusing on the intention. We raise energy and form it with our thoughts. We fuel it with the actions of our body, with each deliberate action of measuring, chopping, kneading, peeling, and stirring. By our thoughts, our words, our breath, and our emotions, the energy is shaped to heal, nurture, empower, gladden, and even compel.

Everyone has the ability to apply this practical craft every day. Through its application, you can bring your Pagan practice to your everyday life, making magick every time you create, no matter the medium.

See part 2 for a list of individual vegetable plants and their magickal correspondences.

Recipe
Asparagus Tart

Asparagus is an early vegetable. The thin, delicate stalks shoot up and are ready for harvest in spring. Asparagus season is short. Harvest the young spears when they have grown 6 to 8 inches above the soil. Cut them off at the base of the soil with a sharp knife. As the spears mature, the stalks become tough and the flavor strong. They will grow to become a 4-to-6-foot tall, feathery plant that will flower and produce tiny red berries. Asparagus dies back in winter's cold but will rise again in spring when the ground warms, returning larger and more abundant.

Magickally, asparagus carries energy for desire, health, love, and virility. Wheat and cheese both carry energy to nurture and comfort. Mustard energy stimulates, while lemon contributes a sunny energy to cheer and brighten.

This recipe makes one 11-by-14-inch tart.

You will need:
* 1 sheet frozen puff pastry
* 1½ pounds asparagus stalks
* flour for dusting
* 1 Tablespoon olive oil

* 2 Tablespoons dijon mustard
* 2 cups shredded gruyère cheese
* 1 Tablespoon fresh lemon zest
* salt and pepper, to taste
* ½ cup shredded parmesan

Set the puff pastry out to thaw as you set your intention. This recipe will support work to make someone feel special, encourage friendship, inspire romance, or arouse passions. When you have your intention firmly in mind, gather the ingredients and tell each what you would like it to do.

Preheat the oven to 400 degrees Fahrenheit. Wash the asparagus and chop off the tough portion of the stalk. Add the discarded ends to your compost bucket if you have one. Dust your work area with flour and mindfully unfold the pastry dough. Cover it with parchment paper, and with a rolling ien, gently roll the dough out to form an 11-by-14-inch rectangle. Discard the parchment and carefully transfer the dough to a baking sheet by folding it, moving the dough to the pan, then unfolding again. Use a fork to prick the dough all over. This will allow the steam to escape and keep the dough from puffing. Bake until golden, about 15 minutes.

In a small dish, mix together the olive oil and mustard. Brush the mustard mixture over the baked pastry dough and sprinkle it with gruyère. Fit the asparagus spears in the center of the pastry, in a single layer over the gruyère, alternating ends and tips. Leave the borders of the pastry uncovered. Brush the asparagus with the remainder of the mustard mixture and top with fresh lemon zest, a pinch of salt and pepper, and the parmesan. Return it to the oven to bake until spears are tender, about 25 minutes. When the pastry is done, remove it from the oven and allow it to cool on the baking sheet for 15 minutes before cutting. Use a sharp knife or pizza cutter to cut it into squares. Serve the tart warm or at room temperature.

Serve as an appetizer to lighten the mood and open the way for opportunities. Serve to an acquaintance to charm them, to a friend to warm the relationship, or to a date to bolster interest.

Recipe
Fresh Tomato and Jalapeño Salsa

Tomatoes and jalapeños hold energy to stimulate creativity and inspire affection.

Exposure to chili oil can cause skin irritation. Wear gloves when handling hot peppers. Avoid direct contact. The oil can cause a very uncomfortable burning sensation that, depending on how sensitive you are to it, can last for hours.

While half the magick comes from the ingredients, the other comes from you. Formulate your intention and say it out loud, sing it, or simply hold it in your mind as you chop each tomato, dice the onion, and mince the cilantro and garlic. It's when we embrace mindfulness that magick happens.

This recipe makes 4 cups of salsa.

You will need:
- ★ 1 or 2 jalapeño peppers
- ★ 3 cups chopped tomatoes
- ★ 1 cup diced onion
- ★ ¼ cup minced fresh cilantro
- ★ 3 cloves garlic, peeled and minced
- ★ juice of 1 lime
- ★ salt and pepper to taste

Put on a pair of food handler's gloves and cut a pepper in half longwise. Remove the stem and most of the seeds and discard. The heat of the pepper is in the seeds, so if you like it hot leave some in or add a second pepper. Put the chopped tomato, onions, cilantro, garlic, and pepper bits into a bowl and mix together. Starting with 2 Tablespoons, add the lime juice to taste. If your lime is really juicy, you may only need ½ the juice. Be present as you mix. Affirm your intention. Mindful preparation evolves our efforts from a half-hearted attempt into a mindful masterpiece. This is the act of conscious creation. Suddenly, the salsa isn't just a tasty treat but a vehicle to refresh thought, encourage creative inspiration, or arouse a lover's affections. Season with salt and pepper and serve with chips at a meeting to inspire a flow of fresh ideas. Serve with a quesadilla at a friendly lunch to loosen tongues and encourage conversation.

When left chunky, this salsa is the classic pico de gallo. Both versions will last several days in the fridge. If you prefer a smoother consistency, simply pulse the mixture lightly in a food processor. Be careful not to emulsify, or you will end up with salsa juice. Serve over tacos to spice up the meal. Serve it to a date to rouse affection.

Recipe

Pumpkin Fettuccine

Pumpkin is a lovely seasonal food associated with the autumn festivals. It holds energy to attract the positive and elicit fondness. The pumpkin also holds energy for protection and can bind, banish, and help you to see what is unseen. This recipe makes 4 servings.

You will need:
* 4 Tablespoons butter
* 1 small onion, chopped (about 1 cup)
* ½ teaspoon dried rosemary, or 1 teaspoon fresh
* ½ teaspoon dried sage, or 1 teaspoon fresh
* 2 cups cooked pumpkin
* 1½ cup vegetable or chicken broth
* 1 cup milk
* 1 Tablespoon brown sugar
* ¼ teaspoon cinnamon
* ¼ teaspoon nutmeg
* ½ cup parmesan, plus more to finish
* 2 ounces goat cheese, cut into chunks
* 1 cup water
* ½ pound fettuccine
* salt and pepper to taste

In a large pan, melt the butter. Add the onion, stirring to coat. Add the rosemary and sage and cook until the onion begins to brown. Add the pumpkin, stirring and mashing to mix. Add the broth and milk. Stir in the brown sugar, cinnamon, and nutmeg. Stir in the parmesan and goat cheese. Add the water and bring to a simmer. When the sauce starts to simmer, stir in the fettuccine, making sure it is covered with sauce, and cook, stirring occasionally, until the noodles are done, about 10 minutes. Season with salt and pepper to taste. Serve a portion to comfort or encourage affection. Eat this dish to gain positive energy for empowerment or enhance psychic sight.

Recipe
Wilted Dandelion Salad

This small flower is maligned as a weed and thought of as a blight to gardens, as it often is a tenacious volunteer, springing up in lawns and growing across open spaces, but dandelion greens are chock full of nutrition and can be eaten raw, sautéed, or steamed. They are loaded with vitamin K, an important vitamin for brain health. Dandelion greens are also a good source of antioxidants and minerals that help a body remain strong and youthful. Harvest the young greens in the spring for culinary uses.

Magickally, dandelions hold positive energy for beauty, health, luck, and psychic ability. Add them to your diet to fight aging and help reduce the appearance of blemishes, wrinkles, and age spots. Cultivate a patch of dandelions to use in recipes and draw positive energy and good luck to your home.

This recipe makes 4 small or 2 medium servings.

You will need:
* 4 cups young dandelion leaves
* 2 Tablespoons sugar
* 3 Tablespoons red wine or champagne vinegar
* ½ teaspoon dry mustard
* 3 bacon strips
* 1 clove garlic, minced

* Salt and pepper to taste
* 2 eggs, hard boiled and chopped

Wash the dandelion leaves and place them in a colander to drain. In a small bowl, stir together sugar, vinegar, and dry mustard. Fry the bacon until crisp, then remove it from the pan and set it aside. Crumble it when it's cooled. Add the garlic to the pan with bacon grease and sauté for about 1 minute. Turn off the heat and add the sugar mixture to the pan. Stir until the sugar is dissolved. Add the dandelion greens to the pan and toss to coat. Transfer the wilted greens to a serving plate. Season to taste with salt and pepper. Finish with a topping of chopped egg and crumbled bacon bits. Serve to boost vitality, gain positive energy for empowerment, or enhance psychic sight.

Recipe
Roasted Summer Squash

Summer squash is a boon for the summer cook as garden plants will produce a steady supply from late June to fall's first frost.

This recipe makes 4 servings.

You will need:
* 2 yellow summer squash, sliced into planks
* 2 zucchini, sliced into planks
* 1 red onion, sliced
* 2 Tablespoons olive oil or more
* 1 teaspoon garlic powder
* salt and pepper

Preheat the oven to 400 degrees Fahrenheit. Place all the vegetables in a large bowl. Drizzle with olive oil and add garlic powder. Stir until the vegetables are evenly coated. Arrange them in a single layer on a baking sheet and roast until tender (about 15 minutes). Season with salt and pepper to taste. Serve as a side dish to fortify health and increase awareness. Eat them to increase energy for fertility.

Recipe
Roasted Parsnips

Roasted vegetables are delicious and very easy to prepare. Parsnips hold an earthy, masculine energy that supports creation and sex magick.

Early parsnips are tender and delicious. Though parsnips are a fall food, some are left in the ground over winter and then are harvested when the ground thaws in the spring. Spending the winter in the cold converts their starches to sugar, making them much sweeter than winter parsnips. Unfortunately, this process also makes the core woody. To find out whether a parsnip has a tough core, halve it lengthwise and stab it with the tip of a paring knife. If the core feels very dense compared to the flesh, you might consider slicing it out.

You will need:
* parsnips
* olive oil
* salt

Preheat the oven to 400 degrees Fahrenheit. Wash, trim, and peel the parsnips. Slice them into 1-inch pieces and toss with olive oil and salt. Arrange the pieces in a single layer on a baking sheet and roast them until tender, about 30 minutes. Serve them to fortify health, boost energy, or empower the beginning of a project.

Recipe
Savory Coconut Flour Zucchini Pancakes

These flavorful gluten-free pancakes are sure to satisfy a craving. They are loaded with the energy of beginnings. Eat one before any important meeting to awaken new ideas. Serve to students before exams to increase their ability to focus. Eat them to increase awareness and intensify your connection with the natural world.

This recipe makes about 8 pancakes.

You will need:
* ★ 2 Tablespoons butter
* ★ ¾ cup diced yellow onion
* ★ 2 cups grated zucchini
* ★ 1 Tablespoon lemon zest
* ★ 3 Tablespoons chopped fresh basil
* ★ ½ teaspoon salt
* ★ ½ teaspoon black pepper
* ★ ¼ cup coconut flour
* ★ 6 eggs, separated

Heat the butter in a pan and add the onion. Stir to coat and sauté until the onion pieces begin to turn golden brown. In a large mixing bowl, add grated zucchini, lemon zest, basil, salt, and pepper and mix to incorporate. Add the cooked onion and coconut flour and mix well. Add the egg yolks and mix until incorporated. In a separate bowl, beat the egg whites until thick but not stiff. Gently fold the egg whites into the zucchini mixture. Do not overmix or the eggs will become flat and the batter will become runny. Spray a nonstick pan with cooking spray and heat. Pour in ½ cup of batter and cook until golden brown, about 2 minutes. Flip and cook until done, about 2 more minutes.

Eat a pancake hot right from the pan when you need some nourishing comfort food. Top it with an egg and serve it for breakfast for a hearty meal with energy to empower creative ventures and spiritual enlightenment. Serve hot with a sprinkle of chopped green onion and a pinch of crushed red pepper to boost intuitive powers. Serve with a dipping spread made of 1 Tablespoon of lemon juice mixed into ¼ cup of mayonnaise and serve to refresh your optimism or brighten your outlook. Or serve them with a dollop of onion sour cream dip to temper words and inspire awareness of others.

Recipe
Onion Sour Cream Dip

This simple dip infuses the savory, bold flavor of onion with the cool satisfying taste of sour cream to create a creamy, delicious dip with energy to soothe and pamper any gathering.

This recipe makes 2 cups.

You will need:
* ★ 2 Tablespoons butter
* ★ 2 cups chopped onions
* ★ 1½ cups sour cream
* ★ 2 teaspoons Worcestershire sauce
* ★ 1 teaspoon sugar
* ★ 1 teaspoon garlic powder

In a large sauté pan, melt the butter. Add the onion and stir to coat. Cook the onion pieces over medium heat, stirring occasionally until they start to brown. Remove the onions from the pan and set them aside to cool. In a medium bowl, mix together sour cream, Worcestershire sauce, sugar, and garlic powder. Stir in the cooked onion pieces and put the dip in the refrigerator to chill for at least 1 hour prior to serving. Serve with roasted vegetables to add a cool, zesty flavor. Serve it as a dip with potato chips to enliven a party or with a tray of raw vegetables to add zest and heighten enthusiasm.

Recipe
Zucchini Bread

This quick bread recipe is just the thing to help you use up your unending supply of summer zucchini.

This recipe makes 1 loaf or 12 muffins.

You will need:
* ⋆ 3 cups flour
* ⋆ 1 teaspoon salt
* ⋆ 1 teaspoon baking soda
* ⋆ 1 teaspoon baking powder
* ⋆ 3 teaspoons ground cinnamon
* ⋆ 3 eggs
* ⋆ 2 cups sugar
* ⋆ 1 cup butter, melted
* ⋆ 1 Tablespoon vanilla extract
* ⋆ 2 cups grated zucchini
* ⋆ coarse sugar to finish

Preheat the oven to 325 degrees Fahrenheit. In a medium bowl, measure out the flour, salt, baking soda, baking powder, and cinnamon and stir together. Set aside. In a mixing bowl, cream together eggs, sugar, butter, and vanilla. Stir in the flour mixture and mix only until incorporated. Stir in the zucchini. Grease and flour a bread pan or muffin tins and fill with batter. Top with coarse sugar and bake 50 to 60 minutes for bread or 30 minutes for muffins. When the bread becomes aromatic, insert a wooden skewer into the center. If it comes out clean, remove the pan from the oven and cool. Slice and serve to promote positive feelings and encourage an optimistic worldview. Serve at a meeting to make ideas more fertile. Give a loaf to a neighbor to sweeten the way they think of you.

Recipe
Rhubarb Chutney

This recipe makes about 2 cups of chutney.

You will need:

* ⋆ 2 Tablespoons olive oil
* ⋆ ½ cup chopped onion
* ⋆ 3 cups chopped rhubarb, chopped into small pieces
* ⋆ ½ cup dried cranberries or raisins
* ⋆ 1 cup brown sugar
* ⋆ ¼ cup cider vinegar
* ⋆ ½ teaspoon ginger
* ⋆ ½ teaspoon cinnamon
* ⋆ ½ teaspoon chili powder
* ⋆ ½ teaspoon garlic powder
* ⋆ 1 dash crushed red pepper flakes
* ⋆ 1 pinch of nutmeg

Measure the olive oil into a dutch oven or a heavy-bottomed pot and add onion. Stir to coat and sauté until the onion pieces are clear. Add the rhubarb, cranberries, and sugar and stir to combine. Add the vinegar and spices and heat to a simmer, then reduce the heat and cook, stirring frequently until the rhubarb is tender, about 10 minutes. Transfer the rhubarb chutney to a heat-resistant bowl and cool. Cover and store the chutney in the refrigerator for up to 1 week. For a flavorful treat, serve the chutney with a sharp cheddar cheese toasted sandwich. Serve with brie and crackers to infuse a party with enthusiasm and encourage optimistic outlooks or serve with a quesadilla to amp up the flavor and inspire affection.

Recipe
Luscious Garden Tomato Pie

I learned to make this pie last year when my tomato plot suddenly had a surplus of fruit all turning ripe at once. The delicious creamy flavor of roasted tomatoes and cheese pairs beautifully with the flaky crust to make the pie incredibly satisfying.

You will need:
* 1 pie crust
* 2½ pounds tomatoes, thinly sliced
* 1 teaspoon salt
* 1 Tablespoon butter
* 1 onion, chopped
* ½ cup basil, chopped
* pepper, to taste
* ½ cup feta cheese, crumbled
* ½ cup parmesan cheese, grated
* ¼ cup mayonnaise
* handful of shredded mozzarella

Preheat oven to 425 degrees Fahrenheit. Place the pie crust in a 9-inch pie pan and bake for 20 minutes. While the crust bakes, arrange the tomato slices in a single layer and sprinkle with salt. Set them aside. Heat the butter in a pan and sauté the onion bits until they turn translucent. Layer tomatoes, onion, and basil in the prepared crust. Season with a grind of pepper. In a bowl, stir together the cheeses and mayonnaise and spread the mix over vegetables in the pie crust. Top with mozzarella and bake at 350 degrees Fahrenheit for 30 minutes. Serve warm or cold. Pair with a salad for a satisfying and healthy meatless meal brimming with energy for love and abundance. Take this pie to a cookout or potluck to inspire friendships and fondness.

Spellwork with Vegetables

Just as any plant can be used in our spellwork, so can garden produce. For example, blackberries hold energy to empower protection magick. Press the ripe berries to make juice and use it to draw protection runes and symbols. Use a sweet potato as a poppet or carve it into an effigy to use in love magick. Or pour boiling water over orange peels and allow the liquid to steep. Strain and pour the liquid into a bath to amplify attraction powers. Use pomegranates to evoke ancestors or dark goddesses. Or grind dried banana slices into powder and use it to empower fertility and prosperity magick.

Spell
Pumpkin Banishing Spell

The pumpkin holds the power to banish habits, unwanted spirits, or abusive people from your life.

You will need:
* pumpkin
* paper
* pen
* 9 bay leaves
* 1 teaspoon cloves
* sprig of rosemary
* handful of garlic skins
* small votive candle, white or black
* matches

Hollow out a pumpkin. Take the paper and write a detailed description of what or who you intend to banish. Place the paper inside the pumpkin and top with the herbs and the garlic skins. Nestle the candle inside and light. Let it burn until the candle burns out. The next morning, bury the remains.

Spell
Love Spell Ink

Beetroot ink is a natural pink ink that is perfect to empower love spells.

You will need:

* ★ 1 large or 2 small beets
* ★ water
* ★ white vinegar

Wash, peal, and trim the beets. Put the roots into a pot and cover with water. Put the pot on the stove and bring it to a boil. Turn the temperature down to maintain a simmer. Cook until the beet is tender. Remove the beets, reserving the liquid. At this point, the beets are a byproduct and may be used however you would like. When the liquid has cooled, mix in ½ teaspoon of vinegar per 1 cup of liquid. And voilà! Your ink is ready to use. Just dip in a quill and write.

Spell
Walnut Water Bath Spell to Shed
the Influence of a Past Lover

You will need:

* ★ 3 quarts water
* ★ 9 black walnuts still in their husks
* ★ matches
* ★ black candle
* ★ slip of paper
* ★ pen
* ★ small fireproof dish

Bring 3 quarts of water to a boil. Drop in 9 black walnuts still in their husks and boil until the liquid reduces to 1 quart. At this point, the liquid should be dark brown. Cool, strain, and bottle.

For the bath spell, light the candle and fill the bath. Add 1 cup of the walnut brew to your bathwater. Write the name of the person you wish to be free of on a slip of paper and set the pen and the slip of paper on the edge of the tub. Place the candle within easy reach and get into the tub. Relax and come to center. When you are ready, dunk yourself under the water and say something like,

> *By this water, I am released from your power.*
> *Your influence washes away.*
> *The power is mine to take back.*
> *I am free. I am free. I am free.*

Scribble out the name and burn the slip of paper in the candle flame over a fire-proof dish. Dunk under the water again, and when you come out, say,

> *The light of the universe shines upon me.*
> *I am filled with peace.*
> *My thoughts are mine and mine alone.*

Scoop out a portion of the bathwater as you drain the tub. If there is any ash left from the paper, dump it into the cup of bathwater and dispose of by dumping it out into the street. If you want help, dump the bathwater out at a crossroads and leave an offering to the energy that is going to deal with your charge. When you are finished, turn and walk away without looking back.

Spell
Bath to Become Irresistible

This beauty bath spell is taken in preparation for a date. Take this bath before you get ready. In the summer months it is done using an avocado, and in the winter it uses the energy of cooked pumpkin.

You will need:

* ½ cup mashed avocado or ½ cup cooked pumpkin, depending on the season
* 1 generous Tablespoon honey
* 2 Tablespoons cream
* sea salt
* matches
* handful each of lavender and catnip
* white candle
* washcloth
* strainer that fits the tub drain

Place the fruit you are using into a bowl and add the honey and the cream. Mix together. Take the bowl and the rest of the ingredients into the bathroom and fill your bath. Add a handful of salt to the water and light the candle. Set the ingredients you need in easy reach and get into the tub. Relax and come to center. When you are ready, mindfully add the lavender to the bowl of mashed fruit as you think of the person finding you irresistible. Mix the herb into the fruit and honey with your fingers. Add the catnip and mix it in, holding the intention of being irresistible.

Let out a long, slow breath, blowing across the mixture as you focus on becoming irresistible. With your fingers, scoop a dollop of the mixture onto your chest as you say,

> Fruit of love, power this enchantment true.
> a charm of becoming,
> as I now become irresistible to you.

Smooth the mixture across your chest and over your breastbone as you say,

> See me, hear me, feel me.
> (Name of desired person),
> see the beauty of my soul and find me irresistible.

Drop another dollop of the mixture onto your chest. With your hand smooth it up onto your neck as you say,

> *(Name of desired person), hear the ring of my voice*
> *and find the sound irresistible.*

Drop another dollop onto your chest and smooth the mixture up over your chin as you say,

> *(Name), feel the fire rise in your heart and*
> *know that my lure is irresistible.*

Scoop another dollop onto your chest and smooth it up until your face, forehead, and shoulders are covered.

> *(Name), look at me. See me now. Hear me now. Feel me now. Know*
> *that I am irresistible.*

Sit back and relax as the enchantment seeps into your skin. Hold the person you desire in your thoughts as you soak. When the bath begins to cool, take the washcloth and wipe off most of the fruit mixture. Then submerge yourself, rinsing the rest from your skin. When you let the water out, be sure to put the strainer in the drain to make cleanup easier and keep the bits from clogging the pipes. Get ready for your date and know that your date will not be able to resist your charms.

Chapter 12

THE CULINARY HERB GARDEN

Culinary herbs enrich our lives with flavor, fragrance, magick, and medicine. A sprig of thyme deepens the flavor of soup and grants energy for courage, luck, and healing. The scent of lavender soothes the psyche. A cup of chamomile tea promotes rest. Herbs hold energy that resonates deep within us to comfort and calm or to heal and refresh, and if you enjoy cooking, a plot of aromatic culinary herbs is a true delight.

What is your favorite herb? Do you sweeten your tea with stevia or flavor it with pineapple sage? Maybe you favor rosemary, or is the basil-topped option the choice that appeals to you? Do you have your own stevia, rosemary, or basil pot? If the answer is no, then why not? There is no reason why you shouldn't grow the herbs you use most often. Most herbs are easy to grow and will grow just as well in a container as in the ground or a raised bed. A plot of cilantro is very handy to the cook who makes a lot of salsa. Oregano and basil are essential herbs for the Italian foodie, while a pot of lemongrass would benefit the cook with a flair for Thai cuisine.

See part 2 for a list of individual culinary herbs and their magickal correspondences.

Drying and Storing Garden Herbs

A convenient herb bed will allow you access to fresh herbs right from the garden. All you need to do is clip off the amount you need at the time and leave the plant to keep on growing. Use clean scissors or pruning clippers to reduce risk to the plant. Pruning encourages a plant to spread and grow and keeps it from flowering, which ends the growing cycle. Also, routinely remove and discard old leaves. This is a good way to control diseases and keep your plants healthy.

Inspect the clipping and remove any discolored leaves, then wash it in cool water. Use the part you clipped immediately or store it by gently shaking off the excess moisture and patting it dry with a clean cloth. Gather leafy herbs in small (one-inch-diameter) bundles and secure the ends with string or a rubber band. Hang each bundle upside down in a cool, shady place with good airflow. This allows for the plant's essential oils to concentrate in the leaves. Make sure to keep the bundles evenly spaced to encourage ventilation. Label each bundle with the name of the herb and the date and immediately discard any herbs that show the slightest sign of mold. Mold can be deadly!

Also consider the space where you choose to store your herbs. Avoid damp areas with a tub or sink. Sunlight and heat will degrade the essential oils, so avoid areas with bright windows, a stove, or a heater. Herbs with small seeds should be gathered into bundles and enclosed in small, individual paper bags to help prevent the seeds from dropping as they dry.

If you live in a damp climate or you are working with an herb with a high moisture content, you might want to invest in a home dehydrator. Most are boxes with stackable trays that are easy to use. You can also use two clean window screens. Lay out your herbs on one screen. Place the other over the top and secure the two together with clamps, rope, or string. Turn the screens daily to ensure even drying.

Whether you use a dehydrator or simply tie your herbs in small bunches and hang them upside down, you will want to make sure that they are completely dry before you put them up. Moisture, heat, oxygen, and sunlight degrade the potency and shorten shelf life. When your herbs have dried, store them whole in airtight containers such as ziplock bags or small glass jars with tight-fitting lids. Whole herbs retain their natural oils much longer than crushed or ground herbs.

Herbs with a higher moisture content, such as basil, chives, lemon balm, and mint, are prone to mold and are better suited to freezing. Simply take your rinsed trimmings and pat them dry. Then place the herbs in an airtight container or a freezer bag and freeze.

If you have space, you can make herbal ice cubes. Just mince your washed herbs and pack the bits into an ice cube tray. Pour boiling water over the herbs in the ice cube tray to blanch before freezing. This will help them retain their flavor and color. Set the tray aside to cool then put it in the freezer. Once the ice cubes have frozen, remove them from the tray and store them in airtight freezer bags.

Another storage method is oil immersion. Make an herbal paste by mixing ⅓ cup of olive oil with 2 cups of fresh herbs. Blend the mixture in a blender or food processor until smooth. Store the mixture in a sealed jar and keep in the refrigerator for up to 2 weeks, or freeze it in ice cube trays and store in an airtight bag for later use.

Magickal Herbal Oils

This process macerates herbs in jars of oil that are stored in a cool, dark cupboard for two to four weeks to create an oil that is infused with the herb's scent and energy. For best results, use clean, dry flowers and herbs and clean, dry jars. Any water that is introduced could create mold growth, which will spoil the oil.

When you mix up your magickal blends, make small batches. Choose a jar to fit your recipe. If you are making a small batch, use a small jar. This will reduce the oil's exposure to oxygen, allowing it to last longer. Oils are delicate. They can quickly turn rancid and moldy. Be precise and neat. But most importantly, remember to add each ingredient with a focused intent. When you make up a batch of oil, you are creating a magickal blend to empower your spellwork. Focus on the work you are doing. Charge each ingredient, programing it with your intent, words, and breath. Tell it what you want it to do. You can do this silently, say it in a whisper, chant it, or even sing it. This is all about energy. The real magick here is weaving your energy, the universe's energy, and the energy of each item into the oil and programing it to do the work you desire. Use the power that is yours to make it magickal.

When making scented oil blends, use a carrier oil with a subtle scent. The first batch of cold-infused rose oil I made smelled heavily of the olive oil I used as a base. The rose scent was almost lost. Also think about the shelf life. Some carrier oils have a relatively short shelf life. Sweet almond oil, jojoba oil, and coconut oil are known for their long shelf lives.

Choosing a Carrier Oil

A carrier oil is a base oil used as a solvent to extract an herb's therapeutic properties. Today there is a huge assortment of butter and oils available for purchase.

Apricot Kernel Oil: This oil is associated with Venus and the element water, and it can be used for attraction, beauty, emotional issues, and love. Its shelf life is around 12 months.

Avocado Oil: This oil is associated with Venus and the element water, and it can be used as an aphrodisiac and for beauty, clear sight, fertility, health, love, and youth. Its shelf life is around 12 months.

Castor Oil: Castor oil is associated with Mars and the element fire. Use it for absorbing negativity, fertility, healing, and protection. Its shelf life is around 12 months.

Cocoa Butter: Unrefined cocoa butter has an amazing chocolaty scent. It can be used in magick for gratitude, happiness, health, longevity, love, luxury, and riches. Its shelf life is 24 to 30 months.

Coconut Oil: This oil is associated with the moon and the element water, and it can be used for beauty, clear thinking, moon magick, healing, protection, purification, and transformations. The shelf life is 18 to 24 months.

Grapeseed Oil: Grapeseed oil is associated with the moon and the element water, and it can be used in magick for abundance, dreams, fertility, garden magick, mental powers, and money. Its shelf life is 6 to 9 months.

Hemp Seed Oil: This oil is associated with the moon, Saturn, and the element water. Use it for healing, love, meditation, and psychic abilities. Its shelf life is 12 months.

Jojoba Oil: This oil is associated with the moon and the element water, and it can be used for abundance, beauty, and healing. Jojoba has a long shelf life: 3 years.

Mango Butter: Use this butter for dream magick, love, and uplifting energy. Its shelf life is 18 to 24 months.

Olive Oil: The olive is associated with the sun and the element fire. It can be used in magick for fertility, healing, love, lust, peace, potency, prosperity, and protection. Note that while olive oil is a thick, luxurious oil, it has its own somewhat heavy scent that could overpower more delicate aromas. The shelf life is 12 months.

Rosehip Seed Oil: This oil is associated with Venus and the element water. Use it for beauty, friendship, healing, and love. Its shelf life is 6 to 9 months.

Sesame Oil: Sesame oil is associated with Ganesha, the sun, and the element fire, and it is used in magick for luck, opportunity, riches, and wealth. Its shelf life is 12 months.

Shea Butter: Try this butter in magick regarding anti-aging, beauty, healing, and rejuvenating. Its shelf life is 12 to 18 months.

Sunflower Oil: This oil is associated with the sun and the element fire. It can be used for abundance, beginnings, confidence, fertility, protection, and success. Its shelf life is 12 months.

Sweet Almond Oil: Sweet almond oil is associated with Mercury and the element air. It supports work for communication, connection to spirit, love, money, riches, and wisdom. Its shelf life is 12 months.

A word of caution: Have care when choosing a carrier oil. Not all oils are created equal. Some oils are rendered by using harsh chemical solvents. Avoid these. The energy they contain has been altered and can be damaging to your health. Choose oils that are cold-pressed or expeller-pressed, to ensure that there are no residual solvents and toxins and that the oil hasn't been heated to a high temperature during manufacturing, as this negatively alters the molecular composition of the fatty acids.

To make your oil last longer, keep the bottle tightly sealed and store it in a dry place out of direct sunlight. Try not to expose your oils to hot or cold temperatures.

Magickal Oils and Spells

Recipe
Prosperity Oil

You will need:
* 1 cup fresh basil
* 1 cup fresh mint
* 3 cinnamon sticks
* carrier oil

In a canning jar, place 1 cup of fresh basil, 1 cup of fresh mint, and 3 cinnamon sticks. Cover with oil to the top and seal the jar. Store it in a dark place for at least 2 weeks. Be sure to check on it every few days to give it a gentle shake as you reinforce your intention. When it is ready, strain out the herbal matter and store the oil in a clean bottle. Use the oil to empower any prosperity spell. Add it to bath salts or use it to anoint candles to empower prosperity spells. Burn it in a diffuser to draw opportunities.

Recipe
Attraction Oil

You will need:
* 1 cup rose petals
* carrier oil
* 1 Tablespoon ground coriander

Stuff a small canning jar half full with the rose petals. Cover with oil and add the coriander. Seal the jar and shake to mix. Place it on a dimly lit shelf. Allow the oil to steep for 4 weeks. Be sure to check on it every few days and give it a gentle shake as you reinforce your intention. When it is ready, strain out the herbal matter and store the oil in a clean bottle. The rose petals will rot and ruin your oil if they are not removed. Wear the oil as perfume to become irresistible. Add it to bath salts to boost an attraction bath's power. Use it to anoint candles in attraction spells to empower the working.

Recipe
Love Spell Oil

Lavender, cinnamon, cloves, and nutmeg all hold energy for love. Science is beginning to confirm what magickal practitioners have held for centuries. Among all the scents deemed sexy, several studies have confirmed that both men and women respond positively to the scents of lavender and pumpkin pie.[48]

You will need:
* ★ 7 wands of lavender
* ★ 1 cinnamon stick
* ★ 1 teaspoon cloves
* ★ 1 teaspoon ground nutmeg

Trim the stems from the lavender wands and drop the budding heads into a small canning jar. Break the cinnamon stick and drop in the pieces. Add the cloves and nutmeg. Cover with oil and seal the jar. Shake to mix. Place on a dimly lit shelf. Allow the oil to steep for 4 weeks. Be sure to check on it every few days to give it a gentle shake as you reinforce your intention. When it is ready, strain out the herbal matter and store the oil in a clean bottle. Use the oil to anoint your pulse points. Wear it as perfume to be noticed. Add it to bath salts and soak to boost your allure. Use the oil to anoint candles in attraction and love spells.

. . . .

48. Lindsay Goldwert, "Pumpkin Pie Smell Stimulates Arousal in Men; Scent is Sexy Aphrodisiac, Says Study," *(New York) Daily News*, November 24, 2010, https://www.nydailynews.com/life-style/pumpkin-pie-smell-stimulates-arousal-men-scent-sexy-aphrodisiac-study-article-1.451682; Alan R. Hirsch et al., "Scentsational Sex Olfactory Stimuli and Sexual Response in the Human Female," *International Journal of Aromatherapy* 9, no. 2 (1998–1999): 75–81, https://doi.org/10.1016/S0962-4562(98)80023-4.

Recipe
Cold Infused Psychic Oil

Mix up this formula when the moon is in Scorpio to concentrate the energy.

You will need:
* 1 part mugwort
* 1 part savory
* 1 part thyme
* 2 whole star anise pods
* carrier oil

Fill a small jar halfway with the herbs and drop in the star pods. Pour oil over the plant matter to the top. Seal the jar and shake. Set it on a shelf and shake daily for 2 or 3 weeks. When it is ready, strain out the herbal matter and store the oil in a clean bottle. Rub the oil on your pulse points to increase psychic ability. Use it to boost intuition, divination, and dream recall and to increase lunar influence. Use the oil to anoint candles to empower moon magick.

Recipe
Banishing Oil

You will need:
* handful of pine needles
* sprig of rosemary
* 1 teaspoon black peppercorns
* ¼ teaspoon cayenne pepper
* carrier oil

Stuff a handful of pine needles into a small jar. Add a sprig of rosemary, the peppercorns, and cayenne pepper. Pour oil over the plant matter to the top. Seal the jar and shake. Let it sit for 1 week. Be sure to check on it every few days to give it a gentle shake as you reinforce your intention. When it is ready, strain out the herbal matter and store the oil in a clean bottle. Use it to empower banishing rituals. Rub it into your hands before dealing with a difficult person. Wear it to keep a difficult person at a distance. Use the oil to mark things you want to be rid of.

To banish a person from your life, pour out a spoonful of banishing oil onto a piece of paper. Spit forcibly on the paper and fold it away from you. Take a pen and draw a line as a symbol of crossing out. To be rid of them, place the paper on their person, in their car, on their windshield, in their desk, or somewhere they have to step over.

Spell
Herbal Spell to Clear Your Home of Bad Luck

You will need:
* ¼ cup mint
* ¼ cup rose petals
* ¼ cup rosemary
* ¼ cup thyme

Combine the herbs and petals together in a large bowl. With your hand, mix them together, breaking them into smaller bits, as you say,

By mint and rose, by rosemary and thyme,
herbs of luck, your true power shines.
To surge and clear this space,
drawing good luck, righting all in its place,
as flow increases with opportunities both large and small,
so that my good luck is supercharged.

Sprinkle the mixture across the floors. Leave it overnight. When you wake the next morning, sweep it up. Then carry it out your door and bury it on the other side of your property line.

Spell
Spell to Instill Harmony

This works wonders to soothe family members who will not get along.

You will need:
- ★ dried catnip
- ★ ground cumin
- ★ dried lavender
- ★ dried violets
- ★ mortar and pestle, or bowl and rock
- ★ olive oil
- ★ white candle
- ★ firesafe candle dish
- ★ matches

Draw a breath and come to center. Put the herbs and flowers into the mortar and crush them into bits as you will them to instill harmony in your home. Dip your fingers in the olive oil and run them over the candle. Roll the candle in the crushed herbal bits. Then set the candle on a fireproof holder and scatter the rest of the flower bits around it. Place the candle in the middle of the kitchen table and light.

> *Clear away the resentment,*
> *heal the hurt feelings,*
> *vanquish what is feared.*
> *Forgive the harsh dealings.*
> *Here and now peace is restored*
> *so that our familial bonds are once more in accord.*
> *All is forgiven and harmony returns once more.*
> *Peace is ours. Peace be mine. Peace is mine.*

Keep an eye on the candle as it burns. Extinguish it before you leave the area. Light it again at mealtime or anytime you need to instill some harmonic energy.

Spell
Good Luck Blessing for a New Project

You will need:
- ★ olive oil
- ★ small dish
- ★ frankincense essential oil
- ★ sandalwood essential oil
- ★ 3 bay leaves
- ★ firesafe dish
- ★ pen
- ★ paper
- ★ white or orange candle (a short pillar would be ideal, as it needs to sit on a folded page)
- ★ pinch of ground nutmeg
- ★ matches

Pour a small amount of olive oil into the small dish. Add 9 drops each of frankincense and sandalwood essential oils. Stir the oils together with the tip of your pen. Arrange the bay leaves on the firesafe dish so that their tips touch. Dip the tip of your pen into the scented oil and write out a short blessing for your project on a small piece of paper. It could be something like "This project is a success," "This project comes together effortlessly," or "With joy, we bring this project to completion." Write whatever you hope to achieve, then fold the page toward you. Dip your fingers in the oil and anoint the page. Blow across it and set the paper on the bay leaves. Set the candle on top of the paper. Sprinkle it with nutmeg and light it. Visualize your project running smoothly as it comes to completion. Success is yours. Feel it. Embrace it and smile as the candle burns down.

Spell
Silver-Tongue Communication Spell

You will need:
* sweet almond oil or olive oil
* small dish
* bay essential oil
* yellow candle
* matches
* small bowl of caraway seeds

Pour a spoonful of carrier oil into the dish. Add 7 drops of bay oil. Dip your fingers in and anoint the candle. Draw a breath and come to center. Light the candle. Dip your finger in the oil and touch your third eye, your lips, and your throat. Take the caraway seeds in one hand and hold the other over them as you visualize the energy of the universe beaming down to spill around you. Draw the energy in and channel it down your arm, out your palm, and into the seeds as you say,

With energy to ease communications, these seeds are empowered.

Pop some seeds into your mouth and chew them mindfully. Swallow them, and when your mouth is empty, say,

As they pass my lips and tongue, I am empowered.
I breathe in the energy of this moment
that my tongue be blessed with eloquence.
As it turns silver, I accept the bliss of easy communication.
My words fill with power.
My ideas excite and entice.
My thoughts win and create,
forging fondness of thought and empowering action.
Forging bonds new and renewed,

to forge bonds new and renewed,
and the bonds form and renew.
For the very best of all. So mote it be.

Carry the remaining seeds in your pocket and chew when you wish to fortify the energy.

Spell
Empowerment Charm

This spell combines the welcoming energy of tarragon and the victorious energy of bay with the confident energy of carnelian to bolster courage, stimulate initiative, and smooth the way forward.

You will need:
* ⋆ candle
* ⋆ nutmeg essential oil
* ⋆ 6 bay leaves
* ⋆ firesafe candle dish
* ⋆ sprig of fresh tarragon
* ⋆ piece of carnelian
* ⋆ offering of milk and honey
* ⋆ matches

Dress the candle with nutmeg oil. Place the 6 bay leaves on the candle dish in a circle and set the candle on them. Pull some of the leaves from the tarragon sprig, strew them over the candle and your offering, and set aside. Set your circle and call up the energies you are going to work with. Light the candle, and when you are ready, say,

I let go of my fear and embrace the abundance life has to offer.
By herb and by stone, I am empowered.
I am empowered.
I am empowered.

Meditate as you hold your stone. See yourself smiling as you speak to your boss. See them leaning toward you, nodding as they listen. See yourself succeeding. Have a clear, concise image of what you desire. See yourself being what you want to be. See yourself getting what you want. Believe that it can be yours as you say,

> *I release all hesitation and open to the infinite possibilities.*
> *For the greatest good, I am blessed.*
> *I am blessed.*
> *So mote it be.*

Take your stone to work. Hold it in your hand or up to your lips when you need resolve to stick to your guns. Place it on your desk, and when it happens to catch your eye, run your fingers over it as you open to the infinite possibilities with a courageous heart.

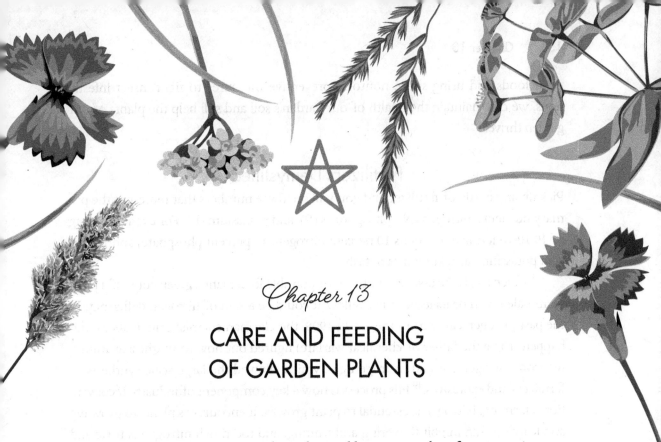

Chapter 13

CARE AND FEEDING OF GARDEN PLANTS

As we create our own unique gardens, the yard becomes a place for restoration not only for the body, mind, and spirit but also for the land. The action of caring for our garden plants awakens a connection deep within us. When we witness the miracle of life unfolding right before our eyes, we come to appreciate nature's artistry as we witness her renewal firsthand. This connection grows into a relationship as we witness the sprouting of a seed, the flower maturing into fruit, the quiet dormancy of winter, and then later the renewal of spring. It is through these cycles we begin to understand the ebb and flow of seasonal energy so that we may reflect these patterns in our own lives. Gardening then becomes a vehicle to exit the busyness of our lives, and as we immerse ourselves in nature's slower rhythms, the labor, the harvest, the entire experience becomes an act of self-care as our mental space expands and we come to see our place in the much bigger picture.

Just as we need care, so does our garden. When we reduce the use of harmful chemicals, we get away from unsustainable practices and help the land heal by building soil health and encouraging natural processes. By applying inexpensive or homemade plant foods and using some nontoxic preventive measures to fight insect infestations, we can maintain the health of our garden's soil and still help the plants of our garden thrive.

Fertilizers Demystified

Pick up any bottle of fertilizer and you will see three numbers that represent the primary nutrients: nitrogen (N), phosphorus (P), and potassium (K). For example, a bag of 10-10-10 fertilizer contains 10 percent nitrogen, 10 percent phosphate, and 10 percent potassium, also known as potash.

Nitrogen (N) is the essential nutrient responsible for a plant's green color. If a plant turns pale green or its leaves turn yellow, it could be a sign of nitrogen deficiency. In the past nitrogen came from the air. In 1908, the German chemist Fritz Haber (who happens to be the father of chemical warfare) figured out how to synthesize ammonia from nitrogen gas and hydrogen gas, which allowed the large-scale synthesis of fertilizers and explosives.[49] His process is now a key component of industrial/conventional farming. Nitrogen is essential to plant growth. It encourages plants to grow big and leafy but can inhibit flowering and fruiting, and too much nitrogen is toxic and will burn or even kill your plants.

Phosphorus (P) encourages strong root growth and flower and fruit production. It is essential for many metabolic processes.[50] Phosphorus is particularly important for annuals to be able to complete their growing process. If your plants are stunted or suffer from poor flowering and fruiting, the cause may be a phosphorus deficiency. While most phosphorus is mined from phosphate rock, it is also available in chicken manure and bone meal.

Potassium (K) is still referred to by many gardeners as potash because a century ago, it was made by boiling wood and other plant ashes in a pot, which would concentrate the naturally occurring potassium from the plants into the ashes, hence "potash." Potassium is essential for many of the plant's important biochemical reactions.

. . . .

49. *Encyclopaedia Britannica Online*, s.v. "Fritz Haber," accessed September 1, 2021, https://www.britannica.com/biography/Fritz-Haber.

50. Hina Malhotra et al., "Phosphorus Nutrition: Plant Growth in Response to Deficiency and Excess,"*Plant Nutrients and Abiotic Stress Tolerance* (2018): abstract, 172, 175, doi:10.1007/978-981-10-9044-8_7.

Today garden potassium is no longer derived from potash or plant ashes but is mined from inland prehistoric ocean beds.

Hardwood ashes are a good source of potassium as long as you use small amounts. Wood ash also contains lime, and it will raise the soil pH slightly, so have care around acid-loving plants like blueberries, azaleas, and rhododendrons.

Hands down the best way to fertilize your garden is by mimicking nature and working compost and manure (cow, horse, sheep, goat, chicken, pigeon, and even bat guano is available to the gardener…) into the soil. Compost and manure build better soil structure. Compost (decayed leaves, composted food scraps, and yard clippings) improves all soil types by boosting soil nutrients and improving soil structure. When worked into soil, compost improves water- and nutrient-holding capacity, and when mixed into clay soils, it increases drainage, aeration, and permeability so that growing roots can spread easier and grow deeper.

Your energy also charges the soil. Every time you dig, spread, or turn the soil, your thoughts and labor are enriching the ground and nurturing the plants, allowing the energy of your mind and body to become a part of the amendment. I am coming across this mindfulness notion, that one's thoughts and energy impact the results, more and more. Today I read it on the instructions of the package of Snapdragon's Vietnamese Pho I made for lunch: "Wait 3 to 5 minutes until noodles are tender and have happy thoughts." Then later I read Nigel Palmer's lovely advice on mixing amendments into water: "In the world of energies and their effects, here is a final thought to consider. The thoughts that course through your mind can also affect the energy structure of the mixture in a bucket as one stirs. Intent defines the future.…Smile and appreciate the clean air, the puffy clouds, the sunlight reflecting off the leaves of the trees, and the breath moving through the body. Know that the water you are preparing for the garden is rich with plant-available nutrition and an energy generated by you."[51] Your thoughts are important. Use them to influence the future of your garden. Hold positive intentions as you work the earth. This exchange inspires a wonderful ethereal feeling of being a part of the web, as you connect to something so much larger.

. . . .

51. Nigel Palmer, *The Regenerative Grower's Guide to Garden Amendments: Using Locally Sourced Materials to Make Mineral and Biological Extracts and Ferments* (White River Junction, VT: Chelsea Green Publishing, 2020), 78.

Recipe
Homemade Liquid Comfrey Fertilizer

Comfrey is a wonderful plant. Also called boneset, it is used to accelerate the healing of sprains, bruises, and broken bones. Its attractive blue to purple bell-shaped flowers are favored by bumblebees, and the leaves can be made into a nutrient-rich liquid plant food.

You will need:
* pair of gloves
* garden clippers
* patch of comfrey
* black bucket with a lid

Comfrey is covered in fine bristles that might cause skin irritation. Put on a pair of gloves and trim off a bundle of comfrey leaves. Take a black bucket if you've got one. Black is preferable because this process uses sunlight to heat the contents, and black retains more heat than a white bucket does. Fill your bucket with comfrey leaves. Stuff the leaves in tightly until the bucket is filled. Set a cover on the bucket and leave it in a sunny spot for 3 to 4 weeks. After a while, the comfrey will break down and become a greenish-brown, funky smelling, nutrient-rich concentrate. Strain the liquid into another bucket and then dump the fibrous remains into your compost pile. Mix the concentrated comfrey liquid with water at a 1 to 4 ratio. Water any plant with the mixture to help it flower and fruit.

Recipe
Produce Scrap Tea

Use your plant-based scraps to make a nutrient-rich garden tea to feed your plants.

You will need:
* 13-gallon garbage pail
* water
* plant-based kitchen scraps
* blender or food processor

Fill your garbage can ¾ full with water and let it sit for 24 hours. Gather your produce scraps. Lettuces and herbs make the best scrap tea, but every vegetable scrap will contribute nutrients. Just be warned when you use crucifers like broccoli and cauliflower, they're pretty smelly and can make your greenhouse stink. Put your vegetable scraps and some water into the processor and whiz until liquefied. Pour this mixture into the water in the garbage pail and let it sit for a day or two. Use the liquid to water any plant that needs a boost of nourishment to improve plant growth.

In zones with mosquito populations, you should avoid leaving standing water for mosquitoes to breed in. Instead use a container with a tight-fitting lid to keep mosquitoes out.

Foliar Feeding

If a plant becomes stressed, with yellow or wilting leaves, a foliar feeding with a solution of liquid seaweed or an organic tomato plant food dissolved in water will often perk it up. Fill a spray bottle with diluted liquid fertilizer and spray directly onto the leaves. Allow the droplets to dry before watering again. Heavy feeders can also benefit from foliar feeding when fed every two weeks throughout the growing season. If the leaves of your squash plant suddenly turn yellow, chances are it could use a feeding.

Soil pH

If your plants fail to thrive, the reason could be lurking in your soil. The abbreviation pH stands for "potential of hydrogen," and in terms of soil, this refers to how hydrogen moves through it. This is important because soil pH directly affects how well your plants are able to absorb nutrients. Nutrients can be withheld from a plant or made too available, which means if the pH is out of whack, your plants could starve or be poisoned. The pH scale is a measure from 0 to 14 of the acidity or alkalinity of soil. A pH of 7 is neutral and 6.5 is the optimal pH level. Many garden plants thrive in soil that is slightly acidic.

Most soils range from an extremely acidic pH of 3 to a very alkaline pH of 10, depending on what the soil is made of. The good news is soil pH can be amended.

Exercise
Home pH Test

If you have access to a pH meter, you can perform a home test to see where your garden soil ranks. A soil meter gives an estimate rather than an accurate determination. Tests are done in threes and the results are averaged to give the gardener a pretty good idea of the range of their soil pH.

You will need:
* garden trowel
* 3 1-quart containers
* 1 gallon deionized or distilled water
* pH meter

Dig 3 small holes in the soil about 1 foot apart. Begin by scooping the top 2 inches of soil away. Then dig down 6 inches to loosen the soil. Put 1 scoop of soil from the bottom of the first hole into a container and fill the container with the water. Do this for each hole, then let the soil-filled containers sit for 5 minutes. Stick your meter in the first container and let it sit for 1 or 2 minutes before reading it. Note down the reading and move to the next container. Wipe the soil from your meter and stick it into the next container. After 1 or 2 minutes, record the reading and move on to the last container. After you have all 3 readings, average them to find an estimation of your soil's pH level.

If you want to do an accurate pH reading, you will need to send a soil sample to a lab to have it tested. But pH is important because every plant has a preferred range of soil acidity. Most vegetables thrive when soil pH is slightly acidic (around 6.5). Blueberry bushes, azaleas, gardenias, and rhododendrons prefer higher acidity and thrive in soils with a pH of 4.5 to 5.5.

When soil pH is too high or too low, it should be amended. Additives can be used to raise soil or lower soil pH. This process takes time and should be done in the fall well ahead of planting season.

Ammonium Sulfate: Ammonium sulfate is a fast-acting, high-nitrogen fertilizer (21-0-0). It also contains sulfur and will lower soil pH more quickly than elemental sulfur.

Elemental Sulfur: Sulfur lowers soil pH slowly over time. When soil pH becomes too alkaline (7.5 to 8.0), an application of elemental sulfur is recommended. Mix into garden soil or water in.

Lime: Lime is used to raise soil pH. It is worked into the soil several months before spring planting. The soil is tilled and the lime spread over it and raked into the top 2 inches.

Nurturing a Sick Plant

On the first of February my husband and I drove to McMinnville, Oregon, to buy some 'Yamhill' hazelnut trees from a hazelnut farm. We were greeted by a young OSU student who was studying agriculture and soil science. The trees were two-year-old seedlings that he'd dug up that morning and were now bare root. He presented us with the ten trees we asked for and three more, explaining we needed to plant a 'York' or a 'Gamma' with the 'Yamhills' for cross-pollination. We bought all thirteen trees and planted them that afternoon. It rained heavily that night and we hoped for the best. By March most of the hazelnut trees were showing signs of budding. By April all but one had new leaves.

I turned my attention to the dormant tree. My husband thought it was dead, but if you looked closely, you could see small, slightly green buds along its limbs. I started offering it a daily bucket of water and talked to it, coaxing it to bud. By the end of April, the other twelve trees were covered with new leaves. The small, bare tree was still dormant but now the green buds along its limbs were swollen with the promise of life. I was encouraged. I started offering it a weekly bucket of chamomile tea and a weak solution of liquid seaweed. In a month's time the small tree had recovered.

Plant First Aid

There are many reasons a garden plant might fall ill. While it is possible for a plant to catch a disease, get a fungal infection, or suffer an insect attack, the usual culprit is an imbalance in the soil or overwatering. If one of your plants begins to show signs of stress, first check to see if the soil is wet. An easy way to do this is by pushing a water meter down into the soil near the plant's roots. If the plant is in a pot and the reading comes back as wet, repot the plant in new dry soil. If the reading comes back in the acceptable range, look at the plant. If the leaves are turning yellow, it could be a sign that it is not getting the nutrients it needs. You can correct this by giving it a dose of liquid seaweed. Liquid seaweed provides a dose of quickly absorbable nutrients to boost the plant's immune system and provide any missing nutrients. It can be watered into the soil or mixed with water and sprayed on the leaves as a foliar feeding.

If the plant looks leggy, or tall and thin like it is stretching toward the sky, chances are it is not getting enough sunlight. You might want to consider planting it in an area with longer sunlight exposure.

If you have difficulty diagnosing the problem, you might want to give a sick plant a dose of cooled chamomile tea. Chamomile is known as the plant doctor. It is planted around herbs and flowers to revive the sick and strengthen the healthy. Its antibacterial and antifungal properties help plants stay resistant to fungus and mold infections. A watering with cooled chamomile tea can help a plant fight off minor infections and boost its immune system.

Exercise
Healing Meditation

Send a plant ally an energy boost with this healing meditation. Stand before the plant if it is tall or sit on the earth and place your feet and root them to the soil. Draw a few meditative breaths and draw your attention in and come to center. When you have reached a meditative state, move your focus down to your feet. Visualize roots or tendrils slowly extending from your feet. See them as they travel down, out of your feet, to meet and sink into the earth. Feel your tendrils push down through the cool, nourishing, and secure soil. Send them down until they reach a pool of earth energy that is waiting beneath the surface.

Visualize the energy as a lovely cool light that pools around your tendrils. Inhale and as you draw in your breath, draw the energy up your tendrils, like a straw. See the energy flowing up through your tendrils, glowing as it flows up into your feet…up your legs…up your spine…to fill your core. Breathe and send the energy down into your hands. Hold your hands over the plant and send the energy through your palms into it.

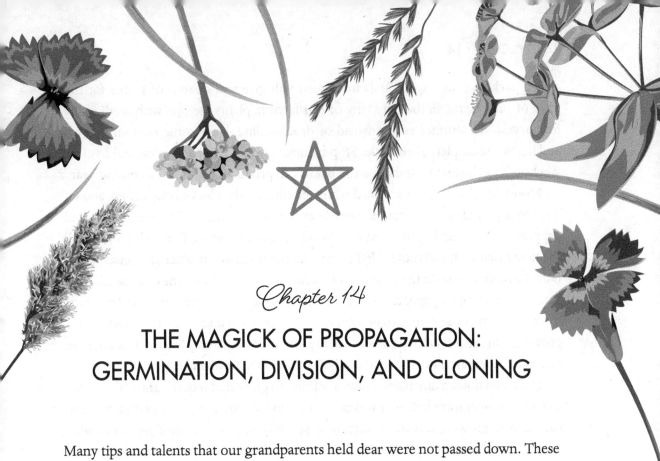

Chapter 14

THE MAGICK OF PROPAGATION: GERMINATION, DIVISION, AND CLONING

Many tips and talents that our grandparents held dear were not passed down. These everyday skills have fallen away, leaving a generation mostly unaware of the life of plants. Now with more people spending time at home, interest in home crafts is reviving. Just as a generation took on the art of home brewing beer and baking sourdough, more and more are taking up the shovel and hoe and dusting off knowledge once antiquated. New interest is surging into the art of gardening. Tasks like how to successfully save and germinate seeds, divide tuberous plants, or clone by cutting are once again being mastered.

Don't worry if your first attempts are not fruitful. Gardening is an art and each act is a lesson. The more time you spend with it, the more you will learn, and the greater your success.

Germinating Seeds

Every spring, nurseries across the country display six-packs of annuals to provide instant gratification to the hobby gardener. For those who are more dedicated, buying a seed pack and starting annuals from seed will give you dozens of plants for the price of one starter. In the fall many of our favorite plants are ripe with seeds ready for harvest. As summer ends, instead of deadheading, leave some of your flowers and herbs to complete their cycle. Stop trimming your cilantro, parsley, and basil six weeks before the first frost date so the plants can produce seeds for the coming year.

Most vegetables you eat are filled with seeds that can be plucked out, rinsed, and set aside to dry. Seeds from tomatoes, peas, beans, melons, pumpkins, winter squash, and peppers can be saved as you prepare the food. Just scrape the seeds free and remove all the fleshy matter. It will mold if left to dry. Put the seeds in a strainer and rinse. When only the seeds remain in the strainer, set them aside to dry. Dump the dried seeds onto a piece of parchment paper and label it with information about the plant and the date. Then when the time comes to germinate them, you will know exactly what you are growing. One year I realized I labeled all my tomato seeds simply "tomato" and had to wait until August to find just what kind of tomato I was growing.

Each seed holds a tiny plant embryo waiting to grow that requires the soil to reach a certain temperature before it wakes. As the cold season comes to an end, you can extend your growing season by starting seeds indoors. A sunny window can provide warmth for the seed to germinate. Seedlings are delicate. The less you handle them the better your success rate. Plant them in a container that will decompose to eliminate damage during transplanting. Cardboard containers, such as an old egg carton, work well, as they can be planted into the soil when the plant is ready to move into the garden.

To decide when to start your seedling, look at the back of the seed packet to see if it lists the days required to mature. Some fruiting plants, like pumpkins and watermelon, can take up to 110 days to produce fruit to harvest, which means that if you want pumpkins by Halloween, you need to plant in May.

If you germinated seeds in a seed tray, you can transplant individual plants to ease crowding. Wait until they develop a set of true leaves. Have the container you are going to move them to ready. Then gently take hold of the leaves and slip a small spoon or a Popsicle stick under to lift the plant, keeping as much of the soil around the root ball as possible. Set the seedling into the prepared pot and gently add soil to fill in around the roots. Water and set in a sunny place.

Division

Division is the method of dividing a mature tuberous plant into several parts. Do not try to divide a plant with a single taproot. You will only injure the plant. This process is for plants with roots that clump or send out runners. If you can see clumps of new growth developing around a mature plant, it could be a candidate for the process. But I suggest you do your research first. Identify the plant and read about it.

Division is done in the early spring or the fall when the plant is not in flower. Every couple of years, I check to see if I need to divide my hostas, iris, or bleeding hearts. I divide my hostas in the spring when the shoots sprout before the leaves unfurl. If they are crowded, I dig up the younger plants clumped around the mother plant. Then I fill in the dirt and water the mother plant in. I immediately plant the young hostas in a different spot and give each a good drenching.

In the fall, every three or four years, the iris bed gets crowded, and rhizomes will grow up on themselves until they are out of the ground. I carefully dig around the mass and lift it from the soil. Next, I examine the root ball and work to pull it apart, gently removing the rhizomes one by one. Then I clip the leaves back, leaving five or six inches. Amend the bed with compost or leaf mold and replant some of the irises back into the bed and move the extra to a new space. After any plant is disturbed, it should be watered to reduce its stress. Through this method, I now have these plants in several sections of my yard.

Bleeding hearts are propagated from root cuttings. Wait until the flowers have faded, then water the plant well the night before you plan to take the cutting. In the morning prepare a pot by filling the bottom with a mixture of compost and coarse sand. Saturate the mixture and carry the pot to where the mother plant is. Carefully dig out a section to reveal the roots. Find a root that has two or more nodes, and using a sharp, clean knife, separate it from the root ball. Place the cutting in the pot and cover it with an inch of sand. Water well and place it in a sheltered, shady place to sprout. This will take four to six weeks. Water regularly and when the cutting sprouts, transplant it to a larger pot filled with potting soil. Your sprouts will be ready to plant out the following spring.

Clumping grasses can also be divided but usually require a strike with a shovel to split apart. Just dig the clump out and split it in two sections. Replant one section back into the hole it came from and drench with water. Then plant the second piece wherever you desire.

Cloning

Nursery workers everywhere propagate plants by cloning, or taking a cutting from a mother plant to clone it and produce another. It works because plants have the amazing ability to change a leaf cell into a root cell. Cloning is a skill that allows a single mother plant to spawn dozens of clones just like it. Learning to clone is a game changer. It means unlimited plants for free! But there are a few things you need to know before you snip just any old cutting.

1. You should ask permission if the mother plant is not yours. In many places, like botanical gardens and parks, taking cuttings is illegal.

2. When you take your cutting, you are working against time to prevent water loss from the plant, so you need to be able to get it into a new source of soil and water it very quickly.

How to Propagate by Cloning

Get out some small pots. I save all my nursery pots and reuse them over and over. For individual cuttings, the small four-inch herb pots work really well. Fill them with potting soil and top with vermiculite, if you have it, to keep the leaves of your cutting from rotting if they touch the soil. You also need a tool to push a hole into the soil to spare the stem injury. You can use a stick, a pencil, the end of a paintbrush, or a Popsicle stick.

Cuttings root more successfully when taken first thing in the morning when the plant is turgid, or full of water. Choose a spot of new growth to improve your success rate. Then take a sharp knife or a pair of small scissors, measure down four or five inches and cut the stem under a leaf node. Starting at the bottom, gently remove the leaves, being careful not to harm the node. Plants lose moisture through their leaves, so you want to remove most of them so the new plant will move its energy to growing roots. Look at the top. If the sprig has a bud at the center, you will want to cut it out too. Take the tool you designated to make the hole and push it into the soil of your pot. Tuck the stem into the hole you made. Immediately water the cutting. Be sure to give it a good soak. Then set it somewhere warm but out of the sunlight. Check on your cutting and water it every day for the next two weeks. Soon roots will grow out of the bottom, and you can plant it into a larger pot or right into your garden.

Saving Seeds

Every time you grow a plant you have a chance to reproduce it by taking cuttings, dividing the root stock, or by saving seeds. Saving seeds is the thriftiest way to gain a supply for next spring's garden. Get to know your plants. Flowers like morning glories, poppies, and hollyhocks produce easy-to-gather seed pouches that only need to be collected. Every tomato, pepper, melon, and winter squash you pick is loaded with seeds to save. Slice a fruit open and look at the seeds. Pepper seeds just need to be picked out into a small dish and set aside to dry, while the small flesh-bound tomato seeds can be soaked in a glass of water overnight to loosen the gel sac. Dump the soaked mixture into a small strainer and stir contents with your fingers, then run the strainer under water to separate the seeds and flush away the membrane. Set the strainer aside to dry and then dump the seeds onto a paper towel. Summer squash, like zucchini and yellow summer squash, is eaten when the fruit is immature and the seeds have not fully developed. You can grow your own summer squash seeds by leaving a chosen fruit to fully mature. Collect the seeds at the end of the season. Cut the squash in half longways and scoop the seeds out. Separate the seeds from the flesh and rinse. Then dump the seeds out on a dish to air dry.

Lettuces, kale, and radish plants must be left to complete their life cycle and go to seed to provide seeds for seasons to come. Just let one grow, and it will shoot up attractive stalks covered with tiny flowers butterflies love. The flowers will become pods you can harvest for seeds. Some crops like beets are biennial and need two years to set seeds.

Label and store your seeds in a dry, cool place. You might think you will remember what is what, but if your seeds are not labeled, come next spring I guarantee you will be looking at a lot of mystery crops.

Part 2

Compendium of
Garden Plants

Every plant has a unique energy that can be used in your magickal practice. Every leaf, seed, and flower contains a unique magickal signature, an enormous potential, stored within that, when aligned with an intention, not only enhances a magickal working but also causes the results to become more predictable. Get to know your plants. Research their history and lore before you begin your experiments. Take detailed notes of your discoveries and your experiences. When we document our results, we can replicate them or learn from our failures. Knowledge is power. When you learn and understand the behavior of an object, you gain the ability to predict a magickal response. To empower your work, do your research. Get to know the energies you are working with.

Within this compendium is a list of plants, their magickal correspondences, and their magickal uses. It is divided into these sections:

- ★ Common Weeds
- ★ Favorite Food Plants for a Wildlife Garden
- ★ Some Favorite Garden Flowers
- ★ Garden Bulbs
- ★ Shrubs, Vines, and Other Perennials
- ★ Magickal Plants for a Witch's Garden
- ★ Some Garden Vegetables Favorites
- ★ Classic Culinary Herbs

Each plant is listed under its common name, followed by its Latin name and a hardiness zone if the plant is a perennial. (Plants that are annuals complete their life cycle in a single year and will die at the end of the growing season.) Each entry also includes practical information and magickal applications. Poisonous or injurious plants also include warnings.

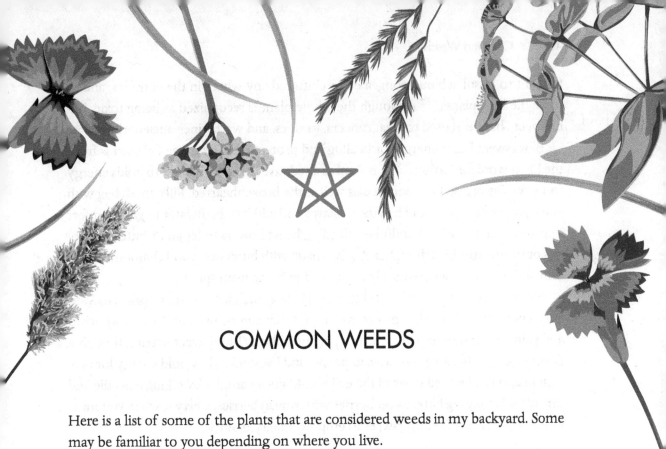

COMMON WEEDS

Here is a list of some of the plants that are considered weeds in my backyard. Some may be familiar to you depending on where you live.

A word of caution: many weeds are magickal and medicinal plants and should be treated as such. If you have any doubt about the identity of a plant, don't experiment with it. *Never* use a plant unless you are 100 percent sure of its identity.

Bittersweet

* *Solanum dulcamara*
* Hardy in zones 4–8
* Balance, healing, and protection
* Warning: This plant is poisonous to people and livestock.

Bittersweet is a perennial vine also known as climbing nightshade, woody nightshade, felonwood, felonwort, scarlet berry, and violet bloom. Bittersweet is a nightshade and the whole plant is considered poisonous. This Old World herb is native to Eurasia but followed the colonists and is now a widespread weed in North America. Sixteenth-century herbalist John Gerard wrote in his *Herball*, "The juice is good for those that have fallen from high places, and thereby brused, or dry beaten: for it is

175

thought to dissolve bloud congealed or cluttered any where in the entrailes, and to heale the hurt places."[52] Although the whole plant is recognized as being toxic, bittersweet "has been used to treat cancers, tumors, and warts since ancient times."[53]

Bittersweet holds energy for healing and protection. The name *Solanum* is from the Latin word for "solace."[54] It is used as a sedative in Iran.[55] This herb holds energy to soothe the bruised and battered as well as the brokenhearted. Fill a mesh bag with equal parts bittersweet and hawthorn leaves and add it to bathwater to gain comfort or ease suffering. Add a handful of bleeding heart flowers to let go of bitter memories or soothe troubled thoughts. A salve made with bittersweet and chamomile may calm inflammation and reduce bruising and swelling from sprains.

Bittersweet is associated with Hermes, Hecate, the element air, Capricorn, Mercury, and Saturn. It holds a protective energy that can be used to drive away aches and pains, from muscle aches to annoying neighbors. Bittersweet berries, though a favorite of wildlife, are poisonous to people and livestock. They hold energy for protection and can be used to repel the evil eye. Make an amulet by taking a needle and thread and stringing bittersweet berries with rowan berries. Carry it when you must face an opponent. Use bittersweet to empower faery magick.

. . . .

52. John Gerard, *The Herball: or the Generall Historie of Plantes* (London: John Norton, 1597), 279.

53. "Bittersweet Nightshade," Drugs.com, last modified January 14, 2020, https://www.drugs.com/npp/bittersweet-nightshade.html.

54. *Merriam-Webster*, s.v. "solanum (n.)," accessed June 1, 2021, https://www.merriam-webster.com/dictionary/solanum.

55. Kourosh Saki et al., "The Most Common Native Medicinal Plants Used for Psychiatric and Neurological Disorders in Urmia City, Northwest of Iran," *Asian Pacific Journal of Tropical Disease* 4, suppl. 2 (2014): S897, doi:10.1016/S2222-1808(14)60754-4.

Bird's-Foot Trefoil

* *Lotus corniculatus*
* Hardy in zones 3–8
* Bird magick, calming, midsummer, and protection
* Warning: All parts of this plant are poisonous.

Bird's-foot trefoil is an invasive low-growing perennial with small yellow flowers that produce long, claw-shaped seedpods. It is known by upward of seventy different common names, including bacon and eggs, granny's toenails, and devil's fingers. Bird's-foot trefoil is a member of the pea family and was introduced to North America by colonialists for livestock fodder and dye. It was brewed into an infusion to treat anxiety and sleeplessness.[56] Here in Oregon bird's-foot trefoil is a favored food of geese, deer, and elk but is considered toxic to humans. If taken in large doses, trefoil can cause respiratory failure and death.

While bird's-foot trefoil is known as a pest plant, it is also a pollinator favorite loved by both bees and butterflies. It is associated with crows and midsummer. It holds energy for protection. Carry a seedpod when you are going into the unknown. Weave its flowers into a wreath and hang it to ward an entry. Make a compress of the leaves and use it to treat skin inflammation. Brew an infusion and add it to bathwater to treat exhaustion or revive a weary spirit. Use the sunny yellow flowers in midsummer rituals.

Burdock

* *Arctium lappa*
* Hardy in zones 3–7
* Animal magick, cleansing, healing, and protection

Burdock is a member of the thistle family native to Siberia, but it has naturalized just about everywhere. The roots, leaves, and seeds have been used for their healing properties since the Middle Ages. The Chinese used the root and seeds as traditional medicine. They introduced burdock to the Japanese, who incorporated the crunchy texture and earthy, meaty flavor into their cooking. Burdock made its way

....

56. Reader's Digest, *Magic and Medicine of Plants* (New York: Reader's Digest, 1986), 99.

to America, where it naturalized and gained its reputation as a weed.[57] Burdock was considered a valuable "blood purifier" in European folk medicine.[58] Poultices of fresh leaves were applied to ease headaches and accelerate the healing of burns.[59]

Burdock is associated with Saturn and Pluto. It is a prominent motif symbolizing abundance and is woven into Turkish rugs for protection from the evil eye.[60] The root is carried for protection, while the large leaves are dried, sewn together, and worn to cover the face to avoid garnering the attention of a spirit. Burn the root, leaves, or flowers as incense to ward off negative energy. Put a burdock root in a small white cotton bag, add a pinch of rue, and carry it for protection from psychic attack. If you have to face a jealous rival, add a pinch of agrimony and carry the pouch to avoid being hexed. Make a tea by pouring boiling water over a chopped burdock root and echinacea. Sip it to fight a cold. If you are moving into a new home, make an infusion by pouring boiling water over a chopped burdock root and adding a handful of rosemary and some lemongrass. Let it steep for 10 minutes and strain. Add it to your washwater and scrub to cleanse a place of negativity left from the previous occupant. Burdock flowers are used to draw abundance; the seed, or burr, is useful when you need help getting something to stick.

Chickweed

* *Stellaria media*
* Birds, glamour, health, love, moon magick, nurture, and regenerate

Chickweed is a small sprawling annual also known as birdweed, chickenwort, starwort, and winterweed. It is an edible member of the carnation family Caryophyllaceae. While it is thought to be a bane by most lawn owners, the high iron content

57. Diane Morgan, *Roots: The Definitive Compendium with More Than 225 Recipes* (San Francisco, CA: Chronicle Books, 2012), 61.

58. Penelope Ody, *The Complete Medicinal Herbal: A Practical Guide to the Healing Properties of Herbs, with More Than 250 Remedies for Common Ailments* (London: Dorling Kindersley Limited, 1993), 38.

59. "Burdock Root," Encyclopedia.com, accessed June 1, 2021, https://www.encyclopedia.com/medicine/encyclopedias-almanacs-transcripts-and-maps/burdock-root.

60. "Turkish Rug Motifs," ABC Oriental Rug & Carpet Cleaning Co., accessed September 1, 2021, https://www.abc-oriental-rug.com/turkish-rug-motifs.html.

makes chickweed a valuable vegetable plant and salad green.[61] Chickweed has a mild pleasant flavor and is eaten raw and cooked. The tiny flowers are used in sandwiches, salads, sauces, and pesto.

Chickweed is associated with the moon and the element water. It holds a nurturing, healing energy that is especially useful to boost the health of birds, animals, and humans. Use chickweed to empower bird magick. Eat chickweed to rejuvenate and enliven the body, mind, and spirit. Use as a cooling remedy to treat sunburns and accelerate the healing process. Whiz chickweed with moonwater in a blender to make a healing beauty paste. Glop it onto your chest and smooth the paste up over your neck and face while soaking in a tub to boost attraction and glamour bath magick. Chickweed also holds energy to attract love and can be used to stop gossip.

Cleavers

* *Galium aparine*
* Hardy in zones 4–8
* Cleansing, determination, love charm, single-mindedness, and vigor

Cleavers is a small common annual. Depending on where you live it is also known as bedstraw, catchweed, goosegrass, grip grass, sticky bob, stickyjack, sticky willy, sweethearts, and the Velcro plant. It is an annual in the madder family. The plant is covered in bristles that cause the stems, leaves, and fruits to stick to clothes and the fur of animals. Geese love to eat it, hence the name goosegrass, and it is called bedstraw because it was once used to stuff mattresses. In the past, herbalists praised cleavers for its powers as a purifier of the blood, the tops being gathered in May and June, "when just coming into flower," and used it as an ingredient in rural spring tonics or made it into an infusion to treat skin complaints and ease insomnia.[62]

The cleavers plant is associated with Saturn and holds a tenacious energy to stick with or hold on. Use it when you need some staying power. Make an infusion by pouring boiling water over the herb and letting it infuse for 10 minutes. Strain out

. . . .

61. Daniel Atha, "Eat the Weeds: Chickweed," *Plant Talk* (blog), New York Botanical Garden, March 29, 2012, https://www.nybg.org/blogs/plant-talk/2012/03/tip-of-the-week/eat-the-weeds/.

62. Maud Grieve, *A Modern Herbal*, vol. 1 (New York: Dover Publications, 1971), 207.

the herb and sip the liquid before going into a confrontation so that you may stick to your resolve. Add the infusion to bathwater and soak to become lucky in love. Make a love charm by sticking a piece of cleaver in the hair of someone you want to catch. Use cleavers in rituals to get in someone's thoughts. Use cleavers in spells to trip up a rival or to stall or tangle an intention.

Coltsfoot
* Tussilago farfara
* Hardy in zones 4–8
* Communication, healing, love, psychic abilities, renewal, tranquility, unblocking energy flow, and wealth

Coltsfoot is an early blooming perennial with bright yellow flowers that produce a fluffy seed head. It is native to Europe but has naturalized the world over and is also known as bullsfoot, coughwort, English tobacco, and hallfoot. Coltsfoot was used as a cough remedy. Grieve writes, "The botanical name, *Tussilago*, signifies 'cough dispeller,' and Coltsfoot has justly been termed 'nature's best herb for the lungs and her most eminent thoracic.'"[63] It was so esteemed in Paris that the flower was painted on apothecary shop doors.[64] A tea made from an infusion of coltsfoot leaves sweetened with honey was used to treat colds and asthma, and a candy called coltsfoot rock was made to remedy coughs and sore throats.[65]

Coltsfoot flowers are one of the first to emerge in the spring. The yellow blossoms are associated with the sun, Venus, and springtime. The leaf, flower, and root are used in love, tranquility, and money formulas. Dry coltsfoot and burn it as incense to inspire feelings of harmony or invoke visions. Crumble dried coltsfoot into bits and roll an anointed candle in the bits of herb to empower love and prosperity spells. Brew an infusion of coltsfoot and pour it into bathwater. Get in and soak to restore energy flow or open psychic channels. Brew it with angelica and add it to bathwater to remove illness

. . . .

63. Grieve, *A Modern Herbal*, vol. 1, 213.

64. Richard Mabey et al., *The New Age Herbalist: How to Use Herbs for Healing, Nutrition, and Body Care* (New York: Fireside Books, 1988), 52.

65. Andi Clevely, *The New Guide to Herbs* (London: Anness Publishers, 1995), 120.

or ease a troubled mind. Crush coltsfoot with celery seed, flaxseed, and star anise and burn the mix on a charcoal disk to open communications with the spirit world. Brew an infusion of coltsfoot and bay leaves and add it to washwater to clear away obstacles.

Dandelion

* *Taraxacum officinale*
* Hardy in zones 5–9
* Divination, health, luck, prophetic dreams, spirit magick, and wish magick

The dandelion is an edible flowering perennial known as the wishing flower or blow balls. Before lawns, gardeners cultivated dandelions, prizing them as food, medicine, and magickal plants. The leaves were eaten as food, the flowers made into wine, and the root roasted and brewed into a coffee-like drink.[66] Colonists carried the flowers with them, and as garden escapees, dandelions have come to naturalize in many countries.

Today the dandelion is gaining popularity as a culinary and medicinal herb, and it is being valued for its importance to the many pollinators who depend on it as a food and pollen source. Dandelion tea is a popular spring tonic and liver detox. The root and young leaves are boiled to make a tea to detoxify the kidneys, bowels, and liver. Dandelion leaves are nutritious greens and can be eaten raw, sautéed, or steamed. The flowers can be made into wine, beer, or jam. They are eaten raw to relieve a headache and restore energy flow.

Magickally, dandelions are associated with Jupiter, Sagittarius, and Hecate and are symbols of hope, summer, and childhood. Drink dandelion tea to bolster spirits and encourage a sunny disposition. Brew a tea from young leaves and sip to enhance psychic sight. Add a dandelion infusion to bathwater and soak to stimulate creative thought. Blow a fluffy dandelion seed head to carry a message to an absent loved one or send a wish off into the universe. Weave the flower heads into a wedding bouquet to bring good luck to the couple. Burn powdered dandelion root with frankincense to promote visions or enhance spirit communications. Allow flowers to grow in your yard to fill the space with positive energy and draw good luck to your home.

. . . .

66. Anna Kruger, *The Pocket Guide to Herbs* (London: Parkgate Books, 1992), 61.

Dead Nettle

* *Lamium* spp.
* Hardy in zones 5–9 (depending on variety)
* Breaking enchantment, empowerment, happiness, persistence, and stability

There are more than fifty species of flowering plants in the family Lamiaceae, all referred to as the dead nettles, as they do not sting. Most are shade-loving ground covers with variegated leaves and small clusters of flowers that bloom from spring to summer. They are known for being enthusiastic growers with a benevolent, empowering energy, and if left to grow, they can fill barren areas, creating habit, adding green to your yard, and offering stability to the energy of your home. *Lamium maculatum,* including 'White Nancy' dead nettle, is a tough perennial that creeps across dry areas, covering places where even grass will not grow. *Lamium album,* also known as white dead nettle, archangel, blind nettle, and stingless nettle, is a European woodland plant that looks a lot like stinging nettle. It was a popular folk remedy, brewed as tea used externally to treat cuts and taken internally to slow internal bleeding and help treat diarrhea.[67] *Lamium galeobdolon,* or yellow archangel, is a common garden plant native to Europe but now found across the world in many shady flower gardens. It is a creeping plant with oval-shaped silvery-gray variegated leaves and produces small yellow flowers. Yellow archangel is a hardy border plant that can be invasive if left unchecked. Plant it in borders to guard and protect. *Lamium purpureum,* also known as red dead nettle, purple dead nettle, and purple archangel, has small purple flowers that bloom in early May. The plant has astringent properties, which makes it a good first aid for cuts. In the garden I will bruise a fresh leaf and apply it to a small cut to staunch bleeding or make a poultice of dried leaves to speed the healing of a bruise or injury.

Magickally, nettle energy is known for its graceful persistence. Use it to instill clear thinking, return confidence, bolster courage, or restore emotional balance. Add dried nettle to formulas to encourage action. Roll a candle that has been anointed in oil in the dried bits and burn it to empower self-motivation. Use purple nettle to overcome obstacles and to heal and cheer. Add it to formulas and infusions to heal

. . . .

67. Reader's Digest, *Magic and Medicine of Plants,* 160.

and comfort. Gather the flowers and add them to bathwater for protection against enchantment, manipulation, or gaslighting.

Dock

* *Rumex* spp.
* Hardy in zones 4–8 (depending on variety)
* Fertility, healing, love, luck, and money

There are more than twenty species of dock in the United States. Here in the Pacific Northwest, two species are considered problem weeds, curly dock (*Rumex crispus*) and broadleaf dock (*Rumex obtusifolius*). Curly dock is a perennial also known as sour dock, narrow dock, garden patience, and yellow dock. In *Today's Herbal Health*, Louise Tenney writes that yellow dock "is an astringent and blood purifier and is used to treat diseases of the blood and chronic skin ailments. It is one of the best blood-builders."[68] Curly dock is high in iron. Broadleaf dock, also known as round-leaved dock and bitter dock, is an effective laxative and was used to treat toothache and skin irritations. It was part of the Angle-Saxon cure for "elf-sickness."[69] When a patient came down with a painful affliction his doctors could not diagnose, the illness was sometimes attributed to being elf-shot of having been caused by an elf.

Docks are traditional bitters used to stimulate the production of digestive enzymes. Both the leaves and the root have restorative properties. Docks are associated with Jupiter and the element air. They are herbs of attraction used to draw luck and attention. Use dried dock in formulas to gain good luck. Dock holds an influencing energy to stimulate interest and attract customers. An infusion of the root is used as a floor wash to attract business. When you want to draw business, brew an infusion and use it to wash your front door and doorknob to draw the eye and inspire curiosity in those passing by. Carry the root in your left pocket to draw attention.

. . . .

68. Louise Tenney, *Today's Herbal Health* (Pleasant Grove, UT: Woodland Publishing, 1997), 172.

69. Reader's Digest, *Magic and Medicine of Plants*, 102.

Herb Robert

* *Geranium robertianum*
* Hardy in zones 5–9
* Binding, cheer, conception, elevating,
faery magick, healing, peace, and refreshing

This common weed is known by many names: crow's foot, fox geranium, red robin, stinking stork's bill, and wild crane's bill are but a few. Herb Robert is an herb steeped in faery lore. Its name hints as much, as Oregon trailkeeper John Sparks discusses: "Another theory has it named after Robin Goodfellow, a pseudonym for the mischievous fairy or forest sprite Puck." Regarding the name fox geranium, he shared that "'fox' is a corruption of 'folks,' as in 'fairy folk.' Calling a fairy by his or her name is considered unwise since fairies are paranoid creatures and always think you are talking ill of them."[70] In Germany herb Robert was called *ruprechtskraut* and associated with the hobgoblin Knecht Ruprecht.[71]

Herb Robert is a relative of the garden geranium. This diminutive flower was once venerated for its healing energy. Today, according to WebMD, "Herb Robert is used for diarrhea, to improve functioning of the liver and gallbladder, and to reduce inflammation in the kidney, bladder, and gallbladder. … The fresh leaves are chewed to relieve sore mouth and throat."[72] Its high tannin content makes it an effective astringent. Steep the herb in hot water overnight using a ratio of 2 teaspoons of dried herb per 1 cup of water. Strain and add the tea to bathwater to soothe, heal, and restore. Soak in the bath to improve mood and lift outlook.

Herb Robert holds a healing, uplifting energy. It is associated with Mars and Venus. Use it to bolster spirit and increase enthusiasm for life. Add dried herb Robert to formulas to draw luck. Herb Robert is also known as a binding herb and can be used to bind an adversary or difficult situation.

. . . .

70. John Sparks, "Herb Robert: Epic Cure-All or Villain of the Piece?" Trailkeepers of Oregon, December 22, 2018, https://www.trailkeepersoforegon.org/herb-robert-epic-cure-all-or-villain-of-the-piece/.

71. Metropolitan Museum of Art, "Saint or Sprite?" *The Medieval Garden Enclosed* (blog), June 17, 2011, https://blog.metmuseum.org/cloistersgardens/2011/06/17/saint-or-sprite/.

72. "Herb Robert," WebMD, accessed June 1, 2021, https://www.webmd.com/vitamins/ai/ingredientmono-24/herb-robert.

Holly

* *Ilex aquifolium*
* Hardy in zones 5–9
* Counter-magick, death and rebirth,
dream magick, luck, protection, and success
* Warning: The berries are toxic. Do not eat.

Christmas holly is a tree native to Europe but now is classified as an invasive species in the Pacific Northwest. The bright red berries are a popular food for wildlife, which disperse this tree through Oregon habitats. A single tree will produce hundreds of sprouts in a single season, and though it must be aggressively managed, it is an attractive addition to a yard and the fruit provides a winter food for hungry birds.

The holly tree has been a symbol of midwinter festivals since pre-Christian times. As a symbol of the sun, holly was brought into the home to add cheer.[73] Hang a branch over your door for luck, or bring a bough of holly into your home as an invitation for the fey to shelter with you. Holly is a warrior tree and a symbol of masculine energy associated with Mars, Saturn, and the element fire. It holds energy for protection. A holly tree planted at the entrance of your home will ward evil from entering. In rural England it was believed that if you grew a holly tree in your yard, it would protect the home from hexes and lightning.[74] Drop a handful of holly leaves into a bowl of spring water. Set the bowl out overnight under the light of a full moon to make a protective water. Use it to anoint the pulse points or the bottoms of feet to fortify the spirit. Dip a finger in the water and trace the inside of your wrists, the center of your palms, and the bottom of your feet. If you need to clear your energy, stand in the tub and pour the water over your head as you visualize rinsing away what is keeping you down or holding you back.

Holly wood is one of the nine sacred woods. It is used in defensive magick and animal work.

73. Tom MacCubbin, "Holly's Magic Traced to Ancient Lore," *Orlando Sentinel*, December 20, 1986, https://www.orlandosentinel.com/news/os-xpm-1986-12-20-0280200006-story.html.

74. Reader's Digest, *Magic and Medicine of Plants*, 168.

Ivy

* *Hedera* spp.
* Hardy in zones 5–11(depending on variety)
* Binding, cooperation, divination, fertility, healing,
   love, luck, peace, and protection
* Warning: All parts are toxic if ingested. Do not eat.

Ivy is a genus of evergreen climbing or creeping vines. It will grow up to cover fences and walls and makes a nice ground cover that creates wildlife habitats in areas where little else will grow. However, its creeping shoots can be hard to manage. I spend hours pulling it out of my lawn. In plant lore ivy symbolizes immortality, love, fidelity, sex, and valor. It is associated with Saturn and the moon. Ivy is known as gort in the Celtic tree calendar.

Ivy is a binding plant often used at weddings, where it symbolizes fidelity. Weave ivy into fidelity and love charms. Intertwine two ivy plants and grow them in a pot to encourage a love that is constant. Ivy also holds energy for protection. Weave it with grapevines into a wreath and hang it on your door to ward against negative forces and discourage unwanted visitors. Grow ivy around doorways and windows for protection. Weave it into a wreath with rowan and blackberry vines for a protection that will return a hex to the sender. Twist it into a braid and wear it around your wrist when traveling for luck and to stay safe from a conman's eye or a faery's enchantment.

Mallow, Common

* *Malva neglecta*
* Hardy in zones 4–8 (biennial variety)
* Comfort, love, protection, and sex magick

An annual or biennial with rounded leaves and a flowering stalk with white or pale violet flowers. Common mallow is also known as buttonweed, cheeseweed, dwarf mallow, and roundleaf mallow. It is a member of the family Malvaceae, which includes cotton, hibiscus, okra, and the marshmallow plant (*Althaea officinalis*), whose root provided the ingredient for the original marshmallows. The leaves, stalks, fruit, and seed of common mallow are edible. The leaves and stems can be added raw to salads or dried and used to make infusions to drink.

Mallows hold energy for love and are associated with Osiris, Althea, Aphrodite, Inanna, Shiva, and Venus. Brew an infusion of mallow leaves and use as a mouth rinse to treat sore gums and freshen breath. Add an infusion of mallow to bathwater to fortify a weary spirit. Add the infusion to a foot soak to comfort and restore someone who is drained. Sip it as tea to lift the mood, bring cheer, or remedy sadness. The leaves contain salicylic acid and can be used for pain relief.[75] Crush the leaves and use them as a poultice to help clear up skin blemishes and restore youthful glow.

Mullein

* *Verbascum thapsus*
* Hardy in zones 3–8
* Courage, divination, healing, love, mental health, protection, and travel

Mullein is a self-seeding biennial native to Eurasia and Africa but is now found growing along roadsides and wastelands across the world. A center stalk grows up from a base of large fuzzy leaves to become a huge spike of blossoms. Mullein was brought to the New World by early American settlers who used it as a medicinal herb. All parts of the plant are helpful. The flowering plant has antispasmodic and expectorant properties.[76] The leaves were smoked to ease asthma and consumption. Mullein tea is a remedy for chest cold and coughs.[77] The flowers and seeds contain an essential oil helpful in the treatment of wounds and earaches.[78] The leaves hold antibacterial properties and are used to bandage wounds.

75. Katrina Blair, *The Wild Wisdom of Weeds: 13 Essential Plants for Human Survival* (White River Junction, VT: Chelsea Green Publishing, 2014), 249.

76. Kruger, *The Pocket Guide to Herbs*, 121.

77. Foster and Johnson, *National Geographic Desk Reference to Nature's Medicine*, 254–55.

78. Ody, *The Complete Medicinal Herbal*, 111.

Mullein is a protective herb associated with the sun, Mercury, Saturn, Jupiter, and the element fire. The tall flower spike was called Jupiter's staff.[79] Mullein holds a strong protective energy that can keep negative energy away. Some magickal practitioners I know string the leaves together to wear as a head covering to conceal their identity when visiting a crossroads or meeting with a cemetery energy. It is a traveler's herb helpful in keeping both the body and luggage safe. To avoid mischief, bruise a mullein leaf and rub it on the bottom of your shoe before venturing out into the world. Place a leaf in your shoes to protect against attacks. Stuff mullein into dream pillows to guard against nightmares. Add a mullein infusion to bathwater to calm the spirit and open psychic channels. Crush mullein with fennel and burn it to dispel a malicious spirit. Use mullein to empower spells that use graveyard dirt.

Plantain

* *Plantago major, P. lanceolata,* and *P. media*
* Hardy in zones 3–12 (depending on variety)
* The dead, divination, dreams, healing, protection, strength, and travelers

Plantain is a wayside weed native to Europe that is now naturalized across North America. It has been called woundwort, snake weed, and Englishman's foot, as it followed the colonists' paths, spreading along with the newcomers who used it as an herbal remedy.[80] Plantain tea was given to treat colds and lung problems.[81] A poultice made of plantain leaves has astringent properties and will help reduce inflammation when applied to a wound, burn, sting, or bite. You can make an instant treatment by chewing a plantain leaf and spitting the mucilage onto a sting.

Plantain is one of the nine sacred Anglo-Saxon herbs mentioned in the *Lacnunga*.[82] It is associated with Venus and the element of earth, as well as Orcus, Persephone, Pluto, and Hades. Plantain energy is empowering and can be used to add strength

· · · · · · · · · · · · · · · ·

79. Folkard, *Plant Lore, Legends, and Lyrics,* 398.

80. "Plantain," Drugs.com, accessed July 26, 2021, https://www.drugs.com/npc/plantain.html.

81. Tenney, *Today's Herbal Health,* 126.

82. "The Nine Herbs Prayer from the *Lacnunga*," Wyrtig, accessed September 1, 2021, http://www.wyrtig.com/GardenFolklore/NineHerbsPrayer.htm.

to other herbs. Brew an infusion from plantain leaves and use it to rinse your hands before reading the tarot to draw cards with a message true. Dry plantain leaves and grind them into a powder. Toss a pinch into a burning flame to instigate a wish to manifest. Add the powder to sachets to keep nightmares away. Use plantain to protect against enchantment and thievery.

Purslane
* *Portulaca oleracea*
* Hardy in zones 3–12
* Counter-magick, happiness, love, luck, protection, and sleep

Purslane is a sprawling annual with thick succulent leaves. It is also known as *herba portulacae*, little hogweed, moss rose, and pigweed. Purslane is a succulent with a cooling nature and is used like aloe to remedy burns and skin irritations. It is a highly nutritious food plant.[83] Purslane is eaten as a vegetable and a salad herb in India and the Middle East and Asia.[84] In traditional Chinese medicine, purslane is known as *mǎ chǐ xiàn* and is used to restore vitality and help treat skin disorders and diarrhea.[85]

Purslane holds a formidable energy for protection. Maud Grieve tells us in ancient times purslane was "one of the anti-magic herbs, and strewn round a bed was said to afford protection against evil spirits."[86] Stuff a pouch with dried purslane and carry it as a charm against jealousy and suspicion. Tie a piece of purslane into a knot and carry it to avoid the attentions of a bully. Knot a piece of purslane with red string and hang it from a closet door to ward a room. Purslane holds a protective energy to guard against fear. Plant it beneath a bedroom window to ward against nightmares. Grow purslane along a front path to keep negative energy away.

. . . .

83. "Common Purslane, *Portulaca oleracea*," *Wisconsin Horticulture Division of Extension*, accessed September 1, 2021, https://hort.extension.wisc.edu/articles/common-purslane-portulaca-oleracea/.

84. Kruger, *The Pocket Guide to Herbs*, 145.

85. "Purslane," Me & Qi, accessed September 1, 2021, https://www.meandqi.com/herb-database/purslane.

86. Grieve, *A Modern Herbal*, vol. 2, 660.

Stinging Nettle

* *Urtica dioica* and *U. urens*
* Hardy in zones 3–10
* Appreciation, balance, boundaries, counter-magick,
protection, restore, strength, and women's tonics
* Warning: The leaves are covered in stinging
hairs that cause irritation to the skin.

Stinging nettle is a common perennial found in Europe, Asia, and North America. It is a member of the Urticaceae family and is covered with small hairs that when handled "sting," or cause the area to itch and burn. *Urtica dioica* is known as big stinging nettle or common nettle, while *U. urens* is known as small nettle or dog nettle. Nettle is a wasteland plant that establishes in abandoned areas where it heals the earth and restores the balance by enriching the soil with minerals and nitrogen.

Nettle has a long history as a helpful plant. Nettle has been recognized as one of the most useful plants for good health. In *Today's Herbal Health*, Louise Tenney explains, "The plant contains alkaloids that neutralize uric acid. It is now understood that decreasing uric acid helps reduce symptoms of rheumatism."[87] Stinging nettle is one of the nine sacred herbs of the Anglo-Saxon Nine Herbs Charm used to treat poisoning and infection.[88] In parts of Scandinavia and Nepal, nettle soup is a staple food.[89] The leaves were boiled to make an early spring tonic to fortify and strengthen. Today nettle tea is drunk to bolster urinary tratk health, treat pain, and manage chronic diseases.[90]

Stinging nettle holds a gentle energy to restore, renew, and balance. Sip nettle tea to restore spirit and reduce brain fog. Add an infusion to bathwater to calm a restless

. . . .

87. Tenney, *Today's Herbal Health*, 117.

88. "The Nine Herbs Prayer from the *Lacnunga*," Wyrtig, accessed September 1, 2021, http://www.wyrtig.com/GardenFolklore/NineHerbsPrayer.htm.

89. Nancy J. Hajeski, *National Geographic Complete Guide to Herbs and Spices: Remedies, Seasonings, and Ingredients to Improve Your Health and Enhance Your Life* (Washington, DC: National Geographic, 2016), 151.

90. Erin Moore, "The Health Benefits of Nettle Tea," Healthline, December 20, 2018, https://www.healthline.com/health/food-nutrition/nettle-tea.

mind. Add an infusion to a footbath to enliven someone weary. Use nettle to redis-cover appreciation for life. Nettle is associated with Aries, Scorpio, Mars, the element fire, and faery places. It holds magickal energy to protect and end restriction. Block a threat by writing the offending person's name on an envelope and stuffing it full of nettle. Burn dried nettle to end thoughts that are limiting your advancement. Stuff a pouch with nettle and carry it when facing an adversary to avoid being hexed. Hang it as a talisman to keep malevolent energy away. Mix nettle with rue or agrimony to break hexes. Use it in knot magick to boost protection powers.

Wood Sorrel

* *Oxalis* spp.
* Hardy in zones 3–7 (depending on variety)
* Balance, fertility, luck, money, protection, stability, and wellness

Wood sorrel belongs to a large genus, *Oxalis*, named for their sour flavor. The name was derived from *oxys*, Greek for "sharp."[91] The leaves contain oxalic acid and can be toxic if consumed in large quantities.

Wood sorrels hold an uplifting, lucky energy and are associated with Venus, the earth, faeries, and woodland spirits. The triple leaves form a triad. Common wood sorrel (*Oxalis acetosella* L.) is thought to be the true shamrock St. Patrick used as a symbol for the Trinity to convert Ireland.[92] The leaves have a pleasant sour flavor and were used as an herb to make sour sorrel sauces.[93]

Creeping wood sorrel (*Oxalis corniculata*) is a creeping perennial found along road-sides, in fields, and in yards. It holds a gentle energy for balance and hearth and home and is favored by faeries, elves, and woodland spirits. A patch of creeping wood sorrel is a good spot to leave an offering if you are seeking a faery ally. Pick a handful and tuck the leaves into your left pocket to protect the heart, or toss them into a bath and soak to quell an infatuation. Dry wood sorrel leaves and use them in good luck formulas.

. . . .

91. *Merriam-Webster,* s.v. "oxalis (*n.*)" accessed November 22, 2021, https://www.merriam-webster.com/dictionary/oxalis.

92. Grieve, *A Modern Herbal,* vol. 2, 751.

93. Gerard, *The Herball,* 1031.

FAVORITE FOOD PLANTS
FOR A WILDLIFE GARDEN

While pollinators appreciate all blossoms, from the lowly dandelion to the lofty rose, certain plants are favored over others. Double flowers, though beautiful, are useless as a food source. Choose simple, open-face flowers to feed the bees and butterflies and tube-shaped flowers to attract hummingbirds. Many moths and butterflies require specific host plants. Research your native species and grow the plants they need to complete their life cycles.

Allium
* *Allium* spp.
* Hardy in zones 4–8
* Banishing negativity; cheer, protection, and stability

For a wildlife garden, choose ornamental onions with large spherical blooms. Bees are drawn to large flower clusters, and there are many beautiful varieties. Two of my favorites are 'Purple Sensation' (*Allium aflatunense*) and 'True-Blue' (*Allium azureum*), a Siberian native with round flax-blue flowers.

Alliums grow best when planted in full sun areas with well-draining soil. Plant allium bulbs in the fall when the soil has cooled for returning spring color. Plant the bulbs six to eight inches deep and about seven inches apart in a repeating pattern in a border or throughout the garden to add a sense of structure to your beds.

Alliums make lovely cut flowers. The flowers are long lasting, and like the edible onion, alliums hold energy to banish the unwanted. Add the cut flowers to wreaths and garlands to boost protection powers. Plant alliums in your garden to ward the space from enchantments. Grow alliums along walkways to keep unwanted visitors away. Cut a few allium flowers and add them to a vase as a focal point when banishing a bad habit or a negative influence.

Alyssum
* Lobularia maritima
* Hardy in zones 9–11
* Balance, calmness, harmony, and protection

Alyssum is a low-growing plant that produces clusters of small flowers. Though often planted for annual color, this small Mediterranean flower is a perennial in warm climates. Sow the seeds directly into garden soil or plant seedlings for instant garden color. Grow alyssum in borders, along walks, and as ground cover in early spring. The flowers may fade in the heat of summer but will often bloom again in fall.

Grow alyssum in your garden to attract happiness. Its sweet, honey-like scent evokes spiritual and emotional balance. Wear a sprig of alyssum to avoid anger and disagreements. Tuck a sprig into your pocket before a hostile encounter to help keep your emotions calm. Add alyssum to a vase of flowers and use it as a centerpiece at any dinner or gathering to promote a peaceful atmosphere. Float flowers in bathwater to soothe emotions when someone has you feeling ruffled. Fill a sachet with dried alyssum flowers and tuck it into your drawer to attract positive energy and scent the clothes with a pleasant, soothing scent. Gather a bouquet of alyssum and tie it with a ribbon. Hang the bouquet in your home to protect from gossip, prying neighbors, and faery glamours. Alyssum is an edible flower and a member of the Brassicaceae family; it has the same spicy flavor as other mustards.

Anise Hyssop

* *Agastache foeniculum*
* Hardy in zones 4–9
* Attraction, dreams, faery flower, healing, and sweeten

Anise hyssop is an aromatic perennial in the mint family native to North America also known as lavender hyssop or blue giant hyssop. Anise hyssop is an easy-to-grow wildflower with spikes of lavender blossoms that bloom from June to September. Because of its name, it is often confused with the Old World cleansing herb hyssop, but the two are not related. The fragrant foliage has a sweet fragrance. The colorful flower spikes are a favorite of bees, butterflies, and hummingbirds. After the last frost, choose an area with full sun exposure and sow seeds or young plants directly into soil. Keep the soil moist until the plants are established.

Anise hyssop is associated with Mercury, Venus, Libra, and the element air. It holds energy to heal, sweeten, and attract. The flower is a faery favorite. Plant anise hyssop in faery gardens to attract devic energies and pollinators. The leaves are aromatic and can be used to flavor jellies and syrups. Brew an infusion from the leaves and flowers to make a pleasant-tasting tea to help treat colds, sore throats, and coughs or to relieve indigestion. Add an infusion to bathwater and soak to rediscover the sweetness of life. Add the leaves to strewing mixtures to instill healing energy. Add dried flowers to potpourri to encourage sweet dreams or stuff them into a dream pillow to end nightmares. Add the flowers to salads or use them to garnish baked goods to boost energy for healing and attraction. The seeds are used in baking as an alternative to poppy seeds.

Bachelor's Button

* *Centaurea* spp.
* Love, power, psychic abilities, and tenderness

The bachelor's button is a vibrant azure blue annual flower also known as cornflower, bluebottle, and boutonniere flower. In Europe these flowers are called cornflowers because they often were seen growing in and alongside wheat fields. The flower came to symbolize reanimation, as each year they would bloom along with the growing crop.[94] This annual grows easily from seed. Sow seed directly into garden soil after the last frost date. Sow in any plot with full sun exposure to add cheery color.

It is said that the flower got its name, bachelor's button, from its use as a lapel flower and the folklore that a man's feelings would stay true as long as the flower held its color. Bachelor's button symbolizes hope in love. The flower is worn on first dates as a love oracle: if it stays fresh, a loving relationship is a possibility, but if the flower fades, their heart belongs to another. Bachelor's button holds energy to enhance psychic abilities. Use the flowers as a gazing focus or make an infusion from the flower tops and sip it to boost intuitive powers. Add 1 teaspoon of dried flowers to 1 cup of hot water and steep. Use the liquid to rinse your forehead to energize the third eye. Or use the infusion as a hair rinse to inspire fresh thought. Add the infusion to bathwater to help reduce anxiety and enhance intuition, or use it to rinse your hands before reading the tarot to intuitively pull meaningful cards. Combine bachelor's button flowers with basil, rosemary, and lavender and use them as an herbal strew, or brew them into an infusion to add to washwater to promote peace throughout the household.

Bee Balm
* *Monarda* spp.
* Hardy in zones 4–9
* Clarity, grounding, happiness, and restoration

Bee balm is a flowering perennial native to the Americas, where it is also known as Oswego tea, Indian nettle, and wild bergamot. It is a pollinator favorite. The leaves emit a strong, citrusy fragrance similar to Earl Grey, a tea flavored with bergamot oil from the citrus fruit *Citrus bergamia*. Though the two have similar scents, they are not related. After the Boston Tea Party, wild bergamot (*Monarda didyma*) became the

....

94. Riklef Kandeler and Wolfram R. Ullrich, "Symbolism of Plants: Examples from European-Mediterranean Culture Presented with Biology and History of Art: SEPTEMBER: Cornflower," *Journal of Experimental Botany* 60, no. 12 (2009): 3297, https://doi.org/10.1093/jxb/erp247.

favored drink of American colonists tired of paying taxes.[95] In 1774 bee balm crossed the ocean to England, where it became known as sweet bergamot.[96] Today there are over fifty commercial cultivars with a wide range of colors. The nectar-rich flowers attract bees, hummingbirds, and swallowtails and silver-spotted skipper butterflies. In the fall the seed heads provide food for finches and sparrows. Plant bee balm in full sun in cool zones or in partial shade in hot climates. This flower thrives in rich, moist soil.

Bee balm holds a calming energy that empowers magick to comfort, relax, and restore. Float leaves and flowers in the bath to instill peace, to ground, and to bring balance. Use the flower and leaves as a strewing herb to improve your sense of well-being. Bee balm is associated with the element air and will lend energy for clarity. Rub the leaves on your hands before an interview or important meeting to keep your thoughts clear and focused. Sprinkle fresh or dried bee balm leaves and blossoms over bathwater and soak to boost creativity and gain inspiration. Dress a yellow candle in oil, roll it in the dried crumbled flower bits, and burn to boost illumination or gain information.

Black-Eyed Susan

* *Rudbeckia* spp.
* Hardy in zones 3–9
* Balance, discovery, healing, legal matters, renewal, and strengthening other energies

Both bees and butterflies feed on the black-eyed Susan. This cheery yellow New World wildflower is a member of the sunflower family, *Asteraceae*, and blooms from June to October. Sow the seeds directly into soil in areas with full sun exposure and well-draining soil. Water sparingly. Black-eyed Susans are susceptible to powdery mildew. Plant in sunny borders and along fence lines for the plant to mass. Grow with bee balm, lavender, and salvia to draw pollinators to your garden.

. . . .

95. Strawbery Banke Museum staff, *The Herb Garden at Strawbery Banke Museum* (Portsmouth, NH: Strawbery Banke Museum, n.d.), 3, accessed June 1, 2021, https://www.strawberybanke.org/garden/HerbGuide.pdf.

96. Carol Benzing, "Bee Balm: History in Your Garden!," *Rome (New York) Sentinel*, June 22, 2014, https://romesentinel.com/stories/bee-balm-history-in-your-garden,61664.

Rudbeckias are associated with Jupiter, the element air, and the sun. They hold a bold magickal energy for renewal and discovery. In the language of flowers, the black-eyed Susan means "for justice" and the flower is often used to gain favor in court cases. Tuck a flower into your left pocket and wear it to court to find a just outcome. Meditate on a blossom to find an answer or clear a roadblock. Float flower heads in bathwater to encourage healing after a hurtful experience.

Butterfly Bush

* *Buddleja* spp.
* Hardy in zones 8–10 (some varieties are hardy to zone 5)
* Beginnings, faery flower, inspiration, opportunities, and whimsy

Buddleja is a genus of flowering shrubs with wands of colorful nectar-producing blossoms. The flowers exude a honey-like fragrance that attracts pollinators. The butterfly bush is a staple plant of southwestern low-maintenance rock gardens. It is easy to grow and in some areas has been declared invasive, as it spreads easily by seed and is hard to get rid of once it has become established.

The butterfly bush attracts faery energy. Plant a butterfly bush in faery gardens. It holds fresh energy for inspiration and hope. Spend some time watching the pollinators enjoy the flowers to renew your perspective and lift your mood. Cut a few flower wands and tuck them into a vase of flowers to lighten a mood or make conversation more playful.

Butterfly Weed

* *Asclepias tuberosa*
* Hardy in zones 10–12
* Divination, cheer, good health, healing, protection
* Warning: The sap is toxic—have care when handling.

Butterfly weed is a milkweed also known as pleurisy root. It is a favorite flower of bees, butterflies, and hummingbirds. Butterfly weed is an important host plant for the monarch and queen butterflies. Have care when handling milkweeds. The sap of *Asclepias* species contains a mix of cardenolides and glycosides that can harm the eyes.[97] Caterpillars have adapted so that when they eat the milkweed, they store the toxins in their body and become toxic themselves, which protects them from being eaten by predators. As butterflies, they retain the toxin, and their colorful wings signal to birds that they are an undesirable food source. Butterfly weed is a hardy perennial. It thrives in areas with full sun exposure. Sow seeds directly into well-draining soil and water them in. Water regularly to maintain soil moisture level.

Butterfly weed is a member of the genus *Asclepias,* named after the Greek god of medicine, Asclepius.[98] It holds a gentle protective energy that cheers the heart and helps inspire feelings of well-being. Gaze upon it during meditation to deepen the experience. Plant butterfly weed in your garden to draw pollinators and inspire happiness.

California Lilac
* *Ceanothus 'Concha'*
* Hardy in zones 8–10
* Cheer, clarity, and true feelings

The California lilac is a fast-growing shrub or small tree with large, glossy green leaves and clusters of blue flowers that the bees adore. California lilacs are hearty, need little care, and propagate easily from cuttings. The sweetly scented flowers are a favorite of bumblebees. Plant California lilacs in full sun and well-draining soil. In hot climates offer the plant shelter from the afternoon sun. Water deeply and allow the soil to dry out between waterings. Plant with lavender, salvia, and lithodora to create a space for pollinators and feed the bees.

California lilacs hold energy to inspire understanding of our truest feelings. Pick a sprig of flowers and bruise it between your fingers. Rub your hand across your forehead before meditation to deepen your connection to your higher self. Use the flowers as a focus during meditation to gain creative insight or to encourage a truthful look at a situation. Burn the blossoms to remove obstacles and activate positive energy flow.

. . . .

97. Susie Reutling, "Gardeners Beware! Milkweed Toxicity," UF/IFAS Extension, Monroe County, October 22, 2019, http://blogs.ifas.ufl.edu/monroeco/2019/10/22/gardeners-beware-milkweed-toxicity/.

98. *Encyclopaedia Britannica Online,* s.v. "Asclepius," accessed September 1, 2021, https://www.britannica.com/topic/Asclepius.

Clary Sage
* *Salvia sclarea*
* Hardy in zones 5–9
* Calming, communication, destiny, healing, protection, restoring, and vision

Clary is a short-lived, aromatic perennial also known as Europe sage, cleareye, and eye bright (not to be confused with *Euphrasia*, eyebright). It is favored by bees and is very adaptable, drought tolerant, and easy to grow, but it will not flower in warm regions. If the conditions are right, clary will readily self-seed. New World settlers brought clary sage and planted it in their gardens. It escaped and naturalized, and now this attractive wildflower can be found growing across North America along roads, in waysides, and in meadows. Sow the seeds in late spring.

Clary sage is an Old World herb in the mint family. It has a pleasant scent that promotes relaxation and eases anger. The leaves are a source of aromatic oil used topically for its astringent and antifungal properties. Clary sage is associated with the moon and holds energy to enhance intuition and visionary states. Crumble dried clary leaves and roll an oiled candle in the bits. Burn the candle to open communication channels with the universe. Rub the leaves between your fingers to expand your perception before divination. Crumble the herb and inhale the fragrance to inspire intuition. Add clary leaves to an evening bath to relax and enhance dreamwork. Dress a candle in oil and roll it in dried clary leaves to empower communication spells.

Comfrey
* *Symphytum officinale*
* Hardy in zones 3–9
* Healing, safety, stability, and travel
* Warning: People with liver problems should avoid consuming this plant.

Comfrey is a perennial herb also known as boneset, bruisewort, and knitbone. It produces attractive blue bell-shaped flowers that bloom from May to August and provide food for long-tongued bumblebees. Comfrey is a vigorous grower that will colonize even in poor soil. Plant it in loamy, well-draining soil in a place where it can clump.

The bruised leaves were used as a poultice to stanch bleeding and accelerate the healing of broken bones, sprains, and bruises.[99] The leaves are rich in minerals and can be made into a brown, potassium-rich liquid that is fed to plants to encourage them to flower and fruit. Keep a comfrey bed to use as garden food. Magickally, comfrey is an herb of protection associated with Saturn and Capricorn. It is used in rituals for stability, meeting life's basic needs, and gaining shelter. Add an infusion to bathwater to soothe sunburns, relieve skin irritations, and calm troubled thoughts. Comfrey is a traveler's herb. Carry its leaves or root when traveling to ensure safety and protect against misfortunes. Tuck a leaf into your suitcase to ensure that it doesn't get lost. Stuff a pouch with a handful of feverfew flowers, some comfrey leaves, and a St. Christopher medal. Hang the pouch from your rearview mirror or place it in your glove compartment to stay clear of accidents. Use comfrey to safely travel the astral realms.

Coreopsis

* Coreopsis spp.
* Hardy in zones 4–9 (most varieties)
* Cheer, luck, and the sun

Coreopsis is a genus of yellow flowering plants also known as tickseed and pot of gold. Most varieties are low-maintenance, drought-tolerant perennials that clump and produce long-blooming, daisylike flowers that attract bees and butterflies. Grow coreopsis in sandy loam with full sun exposure. Settlers thought the small black seeds of this American wildflower resembled bugs, so they called it "tickseed" and stuffed it in their pillows and mattresses to keep the bugs away.[100]

Coreopsis holds a sunny, cheerful energy to lift spirits and inspire gladness. Add flowers to a vase to lift the mood in a room, or give a bouquet with coreopsis flowers to a sick or depressed friend to comfort and cheer them. Stuff a pouch with dried coreopsis flowers, chamomile flowers, and cinquefoil and carry it as a talisman to draw luck. Use the seeds in formulas to repel negativity. Add the seeds to a poppet's stuffing to help repel negative energy and bad luck.

....

99. Foster and Johnson, *National Geographic Desk Reference to Nature's Medicine*, 114.

100. Laura C. Martin, *Garden Flower Folklore* (Guilford, CT: Globe Pequot Press, 2009), 121.

Foxglove

* *Digitalis* spp.
* Hardy in zones 4–10
* Faery magick, health, protection, and sight
* Warning: These tall, elegant flowers are poisonous.
Take care when handling, as they have been known
to cause rashes, headache, and nausea.

The foxglove is a beautiful, showy flower that attracts bees of all sizes. Foxgloves are also known as faery gloves and dead men's bells, for all parts of this plant—the flowers, leaves, roots, and seeds—contain the glycosides digoxin, digitoxin, and gitoxin, which can incite a heart attack.[101] There are many varieties, some biennial and others perennial. The perennial varieties produce a rosette of leaves the first year and flowers in the second. Foxgloves flourish in moist, well-draining soil and prefer afternoon shade.

The foxglove is associated with Venus, Pluto, and Scorpio and holds energy for protection. In Wales a dye made from foxglove was used to paint crossed lines on the floor of the home to ward away evil.[102] Grow foxglove in your garden to provide protection from mischievous spirits. Fill a small bag with dried foxglove leaves and wear to keep from falling under another's charm. Strew dried leaves across doorsteps and thresholds to keep negativity from crossing. Stuff a sachet with dried foxglove leaves, chamomile, and lilac blossoms and hang it for protection from nighttime mischief. Stuff foxglove into a dream pillow to keep night terrors at bay.

Foxgloves are faery flowers and are steeped in faery lore. It is said that a foxglove will indicate faery activity by bobbing or bowing when a faery is near.[103] It is thought to be unlucky to pick a foxglove flower, as it might house a faery and bring their wrath in the form of bad luck or accidents. Foxgloves hold energy to expand awareness. Dip your finger into the dew collected in a foxglove flower and trace the moisture across your forehead. Then sit quietly and watch and listen to become aware of the visiting nature spirits.

. . . .

101. Foster and Johnson, *National Geographic Desk Reference to Nature's Medicine*, 175.

102. Susan Gregg, *The Complete Illustrated Encyclopedia of Magical Plants* (Beverly, MA: Fair Winds Press, 2008), 36.

103. Folkard, *Plant Lore, Legends, and Lyrics*, 344.

Grape Hyacinth
* *Muscari* spp.
* Hardy in zones 4–9
* Cheer, communication, inspiration, and tenacity
* Warning: The bulb is poisonous.

The grape hyacinth is also known as muscari. Its early spring flowers provide a first food source for bees and bumblebees. The small, delicate cobalt-blue flowers have a pleasant musky scent and are lovely when planted in a mass. It is a mass planting of grape hyacinth flowers that make up the famous blue planting known as the Blue River at Keukenhof Gardens in the Netherlands.[104] Grape hyacinths are easy-to-grow perennials. They thrive in well-draining soil and will self-seed and naturalize over time to the point of becoming invasive. Grape hyacinth plantings are hard to eradicate once established. The foliage will yellow and die back in the late spring as the plant becomes dormant. It will not injure the plant to remove the dead leaves. If the plants become crowded, you can dig up the bulbs, separate them, and plant them in new parts of the garden.

Plant grape hyacinth with crocus, daffodils, and tulips for lovely spring color that will boost mood and induce cheer. Grow in borders or along walkways and paths to infuse the area with inspiring, creative energy. Add cut flowers to a vase to boost group communication and encourage networking. Meditate on a grape hyacinth flower when you need resolve or fortitude to finish something you have started.

Hellebore
* *Helleborus* spp.
* Hardy in zones 4–8 (depending on variety)
* Banishing, exorcism, protection, and purification
* Warning: Toxic. Do not eat.

Hellebores are early bloomers. Their flowers provide an important food source for emerging bees. Hellebores begin to flower in February and will flower for months as long as the nights remain cool. They are cold-hardy perennials that thrive in

....

104. Jan Beglinger, "Grape Hyacinths Can Add a 'Blue River' to the Garden," *(Batavia, NY) Daily News*, October 11, 2016, https://www.thedailynewsonline.com/lifestyles/grape-hyacinths-can-add-a-blue-river-to-the-garden/article_8d89c4cb-a867-5bd8-8bc5-2c4745c1cc3d.html.

humus-rich soil and prefer shaded, sheltered areas. Give them plenty of room when you plant them. They do best when planted with deciduous trees, as they like moist beds with winter sun and summer shade. Keep the soil moist and mulch heavily when temperatures warm. Hellebores do not tolerate heat.

The hellebore is sometimes thought of as a baneful herb, and it is toxic, so don't ingest it. Black hellebore (*Helleborus niger*) once known as melampode, after mythological Greek seer Melampus, is now known as the Christmas rose.[105] It was revered for its magickal powers and used as an antidote for madness and to repel evil spirits.[106] Hellebores are associated with Mars and Saturn. They are known for their role in vengeful hex work. They hold energy to empower work for banishing, ending, and invisibility. Dry the flowers and use the bits to bolster protection magick. Strew them across thresholds to keep malicious energies from entering. Grind the dried flowers into dust and carry it when you want to go unnoticed.

Lamb's Ear

* *Stachys byzantina*
* Hardy in zones 4–9
* Bee magick, healing, love, moon magick, and stopping gossip

Lamb's ear is a frost-hardy evergreen with woolly leaves also known as silver carpet, woundwort, woolly betony, and woolly hedgenettle. It produces a stalk of small, spring-blooming, pineapple-scented flowers that attract bees and hummingbirds. The soft, fuzzy leaves are favored by the female wool carder bee (*Anthidium manicatum*), who harvests the fluff from them to line her nest. Lamb's ear is very hardy and easy to grow. Plant it in full sun in soil with good drainage and it will return every year.

Lamb's ear is also known as woundwort because of its battlefield reputation for slowing the flow of blood when used as a wound dressing. The leaves are absorbent and have analgesic, anti-inflammatory, and antibacterial properties.[107] It can be used as

. . . .

105. Grieve, *A Modern Herbal*, vol. 1, 388.

106. Martin, *Garden Flower Folklore*, 247.

107. Gary Antosh, "Is the Lamb's Ears Plant Poisonous?" Plant Care Today, accessed June 19, 2021, https://plantcaretoday.com/lambs-ear-plant-poisonous.html.

a poultice to accelerate healing. Bruise a leaf and press it on a bee sting or insect bite to reduce pain and swelling. The young leaves are edible and quite tasty when added to salads or brewed into a restorative tea. Lamb's ear is associated with the moon and Venus. Magickally, it holds a kind, healing energy to stop, heal, and mend. Add an infusion to bathwater to soothe wounded feelings and help heal a broken heart. Add dried flowers to friendship sachets to facilitate fond feelings. When lamb's ear blooms, it sends up a flowering stalk. This stalk is known as lamb's tongue. It is used in binding and defensive magick to stop gossip or end communication with someone.

Lupine

* *Lupinus* spp.
* Hardy in zones 3–6 (depending on variety)
* Creativity, generosity, healing, and protection

Lupine is a sweetly scented perennial wildflower that grows in poor soils. Pollinators are attracted to the bright flowers. Lupines are the host to several butterfly species. Wild lupine (*Lupinus perennis*) is the only larval host flower of the Midwest's endangered Karner blue, and Oregon lupine (*Lupinus oreganus, L. oreganus* var. *kincaidii*) is the only host for Fender's blue butterfly.[108] The flower gained the name *lupine* because it is often found growing in wasteland areas and was thought to deplete the soil of nutrients, or "wolf them down."[109] But actually, lupines are legumes, and like peas and beans, they have the ability to improve soil by fixing it with nitrogen. Here in the Pacific Northwest, lupines are a wildflower often seen in the early spring growing along roadsides. They bloom in many colors, but their attractive foliage adds interest long after the blooms have faded. Plant the seeds directly in rich, well-draining soil after last frost date. Lupines do not like soggy soils, but they thrive

108. "Fender's Blue Butterfly and Kincaid's Lupine: A Love Story," The Nature Conservatory, May 26, 2020, https://www.nature.org/en-us/about-us/where-we-work/united-states/oregon/stories-in-oregon/endangered-butterfly-pollinator-wildflower-relationship/; Mitchell and Cathy Carnes, "Wild Lupine and Karner Blue Butterflies," US Fish & Wildlife Service, last modified May 29, 2019, https://www.fws.gov/midwest/endangered/insects/kbb/lupine.html.

109. *Encyclopaedia Britannica Online*, s.v. "lupine," accessed September 1, 2021, https://www.britannica.com/plant/lupine.

when soil moisture is even. Water the soil regularly to keep it from drying out. Support your local wildlife by seeking out lupines that are native to your area.

Lupines hold a soothing, uplifting energy to calm and cheer. Cut lupine flowers and add them to a vase to bring cheer into the home. Add lupine flowers to a bouquet of flowers to encourage optimism. Use the flowers to soothe frazzled nerves, calm fears, and encourage creative thought. Brew an infusion from the blossoms and add it to bathwater to soothe a troubled mind. Use it as a hair rinse to inspire a fresh way of thinking. Or soak a rag in the infusion and lay it across your forehead to restore psychic sight.

Meadowsweet
* *Filipendula ulmaria*
* Hardy in zones 4–9
* Happiness, love, peace, protection, and psychic sight

Meadowsweet is in the family Rosaceae and native to Europe, but it has naturalized across the United States. It produces sprays of small, sweetly scented flowers that draw pollinators and attract bees. If you have a damp area, meadowsweet, with its fernlike foliage and clusters of delicate, creamy-white flowers, is an attractive garden plant. Sow seeds in spring directly into the soil.

Meadowsweet contains high levels of salicylic acid, which is known for its ability to reduce pain. It can be used to help treat arthritis, colds, bladder infections, heartburn, and more.[110] Make a cold and flu formula by filling a pan with water and adding a handful of meadowsweet flower heads. Simmer for 10 minutes and then strain out the flowers. Sweeten the liquid with honey and sip it to fight colds and flu. Young meadowsweet leaves are edible. Meadowsweet's sweet, pleasant scent made it a popular strewing herb. It was known as bridewort, lady of the meadow, and queen of the meadow. Gerard writes, "The leaves and flowers far excell all other strowing herbs, for to decke up houses, to strowe in chambers, hals, and banketting houses in the sommertime, for the smell thereof maketh the hart merrie,

---

110. WebMD, "Meadowsweet," accessed September 1, 2021, https://www.webmd.com/vitamins/ai/ingredientmono-108/meadowsweet.

delighteth the senses."[111] Brew an infusion and add it to bathwater to cheer. Add the infusion to a foot soak to comfort. Add a sprig of meadowsweet to a vase of flowers to improve mood. Add dried meadowsweet leaves and flowers to formulas for love and happiness. Add the dried flowers to sachets for harmony. Combine meadowsweet with mint and vervain to make an incense to instill harmony and draw happiness.

Oregon Grape

* *Mahonia aquifolium*, syn. *Berberis aquifolium*
* Hardy in zones 5–9
* Money, nurturing, prosperity, and protection
* Warning: Avoid use during pregnancy or when breastfeeding. Large doses may cause diarrhea and stomach cramps.

The Oregon grape is an evergreen woodland shrub native to North America. Its attractive foliage looks a lot like holly, and the long-lasting yellow flowers are a favorite of nectar-eaters. The early blossoms start to flower in late winter and provide needed sustenance to bees, bumblebees, and hummingbirds. Its tart berries are a favored food source for birds and will draw them to wherever it is planted. The Oregon grape thrives in shaded areas with rich, acidic soil.

The root of Oregon grape contains the alkaloid berberine, which has been shown to have antimicrobial properties. It is sold dried as loose tea to treat infections of the throat, intestines, urinary tract, and psoriasis.[112] Magickally, the Oregon grape holds energy to nurture and protect. Plant it around your house to attract positive energy and ward against negative energy. Plant it near doors and under windows to protect occupants from malicious intentions. Use the sweet-scented flowers to encourage balance and peace. Add sprigs of leaves to a vase of flowers to facilitate amicable communication.

. . . .

111. Gerard, *The Herball*, 887.

112. Cat Ellis, "The Most Important Herbal Remedy: Oregon Grape Root," Herbal Prepper Academy, November 5, 2013, https://www.herbalprepper.com/the-most-important-herbal-remedy -oregon-grape-root/.

Oregano

* *Origanum vulgare*
* Hardy in zones 5–10
* Added energy, dreams, joy, legal issues, love, protection, strength, and vitality

Oregano is a woody flowering perennial herb in the mint family. It is one of the Mediterranean culinary herbs loved by both bees and cooks across the world. Bees are drawn to the small clusters of summer flowers of both oregano and marjoram. Include them in your garden to attract and feed the pollinators. Plant oregano with lavender, sage, and thyme for an aromatic bed of culinary herbs the bees will love. Oregano favors a place in the sun with sandy, well-draining soil. Sow seeds into the soil when temperatures warm to 70 degrees. Choose a location in full sun with fertile, well-draining soil. Allow oregano to flower for a bee treat. Oregano is hardy in many zones and will return year after year. It propagates readily from cuttings. Harvest the leaves by clipping sprigs as you need them.

Oregano is also known as wild marjoram, as it is a close relative to sweet marjoram, and like marjoram, oregano has a long history as a medicinal herb. Agriculture writer Kurt Nolte explains that "the ancient Greeks made creams from oregano leaves and used them to treat sores and aching muscles," while "traditional Chinese doctors used oregano to relieve fever, vomiting, diarrhea, jaundice and itchy skin."[113] Oregano contains carvacrol and thymol, compounds with natural antibacterial and antifungal properties.[114] Oregano is associated with the moon, Juno, Venus, Aphrodite, and Diana. Drink oregano tea to amplify wellness or induce psychic dreams. Use oregano to encourage peace and tranquility or to find comfort when faced with a separation from a loved one. Add leaves to dishes to sweeten affections and encourage freedom of expression. Anoint a candle in olive oil and roll it in dried oregano to

. . . .

113. Kurt Nolte, "Oregano," College of Agriculture & Life Sciences, University of Arizona, accessed September 1, 2021, https://cals.arizona.edu/fps/sites/cals.arizona.edu.fps/files/cotw/Oregano.pdf.

114. Stefani Sassos, "5 Oregano Oil Health Benefits, According to Experts," *Good Housekeeping*, June 16, 2021, https://www.goodhousekeeping.com/health/diet-nutrition/a36674755/oregano-oil-benefits/.

empower a love spell. Oregano also holds energy for protection. Tie a bouquet of oregano with a red string and hang it in a doorway, or crumble and scatter the leaves over a threshold to ward a room. Use oregano in magickal work to repel a meddling neighbor or stop interference or harassment from a coworker.

Primrose
* *Primula vulgaris*
* Hardy in zones 4–8
* Beauty, calmness, joy, pleasure, protection, and youth

The primrose is a shade-loving perennial flower native to the woodlands and moist meadows of Europe. It is one of the first flowers of spring, as noted by its botanical name, which was derived from the Medieval Latin *primula veris*, or "first fruit of spring."[115] Plant primrose flowers to keep worries away. Primrose flowers provide a source of early spring food for bees and other pollinations. Primroses thrive when planted in moist shaded areas where the soil is rich with humus. Water often enough to keep the soil moist and your primroses will return each spring to bloom for years to come.

The primrose symbolized pleasure and self-indulgence, hence the phrase "to walk down a primrose path."[116] In the past the flower was thought to hold the energy to ignite passions. Today the primrose can be used as a sedative to help treat headaches, insomnia, and nervous disorders.[117] Lore holds that the primrose was a key to the Celtic otherworld, and it was customary on May Day eve to strew primrose flowers over a threshold to keep mischievous spirits from entering.[118] Fill a pot with primrose and set it on your doorstep to discourage trouble. In the garden the primrose

. . . .

115. *Merriam-Webster*, s.v. "primula (*n.*)," accessed June 20, 2021, https://www.merriam-webster.com/dictionary/primula.

116. *Merriam-Webster*, s.v. "primrose path (*n.*)," accessed June 20, 2021, https://www.merriam-webster.com/dictionary/primrose%20path.

117. Gather Victoria, "Enchanting Primrose Cordial," *Enchanted Living Magazine*, accessed September 1, 2021, https://enchantedlivingmagazine.com/enchanting-primrose-cordial/.

118. W. Y. Evans Wentz, *The Fairy-Faith in Celtic Countries* (Oxford, UK: Oxford University Press, 1911), 289.

is a cheery faery flower planted to encourage faery visits. Brush the dew collected from a primrose across your forehead to enhance second sight. Use the flower as a meditative focus to become aware of devic energies.

Red Clover

* *Trifolium pratense*
* Hardy in zones 5–9
* Banishing, fertility, love, luck, money, protection, and visions

A flowering plant also known as cow clover, purplewort, purple clover, shamrock, and trefoil. It is grown as a fodder and has naturalized throughout the world. Red clover is valued for its ability to replace nitrogen in the soil it grows in and bees love the flowers. It is a source of isoflavones, water-soluble chemicals that act like estrogens.[119] Red clover tea is a gentle sedative taken to soothe nerves and treat nervous exhaustion, and you can also brew a cup and stir in a spoonful of honey for an effective cough syrup.[120] Clover is high in vitamins, minerals, and protein. Add red clover to salads or cook it as a green.

Clover holds a positive energy to draw good fortune. The druids believed that clover was a symbol of the earth, the sea, and heaven.[121] A clover leaf is an Old World symbol for luck and abundance. A bed of clover planted at the front door will usher in good fortune. If you find a four-leaf clover, pluck it, press it between the pages of a book, and use it as a lucky talisman. Clover is associated with Mercury, Venus, and Taurus and also holds energy to draw a lover. Pluck a clover and tuck it into your pocket to draw the attention of a new love. Stuff a pouch with dried clover and carry it when you want to be noticed by someone.

. . . .

119. Foster, *National Geographic Desk Reference to Nature's Medicine*, 305.

120. Tenney, *Today's Herbal Health*, 132.

121. Foster, *National Geographic Desk Reference to Nature's Medicine*, 304.

Self-Heal

* *Prunella vulgaris*
* Hardy in zones 4–9
* Focus, healing, protecting, and stamina

I have several plants that insistently creep through my lawn. One of them is self-heal also known as prunella, all-heal, heal-all, woundwort, and *xia ku cao*. It is a small, creeping perennial with small purple flowers that the bees love. The flowers bloom from June through October. I don't mind that it spreads through my lawn, but you might, so have care if you decide to grow it. Self-heal thrives in both full sun and partial shade and prefers soils that are damp. It makes a nice ground cover and is a nectar species for Sonoran skippers and many other long-tongued butterflies.

Self-heal has been used as a healing herb down through the ages. It has antibacterial and astringent properties to accelerate the healing of wounds. It is still made into salves and oils to speed the healing of bruises, burns, cuts, and sores, while an infusion can be used to treat infections of the mouth and throat.[122] Magickally, self-heal is associated with Mars and Venus and has energy to heal a broken spirit and to sharpen observation. Mix with bleeding heart flowers to allow a broken sprit to find the ability to heal. Brew a cup of self-heal tea before meditation to deepen your focus. Add the flowers to dishes and serve them to open communication. Crumble and burn self-heal leaves to repel negative energies after an argument.

Sunflower

* *Helianthus* spp.
* Abundance, beginnings, confidence, energy,
   fertility, harvest, success, truth, and wishes

The sunflower genus of plants, belonging to the Asteraceae family, includes about fifty-two species, all of which are native to the Americas. Most sunflowers are summer-blooming annuals. Bees love the flat flowers, and honeybees use the pollen to feed their young. The seeds are a favorite food of many birds and small mammals. Plant sunflowers in areas to provide a source of fall food for backyard birds. Choose a

. . . .
122. Kruger, *The Pocket Guide to Herbs*, 157.

place with a full sun exposure for healthy flowers that will bloom from July to October. Sow the seeds directly into the soil in an area where they can be left to feed the birds and reseed a new crop the next year. Plant large varieties along a fence to provide support.

Sunflowers are a symbol of the sun and are associated with Leo, Apollo, and the element fire. Plant them in the garden to bring joy and draw pollinators. Add its petals to potpourri mixtures to increase energy. Use them in solar rituals. Add dried flower petals to formulas for fertility and confidence. Add them to flower teas to inspire happiness. Sunflowers contain uplifting energy to comfort the sick and inspire friendships. Cut flowers and add them to a vase for a bright, joyous energy that will brighten a room. Fill a vase with sunflowers to add cheer to a sickroom. Give a potted sunflower to someone to inspire friendship. Eat sunflower seeds one at a time while you meditate on something you wish to manifest to give it power.

Toadflax
* *Linaria* spp.
* Hardy in zones 5–9 (depending on variety)
* Attraction, dragons, faery folk, hex breaking, magick, and protection

Linaria is a large genus containing 150 species of herbaceous perennials and annuals, some of which are garden favorites also known as baby snapdragon and faery dust. Some varieties are considered invasive, as they can spread fairly aggressively and are drought resistant, so they can establish with little care. Toadflax produces small snapdragon-like flowers that attract hummingbirds, bees, and butterflies. Plant toadflax seeds in a flower garden to draw positive energy. Toadflax will grow in full sun or partial shade as long as the soil is well-draining. Water regularly in dry periods for flowers that will self-seed a new crop the following spring.

Toadflax is a faery favorite. Plant toadflax with daisies, foxgloves, larkspurs, lupine, pineapple sage, and poppies to create a faery garden. Toadflax is associated with dragons, Mars, and the element fire. It holds a protective energy that can be used to ward areas and break hexes. Use it in protection rituals and anti-hex charms. Float a handful of flowers in a bath to banish negativity. Use toadflax flowers in spells to end hostile activity. Give the flower as an offering to a dragon energy.

Torch Lily

* *Kniphofia uvaria*
* Hardy in zones 5–9
* Freedom, optimism, and strength

An erect perennial also known as red hot poker and tritoma, torch lily is often found in group plantings. Torch lilies bloom in late spring and the tall flower spikes resemble torches or glowing pokers. Native to Africa, these perennials are heat tolerant. Torch lilies thrive when planted in full sun areas with moist, sandy, well-draining soil. They are a favorite hummingbird flower. Plant in a mass in a sunny spot where it can be a focal point.

The torch lily holds a bright, uplifting energy. Plant them in your garden to boost positive energy. Grow torch lilies to attract hummingbirds. Cut a flower and add it to a bud vase to encourage a positive outlook. Grow a mound of torch lilies where you can see them when you leave or return home to lift your mood and inspire an optimistic outlook. Grow them outside your office window so that you can gaze upon them through the glass and find fortitude to finish a project. Plant torch lilies with bee balm, lavender, rudbeckia, and salvia for a magickal, pollinator-friendly spot with expansive energy to inspire appreciation of life.

Yarrow

* *Achillea millefolium*
* Hardy in zones 4–8
* Banishing, courage, exorcism, healing, love, protection, and psychic powers
* Warning: Extended use can cause photosensitivity and skin rashes.

Common yarrow is a flowering plant in the family Asteraceae and was formerly known as soldier's woundwort and knight's milfoil. Its nectar-rich flowers feed pollinators, while its seeds provide food for birds. Grow in full sun to partial shade areas with well-draining soil. Yarrow self-seeds and becomes difficult to eradicate once it is established.

Yarrow is a healing herb, a protective herb, and an herb of love. Its astringent properties help slow bleeding. It was a common practice in the English countryside to stick a yarrow leaf into a nostril to stop a nosebleed.[123] The Scottish made a yarrow ointment to treat wounds and brewed an infusion called milfoil tea to treat melancholy.[124] Yarrow was hung over doors to keep faeries away and was a traditional wedding flower used to ensure a seven-years' love.[125] Add sprigs of yarrow to a wedding bouquet to bless the union. Use yarrow sprigs to decorate a gift-wrapped present to make someone feel special and strengthen friendship. Add yarrow flowers to love sachets to encourage affection. Wish upon the first yarrow flower of the season to gain a favor. Yarrow also has energy to comfort the afflicted. Float flowers in the bathwater to calm a troubled mind. Brew an infusion of lemon balm and yarrow and sip to improve outlook. Yarrow is excellent for eliminating negativity from a person, place, or thing. Tuck a sprig of yarrow into your pocket before meeting with someone who annoys you to keep the conversation light. Add yarrow flowers to a vase of flowers for any family gathering to keep feelings positive. Grow yarrow down walkways to keep negative influences, unwanted guests, and pests away. In the garden a large patch of yarrow indicates an area where there is a concentration of earth energy. Use this as a spot to ground or meditate. Yarrow tea improves psychic powers. It is associated with Venus, Mars, and Libra.

123. Kruger, *The Pocket Guide to Herbs*, 189.

124. Grieve, *A Modern Herbal*, vol. 2, 864.

125. Margaret Picton, *The Book of Magical Herbs: Herbal History, Mystery, and Folklore* (London: Quarto, 2000), 22–23.

SOME FAVORITE GARDEN FLOWERS

The descriptions that follow include a hardiness zone, which indicates the range in which a plant will live as a perennial. Flowers such as calendula, chrysanthemum, dianthus, osteospermum, pansy, petunia, and snapdragon are plants many think of and treat as annuals but are actually perennials in warmer climates, returning each spring to provide another season of color. True annuals are plants that complete their life cycle in a single growing season. They grow, flower, and seed before dying and leaving the seed to produce the next year's generation. Annuals are known for their rapid growth and floriferous color. They can be grown from seed and are often sold in grower's six packs.

A good example is the dahlia. Dahlias come in hundreds of varieties and a variation of colors. They can be grown from seed, planted as tubers, and cloned by cutting. In spring you will often find six packs of small dahlias ready to plant. In cold zones they die away like an annual. I am lucky. Most varieties are cold hardy to my microclimate, zone 8, and thrive from spring to fall. I love my dahlias and have spent time building up a collection by trading plants, buying tubers, and propagating by cutting. I treat my dahlia tubers with special care, and though I don't dig them up and bring them inside to overwinter like those in zones 1 to 7 would need to do, when the season cools and the dahlias' foliage dies back, I mark the place of each tuber with a Popsicle stick. On the coldest days I place a grower's pot upside down over each marked spot to provide some protection from the snow and frost.

Agapanthus

* *Agapanthus* spp.
* Hardy in zones 8–11
* Beauty, confidence, fertility, health, love, and protection

Go to almost any garden center and you will find a variety of agapanthus also known as lily of the Nile and African lily. What begins as a clump of arching leaves produces a tall green stem that blossoms into a large showy cluster of star-shaped flowers that can be blue, purple, and even white. The agapanthus is a lovely accent plant. Plant it in borders and backgrounds to add attractive foliage and dramatic flowers. In cooler climates agapanthus thrives in full sun and well-draining soil. In hot climates it needs to be planted in partial shade.

The name *agapanthus* is derived from the Greek words *agápē*, meaning "love," and *ánthos*, meaning "flower."[126] In the language of flowers, agapanthus means "love letter" and stands for a secret or magickal love. The agapanthus is associated with Jupiter, Saturn, Mars, and Aquarius. Plant this attractive flower in the garden for protection. Anoint a yellow candle with almond oil and roll the candle in the crumbled bits of dried agapanthus flowers to empower a knowledge spell. Add the dried flowers to dream bags and moon magic incense. Float agapanthus flowers in a bath with rose or jasmine to enhance feelings of self-love.

....

126. *Merriam-Webster*, s.v. "agapanthus (*n.*)," accessed June 2, 2021, https://www.merriam-webster
   .com/dictionary/agapanthus.

Aster

* *Aster* spp.
* Hardy in zones 4–9
* Comfort, love, peace, protection, and transition

Aster is a genus of over a hundred daisylike perennials. Asters produce large clusters of lavender, pink, purple, red, or white flowers. These lovely garden flowers grow best in full sun but will tolerate light shade. Asters tolerate poor soil and drought but will bloom poorly if the conditions are too dry. Water to maintain soil moisture and deadhead spent flowers to encourage more blooms.

Asters hold healing energy to encourage positive emotions and ease transitions. Float aster flower heads in a bath to ease feelings of anxiety when going through times of change. Grow asters in the garden to inspire feelings of love and happiness. Pick a mixed bouquet of asters, bachelor's buttons, lobelia, pansies, and strawflowers and give it to someone to grant cheer. Add dried aster flowers to a potpourri and place it in a bedside dish or sew it into the lining of your lover's coat to encourage positive feelings of affection. Add dried aster flowers to love sachets to enhance attraction powers. Plant asters on a grave to grant peace. Burn dried aster flowers to keep unwanted spirits away.

Bleeding Hearts

* *Lamprocapnos spectabilis*
* Hardy in zones 3–9
* Consolation, forgiveness, healing, heartbreak, and love
* Warning: May cause skin irritation and can cause gastrointestinal irritation if ingested in large quantities.

Bleeding hearts are a lovely shade-loving perennial also known as lyre flower, lady's locket, and lady-in-a-bath. I recommend transplanting young plants or propagating by root division after flowers have gone, as the seeds need a period of cooling in order to germinate and can be difficult to start. Grow bleeding hearts in woodland gardens. Water regularly to keep the soil evenly moist. Bleeding hearts thrive in moist soils that are rich in compost and will return every spring.

Bleeding hearts are used to comfort the brokenhearted. Stuff a mesh bag and fill with equal parts of bleeding heart flowers, bittersweet, and hawthorn leaves. Drop the bag into bathwater to give comfort to someone suffering from bitter memories. Burn the dried flowers with carnation to comfort someone who has lost their zest for living. Add bleeding heart flowers to a muslin bag and wear it to gain comfort when dealing with mean-spirited people. Dry bleeding heart leaves and flowers and use them as incense to release attachments to the people, places, and things that are hurtful. Mix bleeding heart flowers with self-heal to allow a broken sprit to find the ability to heal.

Calendula

* *Calendula officinalis*
* Hardy in zones 9–11
* Cheer, healing, legal matters, luck, protection, and success

Though the calendula is also known as pot marigold and garden marigold, it is not related to the New World marigold (*Tagetes* spp.). The calendula is a Mediterranean native and thought to be one of the first flowers to be cultivated for their pungent spicy flavor. "Fresh or dried petals have been used as a saffron substitute since Roman times," writes Emma Callery. [127] Calendulas have been used as food down through the ages: "the fresh flowers are chopped into salads, [and the] dried petals [are] used like saffron, to color butters and cheeses in teas, and to flavor cakes, cookies, puddings, and soups."[128] The cheery edible flower is easily grown as an annual. Sow seeds in the spring for summer and fall color. Plant calendulas in borders, along driveways, and in containers to add long-lasting color and draw positive energy. These low-maintenance beauties need minimal care. Water regularly to keep the soil from drying out.

Calendula is a first-aid flower with a long history of medicinal use. The flowers were made into poultices, brewed into infusions, and macerated into first-aid oils to accelerate the healing of burns, cuts, and bruises.[129] Calendula oil is still sold to treat burns, cuts, insect bites, and bruises. The calendula is associated with the sun, Samhain, and

. . . .

127. Emma Callery, *The Complete Book of Herbs: A Practical Guide to Cultivating, Drying, and Cooking with More Than 50 Herbs* (Philadelphia, PA: Courage Books, 1994), 74.

128. Herb Society of America, "Calendula: An Herb Society of America Guide" (Kirtland, OH: Herb Society of America, 2007), 11.

129. Herb Society of America, "Calendula: An Herb Society of America Guide," 13.

Leo. It holds a bright, cheery energy to brighten thoughts and drive worry away. The Greeks considered calendula to be a lucky plant, and court ladies in Tudor England wore the flowers, while the English youth included them in love charms.[130] Stuff a green velvet bag with calendula flowers. Place it under your pillow to inspire lucky dreams. An infusion of calendula flowers can be sipped to become aware of otherworldly beings. Make a calendula tea and sip it in your garden to become aware of devic energies. Calendula also holds energy for protection. In "Symbolism of Calendula" Mindy Green writes, "Calendula was used as protection against evil influences and disease, including the plague, and victims of thievery were said to be able to identify their robbers if they wore the flower. The flowers were strewn around doors to prevent evil from entering the house and scattered under the bed to protect one during sleep."[131] In Hoodoo calendula is used to win court cases and bring good luck to gamblers. Tuck a flower into your left pocket before a legal proceeding to have a positive outcome.

California Poppy
* *Eschscholzia californica*
* Hardy in zones 8–10
* Dreams, intuition, love, and sleep

The California poppy is a wildflower native to western North America and is usually planted from seed as an annual. It thrives in warm climates when planted in sandy, well-draining soil. Scatter seeds in areas with full sun exposure. Grow along drives, in rock gardens, or in wildflower gardens. California poppies are drought tolerant and will reseed to return year after year.

The California poppy is California's state flower. It has a long history as a medicine plant. It contains sedative alkaloids. The Native Americans of California, such as the Chumash and Yuki, used the plant as a sedative and crushed it to make a compress for pain relief to treat toothache, headache, and insomnia.[132] It was even employed as a love potion, which was a crime that resulted in expulsion from the

....

130. Picton, *The Book of Magical Herbs*, 122.

131. Herb Society of America, "Calendula: An Herb Society of America Guide," 8.

132. Lanny Kaufer, *Medicinal Herbs of California* (Guilford, CT: Falcon Guides, 2021), 192.

tribe if it became known.[133] Make a calming tea from the leaves, stems, and petals. Drink at bedtime for a restful sleep. Brew an infusion of flowers and sip to treat stress and anxiety. Drink a cup before giving a speech or facing a crowd to soothe nervousness. Sip a cup before traveling to alleviate fears. Pour it into your bath and soak to unwind and clear away hostilities. Serve it to someone who is tightly wound to help them find perspective. Brew up a nerve tonic tea by mixing California poppy with passionflower and skullcap for a relaxing brew that will heighten pleasant dreams. Make a potion to inspire love by floating a mix of California poppies, rose petals, and lavender buds in a glass of gin or champagne. Burn dried California poppy flowers with mugwort for a visionary incense to heighten astral travels and deepen dreams.

Carnation

* *Dianthus caryophyllus*
* Hardy in zones 7–10
* Communication, gladness, healing, kindness, love, prosperity, and strength

The carnation is a species of dianthus also known as gilliflower. It is an old-fashioned cut flower and a florist's favorite. Carnations are short-lived garden perennials, living only three to four years, and can take up to two years to bloom. They are often grown in containers, borders, and flowerbeds. Plant carnations in full sun or partial shade in areas with fertile, well-draining soil. Water regularly to maintain soil moisture throughout the bloom period.

Carnations have a lovely, sweet clove-like scent and can be floated in summer drinks to infuse the liquid with their fragrance. They are associated with the sun, fire, Jupiter, kindness, love, and expansion and growth. The frilly, rounded flowers are used in every kind of bouquet and arrangement to celebrate all the cycles of life from birth to death. During the Renaissance, carnations were made into waters and cordials to treat depression.[134] Carnations hold a positive uplifting energy. Float a carnation in a glass of iced tea to lift and sweeten mood. Make an infusion of carnation flowers and

. . . .

133. Reader's Digest, *Magic and Medicine of Plants*, 128.

134. Maggie Oster, *Flowering Herbs* (New York: Longmeadow Press, 1991), 48.

add it to bathwater to comfort or cheer. Place a bouquet of carnations in a sickroom to brighten mood and revive energy flow. Use the dried flowers in formulas to increase luck, advance your career, and gain wealth. Carnation fragrance has properties to open channels for communication with the universe. Burn dried carnations during meditation to grant clarity and spiritual insight. Anoint candles with almond oil, roll them in crumbled dried petals, and burn them to encourage creative inspiration.

Chrysanthemum

* *Chrysanthemum* spp.
* Hardy in zones 5–9 (most varieties)
* Joy, longevity, optimism, protection, and strength

There are hundreds of types of chrysanthemums, and though they are often treated as seasonal decorations, these perennials will come back year after year if planted in rich, moist, but well-draining soil. Plant your holiday chrysanthemums in a sunny spot and they will mound and produce yearly flowers. Chrysanthemums are heavy feeders. Water regularly to keep the soil evenly moist and your chrysanthemums will keep on blooming.

Chrysanthemums, often called mums or chrysanths, were first cultivated in ancient China thousands of years ago.[135] To this day the flowers are highly esteemed, and every year during the Chongyang Festival, families hike up hills and drink chrysanthemum wine to banish evil and gain good health and luck for the coming year.[136] In Japan the chrysanthemum represents power and perfection and were once only grown by the emperor. Across Europe chrysanthemums are grown as funeral flowers and used to honor the dead.[137] In America, chrysanthemums are a popular holiday flower displayed to bring joy and celebration into homes, gardens, and businesses. In the fall yellow, orange, and rust chrysanthemums are favored. In winter the colors change to red and white.

. . . .

135. "History of the Chrysanthemum," National Chrysanthemum Society, USA, accessed September 1, 2021, https://www.mums.org/history-of-the-chrysanthemum/.

136. Andrew Smith, *Strangers in the Garden: The Secret Life of Our Favorite Flowers* (Toronto: McClelland & Stewart, 2004), 10.

137. Smith, *Strangers in the Garden*, 8.

No matter the color, every chrysanthemum holds positive energy to cheer, comfort, and heal. Drop chrysanthemum flower petals in a glass of wine and drink it to ward health. Brew an infusion of chrysanthemum flowers and drink it to reduce inflammation, calm nerves, or fortify the spirit. Give a potted chrysanthemum to comfort someone who is grieving. Chrysanthemum flowers hold healing energy to aid the release of negative feelings and memories. Give a bouquet of chrysanthemums to someone with an apology to encourage forgiveness. Float flowers in the bath to restore and cheer. Make an infusion of chrysanthemum flowers and use it as a hair rinse to release any limiting belief you may hold. Chrysanthemums are associated with Mercury and Uranus and are used to support mental health. Keep a potted chrysanthemum on your desk to improve your outlook.

Daisy
* Bellis perennis
* Hardy in zones 4–8
* Divination, happiness, innocence, love, and luck

The daisy is an attractive perennial grown in beds and borders, edgings, and patio containers. This European native thrives in the cool, moist, fertile soils of a spring garden bed but tends to fade when temperatures warm. The name daisy is from the Old English name *dæges ēage*, or "day's eye," as the flowers open at dawn and close at dusk, appearing to reopen refreshed and inspiring the description "as fresh as a daisy" to describe a good night's sleep.[138]

The daisy is associated with Venus and symbolizes innocence, purity, and loyal love. Maidens wove daisies into their hair to attract an admirer. They wove daisy chains and gave them to their champions to keep them safe during duels and battles. To the Norse daisies are associated with Ostara, goddess of spring.[139] Daisies hold a cheerful restorative energy that evokes feelings of happiness and cheer. Plant daisies in the garden to promote peace and harmony. Give a bouquet of daisies to lift mood

....

138. *Merriam-Webster*, s.v. "daisy (*n.*)," accessed June 19, 2021, https://www.merriam-webster.com/dictionary/daisy.

139. Lizzie Deas, *Flower Favourites: Their Legends, Symbolism and Significance* (London: George Allen, 1898), 134.

or comfort. Add daisies to a vase to inspire happiness. Use the dried flower heads in potpourris to raise the vibration of a room. Crumble the dried flowers into bits and use them in peace formulas. Gift a pot of daisies to inspire an attitude of gratitude. Float flower heads in a bath to fill the heart with peace and gladness. Tuck a daisy behind your ear or wear daisies in your hair to renew creative energy or rouse new interest in a project. Place a daisy under your pillow to inspire good dreams. Tuck a daisy into your pocket to guard mood and avoid becoming the focus of someone's anger.

Delphinium

* *Delphinium* spp.
* Hardy in zones 3–7
* Faery flower, generosity, healing, and perception
* Warning: All parts are toxic.

Delphinium is a genus of tall, showy flowering perennials (for the annual variety, see larkspur). They have both attractive foliage and a dramatic, colorful spike of blossoms. Delphiniums are cold-region plants, and the seeds require a period of chilling before they will germinate. They thrive when planted in beds with full sun to light shade and rich, well-draining soil. Water regularly to keep soil evenly moist. It is common for delphiniums not to bloom the first year.

Delphinium plants and seeds are poisonous. They are associated with Mars and have protective energy to repel unwanted energies when planted along walkways. The flower has a reputation for clearing eyesight. While a delphinium infusion should never be taken internally, an infusion made from blossoms can be used to rinse the third eye to restore psychic sight. Use the infusion to clean crystal balls and magick mirrors. Float delphinium flowers in bathwater to open perception. Grow delphiniums with daisies, foxgloves, lupines, pineapple sage, poppies, and toadflax to create a faery garden. Delphiniums also hold energy to inspire generosity. Give a delphinium to warm a cold heart.

Echinacea

* *Echinacea* spp.
* Hardy in zones 5–8
* Defensive magick, healing, luck, and protection

Echinacea, or coneflowers, are North American perennial wildflowers that come in shades of pink, purple, orange, red, white, and yellow. They thrive when planted in a plot with full sun exposure and well-draining, sandy soil. Echinacea are drought tolerant and become susceptible to disease when overwatered. Sow seeds in fall or plant seedlings in spring to add healing energy to your garden. Echinacea is a garden healer. Grow it in a patch to heal or nurture the plants around it.

Echinacea is a medicine plant that supports the immune system. Modern testing has found that *Echinacea purpurea* contains compounds effective in fighting viral infections such as influenza.[140] Brew an infusion from the leaves and flowers to treat colds and flu, stimulate the immune system, or fortify your inner strength. Add echinacea leaves to comfrey compost teas to strengthen your garden's immune system. Echinacea has positive energy to draw prosperity and luck. Grow echinacea in your garden to draw magick into your life. Sprinkle dried echinacea flowers around your bed to draw energy for a good rest and pleasant dreams. Echinacea is associated with Mars and Scorpio and holds energy with visionary powers. Drink echinacea tea to fortify psychic sight. Add infusion to a footbath and soak to fortify resolve. Add dried flower and leaf bits to endurance formulas to enhance energy. Brew an echinacea infusion and add to bathwater to soothe muscle fatigue and ease mental exhaustion.

. . . .

140. James Hudson and Selvarani Vimalanathan, "Echinacea—A Source of Potent Antivirals for Respiratory Virus Infections," *Pharmaceuticals* 4, no. 7 (July 2001): 1019–31, doi:10.3390/ph4071019.

Fuchsia

* *Fuchsia* spp.
* Hardy in zones 8–10
* Acceptance, affection, blessings, and healing

There are over a hundred species of fuchsia, most of which are native to Central and South America. They produce impressive drooping blossoms and are often purchased in hanging baskets as annuals. Some varieties are climbers that can be planted to cover fences and arbors. Fuchsias thrive in damp soil and will become stressed if they are allowed to dry out. They are sensitive to extreme temperatures and grow best in areas with warm days and cool nights. Grow small varieties in hanging pots in a convenient place where you can keep them well watered. Plant climbing vines in sheltered areas where the roots can stay cool and shaded while the vines climb out to get some sun.

Fuchsias are repeat bloomers producing showy flowers all summer and fall that are favored by hummingbirds and faeries alike. Some believe it's unlucky to bring the flowers indoors, as you could be stealing away a faery's home. Plant fuchsias in areas to invite faery energy. Fuchsias hold energy for acceptance and comfort. Give a basket of fuchsias to comfort someone who is grieving. Hang baskets of fuchsias along a patio to draw positive energy and inspire contentment.

Geranium

* *Geranium* spp.
* Hardy in zones 9–12
* Calming, centering, clearing, fertility, love, health, and protection

Geranium is a genus containing more than three hundred species, most of which are tropical perennials. Unless you bought a hardy variety, the flowers must be brought indoors when temperatures drop below 45 degrees Fahrenheit. When purchasing, check the hardiness zone on the label. Growing geraniums from seed is a slow process. It is much easier to propagate from cuttings, as they are quick and easy to root. Choose a three- or four-inch section with two new leaves and snip it just below a leaf node. The leaf node will switch to growing roots when it is placed beneath the soil. Next, gently cut away any flowers or flowering stems from the top and gently stick the cutting into a pot of soil. Water well. Set the pot in a warm spot out of direct sunlight and watch for any signs of water loss. The trick for a successful cutting is to not let the cutting dry out but not to overwater the soil. Fill a spray bottle with water and give your cutting a spritz throughout the day.

Geraniums hold a gentle, protective, restorative energy that will rid a room of negativity. Keep a pot of geraniums on the porch to keep negativity from entering. Grow geraniums in a border or along a walkway to keep unwanted visitors away. Use geraniums to mend a wounded spirit. Float flowers in bathwater to stabilize emotions and clear the mind and body of negativity or soothe a broken heart. Tuck a geranium leaf into your left pocket to balance aggression when going into a hostile situation. Brew an infusion from dried leaves and flowers and add it to your washwater to clear away hostility and restore harmony to a room after an argument. Use a geranium infusion to wipe down the door and window frames to ward a room and keep the energy positive. Geraniums also hold the healing energy of love and are used in love spells and happiness formulas.

Hollyhock
* *Alcea rosea*
* Hardy in zones 4–8
* Faery sight, fertility, happiness, luck, prosperity, refreshment, and warding

Hollyhocks are short-lived perennials with flowering stalks that can grow up to nine feet tall. They were cultivated in China as ornamentals and edible spring greens.[141] Around the last frost date, scatter seeds directly into soil in an area with full sun exposure. Plant so that they may tower at the back of the garden bed. Water regularly to maintain soil moisture. Hollyhocks are susceptible to rust, so avoid getting leaves wet when watering.

The hollyhock is an edible flower and holds a healing energy. Collect the leaves to use as sandwich wraps. Use the flowers in drinks, in salads, and to decorate baked goods. Tea brewed from the flowers is a refreshing drink and has been sipped to

. . . .
141. Martin, *Garden Flower Folklore*, 161.

soothe a sore throat or treat mouth sores since Roman times.[142] Serve hollyhock tea to lift mood or inspire cheer. Add an infusion to a foot soak to revive after a difficult day. Pour the infusion into bathwater for an uplifting soak that will soothe and comfort. The hollyhock is associated with Ceres, Demeter, Venus, and Libra. It holds a nurturing, generous energy to draw happiness, luck, prosperity, and success to your home. Grow hollyhocks against the east-facing wall of your home to encourage opportunity and inspire fertile ideas. Carry a dried seedpod in your purse or wallet to increase the flow of money. Add dried hollyhock flowers to incense to encourage positive energy flow. According to an old alchemist recipe, an infused oil with hollyhock, marigold, thyme, and hazel will enable one to see faeries.[143] Plant hollyhocks to attract devas and faeries. Hollyhocks are a visionary aid. Add dried hollyhock flowers to formulas to increase psychic abilities. Add hollyhocks to gardens to feed the bees.

Kangaroo Paw
* *Anigozanthos* spp.
* Hardy in zones 10–11
* Courage, empathy, friendship, and interconnectedness

An Australian flower that is becoming very popular as a garden flower in the western states of the US, kangaroo paw is sensitive to cold and wet climates but thrives in the warmth of the western deserts. Plant in full sun in sandy, well-draining soil after the last frost date. If you live outside of the hardiness zone, the plant will have to be dug up and brought inside to overwinter.

Kangaroo paw instills empathy and enhances interconnectedness of both mind and spirit and the spirits of the land. Plant the flower to invite nature spirits into a desert garden. Include dried flowers in a sachet to gain understanding or encourage empathy. Add cut kangaroo paw flowers to a centerpiece to inspire understanding.

. . . .

142. Martin, *Garden Flower Folklore*, 161.

143. Folkard, *Plant Lore, Legends, and Lyrics*, 71.

Larkspur
* *Delphinium* spp.
* Generosity, health, protection, and water magick
* Warning: All parts are toxic.

Larkspurs are annuals that complete their life cycle in a single year. They grow up to thirty-six inches tall with spectacular flowering spires of white, lilac, and pink. Sow larkspurs from seeds, as they do not transplant well. Grow them in areas with full sun exposure and rich, slightly moist soil. Water regularly to maintain soil moisture. Once planted, larkspurs will reseed each year.

Larkspurs are classed in both *Delphinium* and *Consolida*, a name that refers to the plant's ability to stop bleeding and accelerate healing.[144] In the language of flowers larkspur means lightness, swiftness, or openheartedness. It is associated with Venus and the element water. Magickally, larkspurs hold energy to encourage generosity, self-care, and protection. Add cut flowers to vases to add to protective powers. Dry flower stalks and add them to wreaths and garlands or hang them in doorways to keep negativity at bay. Add dried flowers to protection strews and potpourris. Plant larkspurs along walkways to ward entrances from mischievous spirits and ghosts. Use the flowers to inspire generosity of spirit. Add cut flowers to a vase to lighten mood and open conversation. Give a sprig of larkspur to someone you wish to be friends with. Tuck a larkspur in your left pocket and wear it to soften your approach and help make a connection.

. . . .

144. "Consolida ajacis," *Missouri Botanical Garden*, accessed September 1, 2021, http://www .missouribotanicalgarden.org/PlantFinder/PlantFinderDetails.aspx?taxonid=263223.

Lavender

* *Lavandula* spp.
* Hardy in zones 5–9 (Spanish varieties are hardy in 7–9)
* Calm, cheer, clarity, communication, healing,
love, peace, protection, sleep, and transformations

Lavender is a garden favorite with over forty-five different species and more than 400 varieties. Lavender requires a sunny spot with well-draining soil. It is slow to grow from seed but propagates easily from cuttings. Plant it in mass in raised beds or borders to instill an area with a sweet and pleasantly calming scent. The word *lavender* likely comes from the Latin word *lavare*, which means "to wash," and lavender has been used for centuries to scent washwater.[145] A lavender infusion will impart a lovely soothing scent to clothes and bathwater. In Victorian times sprigs of lavender were sold on the street as "tussie mussies" that were carried to cover unwanted odors and keep fevers away.[146]

Lavender buds are used in love formulas and added to wedding cakes to ensure fertility. Stuff a sachet with a handful of violets and lavender buds and carry it to attract love. Hang it in a work space to keep the atmosphere pleasant. Use lavender in spells to attract and protect relationships or to promote harmony in the home. Lavender holds a calming power. Combine lavender flowers with bachelor's button, basil, and rosemary and brew into an infusion. Add it to your washwater and use it to wipe down countertops and floors to promote peace. Add the infusion to your bathwater to encourage a harmonious mindset.

Lavender is an ingredient in many healing rituals. Make a healing bath salt formula by mixing lavender, catnip, and marjoram with salt. Add it to bathwater to lift mood and foster joy. Lavender flowers were used to treat headache pains and cool anger. Collect the buds and add them to teas to encourage balanced emotions. Lavender is associated with Mercury, Gemini, Virgo, and the element air, making it a good addition to any spell that requires fast, clear communication. Use lavender

. . . .

145. Online Etymology Dictionary, s.v. "lavender (*n.*)," by Douglas Harper, accessed June 19, 2021, https://www.etymonline.com/word/lavender.

146. Callery, *The Complete Book of Herbs*, 87.

to enhance divination and dreamwork. The scent of lavender holds energy to clear the mind and open awareness. Breathe in the scent to calm the spirit and encourage clear thinking. Burn lavender as incense to facilitate communication with the spirit world. Lore tells that if you stuff your pockets with lavender, you may gain the ability to see ghosts.[147] Tuscan tradition says it can be used as a remedy for evil eye.[148]

Marigold
* *Tagetes* spp.
* Ancestors, death, happiness, protection, and success

Marigold is a group of flowering plants that produce cheerful orange, red, yellow, or white flowers. Most varieties are annuals that are used in borders and containers. Marigolds are easy to grow and aid garden health, as the plant produces natural pesticides that are effective in reducing the number of nematodes in the soil. They thrive when planted in a spot with full sun exposure and well-draining, fertile soil. After the last frost, when the soil has begun to warm, sow seeds directly into soil or plant out seedlings. Keep the soil evenly watered until plants have established.

Marigolds are native to North and South America. Spanish missionaries have been credited with bringing their seeds to Spain, then France, and North Africa, where they naturalized.[149] Marigolds made their way to India and became a favored wedding flower, braided into garlands and swags for weddings and used to decorate temples for many ceremonies. In an article for the *New York Times*, Catharine Osgood Foster writes, "Until the 18th century, marigolds were used for lotions and ointments to treat skin troubles, taken internally for intestinal difficulties and even wrapped in a head band to draw 'evil humors' out of the head."[150] In their native Mexico, the marigold is called *flor de muerto*, or "flower of the dead," and it is a favored flower

147. Martin, *Garden Flower Folklore*, 169.

148. Folkard, *Plant Lore, Legends, and Lyrics*, 409.

149. Judith Taylor, "The Marigold in California," *Pacific Horticulture*, accessed September 1, 2021, https://www.pacifichorticulture.org/articles/the-marigold-of-california/.

150. Catharine Osgood Foster, "On the Virtues of Sunny Marigolds," *New York Times*, June 3, 1979, https://www.nytimes.com/1979/06/03/archives/on-the-virtues-of-sunny-marigolds.html.

used to decorate family altars to draw the attention of the spirits.[151] Both fresh and dried flower heads are used to decorate family altars, grave sites, and cemeteries. Use marigolds to honor your ancestors. Scatter dried flowers on your altar to invite communication.

The marigold is associated with the sun. It signified pain and grief in the language of flowers and was used to comfort one who was grieving. In Romani magick marigolds are used to draw luck and riches. Plant along walkways or set a pot of marigolds on either side of the front door to usher in prosperity. Place a pot in any room to cleanse the space and rid the room of stagnant energy. String together marigold heads with a needle and thread and hang the garland over a threshold to cheer and ward. Wear a flower crown of marigolds to festivals and gatherings to embody the spirit of celebration.

Nasturtium

* *Tropaeolum majus*
* Cheer, insight, purity, spirituality, and strength

Nasturtium is an herbaceous garden annual that produces a peppery oil similar to that of watercress, which it was named after (*Nasturtium officinale*), but the two are not related. Also known as Indian cress, Mexican cress, and Peruvian cress, nasturtiums are native to Mexico and Peru but now are grown in gardens the world over. In an article for the University of Vermont, horticulture professor Dr. Leonard Perry writes that the nasturtium "was brought to Europe in the 16th century, where it was considered a symbol of conquest and victory in battle."[152] Nasturtiums are easy to grow and will often self-seed after the initial planting. They thrive in light, sandy, well-draining soil. Sow seeds directly into soil after the last frost date or plant seedlings for quick garden color. Water when the weather turns dry to ensure

. . . .

151. Lizz Schumer, "The Most Common Day of the Dead Flowers and Their Meanings," *Good Housekeeping*, October 26, 2021, https://www.goodhousekeeping.com/holidays/a34076822/dia-de-los-muertos-flowers-meaning/.

152. Leonard Perry, "Nasturtium: A Favorite Old-Fashioned Flower," University of Vermont Department of Plant and Soil Science, accessed September 1, 2021, https://pss.uvm.edu/ppp/articles/nasturtium.html.

repeated blooms. Nasturtiums are great companion plants and will help protect squash, cabbage, and cucumbers from pests.

Nasturtiums are edible. Harvest the leaves and flowers as you need them. They have a peppery flavor and add bright color to salads with energy for cheer, health, and vigor. Float flowers in bathwater to strengthen your connection to spirit and lift vibration. Nasturtiums are associated with the sun, Ostara, and Neptune and hold energy to cleanse and inspire. Fight a summer cold by eating a couple of blossoms when you feel it first come on. Float flowers in a glass of iced tea and sip for insight into complicated matters. Add a handful of nasturtium leaves and flowers to a plate of salad greens. Top with feta cheese and walnuts. Dress it in vinaigrette for a light meal to inspire fresh ideas and fuel creative energy. Nasturtiums help us embrace who we are. Use dried flowers in formulas to find destiny, realize life's purpose, or become more authentic.

Pansy
* *Viola tricolor*
* Hardy in zones 4–8
* Cheer, console, love, magick, and rain

The pansy is an early spring flower, and though it is a short-lived perennial, it is often planted as an annual because it does not tolerate heat. Pansies are often planted in borders and containers. They thrive in cool weather. In warm climates they are planted in the fall as cool-season annuals. Plant pansies in a cool, shaded garden bed and keep the soil evenly moist to ensure a long bloom period.

Pansy tea is made from the flowering plant, fresh and dried, and was a treatment for a range of ills from heartbreak to constipation. The plant was used as a love potion, a painkiller, and a sedative and was even used externally to treat skin irritations.[153] The pansy does hold a cheerful, positive energy. Plant pansies in your garden to spread cheer. Float pansies in bathwater to ease grief or console the brokenhearted. Plant a decorative planter with a mix of asters, bachelor's buttons, lobelia, poppies, and pansies and give it to lift the spirits of someone suffering. Add the flowers to formulas to

. . . .

153. Reader's Digest, *Magic and Medicine of Plants*, 263.

draw luck, love, and happiness. Crumble dried pansy flowers and roll candles in the bits to empower bliss magick. Pansies are an ingredient in many love spells and are associated with Eros, Cupid, Pluto, Saturn, and Venus. The flowers are edible and are added to salads and used to decorate baked goods and flavor syrups and honey.

Periwinkle

* *Vinca* spp.
* Hardy in zones 4–8
* Binding, love, and protection
* Warning: Some varieties have a low toxicity.

A woodland flower native to Europe but now common across the United States and much of Canada, periwinkle makes an attractive, and easy-to-grow ground cover that tolerates dry conditions and shade. It flowers throughout summer and fall and spreads to form a mat that controls weed growth. Plant in hard-to-mow areas for an attractive ground cover that will help control weed growth and soil erosion.

The periwinkle is also known as creeping myrtle, vinca, and the sorcerer's violet, as the leaves were eaten to inspire love in a marriage and made into charms to guard against the evil eye.[154] In the language of flowers periwinkle means fond memories and friendship. Stuff the dried leaves into a mattress to improve fidelity, love, and overall happiness. Grow the plant around a home to promote harmony. Include it in bouquets to elicit fond memories. Sew a periwinkle into the hem of your lover's coat to keep them safe and have their thoughts return to you. Stuff a pouch with dried periwinkles and carry it when you are meeting someone new and wish to be well received. Periwinkles are associated with Venus and Saturn and hold energy for love and protection. Weave periwinkles into a wreath and hang on the front door to protect the household from negative forces. Wear a braid of periwinkle when traveling to guard against misfortune. Drop a dried periwinkle into an important letter to help it find its way and encourage a positive response to your words.

. . . .

154. Folkard, *Plant Lore, Legends, and Lyrics*, 108.

Petunia

* *Petunia* spp.
* Hardy in zones 9–11
* Beauty, happiness, hope, and love

Petunias belong to a popular genus of tender perennials native to South America. They bloom prolifically from June through to October and are grown in flowerbeds, borders, patio pots, hanging baskets, and window boxes by gardeners across the country. Petunias thrive in sun and shade but cannot tolerate the cold. They are a warm weather plant usually bought as seedlings since the seeds only germinate when temperatures reach 70 degrees. Petunias add color and beauty to a flowerbed. Plant the flowers in borders and along walkways to add beauty to a garden. Deadhead old flowers to encourage constant blooms.

Petunias hold positive, hopeful energy to inspire happiness and love. Float flowers in bathwater to empower feelings of well-being and self-love. Fill patio pots with petunias to draw positive energy to your home. Plant them in hanging baskets or fill window boxes with petunias to energize an area. Give a potted petunia as a house-warming gift to encourage feelings of welcome.

Pinks

* *Dianthus* spp.
* Hardy in zones 7–10
* Good fortune, happiness, health, love, luck, and success

Pinks are members of the genus *Dianthus*, which also includes carnations. They are often planted as annuals to add quick color to flowerbeds and patio pots and have become a staple flower of gardeners around the world. Pinks thrive when planted in full sun in light, fast-draining soil. They have a lovely spicy fragrance with notes of cinnamon or clove and get their name not from their color but from the jagged edges of their petals that appear to have been cut with pinking shears. "In the 18th century the color we refer to as pink was called blush, pale red, rose, light red, or flesh," explains gardener Robin Sweetser. "The color we now call pink got its name from the flowers."[155]

. . . .

155. Robin Sweetser, "Dianthus Flowers: A Rock Garden Favorite," *Old Farmer's Almanac*, June 5, 2020, https://www.almanac.com/dianthus-types.

Pinks were associated with happiness and feeling carefree. They were made into remedies to combat melancholy. In *The Complete Illustrated Encyclopedia of Magical Plants* Susan Gregg writes, "A tea made from the flowers will relax the nervous system and help in the healing process."[156] Float flower heads in wine and serve it to add cheer to a meal or keep the conversation happy and bright at a family gathering. Float flowers in a bath to cheer a weary spirit. Pinks are associated with the Roman god Jupiter, the element fire, and the sun and hold energy for career advancement, success, and good luck. The flowers can be used in formulas to attract positive feelings for friendship and romance. Add pinks to a bouquet to use as a focus or give them to comfort someone downhearted.

Poppy

* *Papaver* spp.
* Beauty, fertility, invisibility, love, luck, money, peace, protection, remembrance, and sleep
* Warning: Some varieties have a low toxicity, and some are narcotic.

The poppy is a colorful flower cultivated as an ornamental annual, although in cooler zones some varieties can live for several years. Poppies thrive in sunny garden beds with rich, moist soil. They grow into a tall, erect garden flower with brightly colored petals that later become a seed head containing hundreds of tiny black seeds. Poppy flowers are self-seeding and once planted will return year after year.

Down through the ages, the poppy has represented rest, sleep, and death. Greek lore holds that Demeter was gifted the flower so that she might sleep and forget her great grief after Hades carried off her daughter, Persephone.[157] Because of its sedative qualities, the poppy often represented rest and even eternal sleep. The Victorians embraced this symbolism, and the poppy became a popular tombstone motif.[158] Today the red poppy is an emblem of remembrance and is often left at grave sites

156. Gregg, *The Complete Illustrated Encyclopedia of Magical Plants*, 200.

157. Pam Shade, "The Supernatural Side of Plants," *Cornell Botanic Gardens*, October 27, 2020, https://cornellbotanicgardens.org/the-supernatural-side-of-plants/.

158. "Headstone Symbols and Meaning," Headstone Symbols, accessed September 1, 2021, https://headstonesymbols.co.uk.

as a tribute. Poppies also hold energy for protection. In the Highlands of Scotland yellow horn poppies (*Glaucium flavum*) were burned to drive away evil spirits, while in the New World flowers of the California poppy were laid under children's beds to help them sleep.[159] Grow poppies in the garden to add color and invite faery energies. Grow them to keep negative energies away. The fresh flowers have a lovely scent and can be floated in bathwater to revive and comfort. Dried poppy flowers can be added to dream pillows and used in love spells and enchantments. Bake the seeds into sweet breads and mix them into salad dressings to encourage affection and increase fertility. Stuff the seeds into a poppet to deepen the connection. In Hoodoo poppy seeds are used to cause a delay and to dominate and confuse your enemy.

Snapdragon

* *Antirrhinum majus*
* Hardy in zones 7–10
* Friendship, glamour, hex reversal, protection, and truth

Snapdragons are tender perennials with small flowers that resemble a dragon's face. The name is derived from the Greek words *anti* and *rhis*, comparing the shape of the flower to a snout or nose.[160] Plant snapdragons in well-draining soil in full sun for abundant blooms. Though usually bought in six-packs as annuals, in their limited hardiness zone these flowers will return to flower the following year. Water snapdragons regularly during dry weather to keep the soil from drying out. Stake tall varieties to avoid damage to the flower.

In the language of flowers, snapdragons represent both graciousness and deception, and the flowers are used in charms for truth-telling. Grow snapdragons in your garden to repel those trying to manipulate you. Drop a snapdragon into your pocket before meeting with someone to gain the ability to see through deceptions. Bring a bouquet into the office and place it near someone you suspect is being deceitful to have the truth revealed. The flower also carries a glamour to allow one to appear

159. Gabrielle Hatfield, *Encyclopedia of Folk Medicine: Old World and New World Traditions* (Santa Barbara, CA: ABC-CLIO, 2004), 274.

160. NC State University, "Antirrhinum majus," *North Carolina Extension Gardener Plant Toolbox*, accessed September 1, 2021, https://plants.ces.ncsu.edu/plants/antirrhinum-majus/.

more interesting. Pin a snapdragon on your lapel to improve the way others see you. Float a handful of snapdragon blossoms in bathwater and soak to intensify your allure. Before date night, brew an infusion of snapdragon flowers and cardamom. Add it to bathwater to boost your ability to charm. The flower is associated with Gemini, Mars, the element fire, sylphs, and dragons. Use it in dragon magick.

Stock

* *Matthiola incana*
* Hardy in zones 7–10
* Cheer, contentment, happiness, and pleasures

These bright, cheerful flowers, sometimes called Virginia stock, perfume flower, and gillyflower, are known simply by the generic name "stock," and they should be a stock flower for the cool-weather garden. Stock performs well when temperatures do not exceed 75 degrees Fahrenheit. Not only are they easy to sow from seed, but these bright flowers are one of the first to bloom and exude a wonderful sweet and spicy fragrance. The scent makes them a favorite of pollinators. Stock thrives in full sun but will tolerate some shade. Sow seeds indoors six weeks before the last frost date or plant seedlings directly into soil one week after last frost date. Stock flowers thrive in full sun when planted in rich, well-draining soil. Deadhead spent flowers for repeating blooms.

Stock is associated with Taurus and holds positive energy to draw happiness and contentment. Its message in the language of flowers is "enjoy the moment." Plant stock in your flower garden to inspire appreciation of what you have and where you are in the present moment. Add cut flowers to a bouquet to add energy for happiness. Crumble dried flowers and roll candles in the bits to empower happiness spells. Add dried flowers to formulas for finding contentment. The flowers are edible and have a spicy flavor. Add them to salads to add beauty and cheer. Use stock flowers as a garnish to heighten enjoyment. Use the flowers to decorate desserts to add energy for celebration and inspire joy.

Strawflower

* Xerochrysum bracteatum
* Hardy in zones 8–10
* Lasting, longevity, luck, and remembrance

Though often planted as an annual, this short-lived perennial is a summer-blooming flower with stiff, papery bracts that allow the flower to retain its shape and color for so long that it is also known as everlasting. These Australian natives thrive in warm-weather gardens. Start the seeds indoors and plant the seedlings when night temperatures reach 60 degrees Fahrenheit. Strawflowers thrive in gardens with full sun exposure and well-draining soil. Have care when companion planting, as these flowers prefer dry conditions. They do well in beds with balloon flowers, bee balm, lavender, rudbeckia, sage, yarrow, and zinnias. Though they are drought tolerant, strawflowers do need light watering in dry periods. Plant strawflowers in garden beds, borders, and edgings.

The strawflower is a crafter's favorite because the flowers will continue to look fresh for thirty days or more with little care. Use them to decorate wreaths or garlands. Weave them into floral crowns for long-lasting beauty. Strawflowers are lovely garden flowers with a positive energy to improve luck. Include them in your flower garden to draw positive energy. Add the dried flowers to luck formulas, or craft one with a combination of strawflower, honeysuckle, red clover flowers, thyme, and dandelion fluff. Set the mixture out to dry. Crumble the dried mixture and roll your candles in the bits to empower luck spells. Burn strawflower as an incense to usher in positive energy to open the way to an opportunity. Use the dried mixture to empower wish magick.

Zinnia

* *Zinnia* spp.
* Abundance, affection, character, endurance,
friendship, health, and strength

Zinnia is a genus of mostly annuals native to the New World. They are also known as old maids and are a butterfly flower, as pollinators are drawn to the nectar-laden blossoms. Plant zinnias to attract butterflies and draw faeries to your yard. Scatter seeds in an area with full sun exposure and fertile, well-draining soil. Keep the soil moist until seedlings have sprouted. After the plants have grown, water sparingly. Zinnias are susceptible to powdery mildew. When the blooms begin to fade, snip them off to prolong the bloom season. As winter nears, allow a few flower heads to remain to drop seeds and plant a new crop of spring zinnias.

Zinnias are known as a friendship flower. In the language of flowers zinnia means "far away friends." It celebrates fond thoughts of an absent friend. Zinnias make good cut flowers. Add them to a bouquet for harmonic energy to end a quarrel. Give a bouquet to a friend to sweeten your relationship. Zinnias also hold energy for fortitude. Tuck a zinnia into your left pocket when you need strength to stand up for your ideals. Add dried zinnias to a potpourri for energy to be your own person. Add dried zinnias to incense formulas that support individuality. Make a flower crown by weaving fresh zinnias into a circlet of hydrangea. Add sprigs of rosemary, aster, and peony flowers. Wear it to embrace the spirit of celebration.

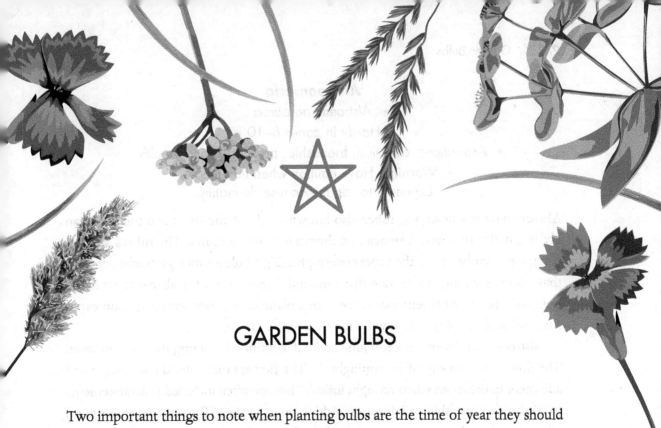

GARDEN BULBS

Two important things to note when planting bulbs are the time of year they should be planted and the depth at which they should be planted. There are two types of bulbs: hardy and tender. Hardy bulbs, or those that need a period of cold temperatures to break their dormancy, should be planted in fall. These include alliums, crocuses, daffodils, irises, and tulips. Tender bulbs, or summer bulbs, are planted in the spring and often need to be dug up and stored indoors in order for them to survive the winter.

The old gardener's rule for planting bulbs is to dig a hole two or three times the height of the bulb. This means to plant most large bulbs six to eight inches deep and plant small bulbs three or four inches deep. There are exceptions. Iris, for one, will not flower if planted too deep, and some of the bulbs will not even break dormancy.

Alstroemeria

* *Alstroemeria aurea*
* Hardy in zones 8–10
* Aspirations, devotion, friendship, prosperity, and wealth
* Warning: Have caution when handling.
Exposure to sap may cause dermatitis.

Alstroemeria is a flowering tuber also known as lily of the Incas and the Peruvian lily. It is native to South America and thrives in warmer zones. The tubers are best planted in October. Soak the tubers overnight. Dig a hole about eight inches deep so that it is large enough to contain the roots and rhizomes. Set the alstroemeria in the hole and bury it. Alstroemerias thrive when planted in a spot with good sun exposure and well-draining soil. It will tolerate dappled shade.

Alstroemerias bloom in early June and will continue flowering through summer. The flower is a favorite of hummingbirds. The flowers make good cut flowers and add cheer to the room when brought inside. They are often included in arrangements to symbolize friendship and devotion. Add them to a vase of flowers to increase good vibrations. Use them as a centerpiece for a friendly lunch to make guests feel welcome and more sociable. Use an alstroemeria flower as a meditative focus to help you realize your dreams.

Anemone

* *Anemone* spp.
* Hardy in zones 5–9
* Anticipation, faery flower, grounding, healing, and protection
* Warning: Take care when handling; may cause severe topical irritation.
Do not eat, as it will upset the stomach.

Anemones are perennial flowers in the buttercup family. They are also known as windflower and poppy anemone. The name *anemone* comes from the Greek word *anemos*, meaning "wind," hence the name windflower.[161] Anemones grow from tubers or rhizomes to form colonies and will naturalize in an area. They are popular

....

161. Online Etymology Dictionary, s.v. "anemo-," by Douglas Harper, accessed July 1, 2021, https://www.etymonline.com/word/anemo-#etymonline_v_41403.

in cottage gardens, woodland gardens, and perennial borders. Most varieties require moisture and partial to dappled shade. Plant anemones in the fall. Soak the corms overnight to encourage sprouting. Plant them in an area with rich, well-draining soil. Dig a hole three inches deep, set the corm in, and cover. When the flowers grow, stake the tall varieties before they have a chance to flop over and break. Anemones do best in partial shade but will grow when planted in areas with morning sun and afternoon shade. They require regular watering.

In the language of flowers anemone means fragility. The flower holds a grounding, healing energy. Float the flowers in a bath to alleviate anxiety. Anemones are associated with Venus, Cupid, Adonis, Mars, and the element fire. It was the symbol of forsaken or forgotten love. Down through history, the flower has been worn to ward against sickness first by Egyptians and later the English, who wore them around the neck or arm.[162] Pick the first anemone to bloom and hang it to dry to act as a protection talisman. Use anemone petals in healing formulas. Roll candles in dried petals to boost healing or protection powers.

Begonia
* * Begonia spp.
* * Hardy in zones 8–11
* * Balance, caution, and psychic sight

Begonia is a genus of over a thousand species. Because begonias are cold-sensitive, they are often planted as annuals. You can start begonia bulbs indoors by planting them in containers. Set the bulbs in and cover them with four inches of soil. Water well so the soil is evenly moist. Transplant them into the garden after all threat of frost has passed for blooms that will flower from summer through fall. Begonias are shade-loving plants and are often planted in patio pots and hanging baskets.

Begonias hold a balanced energy for heightened awareness and intuitive thought. Use them as a meditation focus to deepen concentration. Drop a begonia flower in your left pocket to help you see through illusions. Keep a small pot of begonias on your desk to add cheer and ward from gaslighting. Fill a window box with begonias to deter gossip.

. . . .

162. Martin, *Garden Flower Folklore*, 225.

Bluebell

* *Hyacinthoides non-scripta*
* Hardy in zones 4–8
* Faery favorite, preventing nightmares, and truth
* Warning: Do not eat. The bulb and plant are poisonous.

Bluebells are shade-loving perennials that grow wild in woodland areas. Two of the most common are the English (*Hyacinthoides non-scripta*) and the Spanish bluebell (*Hyacinthoides hispanica*), which are hardy down to zone 4. Bluebells are easy to grow in areas with dappled sun or partial shade. Dig a hole three inches deep and set the bulb in root-side down. Cover over and water in. Bluebells thrive in moist, well-draining soil and naturalize well to the point of becoming invasive. Bluebells are early spring and late fall bloomers and will go dormant as temperatures warm or cool. They are often planted in woodland gardens, in natural areas, on hillsides, in borders and along walks, or in containers with other bulbs.

Bluebells contain glycosides, which means they are toxic.[163] They are associated with a dreamless or eternal sleep. In Celtic lore the bluebell was "a fairy flower, and thus dangerous."[164] Stories tell that if a child enters an area with bluebells to pick a flower, they might vanish, never to be seen again. Places where bluebells grow in mass are thought to be unlucky to cross and are avoided, as disturbing them could result in a faery's curse—which is of great service to the delicate flowers because they are greatly harmed when trampled and could take years to recover. Bluebells are associated with the moon goddess Selene, Saturn, sleep, death, and comfort in grief. They are planted in faery gardens to attract nature spirits and friendly faeries.

163. Nicola Bates and Alan Murphy, "Bluebell (Glycoside) Poisoning," *Vetlexicon*, accessed June 22, 2021, https://www.vetstream.com/treat/bovis/diseases/bluebell-(glycoside)-poisoning.

164. Lois Tilton, "Whose Name Is the Bluebell: Hyakinthos or Endymion?," Dave's Garden, April 18, 2008, https://davesgarden.com/guides/articles/view/980.

Calla Lily
* *Zantedeschia aethiopica*
* Hardy in zones 8–10
* Beauty, faithfulness, fertility, rebirth, and sex
* Warning: The raw bulb and plant are poisonous.

The calla lily is a graceful flowering plant in the family Araceae, native to southern Africa, and though it is named calla lily, it is neither a true calla (Calloideae) or a lily (*Lilium*). With its large attractive leaves and beautiful trumpet flowers, the calla lily makes a lovely addition to any bulb bed. Plant the rhizomes in the spring after the last frost. Choose an area with full sun to partial shade and rich, moist soil. The white varieties like wetter soil than the colorful hybrids do. Dig a hole and plant the rhizome four inches deep. Water regularly during dry periods to keep the soil evenly moist. White calla lilies do well around ponds, in water gardens, and under birdbaths. Plant with alliums, dahlias, and gladiolas for a colorful cut flower garden.

The calla lily is both a wedding flower and a funeral flower associated with Hera, Venus, faeries, and satyrs. Callas hold energy to empower illusions. Use the flower in glamour spells and sex magick. Add cut flowers to a bouquet to boost glamour. Use it as a meditative focus to explore inner beauty and sexual power.

Crocus
* *Crocus* spp.
* Hardy in zones 3–8
* Fertility, happiness, love, lust, optimism,
psychic abilities, reconciliation, renewal, and visions
* Warning: The bulb and plant are poisonous if eaten in large amounts.

The crocus is a cold-climate flower. It is one of the first flowers to bloom, a reminder of spring even while winter still has a grip on the world. Crocuses naturalize easily and most are cold hardy. Plant crocus corms in the fall for a spring surprise. They grow well in full sun but will tolerate partial shade. Dig a hole three inches deep and set the corm in pointy end up. Cover it with soil and water it in. Planting in drifts will create a swath of color and provide an early food source for bees and other pollinators. Plant crocuses in lawns for early spring flowers while the grass is dormant.

The sight of crocus flowers on a cold day lightens the heart. In the language of flowers crocus means youth and gladness. Plant crocuses to bring spring cheer. Plant crocus bulbs in areas you see often to brighten your mood and gain a surprise appreciation of beauty. The crocus is associated with Venus, the sun, and the element of fire. Use crocus flowers to empower love and lust spells. Use a crocus as a meditation focus to open the mind to psychic sight.

Daffodil

* *Narcissus* spp.
* Hardy in zones 3–8
* Beauty, cheer, counter-magick, fertility, inspiration, love, luck, and protection
* Warning: Some varieties are poisonous.

There are many varieties of daffodils. Most are hardy and easy to grow, but for best results, select a variety that thrives in your zone. Most varieties are winter hardy and, once planted, only need an occasional feeding to multiply. In fall choose a spot with well-draining soil and at least six hours of full sun. Dig a hole about eight inches deep. Set the bulb in, pointed end up, and bury. Do this for each bulb and then water them in. Plant daffodils with crocus, grape hyacinth, and tulips for a bed with lovely spring color.

The daffodil is associated with Mars, Venus, and Saturn. Daffodils repel negative energy and can be used in counter-magick. They hold a bright energy and are given to cheer the downhearted. Give a potted daffodil to help motivate someone who has lost their zest for life. Use a daffodil as a focus to fuel a project that has stalled with new energy. Bring a bouquet of daffodils into a winter's gray home to activate energy flow. Use a daffodil as a meditative focus to inspire new ways of thinking. A pot of daffodils holds optimistic energy. Set a pot of bulbs in the kitchen window to bring the fresh, rejuvenating energy of spring into the home. Add cut daffodils to a vase of fresh flowers to increase energy for fertility. Give a bouquet of cut daffodils to lift someone's spirits and inspire affection. The bulbs are poisonous and cause paralysis of the central nervous system. They can be used in magick to compel someone to keep a secret.

Dahlia

* *Dahlia* spp.
* Hardy in zones 8–11
* Dreams, friendship, fortune, happiness, inspiration, luck, refinement, and success

Dahlia is a genus of flowers in the Asteraceae family. They are native to Mexico, where they are the national flower. In the early 1800s a French minister brought dahlia tubers to France. They were given to Empress Josephine, and under her care, they thrived. Her gardens were the envy of everyone until a Polish count brazenly stole as many as 100 plants. He spirited them away, and by 1826 there were as many as sixty dahlia varieties recorded.[165]

Dahlias are my favorite garden flower. They come in so many styles and sizes, from small, single-flower varieties to towering plants with ruffled, dinner-plate-size flowers, all with abundant blooms in spectacular colors. And they are so easy to grow, whether planted from seed, propagated by cutting, or planted as tubers. Plant in rich, well-draining soil and full sun exposure, and you will find they outperform most of the other garden flowers. Dig a hole large enough to contain each group of rhizomes and cover over. Do not bury them too deep or the plants will not bloom. Water them in. Dahlias are heavy feeders and should be fed monthly while in bloom. Stake tall dahlias to add support. Dahlias are tender perennials and must be lifted in the fall and stored indoors in most regions. Carefully dig up the tuber. Shake it gently to remove the remaining soil, and set it in a box or crate of dry vermiculite or peat moss. Cover and store the box in a cool garden shed or garage (45 degrees Fahrenheit is ideal) until the following spring.

Dahlias make lovely, long-lasting cut flowers. They are associated with the moon, the element water, and inspiration. They brim with positive energy for manifesting happiness and success. Fill a vase with cut flowers to add beauty and positive energy to a room. Give a bouquet to a friend to sweeten friendship, or grow a potted dahlia and give to a friend who has a passion for gardening to share the joy and gel your relationship. Dahlias hold energy to boost creative inspiration. Plant a bed of dahlias

. . . .

165. Smith, *Strangers in the Garden*, 58.

outside an office window to gain inspiration by gazing upon them through the glass. Dry the petals from a spent flower head and use them in formulas to increase creative inspiration, happiness, or luck. Add dahlias to flower teas to empower cheer.

Gladiolus

* Gladiolus spp.
* Hardy in zones 7–10
* Fertility, generosity, integrity, remembrance, strength, and stability

Gladiolus is a genus of over 260 species of corm-bearing plants. The gladiolus is one of the iconic flowers of the bulb garden. Known for its tall flower spikes and large, colorful blooms, this flower is available in every color. Plant the bulb in a sunny spot. Plant each corm twice the depth of the bulb, pointy side up. Cover and water well. Gladioli thrive when planted in a sunny spot with sandy, well-draining soil.

Gladioli are associated with Jupiter and Leo and represent generosity, strength of character, and sincerity. Gladioli are showy, glamorous, and long-lasting cut flowers, a standard in the florist trade. Fill a vase with gladioli and use it as a centerpiece for any gathering where you need to help remind your guests to be at their best. Use it at family holiday gatherings to help ensure everyone acts kindly. Plant them along your fence line to keep neighbors friendly. The bulbs and leaves are used in luck, love, and fertility charms.

Glory-of-the-Snow

* Chionodoxa luciliae
* Hardy in zones 3–8
* Cheer, friendship, inspiration, luck, and optimism

Glory-of-the-snow is an early hardy perennial also known as chionodoxa. It often can be found blooming through the snow. As its name suggests, glory-of-the-snow is one of the first flowers to bloom in the spring and can often be seen blooming in large patches like bluebells and scillas. These hardy perennials will naturalize in cool climates when planted in well-draining soil. They thrive in full sun or dappled shade but will not flower if the shade is too deep. Dig a hole three inches deep and set the bulb in, pointy side up. Cover and water it in. Plant bulbs in a mass, setting bulbs two to three inches apart for a spring carpet of color. Avoid cutting or mowing until the leaves have yellowed and died back.

Glory-of-the-snow holds a gentle optimistic energy to encourage a positive outlook. Plant a bed where you can gaze upon them through a window to infuse your outlook with hope and cheer. Add cut flowers to a bud vase to cheer a gloomy room. Add flowers to a bouquet and use them as a centerpiece for any luncheon to encourage friendship and open conversation. Use the flowers to cheer a sick or downhearted friend.

Hyacinth
* Hyacinthus orientalis
* Hardy in zones 4–8
* Comfort, happiness, healing, love, protection from enchantment, and rebirth
* Warning: The bulb is poisonous. The sap can cause dermatitis.

Hyacinths are easy-to-grow spring-blooming bulbs. The flowers have an incredible fragrance that can perfume your garden or room. Plant with other early spring bloomers such as daffodils, grape hyacinths, and early tulips for a sweetly scented bed of luscious color. Plant the bulbs in fall. Dig a hole four inches deep and set bulbs in with the pointy end up. Plant in a mass, setting bulbs three inches apart, and cover. Hyacinths grow well in pots that can be brought inside to add spring color to cheer a dull room.

The scent of hyacinth holds soothing energy to comfort grief and ease life transitions. Keep a potted hyacinth on your desk to combat apathy. Burn dried flowers as an incense to combat feelings of melancholy. Give a potted hyacinth to someone sick or heartbroken to comfort them. The flowers hold energy to relieve anxiety and fear. Give a potted hyacinth to a new neighbor to welcome them to the neighborhood and ease their transition. Set a potted hyacinth in the center of the kitchen table to facilitate change after a breakup. Breathe in the scent to sever enchantment. Hyacinths are associated with Venus, the element water, spring, and rebirth. Drop dried flowers into your left pocket and wear them to find ways to better express yourself.

Iris

* *Iris* spp.
* Hardy in zones 3–9
* Communication, creativity, empowerment, love, money, and wisdom
* Warning: The rhizomes and leaves contain a substance that can irritate the skin if touched and cause stomach troubles if ingested.

Iris is a genus of stately flowering plants with more than three hundred species of May to June bloomers that come in a rainbow of colors. As a garden flower, the iris is a reliable bloomer that requires little care and attracts butterflies and humming-birds. Plant iris rhizomes in late summer in an area with well-draining soil and full sun. Dig a shallow hole and plant the rhizome just below the soil surface. If the rhizomes are buried too deep, they will not flower and might rot. Cut back the flowering stalks after the flowers fade. Leave the attractive foliage to feed the rhizomes to ensure next year's flowers.

The iris is a long-lasting cut flower. It gets its name from the Greek *iris*, "rainbow," which is also the name of a goddess who was a messenger to the Olympian gods.[166] She walked between the worlds, carrying communications and information between the gods and between the gods and humans, outwitting even the trickiest of the tricksters. Use the iris to act as a communication bridge to aid in any communication spell or heighten contact with the Divine. Associated with the moon and Mercury, the iris symbolizes creative freedom. Employ the creative energy to gain eloquence, unblock creativity, or stimulate inspiration. The iris holds a transformative energy that can ease journeys and aid in exploring liminal spaces. It is a funeral flower often used in funeral rites to aid transition. Orris root is the root of *Iris germanica* and *Iris pallida*.

166. *Merriam-Webster*, s.v. "iris (n.)," accessed June 22, 2021, https://www.merriam-webster.com /dictionary/iris.

Lily

* *Lilium* spp.
* Hardy in zones 5–8 (with some varieties hardy to zone 3)
* Abundance, fertility, innocence, luck, protection, renewal, and strength

Lilium is a genus with up to a hundred known species, prized for their spectacular and elegant flowers. Plant bulbs in the fall to add elegance to any garden space. Dig a hole six to seven inches deep in an area with rich humus, full sun exposure, and well-draining soil. Set the bulb in root-end down and cover over.

Lilies are associated with spring, Easter, death, renewal, the moon, and Venus. They hold energy for strength and protection. Cut the first lily to bloom and display it in a vase. Use as a meditative focus to find inner strength. Grow lilies next to a front gate or along a path to guard against wandering ghosts. Use lily energy to antidote enchantments or reveal a cheat or a liar. Wear the image to protect against the evil eye. Lilies are a common funeral flower given to ease transitions. In the *Book of Secrets*, thirteenth-century philosopher Albertus Magnus recorded a curse made by mixing lily and bay into a powder to render sleeplessness.[167]

Lily of the Valley

* *Convallaria majalis*
* Hardy in zones 3–8
* Cheer, contentment, faery flower, happiness, love, and mental powers
* Warning: All parts of the plant are poisonous.

Lily of the valley is a beautiful, low-growing woodland flower native to most of Europe. It naturalizes easily and is an aggressive spreader—in fact, it escaped early gardens across the world and now can be seen growing across the cooler temperate regions of most of the Northern Hemisphere. Grow it in woodland gardens as a ground cover under trees or along shaded borders and walkways. Lily of the valley thrives in moist soil in areas with partial to full shade. Dig a shallow hole and place

....

167. Michael R. Best and Frank H. Brightman, eds., *The Book of Secrets of Albertus Magnus* (Newburyport, MA: Weiser Books, 1999), 11.

the rhizome inside it, pointy side up. Cover with a half inch of soil and water it in. Space rhizomes about six inches apart for mass plantings.

Though a bed of lily of the valley flowers, with their dainty cluster of little white bells, is a lovely sight, and the scent is pleasant to the senses, the flower is poisonous to both people and pets. If you are out on a spring walk and you come across a sighting, take a moment to appreciate their beauty before going inward. The sight and scent of lily of the valley swells the heart with happiness and the mind with peace as it opens communication channels to our higher self. Lily of the valley is associated with Apollo and Mercury. Plant it in meditation gardens to facilitate communication. The flower is a faery favorite. Plant it to attract nature spirits. The small flowers hold a positive energy to inspire gladness. Use it to repel negative energy or thwart melancholia. Add it to cut flower bouquets to lift mood and evoke happiness. Breathe in the fragrance before meditation to expand concentration and perception. Wear a sprig when you wish to maintain your personal barriers, empower your ability to speak, or keep your thoughts on track.

Tulip

* *Tulipa* spp.
* Hardy in zones 3–8
* Abundance, beginnings, declaration of love, fame, luck, and protection

There are over a hundred species of this popular spring-blooming perennial. Tulips are cool-weather flowers. They are sensitive to hot, sunny conditions and should be planted in shaded areas in hot regions. Plant tulip bulbs in the fall for spring color. The old gardener's rule for planting a tulip is to plant the bulb at a depth two to three times the size of the bulb. Plant the bulbs in groups two inches apart. Cover over with soil, mulch, and water well. Grow tulips around trees, in drifts at the back of a perennial border, and under annual beds for magnificent spring color.

The Dutch fell in love with the flower, and today tulip production is one of the Netherlands' main industries. Though tulips are the national symbol of the country, they are native to Eastern Europe, Western Asia, and China.[168] The tulip is the

. . . .

168. "Tulip Species," Chicago Botanical Garden, accessed June 22, 2021, https://www.chicago botanic.org/plantinfo/tulips_species.

national flower of Turkey, where it is a favored motif in folk art, representing feminine beauty, perfection, paradise, and protection from evil.[169] The tulip motif is featured in the folk art of the Pennsylvania Dutch, German immigrants who first settled in Pennsylvania several hundred years ago, who carve tulip designs into chests and butter molds and feature it in paintings, on quilts, and in embroideries. Grow a pot of tulips near your door to repel bad luck and draw prosperity. Wear the image of a tulip as a charm to draw luck and protection. Pack the image of a tulip in your luggage when traveling or carry it in a backpack to avoid losing your way. Carry it to shield from the attentions of a thief or con man. Tulips are associated with Venus and also hold energy to attract love. Float petals in your bathwater to encourage your inner goddess. Soak in a bath of red tulips to find love. Yellow tulips foster friendship and inspire charisma. Give a pot of yellow tulips to a neighbor to warm their feelings and encourage communication.

169. Valerie Behiery, "Islamic Art: Beloved Bloom: The Tulip in Turkish Art," *Islamic Arts Magazine*, July 14, 2017, http://islamicartsmagazine.com/magazine/view/beloved_bloom_the_tulip_in_turkish_art.

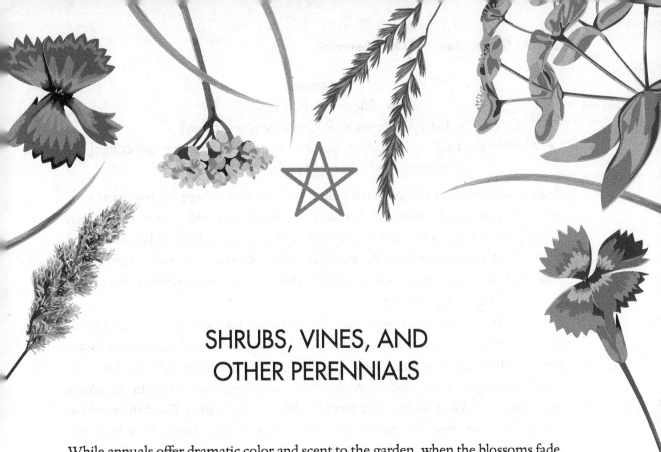

SHRUBS, VINES, AND OTHER PERENNIALS

While annuals offer dramatic color and scent to the garden, when the blossoms fade, it is the plants with interesting foliage that give the garden a point of four-season interest. The wide leaves of hostas, the colorful mounding foliage of coral bells, the movement and sound of ornamental grasses, and the fine, delicate leaves of fern and bamboo all provide delight long after flowers have faded. In the winter these plants provide the bones of the garden.

Perennials are an investment. Unlike the fleeting annual, most perennials will be around for years. Including shrubs, vines, and other large garden plants in your garden plan might elevate the cost, but it is a lasting investment that will add layers, height, and depth, dramatically increasing the sensory output and making your garden more stimulating. Choose a theme and repeat colors and textures throughout to draw the eye and make the planting appear ordered.

Azalea
* *Rhododendron* spp.
* Hardy in zones 4–9 (depending on variety)
* Abundance, caution, happiness, passion, personal power, and self-control
* Warning: The leaves and pollen are poisonous.

Azaleas are flowering shrubs in the genus *Rhododendron*. There are two basic varieties: evergreen and deciduous. Brilliant and floriferous with glossy, deep green foliage, the azalea is a treasure in the garden. The fragrant blooms last for several weeks. Azaleas are shade tolerant and thrive when planted under trees. They appreciate soil that is evenly moist and will suffer when over- or underwatered. Plant them in woodland or cottage gardens.

The azalea symbolizes temperance, fragility, and even passion. Like many other rhododendrons, azaleas are toxic, so it's not surprising that one of the flower's meanings is caution and, if sent in a black vase, it suggests a death threat.[170] In China, the azalea is thought to be a more pensive flower and is referred to as the "thinking home bush."[171] Plant azaleas to attract bright, positive energy. Plant them where you can see them from the road to elicit fond feelings upon return. Float buds in a bowl of water to brighten a room. Float flower heads in a bath to increase feelings of happiness. Breathe in the scent of azalea to lighten the heart and lift mood.

Bamboo
* Bambuseae spp.
* Hardy in zones 4–9
* Balance, flexibility, hex breaking, immortality, luck, and wishes

I spent an afternoon hiking through a bamboo forest in Maui, and it was magickal. I spent a summer trying to eradicate a large plot of running bamboo that had crept under a wall and taken over a back corner, and it was a nightmare. Bamboo comes in

170. Jessica Phippard, "Stopping to Smell the Rhododendron," *Natural Selections Magazine*, June 13, 2013, https://selections.rockefeller.edu/stopping-to-smell-the-rhododendron/.

171. Isabel Prontes, "What Is the Meaning of Azaleas?," Garden Guides, September 21, 2017, https://www.gardenguides.com/108915-meaning-azaleas.html.

running varieties and clumping varieties. Many varieties are aggressive growers that can quickly become invasive. Research the variety before you plant to avoid remorse. Running bamboos spread aggressively by underground rhizomes. Avoid this variety. Choose a clumping variety. These expand more slowly and stick to the same area.

Plant bamboo outside your home for protection. A row of bamboo will prevent malicious energies from entering. Place a stick of bamboo over your doorway to bring good luck. Carve a symbol into the bark to empower it. Carve a wish into a piece of bamboo and bury it for a simple wishing spell. Use a bamboo wand to facilitate work with water elementals. Leave hollow stalks of bamboo around your garden to serve as homes for bees. Bamboo is associated with the moon, Mercury, Mars, Saturn, and Gemini.

While lucky bamboo (*Dracaena braunii*) is not a true bamboo, it is a feng shui favorite used to improve luck and joy and its magickal correspondences are similar. Lucky bamboo holds a positive energy to stimulate the mind so that the simple act of gazing upon it increases the flow of creative energy. If you feel stuck or find your creative spark in need of a boost, sit next to your lucky bamboo and look at it. As you move your attention to it, draw a few meditative breaths. The plant will respond by offering energy for mental stimulation.

Banana

* *Musa* spp.
* Hardy in zones 9–11 (cold-hardy varieties: 5–11)
* Energy, fertility, love, luck, prosperity, and spirituality

Bananas are herbaceous perennials that are not really trees but are large herbs. They are dramatic, fast-growing, palmlike plants with broad leaves. Plant bananas in an area with full sun exposure and rich, loamy, well-draining soil. Choose a sheltered area where they will be safe from blowing winds. Water regularly to keep soil evenly moist. Bananas do best when grown in groups, and they thrive in regions with moist, temperate weather. Plant a banana as a focal point or use it as a backdrop to add tropical flavor.

Bananas are associated with Jupiter. They contain energy for fertility and love. It is lucky to be married under a banana tree. Use dried banana flowers to empower prosperity spells. The bright yellow, phallic-shaped fruit symbolizes love, sexuality, and fertility. In ancient India and Persia, the fruit was eaten to retain youth. A banana is a perfect portable snack and can offer a traveler both a burst of quick energy and protection from misfortunes. Carry dried banana chips when hiking to avoid accidents.

Bougainvillea

* Bougainvillea spp.
* Hardy in zones 9–11
* Beauty, cleansing, healing, passion, protection, and radiance

Bougainvillea is a genus of thorny vines and bushes native to South America. They are drought-resistant and thrive in warm climates when planted in well-draining soil. The arching branches covered in their brightly colored flowerlike leaves add form, and their bright, long-lasting color makes them a favorite garden plant in gardens across the Southwest.

The bougainvillea is associated with Mars and the element fire, and it resonates with restorative energy to heal the battle weary, renew awareness of magick, and reveal a vision of one's destiny. Float the colorful leaves in bathwater to soothe a weary soul. Combine bougainvillea leaves with yarrow to help heal a wounded spirit. The bougainvillea holds energy for insight. Use it in rituals when facing a crossroads to reveal the best way forward. Use a wand of bougainvillea in meditation to gain perspective. Use bougainvillea in truth spells to reveal what is hidden. Use bougainvillea thorns in protection rituals to boost the working.

Camellia

* Camellia spp.
* Hardy in zones 7–10 (some varieties hardy to zone 6)
* Appreciation, beauty, Divine Feminine, friendship, hospitality, love, spirituality, and wealth

The garden camellia is a flowering shrub with luscious, showy flowers that bloom through the spring. Camellias, like azaleas, gardenias, and hydrangeas, thrive in moist, slightly acidic soil. Plant a camellia in an area with partial shade and well-draining soil. Mulch with bark to help soil hold moisture. Camellias are slow growers but over time can grow to the height of a small tree.

Camellias hold energy for spiritual advancement and appreciation. Use the flowers in rituals for authenticity and finding contentment. They are associated with the moon and the element water. The camellia is a flower of welcome and friendship. Give a camellia to a friend to make them feel valued. Display a camellia in a bud vase to make a guest feel welcome. Float camellia blossoms in bath magick to channel goddess energy.

Cape Plumbago

* *Plumbago auriculata*
* Hardy in zones 9–11
* Beauty, faery garden, hexing, and protection
* Warning: This plant is poisonous and can cause contact dermatitis.

Cape plumbago is a vigorous evergreen shrub with a sprawling habit. It is a sun-loving, easy-care, drought-tolerant plant that can be found growing across Florida and the Southwest. Once established, plumbago requires little maintenance. Plant in full sun for abundant May to November blooms. Water regularly until the plant has established.

With its abundant and fragrant clusters of sky-blue flowers, plumbago is a butterfly favorite. The roots are a source of plumbagin, a novel inhibitor that has been shown to reduce breast cancer tumor growth in mice.[172] They also have strong antimicrobial and antifungal properties but are an irritant and toxic if ingested. The powdered root is used by the Zulu to create decorative welts on their skin. In India the powder is used to remove warts.[173] In Africa plumbago is known for its ability to prevent nightmares and ward off lightning.[174] Tie a handful of twigs into a bundle and hang to ward a room from bad dreams and negative energy. Dress a candle in oil and roll it in the dried and crumbled flower bits to empower a protection spell. Tuck a handful of flowers into your backpack to avoid provoking a bully. Use plumbago to empower spells to confound an enemy.

. . . .

172. Wei Yan et al., "Plumbagin Attenuates Cancer Cell Growth and Osteoclast Formation in the Bone Microenvironment of Mice," *Acta Pharmacologica Sinica* 35 (January 2014): 124–34, doi:10.1038/aps.2013.152.

173. Horace F. Clay, *The Hawai'i Garden: Tropical Shrubs* (Honolulu, HI: University of Hawaii Press, 1987), 162.

174. Jerry Parsons, "Plumbago: A Lovely Blue-Flowered, Butterfly Plant for Texas," Plant Answers, accessed June 22, 2021, https://www.plantanswers.com/plumbago_best.htm.

Clematis

* *Clematis* spp.
* Hardy in zones 5–9
* Bind, ingenuity, joy, and lightheartedness

There are hundreds of varieties of garden clematis. Most produce showy single or double flowers. Clematis like sun on their leaves and shade on their roots and will thrive when planted in a sunny area that allows their feet to remain cool. Plant it on a wall or fence for support or use a trellis for the vine to climb. Dig a hole that is deeper than the pot the clematis is in. Pour in some compost and set your plant in. Completely fill in the hole. You will want to bury up to three inches of the clematis to stimulate new growth. Water it in well.

Clematis was a favorite of Bacchus. The vines were used in celebrations, woven into crowns and garlands.[175] In the language of flowers, clematis means beauty of the mind and ingenuity. Wear a flower in your hair when you need energy for cleverness. Use a flower in meditation to enhance concentration. Burn dried leaves to find pragmatic solutions. Gather the vines and use them in binding rituals. Stuff the seed fluff into poppets to boost energy to bind.

Coral Bells

* *Heuchera* spp.
* Hardy in zones 4–9
* Healing, love, protection, and strength

Coral bells, also known as alumroot, is a lovely plant native to America. They come in a range of colors with interesting-looking leaves and stalks of small flowers. Coral bells are easy to grow and grow best when planted in partial shade. Coral bells are woodland flowers and thrive when planted in a woodland setting. Amend the soil if it is heavy.

Coral bells hold a gentle, uplifting energy. Grow them in a woodland garden to protect the area from encroachment. Snip the flower stalks and add them to flower bouquets to add nurturing energy. Dry the tiny flowers, crumble them, and add the bits to formulas to draw love or gentle strength. Mix them with dried pansies and chamomile flowers and burn to ease bitter memories.

....
175. Smith, *Strangers in the Garden*, 22.

Corydalis

* *Corydalis* spp.
* Hardy in zones 5–8 (or 6–9, depending on variety)
* Communication, faery energy, friendship,
  good health, and psychic enhancement

Corydalis is a member of the poppy family and a distant relative of bleeding heart. It is a delicate-looking faery plant with lacy foliage and small tubular flowers that come in shades of blue, pink, white, and yellow. Corydalis will add grace to any woodland garden. Plant it in a shaded area with rich, well-draining soil. Corydalis is a shade-loving plant and will self-seed, but it spreads more effectively through its root rhizomes. The seeds must chill for a period to germinate.

Corydalis is a faery flower. Just the sight of it adds to the mystic qualities of a place. Grow it to invite communion with devic energies. Use the dried flowers in formulas for expanding perception. The roots and tubers of some varieties have been used as remedies to help treat pain and high blood pressure in Eastern medicine.[176] Float flowers in bathwater to add healing energy or ease anxiety. Place a handful of blossoms in a bowl and place it under a full moon's light to make an infused moon water with energy to expand perception. Dip a cloth in and use it to rinse your forehead to awaken psychic sight. Use the water as a hair rinse to refresh thought.

Forsythia

* *Forsythia* spp.
* Hardy in zones 5–9
* Enthusiasm, longevity, the sun, and sustainability

The forsythia is a hardy spring-flowering bush. The flowers precede the leaves, so one moment the branches are bare, and then *pop*—overnight the blossoms open to create bright wands of yellow flowers loved by both bees and butterflies. Forsythias thrive when planted in well-draining soil in areas with full sun to part shade. They are quick growers, gaining as much as twenty-four inches in height a year. Plant to provide habitat for birds and small mammals.

. . . .

176. *Encyclopaedia Britannica Online*, s.v. "Corydalis," accessed July 26, 2021, https://www
     .britannica.com/plant/Corydalis.

In the language of flowers forsythia means anticipation, as the sudden appearance of blossoms symbolizes something wonderful about to happen. Forsythias are associated with spring, Ostara, the element air, and the sun. They hold a bright, optimistic energy for manifesting things with long-term effects. The flowers are edible and can be used to decorate baked goods or floated in iced teas. Use the flowers in sun rituals. Float flowers in bathwater for a gentle effervescent energy that will brighten your mood and enhance your ability to influence. Cut wands and bring them in to add to floral displays to brighten a room. Add flowers to potpourri to increase positive energy flow.

Gardenia
* *Gardenia jasminoides*
* Hardy in zones 8–11
* Goddess rituals, healing, love, peace, possibilities, protection, and spirituality

Gardenia is a genus of flowering plants known for their sweet fragrance, waxy petals, and glossy foliage. Gardenias thrive in well-draining, rich soil. And like azaleas, camellias, and hydrangeas, gardenias prefer soil that is slightly acidic. Plant a gardenia on a mound with the root ball about an inch higher than the surrounding soil. Mound up the soil to the top of the exposed root ball and pat it down to provide adequate drainage. Add a layer of mulch and water it in.

Gardenia flowers are strongly scented and promote feelings of love, healing, and peace. Float flower heads in the bath to channel your inner goddess. Use the flowers in moon rituals. Float flowers in a bowl of water and gaze upon its surface during meditation to raise vibration and facilitate communication with the higher self. Dry some flowers and crumble them into bits. Use them in love formulas or roll oiled candles in the flower bits to empower spells for love and harmony. Wear a gardenia to attract love or friendship. In the language of flowers, the gardenia is a symbol of courtesy. Wear a flower to encourage politeness. Fill a vase with gardenia flowers to scent a room and provide a gentle protection against unwanted drama. This works especially well for family gatherings.

Hibiscus

* *Hibiscus* spp.
* Hardy in zones 5–9 (tropical varieties require warmer temperatures)
* Attraction, beauty, heart health, love, and sexuality

Hibiscus is the name of a genus of flowering herbs, shrubs, and small trees in the mallow family. It contains more than 250 species, of which there are two main types: perennial and tropical. Perennial varieties are cold hardy down to zone 5. Tropical varieties require temperatures between 60 and 90 degrees Fahrenheit. Both varieties thrive in full sun and do best in rich, moist soil. When purchasing a hibiscus, make sure to choose a variety that will be happy growing in your microclimate.

Hibiscuses are grown in gardens across the world for their attractive foliage and large, showy flowers. Many varieties are edible. The flowers are made into a popular tea that is used to encourage the healing process and relax the nervous system. An infusion of hibiscus flowers is a popular hair rinse used to accelerate growth.[177] Hibiscus flowers are associated with Venus and Ganesha. They are used in beauty, love, and attraction formulas. Brew up a hibiscus infusion and add to bathwater, and toss in a handful of sea salt and rose petals for a comforting bath that will inspire love and beauty. Wear a flower in your hair when you wish to attract attention. Dry hibiscus flowers and use in formulas to instill lust, instill passion, or find sexual freedom. Add dried flowers to attraction sachets and incenses or crumble into bits and roll your candles in them to bolster attraction energy.

Honeysuckle

* *Lonicera* spp.
* Hardy in zones 4–9
* Abundance, communication, inspiration,
love, luck, prosperity, and protection

The name honeysuckle refers to over 100 species of hardy twining vines in the family Caprifoliaceae. Choose a variety hardy to your microclimate for a wonderful, fast-growing climber. Plant honeysuckle vines on sunny trellises, walls, and fences

....
177. Gregg, *The Complete Illustrated Encyclopedia of Magical Plants*, 201.

in areas protected from the wind. Water regularly during dry periods for a healthy plant with sweetly scented flowers that will attract wildlife to your garden.

Honeysuckles are associated with Mercury, Mars, and Cancer. In traditional Chinese medicine honeysuckle is prescribed to cleanse toxins from the body.[178] The stems are used by acupuncturists to stimulate qi circulation, and the flowers are combined with mullein or marsh mallow to make a cough syrup.[179] Make a batch of honeysuckle flower water by adding a handful of blossoms to a pitcher of spring water. Let it sit overnight and use it as a hair rinse or wear it as a light perfume to encourage feelings of love. Put the water into a spray bottle and use it to spritz yourself to lift mood and inspire creative thought. Place a handful of blossoms in a bowl and place it under a full moon's light to make an infused moon water with energy to stimulate psychic sight and empower love spells.

The scent of honeysuckle inspires love. Plant a honeysuckle outside your window so the lovely perfume drifts in on the summer breeze. Plant near the entrance of your home to draw prosperity and offer protection. Wear honeysuckle flowers to attract love or to sweeten someone's thoughts toward you. Float flowers in bath before a date to boost sex appeal. Add honeysuckle flowers to prosperity spells and charms to enhance the effectiveness of other herbs. Anoint a green candle with oil, roll it in dried honeysuckle bits, and burn to attract riches. Use dried honeysuckle in formulas to draw happiness and harmony. Burn them to remove obstacles and activate positive energy flow. The sweet fragrance of honeysuckle lifts thoughts to grant creative insight. Bruise the flowers and rub them on your forehead before meditation to deepen connection to higher self.

. . . .

178. Gregg, *The Complete Illustrated Encyclopedia of Magical Plants*, 223.

179. Ody, *The Complete Medicinal Herbal*, 76.

Hops

* Humulus lupulus
* Hardy in zones 5–9
* Banishing worries, calming, healing, prosperity, and sleep
* Warning: May cause dermatitis.
This herb should not be used during pregnancy.

Hops are hardy climbing perennials that will grow twenty-five feet in a single season. Shoots rise from the ground to twine up over anything it can grab on to. This vigorous grower loves to be planted in a sunny location in well-draining soil that is rich in organic matter. Provide support for the vines to grow up. It will die back when temperatures cool but will regrow the following spring.

Hops is associated with Jupiter, Mars, and the element air. It holds positive energy to inspire relaxation and happiness. Hops is a species of flowering plant in the Cannabaceae family, which also includes cannabis, and like its cousin, hops flowers have a calming energy that is used to remedy anxiety, stress, and insomnia. The hops flower is a cone-like leafy bract with a slightly bitter, piney-citrusy flavor that has been used as far back as the fourteenth century to add a bitter taste to beer.[180] The history of hops as a sedative and a sleep aid goes back to the ninth century and the Arabian physician Mesue, who used hops to induce sleep. King George III used a pillow stuffed with hops to help calm himself when dealing with bouts of mental illness. It was prescribed to remedy "a quarrelsome nature."[181] Today hops is recognized as a nervine relaxant for treating insomnia.[182] For a tea that naturally promotes relaxation, pour 1 cup of boiling water over 1 teaspoon of hops flowers; cover and steep for 5 minutes. Strain and drink to induce sleep, enhance dreams, or simply wind down after a difficult day. Add a teaspoon of valerian root to quiet troubled thoughts. Stuff a sleep pillow with hops to gain a good night's sleep. Make a sleep

180. Ben McFarland, *World's Best Beers: One Thousand Craft Brews from Cask to Glass* (New York: Sterling, 2009), 12.

181. Ernest Small, *North American Cornucopia* (Boca Raton, FL: Taylor & Francis, 2014), 382.

182. Vincent Minichiello, "Botanical Medicines to Support Healthy Sleep and Rest," VA Office of Patient Centered Care and Cultural Transformation, 2018, 3, https://www.va.gov/WHOLE HEALTHLIBRARY/docs/Botanical-Medicines-to-Support-Healthy-Sleep-and-Rest.pdf.

talisman by filling a muslin bag with hops flowers, rosemary, and thyme. Tuck it under your pillow to keep nightmares at bay. Add hops flowers to healing rituals and incense formulas to instill peace. Add hops flowers to potpourris to raise the vibration of a room. Add to formulas for happiness and cheer. Use hops to usher luck and prosperity into the home. Hang a sprig of hops in the kitchen to ensure plenty. Hops leaves can be blanched and eaten like spinach.

Hosta

* *Hosta* spp.
* Hardy in zones 3–8
* Friendship, healing, love, protection, and strength

Hosta is a genus of over seventy herbaceous shade-loving perennials. They are elegant plants with attractive and sometimes dramatic foliage and are also known as the plantain lily. Hostas are native to Japan but have naturalized to the temperate regions of the Northern Hemisphere. These woodland plants grow in clumps and thrive when planted in shaded areas with rich, well-draining soil. Dig up and divide clumps every four years. Plant one section back in the original spot and the other in a new area. Grow them in shaded walkways, around ponds, and in woodland gardens. Blue-leaf varieties require more shade than the green-leaf types.

Grow hostas under windows to protect against enchantment and thievery. Hosta energy is empowering and can be used to strengthen the energy of other herbs. Add dried hosta flowers to power up protection formulas. Add them to sachets to keep nightmares away. Float hosta flowers in bathwater to add healing energy.

Hydrangea

* *Hydrangea* spp.
* Hardy in zones 4–9
* Boundaries, friendship, hex breaking, love, and protection

Hydrangea is the genus of shrubs and small trees with showy, large globes of flower heads. They are native to most of the world and will grow quickly into large shrubs when planted in their grow zone. In hot climates hydrangeas should be protected from afternoon sun. Hydrangeas thrive in moist, well-draining soil. To plant, dig a hole twice the size of the root ball, making sure to keep the base of the plant even with the soil level. Fill in with good soil and water well. Hydrangeas thrive in moist soil and suffer when it is allowed to dry out. Hydrangeas propagate easily from cuttings. They can grow to the size of a car and live for decades; some have been known to live more than 100 years.

Hydrangeas hold a protective, tolerant energy and, when planted around the perimeter of your property, will help establish boundaries. Plant a bush between your house and a bothersome neighbor's to instill privacy and discourage gossip. Plant between your house and an enemy's to redirect curses and counter psychic attacks. Give a bouquet of hydrangea flowers to safeguard a friendship or end gossip. Add hydrangea bark and buds to potpourris to change the vibration of a room. Add flower heads to a floor wash or bath to change luck and break jinxes or curses. Add hydrangea flowers to bathwater to lift mood. Float a handful of flowers in a bowl of spring water and set out overnight in the light of the full moon. Strain out the plant material and use the water to boost protection magick, or use the water as a hand wash before dealing with a difficult person. Add hydrangea-infused water to bathwater and soak to fortify personal boundaries. Hang the image of a hydrangea in your work space to ward and safeguard the area. Tack it to the wall, then dip your thumb into the hydrangea water and press it to the image to ward your desk of a negative coworker. Add hydrangea water to an atomizer and spritz an area to neutralize negative energy.

Jasmine

* *Jasminum* spp.
* Hardy in zones 9–10 (cold-hardy varieties to zone 7)
* Attraction, hope, love, peace, prophetic dreams, and prosperity

Jasminum is the genus of 200 species of flowering shrubs and vines known for their small fragrant flowers. Before you purchase a jasmine, consider if it will grow in your microclimate. Most varieties are tropical plants that thrive in warmer climates. They can be deciduous or evergreen. Some varieties love the sun, while others prefer shade. And strangely, one of the most popular jasmines is not even a jasmine at all but a member of the dogbane family. Star jasmine (*Trachelospermum jasminoides*) is hardy in zones 8 to 10 and can be found in gardens across the world growing up walls, covering fences, and even as ground cover. Just like jasmine, its small white flowers are highly fragrant and emit a sweet, exotic scent.

Jasmine is associated with Jupiter, Cancer, the moon, the element water, Diana, Vishnu, and Quan Yin and is known for its feminine energy. The flowers are a favored offering of many deities and are often floated in ritual drinks. The scent of the blossoms lifts mood, stimulates mental creativity, and attracts abundance. Plant beside the bedroom window so that the scent will drift into the room and infuse the space with a loving harmonic energy. Add dried jasmine flowers to prosperity formulas to boost energy. Add to love sachets to sweeten the working or burn to carry prayers out into the universe. Float flowers in bathwater to inspire new ideas. Make a batch of jasmine water by rinsing 2 cups of jasmine blossoms and adding them to a pitcher of water. Cover the pitcher with a kitchen towel and put in the refrigerator to infuse overnight. Strain out flowers and use the floral water as a hair rinse to bolster an optimistic outlook or increase your attraction. Pour a cup of the infused water into a bowl, dip in a finger, and trace down the inside of both your wrists. Anoint your throat, your heart, and your belly to open the mind, stimulate inspiration, and increase your appreciation of life. Anoint your lips to sweeten your words. Use jasmine water to empower candle magick. Anoint a red candle with it and use it in love spells. Anoint a green candle to draw prosperity. Anoint a yellow candle to inspire creativity or gain wisdom.

Lilac

* Syringa vulgaris
* Hardy in zones 5–7 (some cultivars hardy to zone 8)
* Banish, beauty, beginnings, love, nostalgia, and protection

The lilac is a flowering plant in the olive family. Lilacs are known for the heady, nostalgic scent of their blossoms. Most lilac bushes are hardy, need little care, and propagate easily from cuttings. They thrive in well-draining soil and bloom best when planted in full sun. Plant to attract pollinators. Lilacs are an important food source for some lepidopterans.

The lilac symbolizes beauty, love, and passion, and because lilacs bloom early in the spring, they are associated with beginnings, new life, and renewal. Pan, the Greek god of forests and fields, is said to have created the first panpipe from the lilac.[183] The lilac is a faery favorite. Plant a lilac in your yard to encourage nature spirits. Leave an offering of milk and honey or beer and bread under a lilac bush to gain favor. Lilacs hold energy to clear a home of mischievous ghosts. A lilac planted near a home will deter wandering spirits. Add lilac blossoms to chamomile and foxglove flowers to make a protection sachet that will clear an area of unwanted spirit energy and induce feelings of peace. Burn dried lilac blossoms with rose petals and a pinch of powdered lemon peel to soothe hurt feelings. Make a batch of lilac infused oil by filling a jar with lilac blossoms. Cover with olive or sweet almond oil and macerate for 2 weeks. Strain out the flowers and use the oil to anoint candles in rituals for recalling past lives, or wear it as perfume to facilitate the start of something new. Add 9 drops of lilac oil to ½ cup of salt and add it to bathwater for uncrossing.

Moonflower

* *Ipomoea alba*
* Hardy in zones 10–12
* Happiness, luck, money, peace, protection, and visions
* Warning: The seeds are poisonous.

The moonflower, with its heart-shaped leaves and sweetly scented flowers, is the nocturnal version of the morning glory. The flowers open in the late afternoon and stay open for a single night. Their delicate scent draws moths and bats. Moonflowers thrive when planted in moist, well-draining soil. Plant moonflower seeds where the vines can climb. Provide support and water when the weather is dry.

Plant the seeds in a moon garden to draw peace and happiness to your home. Plant them beside a bedroom window so the scent will fill the room and induce prophetic dreams. Float the flowers in bathwater to channel moon goddess energy. Use the flowers in moon magick. The vines can be used for binding magick. Moonflower roots are often substituted for the Hoodoo root High John the Conqueror (*Ipomoea purga*) and used in spells to draw luck and money.

. . . .

183. Jenny Krane, "6 Little-Known Lilac Facts That May Surprise You," *Better Homes & Gardens*, May 21, 2019, https://www.bhg.com/gardening/flowers/lilac-facts/.

Morning Glory

* *Ipomoea* spp.
* Hardy in zones 10–11
* Banishing, binding, contentment, love, peace, and protection
* Warning: The seeds are poisonous.

The morning glory is a flowering vine with slender stems and heart-shaped leaves. The flowers open in the morning and last only a day. Morning glories are frost tender and are often planted as annuals in spring when the ground warms. Plant them in a sheltered location and provide support for the vines to climb. Leave some of the seedpods in place to seed a new crop of flowers the following spring.

Morning glories hold a harmonious energy for contentment. Float the flowers in a bath to relax and let the mind rest. Use the blue blossoms in formulas for harmony and love, the pink for friendship and affection, and the white in formulas to refresh thought and to open perception. The morning glory is associated with Saturn and the sun. The foliage and blossoms can be incorporated into protection spells. Plant them to safeguard your home. The morning glory is one of the "bindweeds" used in binding magick. The roots are used in folk magick as a substitute for High John the Conqueror root. The seeds are considered to be toxic and can induce hallucinations.

Passionflower

* *Passiflora* spp.
* Hardy in zones 6–10 (with hardy varieties 5–11)
* Beauty, calmness, friendship, harmony, and sleep

The passionflower is a fast-growing perennial vine with beautiful fruit-producing flowers. Passionflower vines thrive when planted in an area with full sun and moist, rich soil. In hotter climates provide afternoon shelter or plant in dappled shade. Provide a sturdy support. Passionflower can grow up to thirty feet in a single season. It is easily propagated from cuttings. The wide, flat flowers are a favorite of butterflies.

Passionflowers are native to the New World. The native peoples of South America knew it held sedative and antispasmodic properties, and they used the plant and the flower as medicine. When Spanish explorers invaded in the sixteenth century, they observed the calming properties of the plant and carried it back to Europe, where it became a part of folk healing there.[184] Today the dried fruit and flower tops are ingredients in many sedatives.[185] The leaves are infused to make a tea to soothe the nerves and treat depression. Drink a cup of passionflower tea to soothe anxiety, calm restlessness, or alleviate insomnia. The passionflower is associated with Neptune, Venus, and the moon. It holds a harmonious energy to calm, relax, and soothe. Serve passionflower tea during reconciliations to ease annoyance and encourage an amicable attitude. Serve an infusion to stem jealousy. Add the infusion to your bathwater and soak to release anger or fear. Add the dried leaves and flowers to formulas to bring peace or instill harmony. Stuff them into dream pillows to quiet troubled dreams. Use passionflowers in charms to encourage friendship.

Peony

* *Paeonia* spp.
* Deciduous Peonies: Hardy in zones 3–8
* Tree Peonies: Hardy in zones 4–9
* Abundance, attraction, calming, healing, prosperity, protection, spring, and wealth
* Warning: Some varieties are poisonous.

Paeonia is a genus of stately flowering shrubs that are divided into three types: herbaceous, which die back to the ground at the end of the growing season; tree peonies, which are actually deciduous shrubs; and intersectional peonies, which are a cross between the two. Herbaceous peonies require staking for support. Tree peonies do not. Intersectional peonies, also known as 'Itoh' hybrids, are strong, healthy plants that grow more compact than the other types. They do die back to the ground after a frost like the herbaceous type. Peonies thrive in rich, moist soils. Choose a sheltered area with full sun exposure. Find out which types grow best in your zone and plant accordingly. Some varieties have been known to live up to fifty years.

Peonies are associated with the sun, the element fire, Leo, Pan, and spring. They symbolize beauty, good health, good fortune, and nobility of spirit. Peonies are used

184. "Passionflower," National Center for Complementary and Integrative Health, last modified August 2020, https://www.nccih.nih.gov/health/passionflower.

185. Reader's Digest, *Magic and Medicine of Plants*, 266.

in spells to attract positive energy and draw luck and abundance. Wear a peony when you need to exude confidence. Add dried peony flowers to wealth spells. Anoint a green candle with olive oil and roll in dried peony bits and burn to draw prosperity. Add cut peonies to a vase to boost business and draw customers. Cut peony flowers and bring in to add charm and glamor to any space. Give cut flowers to cheer or comfort. Use a peony flower as a meditation focus to rediscover appreciation of beauty and wonder. Peonies also hold energy for protection. Plant peonies around the home to protect and keep evil away. Smith writes in *Strangers in the Garden* that the root was a medieval remedy for "the Incubus we call the Mare" (nightmares) and "falling sickness" (epilepsy).[186] Tuck a piece of peony root into your left pocket to avoid being enchanted. Make an amulet by wrapping a piece of root with red thread and wear to avoid the evil eye or protect against falling under the influence of someone with a silver tongue.

Rhododendron

* *Rhododendron* spp.
* Hardy in zones 3–9 (depending on variety)
* Abundance, confusion, empathy, and personal power
* Warning: Leaves and pollen are poisonous.

Rhododendron is the name of an entire genus of shrubs and small trees that produce large clusters of showy winter and spring flowers in shades of lavender, pink, red, and white. Most are broadleaf evergreens that thrive in partial shade and, like their cousin the azalea, do best in acidic soil. Rhododendrons have toxic compounds in both the leaves and flowers that if ingested can cause life-threatening blood pressure and heart issues. Honey contaminated with these compounds is known as "mad honey" and can cause confusion and dizziness even when eaten in small quantities.[187] Even so, rhododendrons are very popular here in the Pacific Northwest. You can find them growing everywhere. They need little care, can live hundreds of years, and grow into

. . . .

186. Smith, *Strangers in the Garden*, 102.

187. Suze A. Jansen et al., "Grayanotoxin Poisoning: 'Mad Honey Disease' and Beyond," *Cardiovascular Technology* 12, no. 3 (2012): 208–15, doi:10.1007/s12012-012-9162-2.

huge bushes that produce beautiful, long-lasting blooms. Plant a rhododendron in a sunny spot with room for it to grow and water during dry periods.

Magickally, rhododendrons hold energy for abundance, defense, and personal power. In Victorian society they represented fragile love and were a death threat when sent in a black vase. Use a rhododendron as a focus in meditation to discover what conditions lie under the obvious. Dry the leaves and flowers and burn them as incense to quiet an overactive mind. Burn them during meditation to absorb knowledge or enhance awareness of an enemy's activities and motivations. Float the flowers in a bowl of water and use it as a gazing pool to see what lies beneath what was spoken or find a way through a deception. Use them in rituals to confound your enemies or hide something you do not want revealed.

Rose
* *Rosa* spp.
* Hardy in zones 3–11 (depending on variety)
* Acceptance, attraction, divination, dreams, feminine power, happiness, healing, love, protection, secrecy, and wish magick

The rose is one of the oldest-known perennial shrubs. Today there are thousands of varieties and colors, one for just about every hardiness zone. Choose the right rose for your microclimate and soil. Most grow best in clay and loam soils that have been richly amended with organic matter. Plant your rose in an area with full sun exposure and well-draining soil. Water regularly to keep the soil moist. Roses are heavy feeders. To keep them blooming, keep them well watered and feed with a rose or multipurpose fertilizer. Deadhead the spent flowers as they fade. Roses need regular pruning to stay healthy. Treat problems as they arise. Mulch to hold in soil moisture when the weather is hot and protect rootstock when the weather turns cold.

Roses are best known for their nurturing energy for peace and love. They are associated with Taurus, the moon, and many goddesses, including Hulda and Aphrodite. The flowers are steeped in lore, each color with its own meaning: pink for happiness, red for passion, yellow for friendship, and white for purity. The sweet scent encourages both acceptance and affection. Add fresh rose petals and honey to a warm cup of tea and sip to lift spirits. Bring cut roses inside to lift vibration and encourage happiness. Toss a handful of rose petals into bathwater to boost beauty or attraction spells. Use rose petals in love, luck, grief, and healing rituals. Make an attraction salve by infusing a jar of sunflower oil with rose petals. Fill a small jar with fresh rose petals and cover with sunflower oil. Seal the jar tightly and allow it to sit for one week. Strain out the plant material and sniff. The oil should be sweetly scented. Rub it into the skin to increase charm and appeal. Use as a massage oil to promote affection. Use the oil to anoint candles in love magick. Add dried rose petals to love formulas to bolster energy and quicken results. Add dried rose petals to dream sachets to encourage prophetic dreams. Make a love-drawing powder by grinding dried rose petals with basil, ginger, lavender, and yarrow. Anoint a candle with olive oil and roll it in the crushed bits to empower a love spell.

The rose is also a keeper of secrets and a symbol of secret societies. The Latin phrase *sub rosa* means "under the rose" and is used to denote secrecy or a confidence.[188] To this day ornamental plasters used to decorate ceilings are called ceiling roses. Give a rose when you express something you wish to be kept secret. Fill a vase with cut roses and use it as a table centerpiece when you wish to keep a conversation private. To keep a secret from being discovered, write it cryptically on a piece of paper. Cover the page with rose petals and then fold the paper in half twice, folding it toward you to enclose the petals. Secure it with ribbon and tuck the packet into a drawer where it is out of sight.

188. *Merriam-Webster*, s.v. "sub rosa," accessed June 4, 2021, https://www.merriam-webster.com/dictionary/sub%20rosa.

Viburnum

* *Viburnum* spp.
* Hardy in zones 5–7 (depending on variety)
* Binding, conjuring, hex breaking, hexing, luck,
money, protection, and success

Viburnum is a genus of over 150 different species of shrubs and small trees that produce clusters of lightly fragrant flowers followed by dark blue-black fruit that is food for birds and other wildlife. Many cultivars of this diverse group are garden favorites. Choose one for your microclimate and plant it accordingly.

Black haw (*Viburnum prunifolium*), cramp bark (*Viburnum opulus*), hobble bush (*Viburnum alnifolium*), and witches hobble (*Viburnum trilobum*) are folk herbs known as devil's shoestring and are used to attract luck, to gain a job, and to trip up the devil or keep him out.[189] A spell to conjure luck is worked by tying 9 roots together with string and knotting with 9 knots. The knotted root is splashed with whisky and kept in a mojo bag.

. . . .

189. Catherine Yronwode, "Devil's Shoe String," Lucky Mojo Curio Co., accessed September 1, 2021, https://www.luckymojo.com/devilsshoestring.html.

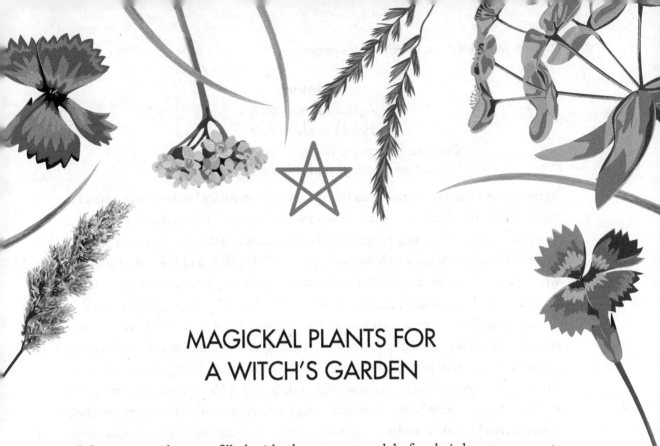

MAGICKAL PLANTS FOR
A WITCH'S GARDEN

While many gardens are filled with plants grown solely for their beauty or scent, a witch's garden contains plants cultivated for their magick and medicinal powers. If you choose well, you will find it is this type of herb garden that fuels your practice and brings out your inner witchiness. Do your research as you start your collection. Long for knowledge and hold it tight. Experiment and keep a written record. Apply what you learn as often as you are able and your practice will expand and deepen.

As you begin a plant collection, gather all the information you can find. You will discover that while some will grow like weeds, others must be coaxed in indoor pots, but it is these unique plants, vibrating with potential, collected, and cared for—nurtured and researched, and grown for no other purpose but to empower our spellcraft—that stimulate and fuel our magickal natures. It is through this interaction, through the practice of the Green Craft, that we grow our power and, with its knowledge, nurture our inner life and come to deity.

Agrimony

* *Agrimonia eupatoria*
* Hardy in zones 6–9
* Dispersing negative energy, healing, protection, rest, uncrossing, and voice enhancement

Agrimony is a wildflower native to Europe and North Africa but now widespread in other northern temperate regions. It is a medicine plant, still used today as an eye-wash for conjunctivitis, an astringent to treat wounds and skin conditions, a poultice to treat migraines, and a gargle for sore throats.[190] If planted in full sun, this flower will grow in just about any kind of soil. Sow seeds directly into the soil after the last frost date. Water regularly until the plant is established. This flower will self-seed.

Agrimony is associated with Jupiter, Cancer, and the element air. It was brewed into an infusion and used as a mouthwash by singers and public speakers.[191] Use an agrimony infusion to loosen your voice and set the words to fall upon receptive ears. Sip a cup of agrimony tea next time you must have a difficult conversation to ease your words. Agrimony holds a calming energy to reduce troubled thoughts and help calm the mind to gain a restful sleep. Add an infusion of agrimony to bathwater to lift vibration and find peace. Add a sprig of agrimony to a dream pillow with mugwort or lavender to induce a deep sleep. Agrimony is also a banishing herb used in counter-magick to break a curse, repel ill will, or return a hex to its creator. Brew an infusion with agrimony and wormwood or chicory. Pour the infusion into your bathwater and submerge to counter a hex and return it back to the ill-wisher. Or grind agri-mony, peppermint, and rue and burn as incense to end mischievous behavior. Burn agrimony with slippery elm bark to stop gossip. Stuff a mojo bag with agrimony and a handful of rue and wear to send back the evil eye. If you have to face a jealous rival, make a protective amulet with a pinch of agrimony, rue, and a piece of burdock root. Carry it to avoid being hexed. Burn dried agrimony as incense during circle work to protect against unwanted astral intruders. Add an infusion of agrimony to your

. . . .

190. Ody, *The Complete Medicinal Herbal*, 31.

191. Kruger, *The Pocket Guide to Herbs*, 9.

washwater and use it to dispel residual energy after a fight or an argument. Use as a floor wash to rid a dwelling of energy left by the past occupant. Dispose of the leftover washwater by pouring it out on the other side of your property line.

Angelica

* *Angelica archangelica*
* Hardy in zones 4–9
* Healing, protection, purification, and visions

Angelica is a genus name of over sixty separate herbs, some of which are poisonous. This description is for the Old World herb, *Angelica archangelica*, an edible biennial native to northern Europe. To grow angelica, choose an area with rich, moist, well-draining soil and full sun exposure. In hot regions choose a place sheltered from afternoon sun. Plant the seeds directly into soil and water to keep the soil moist until the plants are established. It will self-seed once it is established.

Angelica is an herb of protection. All parts of the plant were used to repel enchantments and hexes.[192] In medieval times angelica leaves were worn as protective necklaces for protection from evil spirits and hexes. Angelica root was steeped in water to make a "holy water" used to ward off the plague.[193] Angelica is associated with the sun, Leo, and Jupiter and is used to drive darkness from a place. All parts are aromatic and, when brought inside or burned as incense, will restore freshness to a stagnant or musty space. Use angelica when moving into a new home to instigate fresh energy flow. Angelica can repel negative energy and attract positive energy. Use it as a strewing herb to dispel the old energy and draw in new. Use angelica in rituals for blessing and banishing. To make a protective oil, take a wide-mouthed jar and fill it with angelica leaves. Cover the leaves with sunflower oil. Seal the jar tightly and allow it to sit for a week. Strain out the plant matter and use the oil to anoint candles in protection rituals. Anoint your threshold with the oil to ward your home. Angelica root is warming, and angelica tea is drunk to calm the stomach and the spirit.

. . . .

192. Grieve, *A Modern Herbal*, vol. 1, 36.

193. Kruger, *The Pocket Guide to Herbs*, 16.

Dong quai (Angelica sinensis) is another herb in the family Apiaceae whose root is often used as a substitute for angelica. Dong quai a protective herb that is indigenous to China. It is known as a healer, guardian, and a giver of strength to women.

Arnica
* *Arnica montana*
* Hardy in zones 4–9
* Abundance, awareness, favor, healing, protection, and psychic abilities
* Warning: This plant is poisonous if ingested.

Arnica is a perennial flowering plant with bright yellow daisylike flowers. It is known also as leopard's-bane and wolfsbane, not to be confused with the deadly plant aconite, also called wolfsbane. Arnica is an alpine plant and favors a cool climate with full sun exposure. It does not fare well in regions with overly wet winters. Grow arnica in your garden to gain the favor of devic energies.

Arnica is associated with Apollo, the sun, and the element fire. The yellow flowers are made into salves and ointments that are used topically to reduce the pain and swelling of bruises and sprains.[194] Macerate arnica flowers in safflower oil to make an anti-inflammatory massage oil to rub into skin to remedy aches and pains. Arnica helps heal all sorts of traumas. Float arnica flowers on bathwater to quicken a recovery or heighten awareness of your higher self. Use arnica in shadow work to deepen the experience. In Germany arnica was used to gain favors from spirits: "Bunches were gathered and set on the corners of fields to spread the power of the corn spirit and to ensure a good harvest," writes Nancy Allison of *Mother Earth Living*.[195] Burn dried arnica as incense to enhance spirit communication. Add sprigs of arnica to bouquets or a vase to improve the mood of a room. Tuck a flower into your left pocket when you need luck on your side. Arnica also holds energy for protection. Plant it along a path to keep unwanted visitors away. Add an arnica infusion to washwater and use it to wipe down the door and front step to keep away trouble.

. . . .

194. Andi Clevely and Katherine Richmond, *The Complete Book of Herbs* (London: Smithmark, 1998), 77.

195. Nancy Allison, "Arnica Montana: Natural Magic," *Mother Earth Living*, May 1, 2003, https://www .motherearthliving.com/health-and-wellness/natural-healing-arnica-montana-natural-magic.

Betony

* *Stachys officinalis*
* Hardy in zones 5–10
* Banishing, healing, protection, and soothing

Betony is a perennial wildflower also known as bishop wort and common hedge-nettle. It grows in damp meadows, around ponds, and in boggy spaces. Betony does well in both full sun and full shade. Its only requirement is wet, heavy soil. Sow seeds in late summer for blooms that attract bees and butterflies next June to August. Grow betony in wildflower and meadow gardens.

Throughout the centuries, betony was prized for its healing powers. It is still used today as a remedy to help relieve tension and headaches.[196] For a calming infusion, brew equal parts betony, chamomile, skullcap, and valerian. Sip a cup before bed to relax the mind and discourage disturbing dreams. Betony holds a protective cleansing energy. Both the Egyptians and Anglo-Saxons believed betony to be a magickal herb with power to repel evil.[197] Tuck a sprig of betony into your left pocket for protection. Brew an infusion of betony and add it to bathwater to alleviate a psychic attack. Burn betony leaves as incense to rid a room of negative energy. Betony can be used to soothe feelings and end quarrels. Use it as a strewing herb to instill harmonic energy. Burn betony with lavender to clear a room after an argument. Tuck a sprig into your left pocket before you go into negotiations to bolster confidence and alleviate fears. Press your hand over your pocket whenever you find you need to come back to point. Grow betony in your garden to protect your home from negative energy, gossip, and fear. Betony is associated with Jupiter and Pluto. Rinse your forehead with an infusion of betony to clear your third eye and improve psychic abilities.

196. Amy Jeanroy, "Grow and Use the Betony Herb (Stachys Officinalis)," The Spruce, last modified January 5, 2021, https://www.thespruce.com/betony-stachys-officinalis-1762351.

197. Paul Whitmer, "Herb to Know: Wood Betony," *Mother Earth Living*, November 11, 2009, https://www.motherearthliving.com/plant-profile/wood-betony.

Borage

* *Borago officinalis*
* Beauty, courage, forgetfulness, gladness,
happiness, harmony, protection, and psychic powers

Borage is a hardy, easy-to-grow garden annual also known as bee bush and star-flower. It thrives when planted in full sun to partial shade and readily self-seeds, so if you plant it once, new plants will sprout the next year.

Borage is associated with Jupiter and Leo. It is an herb of cheer thought to inspire euphoria. Grow in your garden to cheer the spirit. Tea made from borage leaves is used to restore vitality. Brew young leaves to make a green tea and drink to improve mood and lift spirits. Float flowers and young shoots in iced summer drinks to add cheer. Add flowers to salads to promote cheerfulness or end melancholy. Add a hand-ful of borage leaves to a hot bath to ease exhaustion and aching muscles and to fortify the spirit. Steep the flowers in boiling water for 10 minutes, then drink to enhance psychic abilities. Borage can also be used to restore peace to the home. Brew a peace-restoring infusion of borage flowers, bachelor's buttons, periwinkle, and rosemary. Strain and add it to washwater to wash away resentments and restore harmony.

Cannabis

* *Cannabis sativa*
* Divination, dreams, relaxation, transition, and visions
* Warning: The plant is a narcotic.

Cannabis is a genus of fast-growing annual flowering plants in the family Cannaba-ceae. Though cannabis grows easily from seed, commercial plants are grown from cuttings or seedlings. Plant cannabis in full sun and water regularly, but do not over-water. Feed the plants after four weeks but do not over fertilize, or it will burn your plant. Cannabis grows very quickly. It is a bee favorite.

Cannabis is a medicine plant and a hallucinogen. Today it is a subject of contro-versy even though medical studies have shown it helps remedy a long list of ailments. The *Economist* printed a 2006 story that stated, "If cannabis were unknown ... its discovery would no doubt be hailed as a medical breakthrough. Scientists would praise its potential for treating everything from pain to cancer, and marvel at its rich pharmacopoeia—many of whose chemicals mimic vital molecules in the human body."[198] Cannabis is used to treat everything from sleeping disorders to stress to body pains. It provides relief for patients suffering from seizures, glaucoma, and cancer. Cannabis has been used to trigger astral travels and induce visions for thousands of years. It is associated with Saturn and Neptune as an herb of transitions and gateways, granting passage into other realms. Use the smoke to make a spirit ladder to carry your consciousness up or down to the otherworlds. While the bud and leaf are usually smoked, the stems can be brewed into a lovely calming tea. Infuse the tea with lavender buds to soothe an injured spirit. Infuse with rose petals to inspire a romantic mood. Add a splash of cream to increase the potency.[199]

Catnip

* *Nepeta cataria*
* Hardy in zones 3–9
* Beauty, familiar magick, friendship, joy, and love
* Warning: Do not smoke or ingest while pregnant.

Catnip is a vigorous herbaceous perennial also known as catmint. It has attractive green-gray foliage and spires of small white flowers. Catnip thrives when planted in areas with full sun exposure and rich and loamy but well-draining soil.

Many cats gain feelings of ecstasy from bruising the leaves and rolling in the oil. Grow catnip near the home or hang over the door to attract positive energy. In France catnip was a kitchen herb, and in England it was infused into a tea to treat nervous headaches, colds, and fevers and to aid sleep.[200] Brew a calming cup of catnip tea by pouring boiling water over the herb. Let it steep and then strain and sip

. . . .

198. "Refer Madness: Marijuana Is Medically Useful, Whether Politicians Like It or Not," *Economist*, April 27, 2006, https://www.economist.com/science-and-technology/2006/04/27/reefer-madness.

199. Atheer Zgair et al., "Dietary Fats and Pharmaceutical Lipid Excipients Increase Systemic Exposure to Orally Administered Cannabis and Cannabis-Based Medicines," *American Journal of Translational Research* 8, no. 8 (August 2016): 3448–59, https://www.ncbi.nlm.nih.gov/pmc/articles/PMC5009397/.

200. Grieve, *A Modern Herbal*, vol. 1, 174.

while warm. Add lavender to calm the spirit or skullcap to induce pleasant dreams. Catnip is an herb of beauty associated with Libra and Venus. Use it to boost beauty, love, and fertility charms. Brew a catnip infusion and add to bathwater to boost attraction and beauty baths. Brew catnip with lavender and marjoram to lift spirits and foster joy. Catnip can draw a love that's true. Stuff a sachet with catnip and rose petals to attract love. Sprinkle across your bed to attract a new lover.

Centaury
* *Centaurium erythraea*
* Counter-magick, protection, psychic ability, and unhexing

A small annual wildflower with clusters of pink star-shaped blossoms also known as bitterwort, European centaury, Christ's ladder, and feverwort. Centaury is native to Europe and North Africa but has naturalized in the United States and Australia. It is a wildflower that thrives in warm regions. You can find it growing in meadows and in dappled woodlands. Grow centaury in an area with partial shade and light, sandy soil, and it will reseed and grow back the following spring.

Centaury is associated with the sun and the element fire. It was named after the centaur Chiron of Greek myth, who used it to cure a wound cause by a poison arrow.[201] Centaury is a bitter herb eaten to aid digestive function. It is also used as a poultice to treat skin disorders. Magickally, centaury holds a protective, calming energy. Use centaury blossoms to repel anger and spite. Add dried flowers to sachets to neutralize negative energy. Add them to a potpourri to encourage a positive outlook. Use centaury in counter-magick. Add centaury flowers to formulas to break a hex. Brew an infusion of equal parts centaury leaves, chamomile, marsh mallow root, and meadowsweet. Add the infusion to your bathwater and soak to break an influence. Add it to washwater and use it to clean with to banish bad luck.

. . . .

201. Kruger, *The Pocket Guide to Herbs*, 47.

Chamomile
* *Chamaemelum nobile* and *Matricaria chamomilla*
* Hardy in zones 3–9 (Roman variety)
* Abundance, communication, healing, peace, rest, and water elemental

Chamomile is a member of the daisy family. The name chamomile refers to *Chamaemelum nobile* (Roman chamomile) and *Matricaria chamomilla* (German chamomile), two plants belonging to different species but used to treat the same problems. Roman chamomile is a creeping perennial often used as a ground cover. German chamomile is a shrubby annual wildflower. Roman chamomile isn't as floriferous as the German variety, but it has a lovely apple-like scent. Both species produce white flowers with yellow centers in the spring and summer and both thrive in full sun. Start from seed after the last frost or plant seedlings. Chamomile is known as a "plant doctor" and will revive a sickly plant when planted nearby. Spray a sick plant with a cooled dose of chamomile tea to help it revive.

Chamomile is an Old World medicine plant that has been used for centuries to treat upset stomach, gas, headache, insomnia, and anxiety.[202] Today the dried flowers are brewed into a tea that is drunk to calm the nerves and induce sleep and used externally to soothe the skin.[203] Drink before bedtime to calm the nervous system. Drink a cup of chamomile tea to prepare the mind and body for magick work. Add a chamomile infusion to your bathwater and soak to soothe a frazzled spirit or dispel nervousness. Chamomile is associated with the sun and holds a calm, grounding energy. Use the flowers in formulas to manifest abundance. Mix the dried flowers into potpourris or stuff them into sachets to scent linens and clothes with a feel-good fragrance. Chamomile also holds energy for protection. Brew a chamomile infusion and add it to your bathwater to remove negative energy. Brew an infusion of chamomile and basil and soak to remove a curse. Stuff a sachet with chamomile, foxglove, and lilac blossoms and hang it from the closet door to ward a room. In Hoodoo chamomile is brewed into a good-luck hand wash for gamblers to increase winnings.

. . . .

202. Foster, *National Geographic Desk Reference to Nature's Medicine*, 94.

203. Jekka McVicar, *Jekka's Medicinal Herbs* (New York: William Morrow & Company, 1995), n.p.

Costmary

* *Tanacetum balsamita*
* Hardy in zones 4–8
* Clear thoughts, communication, emotions, and good luck
* Warning: This herb should not be used during pregnancy.

Costmary is a daisylike perennial also known as alecost, balsam herb, and Bible leaf. It is a low, bushy plant that produces clusters of yellow flowers from spring to summer. Sow seeds in the spring directly into rich, well-draining soil in an area with full to part sun exposure. Water to keep the soil evenly moist. Divide a clump in the fall and replant the divisions at the same depth. Plant costmary with lavender, oregano, sage, and thyme for an aromatic bed of useful herbs.

Costmary is an aromatic plant with a long history as an old-fashioned English strewing herb.[204] The sweetly scented foliage is used to make sachets and potpourris. A leaf of costmary was often used as a scented bookmark to hold places in Bibles.[205] Magickally, costmary is associated with Jupiter and holds positive energy to calm emotions, activate thought, and draw good luck. Tuck a leaf into your pocket to stimulate the flow of positive energy. Fan yourself with a costmary leaf to find inspiration. Add costmary to hair rinses, bathwaters, and floor washes for a pleasantly scented rinse with energy to calm the mind and refresh the outlook. Collect costmary leaves and lavender sprigs and tie into bunches. Hang it in a closet to scent clothes, or wear it to aid communication. Stuff a sachet with costmary, lavender, and mint, and tuck it into your left pocket to stimulate thought. Press your hand over it to find focus or see around an obstacle. Tuck a costmary leaf into a manuscript to activate ideas. Add a costmary leaf to a glass of iced tea and sip to stimulate conversation.

. . . .

204. Thomas Tusser, *Five Hundred Points of Good Husbandrie* (London: Tuber & Co. 1573; Project Gutenberg, 2016), 95, http://www.gutenberg.org/files/51764/51764-h/51764-h.htm.

205. The Herb Companion Staff, "Herb to Know: Costmary," *Mother Earth Living*, June 1, 2002, https://www.motherearthliving.com/plant-profile/costmary.

Cowslip

* *Primula veris*
* Hardy in zones 5–9
* Beauty, calm, flower, soothing, and unlocking

Cowslip is an easy-to-grow primrose native to Europe also known as key flower. It is known for its fragrant, funnel-shaped yellow flowers. Sow seeds in the fall in sunny areas. Include cowslip in wildlife, wildflower, and meadow gardens. Cowslip is a clumping flower that likes to grow in groups. It thrives when planted in a shady area with rich, moist soil. Cowslip favors areas that are damp, such as the bank of a stream, the edge of a pond, or under a birdbath.

Cowslip is associated with the Divine Feminine, Freya, faeries, Ostara, the sun, Aries, Venus, and Libra. The pleasant scent soothes the spirit. The young leaves are edible and can be added to salads and brewed into a tea to ease restlessness. Float flowers in bathwater to relieve headache. Fill a jar with clean flower tops and pour cold-pressed sunflower oil in to fill. Seal the jar tightly and place it in a sunny windowsill for at least 2 weeks. Strain out the herb and use the oil topically to treat aches and pains. Use cowslip to empower beauty and glamour magick. Add an infusion to bathwater and soak to restore youthful glow. Drop a handful of cowslip blossoms into a bowl of fresh water and leave it out overnight in the light of the moon. Use the water as a face rinse to ease worries and fortify charm. Cowslip is a faery flower. Plant it in a faery garden to attract nature spirits.

Dittany

* Origanum dictamnus
* Hardy in zones 7–11
* Affection, astral projection, divination, healing, love, and visions

Dittany is an attractive flowering herb with fuzzy oval-shaped leaves and small flowers. It is also known as Cretan dittany, dittany of Crete, and hop marjoram. It is native to the island of Crete, where it has been used as a painkiller and wound healer since the Bronze Age.[206] Plant seeds directly into the soil in an area with full sun

. . . .
206. Clevely and Richmond, *The Complete Book of Herbs*, 105.

exposure. Dittany needs soil with good drainage. It grows wild on the rocky island of Crete, and like other Mediterranean herbs, dittany prefers dry conditions. Once it is established, it needs little water.

Dittany is a solar herb associated with Venus and Samhain. It holds energy to inspire affection and warm the heart. Use dittany in love formulas to inspire new relationships or deepen existing ones. Dittany also holds energy to aid communications. Burn dittany with dragon's blood to communicate feelings of affection. Mix dittany with benzoin and sandalwood and burn it on a charcoal disk to receive communications from the astral realms or help spirits manifest. Rub dittany leaves over your forehead to stimulate psychic vision. Make a tea out of the flowering tops and drink it to aid astral projection. Use dittany with frankincense for protection.

Elecampane
* Inula helenium
* Hardy in zones 5–8
* Beauty, communication, healing, joy, love, protection, and psychic powers

Elecampane is a bushy plant with large leaves and bright yellow flowers that bloom from July to October. It is a perennial wildflower in the aster family and is also known as horse-heal, elfwork, and elfdock. Elecampane has a long medical usage that can be traced back to ancient Greece, and now the flower is found naturalized across Europe, Asia, and North America, growing in fields and along roadsides.[207] Plant elecampane where it will have space to grow. It thrives in moist, well-draining soil in areas with full to part sun exposure.

Elecampane has a long history as a medical plant and all parts of the plant have medicinal applications. In the nineteenth century elecampane candy, made by boiling the root with water and sugar, was a lozenge eaten to treat asthma.[208] In Denmark elecampane was known as elfdock and was used to ward off afflictions caused

....

207. Foster and Johnson, *National Geographic Desk Reference to Nature's Medicine*, 140.

208. Grieve, *A Modern Herbal*, vol. 1, 279.

by being elf-shot.[209] In the past when someone suffered from an unexplained illness or sudden shooting pains, it was sometimes attributed to being "elf shot," or shot with an elf's arrow. Offer elecampane flowers to faeries, elementals, and nature spirits to open communications. Grow the plant in your garden to enhance communication with plant devas. Elecampane is associated with the sun, Mercury, Uranus, and Gemini. It holds a positive energy to open opportunities and attract love. Strew dried elecampane around a room or bed to draw positive energy. Crush dried elecampane with mistletoe and vervain to make a true love powder. Dust it over your body before an encounter to boost your charm. Roll candles in the herbal bits to empower love magic. Stuff elecampane, mistletoe, and vervain into a poppet to draw a love that is true. Burn elecampane as incense to ground energy and sharpen psychic powers.

Evening Primrose
* *Oenothera* spp.
* Hardy in zones 4–8 (depending on variety)
* Attraction, hunting rituals, and protection

Evening primrose is a wildflower native to North America. It was used as food and medicine by the Native American Blackfoot tribe. The New World settlers adopted evening primrose as a folk remedy for colds and coughs and named it *scabbish*.[210] It was taken to Europe, where it naturalized, and now it is found growing in many parts of the world. Many varieties of evening primrose are vigorous growers. Plant it in a sunny spot with well-draining soil, and if you are in its hardiness zone, this flower could become almost invasive.

Today evening primrose is best known for being a woman's herb used to relieve PMS symptoms and help treat eczema.[211] Evening primrose is associated with Venus, Freya, the Divine Feminine, Libra, and immortality. Magickally, it holds energy to

. . . .

209. Ruthie Hayes, "Elecampane Monograph," Eclectic School of Herbal Medicine, accessed January 5, 2022, https://www.eclecticschoolofherbalmedicine.com/elecampane-monograph/.

210. Nancy Burke, *The Modern Herbal Primer: A Simple Guide to the Magic and Medicine of 100 Healing Herbs* (Dublin: Yankee Publishing, 2000), 29.

211. Glenda Taylor, "Health Benefits of Evening Primrose Oil," *Facty Health*, last modified December 10, 2021, https://facty.com/lifestyle/wellness/health-benefits-of-evening-primrose-oil/.

gain what you desire. Tuck a dried primrose flower into your lover's pocket to keep their thoughts on you. Float primrose flowers on bathwater and soak in the bath to enhance inner beauty. Use primrose in magick to attract faeries. Tuck a handful of primrose flowers into your pocket to find your perfect job. Rub a flower on your pulse points before you go out on a quest to zero in on what you are looking for.

Feverfew

* *Tanacetum parthenium*
* Hardy in zones 5–9
* Anti-accident, cheer, headache, and protection
* Warning: This herb should not be used during pregnancy.

Feverfew is a perennial native to southeastern Europe but is now widespread across North America. It is a bushy plant with yellowish-green leaves that have a bitter citrus scent. It produces clusters of white flowers from July to September. Feverfew requires moist soil but does well in both sandy and clay soils. Sow the seeds directly into the soil after the last frost date. Plant in full sun or partial shade and keep the soil moist until seedlings have established. Water it regularly to keep soil evenly moist. Feverfew is not drought tolerant.

Today feverfew is known as a headache remedy. It was once used so widely it was described as the "aspirin of the eighteenth century," and "weed sandwiches" filled with feverfew leaves were eaten to help end migraines.[212] Feverfew has a calm, cheering energy. The leaves can be brewed into an infusion and the liquid drunk to relieve sadness, stress, and anxiety. Brew feverfew and lemongrass for delightful citrusy tea with energy to encourage wellness. Dry feverfew leaves and burn them with lavender or frankincense for a pleasantly scented incense with relaxing, anti-anxiety properties. Feverfew is an effective herb against enchantment. Stuff feverfew leaves into a pouch and wear when dealing with an old love to keep your thoughts clear and your feet on the right path. Wear feverfew leaves when dealing with anyone who is manipulative to avoid falling under their charm. Feverfew is also used to guard against accidents. If you suddenly seem to be having a lot of accidents, brew an

....

212. Smith, *Strangers in the Garden*, 21.

infusion of feverfew and add to your bathwater to break a hex. To guard against accidents while traveling, stuff a few feverfew leaves into a muslin bag with hyssop and rosemary and wear it under your clothing to avoid trouble.

Horehound

* *Marrubium vulgare*
* Hardy in zones 3–10
* Exorcism, healing, mental powers, protection, and unhexing
* Warning: Large doses may affect glucose levels, heart rhythm, and blood pressure. Avoid during pregnancy and while breastfeeding.

Horehound is a member of the mint family and also known as houndsbane. It is a bushy plant with crinkly gray-green leaves that have a musky scent. It is a hardy plant that does best in dry, neglected soil. Sow the seeds in spring in an area with full sun exposure and well-draining soil.

Horehound is associated with Mercury, Gemini, and the element air. It is a healing herb used to combat illness, boost psychic abilities, and break hexes. The wrinkled leaves are used to make cough syrup and hard candy lozenges. Sixteenth-century botanist and herbalist John Gerard wrote that horehound syrup was "a most singular remedy against the cough, and wheezing."[213] Horehound energy has stimulating properties. Brew an infusion and sip it to stimulate mental powers. Drink the infusion to sharpen psychic sight. Use the infusion to anoint your heart, your throat, your third eye, the inside of both your wrists, the center of your palm, and the bottom of your feet to balance energy and open creative channels. Brew a horehound infusion and add it to bathwater for a psychic reset. Brew horehound with a handful of ash leaves to activate healing energy. Add the infusion to bathwater and soak to fortify wellness. Horehound is also an herb for anti-magick. Add a horehound infusion to bathwater to break a hex. Use it as a hair rinse to get rid of a bad habit. Use the dried leaves in purification rituals or to banish unwanted energies. Strew them around thresholds to guard and ward. Add a horehound infusion to your washwater when you need to amp up your protection power.

. . . .
213. Gerard, *The Herball*, 563.

Hyssop

* *Hyssopus officinalis*
* Hardy in zones 4–9
* Healing, protection, psychic ability, and purification

Hyssop is a bushy evergreen herb with violet-blue flower spikes that bloom from June to September. It is a member of the mint family and, like mint, is easy to grow. In the spring sow hyssop seeds directly into well-draining soil in an area with full sun or part shade. Do not overwater. Hyssop prefers drier soils. Grow hyssop in patio pots or along a path for an aromatic border. Plant a border with hyssop, lavender, and rosemary for an aromatic planting that will attract pollinators and draw positive energy.

Hyssop is associated with Jupiter, Cancer, Sagittarius, and the element fire. It is a medicinal herb with sedating and antispasmodic properties. Hyssop has a wide range of uses, including treating colds and anxiety.[214] Hyssop tea is an infusion of hyssop leaves and flowers drunk to ease cold symptoms. Add a hyssop infusion to bathwater to relieve aches and pains. Dry hyssop flowers and add them to healing formulas to empower healing energy. Hyssop also holds energy for protection. Hang a bouquet on the front door to deflect unwanted energy from entering. Add an infusion of hyssop to washwater to cleanse a room of a negative emotion or dispel fear. Stuff a muslin bag with hyssop, feverfew, and rosemary and wear it to gain safety while traveling. Add dried hyssop to incense and burn to raise vibration. The rising smoke will evoke spiritual protection. Grow hyssop to guard against gossip, trespassers, and thieves. Plant hyssop on a grave to end a haunting.

....
214. Nancy Burke, *The Modern Herbal Primer*, 116.

Lemon Balm

* * Melissa officinalis
* * Hardy in zones 4–9
* * Friendship, happiness, healing, love, peace, and success
* * Warning: This herb should not be used during pregnancy.

Lemon balm is a fragrant, easy-to-grow, lemony herb that is a member of the mint family. It is also known as sweet Melissa and bee balm as it is a bee favorite. Lemon balm will grow in most soils, but it thrives when planted in rich soil in an area with full sun exposure. It will self-seed to the point of being invasive. Plant lemon balm in patio pots or herb plots. Water it throughout the growing season.

Lemon balm has soothing, anti-inflammatory, and antibacterial properties. Brew an infusion from fresh or dried leaves to console the melancholy or comfort the brokenhearted. The tea is calming. Sip to relieve anxiety, balance emotions, and improve outlook. Use a lemon balm infusion to treat sunburn and skin irritations. Brew up a batch of lemon balm syrup. Rinse ¾ cup of fresh lemon balm leaves and place them in a saucepan. Cover with water and simmer until the liquid is reduced by half. Strain out the herb. Pour the liquid into a jar and stir in ¼ cup of honey. Store the liquid in the refrigerator for up to a week. Take a spoonful whenever you feel sad or stressed. Add a spoon to your morning tea to improve your outlook. Lemon balm is associated with Diana, Jupiter, the moon, and the element water. It holds energy for attraction. Have a hot date? Fill a bath sachet with lemon balm leaves and rose petals. Toss the sachet into the bath and soak. Pour a drop of jasmine, rose, or vanilla essential oil into your palm and rub into your skin, and you will be ready to woo. Use lemon balm in formulas for love and friendship spells. Anoint a pink candle with oil and roll it in crumbled bits of dried lemon balm to inspire compassion and kindness. Burn it as incense to encourage patience. Stuff a sachet with dried lemon balm and hang it to inspire affection. Tuck a sprig of lemon balm into your left pocket to be lucky in love.

Lemongrass

* *Cymbopogon citratus*
* Hardy in zones 8–11
* Inspiration, mental clarity, psychic powers, and purification

Lemongrass is a frost-tender scented grass native to India. It grows in clumps. Plant lemongrass in an area with humus rich soil and full sun exposure. Water regularly to keep the soil evenly moist. Grow lemongrass in an herb bed, along walkways, or in borders. In colder zones grow lemongrass in patio pots and bring them inside to overwinter.

Lemongrass is a fragrant herb used in cooking. Cut through the bulbous lower leaf section to harvest. Lemongrass tea has a citrusy flavor and holds energy to lift and open. Drink it to refresh your outlook. Add an infusion to a footbath to restore energy and awaken the senses. Use it as a hair rinse to open communication channels or use it to fill a spray bottle for a refreshing spritz to inspire creativity. Spritz yourself before going out to brighten your outlook and boost allure. Burn lemongrass during ritual work to increase intuitive abilities. Lemongrass also holds energy to clear away the negative. Add an infusion of lemongrass to washwater and wipe down the threshold, doorways, and floors to cleanse an area of residual energy. To rid a room of a haunting or a hex, pour boiling water over a chopped burdock root, a sprig of rosemary, and a handful of lemongrass. Let steep for 9 minutes and strain. Add the infusion to your washwater and use it to rinse away the negative and raise vibration. Lemongrass is a Hoodoo herb used to inspire lust. Brew an infusion and sip it with your lover to heighten awareness of each other. Lemongrass oil is a traditional insect repellant used to repel mosquitoes and fleas.

Mugwort

* *Artemisia vulgaris*
* Hardy in zones 3–9
* Astral projection, clairvoyance, dreaming, psychic abilities, and spiritual protection
* Warning: This herb should not be used during pregnancy.

Mugwort is a tall herbaceous perennial also known as mother herb. It is a meadow and woodland plant that can grow up to five feet in height and has been known to be invasive in some areas. Plant or sow seeds directly into a bed with full sun or partial sun exposure with well-draining soil. Water to keep soil moist but not soggy.

Mugwort is associated with Artemis and the moon. It holds nourishing energy with properties to heal. Mugwort leaves are bruised and used as a poultice to treat poison oak and the aches and pains of rheumatism. Mugwort tea is drunk to open psychic abilities and stimulate lucid dreams. Drink a cup before meditation or divination to enhance clear-sightedness and deepen insight. Brew an infusion of mugwort and add it to bathwater to balance mood and embrace the mystical. Use it as a hand wash before reading the tarot. Rinse your third eye to unblock psychic channels. Wash your gazing ball in a mugwort infusion to strengthen visions. Stuff mugwort, chamomile, and agrimony into a dream pillow to induce a restful sleep. For prophetic dreams, stuff a dream pillow with mugwort, eyebright, lemongrass, rose petals, and yarrow. Grind dried mugwort with sandalwood and cinnamon and burn as incense to aid astral projection.

Mugwort is a traditional traveler's herb carried for protection. Before stepping out on a new path, bruise a leaf and rub it on the soles of your feet to avoid trouble, prevent fatigue, and keep from getting lost. Wear mugwort to deflect malevolent thoughts. Stuff a pouch with mugwort and wear it to guard against the evil eye. Tuck a sprig into your left pocket when going into an unpleasant situation. Brew an infusion and soak your feet after you return from a hostile encounter to remedy the negative exchange. Add an infusion of mugwort to your washwater and scrub down your front step to keep an unwanted visitor from returning. Toss a handful of mugwort into a fire after a negative encounter to counter negativity.

Patchouli

* *Pogostemon cablin*
* Hardy in zones 9–11
* Fertility, healing, love, luck, protection, reversals, and wealth

Patchouli is a species of bush in the mint family that produces a scented oil that is used to make perfumes, soaps, incense, and insect repellent. Patchouli is a warm-weather plant that thrives when planted in fertile, damp, but well-draining soil with full or partial sun exposure.

Patchouli is associated with Saturn, Earth, Scorpio, Aphrodite, Pan, and Osain. It holds energy to draw love, wealth, and passion. Wear as perfume to draw love. Add dried patchouli leaves to charms or incense to promote fertility. Crumble dried patchouli over the money in your wallet to ensure it returns to you. Anoint a green candle in oil and roll it in crumbled patchouli to empower prosperity spells. For a luck-drawing powder, grind 1 cinnamon stick with 1 spoonful of dried patchouli leaves and 1 vanilla bean pod that has been scraped of its seeds. Use the herbal blend to draw good luck, or dust it over your body when you need to boost your own. Use it to draw good luck, or dust it over your body when you need to boost your own. Patchouli also holds protective power to return negative energy to its source. Make a hex-breaking incense with a pinch of powdered myrrh, a pinch of powdered sandal-wood, and a pinch of crumbled patchouli leaves. Burn it on a charcoal disk to break a hex or return ill will.

Pennyroyal

* *Mentha pulegium*
* Hardy in zones 5–9
* Banishing, peace, protection, and storms
* Warning: This herb is toxic. Do not ingest.

Pennyroyal is an aromatic mint-like perennial native to Europe. It was cultivated as a garden ornamental and as a medicinal plant, and it escaped its gardens and rapidly naturalized in California, Oregon, and Washington. Pennyroyal is a low-creeping herb that thrives in damp soil. Plant it in borders or in walkways to fill in between the stones.

Pennyroyal is an herb of peace and protection associated with Venus and Demeter. Its energy will support work to clarify communications, aid negotiations, or facilitate a truce between quarreling parties. Wear a sprig of pennyroyal in your left pocket when going into negotiations to ensure a fair and positive resolution. Burn dried pennyroyal to inspire a compromise or defuse a hostile situation. Add pennyroyal to sachets to bring harmony to the home. Pennyroyal is a traveler's herb carried to ward against danger and tucked into shoes to avoid becoming weary. Because of its fragrant aroma, it has been employed through history as a strewing herb and an insect and rodent repellent. Its fragrant leaves made it a popular herb to crush and carry to ward off noxious odors. In Hoodoo pennyroyal is mixed with nettle and graveyard dirt to break a run of bad luck or end a curse. Pennyroyal is toxic and causes liver damage. In the past it was used to end unwanted pregnancies, a practice that sometimes also killed the mother.[215] Pennyroyal essential oil is poisonous. Please never ingest pennyroyal in any form.

Peppermint

* *Mentha ×piperita*
* Hardy in zones 5–10
* Healing, love, psychic powers, purification, and sleep
* Warning: This herb should not be used during pregnancy.

Peppermint is a hybrid cultivated from water mint and spearmint in the late 1600s.[216] It is now one of the most popular varieties of mint found in gardens the world over. Peppermint thrives in full sun when the soil is kept evenly moist. Like other mints, peppermint has a creeping habit and can quickly take over an area.

Peppermint is a festive herb prized for its refreshing taste and pleasant aroma. It holds a refreshing, uplifting energy and is associated with Venus, Zeus, Pluto, and the underworld. Peppermint tea grants energy and clarity of mind. Sip it to inspire

215. Barbara Pleasant, "What You Need to Know about Pennyroyal," *Mother Earth News*, September 3, 2020, https://www.motherearthnews.com/natural-health/herbal-remedies /pennyroyal-safety.

216. "Peppermint," *Encyclopedia.com*, last modified May 18, 2018, https://www.encyclopedia.com /plants-and-animals/plants/plants/peppermint.

creative thought and enhance psychic abilities. Brew an infusion and add it to bath-water to revive. Use a peppermint infusion as a hair rinse for a refreshing mental lift. Add it to a footbath to revive after an exhausting day. Like pepper, peppermint is good for inducing action. Add peppermint leaves to your wallet to attract money. Use it to empower health and money spells. Grow a bed of peppermint near the door to keep negative energy away. Add a peppermint infusion to a spray bottle and mist your place of business to attract customers. Crush the leaves and rub the oil over the threshold when selling your home to make a buyer feel welcome. Stuff a handful of peppermint leaves into your pocket to avoid being cursed. Protect your-self from the wrath of a jealous neighbor by mixing peppermint with equal parts cinnamon, galangal, rue, and vervain. Sprinkle the mixture across your windowsills and thresholds to repel negativity energy.

Rue

* *Ruta graveolens*
* Hardy in zones 2–9
* Exorcism, grace, hex breaking, protection, safe travel, and vision
* Warning: All parts of this plant are poisonous. This herb should not be used during pregnancy. May cause dermatitis.

Rue is a shrubby evergreen with small yellow flowers. It is native to southern Europe and is considered toxic to people and animals. Exposure to rue sometimes causes skin irritation that gets worse with sun exposure, so have care when handling. Rue is easy to grow from seed even in poor soil. It is drought tolerant and thrives when planted in well-draining soil with full sun exposure. Rue is a host plant for several types of butterflies.

Rue is associated with the sun, Mars, and Leo. It is often used in counter-magick to reverse hexes and counter curses. Plant rue along walkways and under windows to deter negative energy. Tuck a sprig into your pocket when you know you must face someone who is antagonistic to counter a psychic attack. Use rue with pars-ley to prevent a haunting. Protect your family from the wrath of a jealous neigh-bor with an infusion of equal parts of rue, cinnamon, galangal, peppermint, and vervain. Wash down thresholds and front steps or asperge rooms to neutralize the negativity energy. Add a rue infusion to a bucket of water and spit into it forcibly three times. Then carry the bucket out into your yard and toss the water out toward the troublemaker to neutralize the hostility and end the unwanted attention.

St. John's Wort
* *Hypericum perforatum*
* Hardy in zones 3–8
* Abundance, happiness, health, love, luck, protection, and strength
* Warning: May cause photosensitivity.

St. John's wort is a small herbaceous perennial native to Europe and Western Asia, but it was carried by settlers as a medicine plant and now grows across the world. St. John's wort is invasive in many areas and is considered harmful to livestock, as it causes animals to be highly sensitive to sunlight.[217] Plant it in containers or in restricted borders. It is hard to get rid of if you decide you don't want it in your garden.

St. John's wort has been revered for its medicinal properties since the Middle Ages, when it was used to dress cuts, burns, and sword wounds.[218] The herb was thought to be quite magickal, as Jekka McVicar writes in *Jekka's Medicinal Herbs*: "In England it cured mania, in Russia it gave protection against hydrophobia, and Brazilians knew it as an antidote to snakebite."[219] Today we know St. John's wort has astringent, antibacterial, and sedative properties, and we use it most often to treat headaches and mild depression.[220] St. John's wort holds a calming energy. Brew an infusion and add it to bathwater to revive a weary spirit or use it as a foot soak to relax and renew. Make a healing massage oil by stuffing a canning jar with St. John's wort flowers. Cover the flowers with olive oil and seal. Set the jar on a sunny shelf and let it macerate until the oil becomes a rich red, about 3 weeks. Strain out the herb and rub the oil into aching muscles and varicose veins. Smear across the

217. Kris Zouhar, "Hypericum perforatum," Fire Effects Information System, US Department of Agriculture, 2004, https://www.fs.fed.us/database/feis/plants/forb/hypper/all.html.

218. Kruger, *The Pocket Guide to Herbs*, 154.

219. McVicar, *Jekka's Medicinal Herbs*, n.p.

220. Ody, *The Complete Medicinal Herbal*, 63.

forehead to deepen spirituality during meditation. Use as a magickal oil to anoint candles to empower abundance spells. St. John's wort is associated with the sun, Leo, the element fire, and Midsummer. Magickally, it holds energy to heal, repel negativity, and attract abundance. Pick flowers and float them in a bowl to protect the home from lightning, fire, and malicious spirits. Plant St. John's wort with heather and marigolds to keep troubles away and encourage happiness and luck. St. John's wort is a protective herb hung to ward against faery mischief. Carry a sprig of St. John's wort to avoid falling under the enchantment of another. Tuck a sprig into your pocket when traveling or hiking to avoid losing your way.

Silverweed
* *Argentina anserina*, syn. *Potentilla anserina*
* Hardy in zones 4–8
* Faery attraction, love, moon magick, peace, and wisdom

Silverweed is a flowering perennial native throughout the temperate Northern Hemisphere also known as potentilla, goose grass, crampweed, and silver cinquefoil. Silverweed is one of the most common potentillas. Garden silverweed thrives when planted in an area with full sun exposure and fertile, well-draining soil. Water regularly to keep the soil evenly moist.

Silverweed is edible. The spring root was eaten raw, boiled, and roasted, having a flavor similar to parsnips. It was brewed into an infusion for menstrual cramps and gargled as mouthwash for teeth and gum problems.[221] Silverweed is one of the all-purpose magickal herbs, and, like its cousin cinquefoil, each leaflet holds a different power, one for wisdom, one for love, another for money, another for good health, and the last for power. Use an infusion of silverweed for house blessings. Use silverweed to restore peace between quarreling parties. Carry a sprig to quicken thought and gain eloquence. Lore holds that if you dig up the root on Midsummer Day before sunrise, it can be made into an amulet that will win the love of someone you desire. Silverweed is a faery favorite. It is associated with geese, the moon, Jupiter, and faeries. Add it to faery and moon gardens to attract nature spirits.

....
221. Reader's Digest, *Magic and Medicine of Plants*, 297.

Skullcap

* *Scutellaria lateriflora*
* Hardy in zones 5–8
* Fidelity, love, peace, and rest
* Warning: This herb should not be used during pregnancy.

Skullcap is a member of the mint family. It gets its name from its small, helmet-shaped flowers. It is also known as Quaker bonnet, mad-dog, and madweed, as it was once a treatment for rabies.[222] Skullcap is a mint and grows easily when the conditions are right. It does prefer damp soil, and the seeds need a chilling period to germinate. In areas with a cool spring, you can sow seeds directly into the soil. Rake the area to expose the soil and evenly distribute the seeds throughout the area, then cover them lightly with soil and gently water them in.

Skullcap is used to treat stress, anxiety, insomnia, and nervous disorders.[223] It has a gentle, calming, sedative energy that, when taken internally, soothes anxiety and lifts mood without decreasing energy. Drink an infusion of skullcap to relax. Sip an infusion to break habits, ease withdrawal symptoms, or gain the ability to be present in the moment. Drink a cup before bed to gain a peaceful rest and reduce nightmares. Make a dream tea by combining skullcap with hops, passionflower, and/or wild lettuce. Sip it before bed to inspire lucid dreams. Skullcap is associated with Mercury, the moon, Neptune, Pluto, Saturn, and Venus. It is used to bind oaths and consecrate vows. Drink an infusion to bolster resolve and keep your thoughts clear. Drink as a tonic to soothe the psyche and restore peace of mind. Use skullcap to restore strength to the overwhelmed. Skullcap is also an herb of love with energy to both woo your lover and keep your lover faithful. Sew dried skullcap leaves into the hem of your lover's coat to encourage fidelity and remain unaffected by another's charms. Tuck a few leaves into your left pocket when you need energy to avoid straying.

. . . .

222. Kruger, *The Pocket Guide to Herbs*, 160.

223. Rebecca L. Johnson et al., *National Geographic Guide to Medicinal Herbs* (Washington, DC: National Geographic Society, 2010), 45.

Soapwort

* *Saponaria officinalis*
* Hardy in zones 4–8
* Beauty, cleansing, glamour, and health
* Warning: This herb should not be used during pregnancy.

Soapwort, also known as bouncing Bet, wild sweet William, latherwort, and soap-weed, is a perennial in the carnation family Caryophyllaceae. It is a vigorous grower that needs little care. Soapwort thrives in full sun and is considered invasive in many regions. Plant it in well-draining soil. Soapwort flowers throughout the summer in attractive fragrant clusters that smell like cloves. Keep it away from ponds and streams, as the herb contains saponins that are toxic to fish.

Soapwort is a popular washing plant. The leaves, stem, and roots are rich in saponins that produce a foaming lather in water.[224] Colonists brought soapwort to the United States from Europe and used it to wash just about everything, while the Pennsylvania Dutch used it to give beer a foamy head.[225] To make your own liquid soapwort, bring 2 cups of spring water to a boil. Add 1 cup of bruised fresh leaves and simmer for 30 minutes. Remove the pot from heat and let cool. Strain and use the liquid as a gentle cleanser for skin and hair. Add a portion to beauty baths to empower energy. Infuse the liquid with chamomile flowers for a calming shampoo or lavender for a soothing bath. Soapwort is associated with Venus, Mars, Neptune, and the moon. Plant soapwort in a moon garden to add sweet fragrance and boost charm.

. . . .

224. US Forest Service, "Soaps," US Department of Agriculture, accessed September 1, 2021, https://www.fs.fed.us/wildflowers/ethnobotany/soaps.shtml.

225. Reader's Digest, *Magic and Medicine of Plants*, 118.

Sweet Woodruff

* *Galium odoratum*, syn. *Asperula odorata*
* Hardy in zones 4–8
* Balance, courage, justice, protection, strength, and wealth

Sweet woodruff is a hardy ground cover also known as scented bedstraw, wild baby's breath, and master of the woods. It is a shade-loving creeping perennial that spreads by runners and can be invasive. Its tiny white blossoms are vanilla scented. Plant sweet woodruff as ground cover in any shady garden bed. Water regularly until it is established.

Sweet woodruff was cultivated for its sweet-smelling foliage, which is faint upon harvesting but develops, as the herb dries, into a deeper, refreshing, newly mown hay scent, which it retains for years. Tie sprigs into bundles and place them in drawers or hang them in closets to scent cloth. In Germany a spring wine known as *Maibowle* is made by steeping fresh sprigs of woodruff in Rhine wine. It is the traditional May Day drink.[226] Make your own version by picking a handful of young sweet woodruff (the herb shouldn't be in bloom). Wash it thoroughly and place it in a bowl. Pour a bottle of sweet wine over it and stir in 2 tablespoons of sugar. Let the mixture stand for an hour. Strain and serve to lighten the heart and cheer the spirit. Magickally, sweet woodruff is known for restoring balance. Add a handful to a mojo bag to strengthen and fortify. The scent of woodruff brings clarity. Anoint a yellow candle with almond or sunflower oil. Roll it in crumbled woodruff and burn it when seeking information. Sprinkle a pinch of dried woodruff over a candle flame to conjure visions. Add an infusion of woodruff to bathwater and soak in it to find way through obstacles or gain wisdom to deal with adverse conditions. Make a sweet dreams pillow by stuffing it with a handful of dried woodruff, dried hops, and oakmoss. Tuck under your pillow to safeguard your dreams.

. . . .

226. "What Is May Wine?" EHL Insights, accessed September 1, 2021, https://hospitalityinsights .ehl.edu/may-wine.

Valerian

* *Valeriana officinalis*
* Hardy in zones 4–7
* Animal magick, charisma, harmony, love, protection, purification, sleep, strength, and valor
* Warning: Prolonged use may lead to addiction.

Valerian is a perennial flowering plant also known as all-heal and garden heliotrope. It is a tall, attractive plant with clusters of pale-pink or white flowers that bloom from June to September. Valerian will self-seed to the point of being invasive. It is native to Europe and Western Asia but has escaped gardens and naturalized across much of North America. Grow valerian in an area with full sun exposure. Water it regularly to maintain soil moisture.

Valerian is a cat favorite. The leaves, stems, flowers, and roots have a musky scent that some animals are attracted to. Lore tells that a piece of valerian in the Pied Piper's pocket might have contributed to his ability to lure rats away.[227] Anoint a yellow candle in sweet almond oil, roll it in crushed valerian bits, and burn it to enhance communication with your animal guides and familiar spirits. A tea made with valerian root is taken to ease tension, calm anxiety, and treat insomnia. Drink a cup before bed to relax and make sleep come quicker. Combine valerian with hops and lemon balm to fight insomnia. Mix valerian with skullcap to gain a deep and dreamless sleep. Valerian holds a calming energy. Use the fresh leaves and flowers in magick to instill harmony and end bickering. Add dried valerian root to formulas for peace. Valerian is associated with Jupiter, Mercury, Virgo, and Aquarius and also holds energy for protection. Hang a bundle of valerian above a door to keep out malicious spirits. Plant it along walkways to deter negative energy. Sprinkle dried valerian across a threshold to keep away intruders or deter unwanted guests. When traveling, tuck a piece of valerian root into your left pocket to avoid trouble.

. . . .

227. Jackie Johnson, "Getting to Know the Valerian Plant," The Herbal Academy, June 24, 2015, https://theherbalacademy.com/getting-to-know-the-valerian-plant/.

Vervain

* Verbena officinalis
* Hardy in zones 4–8
* Communication, health, love, money, peace, protection, purification, and sleep
* Warning: This herb should not be used during pregnancy. Do not give it to children or use it while breastfeeding.

Vervain is a perennial herb native to Europe but is now naturalized across North America. It is an attractive plant with delicate jagged leaves and clusters of delicate, small pink or purple flowers. It thrives in sunny areas with moist, lime-rich soils. Sow seeds in an area with full sun exposure and moist, well-draining soil. Plant in an herbaceous border or add it to a bee or butterfly garden.

Vervain tea is prescribed to relieve stress and treat insomnia, but it is not suitable for children and may cause addiction and miscarriage. Vervain tea is used to relieve symptoms of menopause.[228] Vervain energy is calming and purifying. It supports work for balance, clear communication, and dreamwork. Stuff a sachet with vervain, clover, roses, and rue and tuck it under a pillow to inspire prophetic dreams. Brew a vervain infusion and use as an aspersion to cleanse a ritual space. Vervain is associated with Virgo, Libra, Gemini, Jupiter, Venus, Cerridwen, Diana, Midsummer, and the underworld. The druids, Greeks, Romans, and Egyptians regarded vervain as a sacred plant and used it in religious rites and as an anti-magick herb.[229] Vervain was also used in love potions. Folkard writes that vervain was an herb of enchantment and that "by smearing the body over with the juice of this plant, the person would obtain whatever he set his heart upon, and be able to reconcile the most inveterate enemies, make friends with whom be pleased, and gain the affections."[230] In the language of flowers, vervain means enchantment. Place a sprig in your pocket or wear it in your hair to boost charisma and power of persuasion. Crush with dried

228. Christine Mikstas, "All About Herbal Tea," WebMD, January 28, 2020, https://www.webmd.com/food-recipes/ss/slideshow-herbal-tea.

229. Pam Shade, "The Supernatural Side of Plants," Cornell Botanic Gardens, October 27, 2020, https://cornellbotanicgardens.org/the-supernatural-side-of-plants/.

230. Folkard, Plant Lore, Legends, and Lyrics, 573.

elecampane and mistletoe to make a true love powder. Combine dried vervain with meadowsweet and mint to make an incense to instill harmony and draw happiness.

Vervain is also an herb of protection. Add an infusion of vervain to bathwater to rid yourself of negative energy. Use it in work to banish harmful habits and hurtful people from your life. Fill a pouch with vervain and carry it to ward off energy vampires. Bundle it with St. John's wort and hang it over your bed to repel malicious spirits and end nightmares. Grind dried vervain root and add it to protection sachets to amplify protection. Protect your family from the wrath of a jealous neighbor by mixing vervain with cinnamon, galangal, peppermint, and rue. Sprinkle the mixture across your threshold to neutralize the negative energy.

Witch Hazel

* *Hamamelis virginiana*
* Hardy in zones 3–9
* Balance, beauty, communication, dowsing, and protection
* Warning: This herb should not be used during pregnancy or while breastfeeding.

Witch hazel belongs to a genus of deciduous shrubs or small trees also known as winterbloom. It is an attractive bush with stringy yellow blossoms that bloom from October to December. Witch hazel adds dramatic color and fragrance to a winter garden. It grows well in sun or shade and requires little care. Plant it as an accent plant or include it in a border. Give witch hazel plenty of room to grow and water regularly its first year.

Witch hazel holds protective qualities. Carry a twig in your pocket when facing a jealous rival to avoid being hexed. Burn witch hazel to banish negative energy. Brew an infusion of witch hazel leaves and add it to bathwater to banish troubling emotions or break a hex. Add the infusion to washwater to deter negative energy. Witch hazel wood is associated with Saturn. It is a favored wood for diviners to find lost things. Witch hazel holds energy to heal and comfort. Break twigs into pieces and soak them in water overnight. Strain and add the water to bath magick to ease depression and comfort the grieving, or add it to a foot soak to revive the spirit after a difficult day. Rinse your forehead with a cloth that has been dipped in witch hazel water to heighten psychic powers.

Witch hazel extract is a natural astringent distilled from the roots, bark, and young stems. It is one of the few American medicinal plants still approved by the FDA to relieve minor skin irritations due to cuts, scrapes, and insect bites and relieve the pain and discomfort of varicose veins. Witch hazel has energy for beauty, and when used as a facial astringent, it will tone skin and heal the complexion. It makes an excellent aftershave lotion, as it soothes razor burn.

Wormwood

* *Artemisia absinthium*
* Hardy in zones 4–9
* Change, enhancing psychic ability, love, protection, uncrossing, and visions
* Warning: This plant is poisonous.

Wormwood is a species of *Artemisia* grown as an ornamental plant. It has attractive silver-gray foliage and a strong, sage-like scent. It will grow in most soil as long as it has good drainage. Wormwood is found growing on roadsides and in waste places. Transplant seedlings after the last frost into an area with full sun exposure and well-draining soil.

Wormwood is the notorious ingredient in absinthe. It contains the neurotoxin thujone, which can cause a state of psychosis when ingested. Wormwood was a strewing herb, as it is a bane to fleas. Make your own repellent by mixing equal parts of wormwood, lavender, and mint and stuffing into a mesh bag. Hang it in a closet or tuck it into a drawer to repel insects. Wormwood is associated with Diana, Artemis, Isis, Mars, Pluto, and the elements fire and air. It holds positive energy to clear away what has become stagnant. Burn wormwood to restore energy flow. Use wormwood flowers to empower a vision quest. Wormwood is used to inspire love magick and enhance psychic abilities. Crumble it with mugwort and burn as incense to improve all acts of divination. Burn wormwood with sandalwood to enhance visionary states. Burn with myrrh resin and dittany of Crete to enhance spirit communications. Make a Samhain incense with a mix of wormwood, marigold, and sunflower petals. Wormwood has energy for protection and can be used in spells to send hexes back to the sender. It will protect the traveler from accidents and, if hung from the rearview mirror, will aid in avoiding collisions.

SOME GARDEN
VEGETABLE FAVORITES

The home vegetable patch is gaining popularity once again as a new generation is discovering the miracle of planting seeds and minding young plants. Lawns are being converted into vegetable patches. Even those with small spaces are growing food in pots on patios, porches, balconies, and staircases.

Growing garden vegetables is an incredibly rewarding experience. To grow a plant that produces a food you can harvest and prepare for yourself or your family creates a bond with your land that grows with each moment you spend working with it. The act of gardening becomes a vehicle to rediscover awe and reclaim our relationship with the world as a whole. When we work with the earth, we reinforce our link to her as we become witness to the vastness and power of nature around us. Forging a relationship with a plant that we take under our care is a rich learning experience, and caring for a garden connects us to the traditions of our ancestors and the practices they performed for thousands of years, reaching back through time to grant knowledge that is being lost.

Favorite Garden Vegetables

Cucumber

* *Cucumis sativus*
* Grow in zones 4–11
* 55–65 days to harvest
* Beauty, fertility, healing, and refreshment

The cucumber is a creeping vine in the gourd family grown as a vegetable crop. It is a warm-weather plant and should not be planted out until soil temperatures reach 60 degrees Fahrenheit. You can extend their growing season by starting seeds indoors three weeks before your planting date. Cucumbers are sensitive to being replanted. In order to not injure the roots, start seeds in a container like a cardboard egg carton or a coir planter and plant, container and all, right into the soil. Harden the young plants off by setting them outside a few hours every day to acclimate them to being outside before transplanting. Cucumbers require full sun exposure and rich, well-draining soil. If you live in a hot climate, provide some afternoon shade. Amend the soil before planting by mixing three inches of compost into the top six inches of soil. If you live in a cool climate, add mulch around each plant to help heat the soil and retain moisture. Keep the bed weeded and watered so that the soil stays moist. If you have problems with insects, use a row cover to shelter new plantings and remove when the plants flower.

Cucumbers are native to Africa and made their way to Europe via the silk and spice route. By the second century BCE cucumbers had reached Italy, where they gained their name *Curvimur*.[231] Cucumbers have a cool, healing energy to refresh and restore. They are an age-old remedy, mixed with oatmeal and smeared on the skin, to treat skin conditions. In a food processor, whiz ½ cup of sliced cucumber with 2 tablespoons of uncooked oatmeal and a teaspoon of honey for a healing face mask paste. Spread it over your skin and wait 15 minutes before rinsing. Or drink your cucumber by whizzing a cucumber with ice and coconut water for a refreshing drink to inspire creativity and refresh thought. Cucumbers are rich in vitamins and minerals that nourish skin. They contain phytochemicals to improve skin tone

· · · · · · · · · · · · · · · · ·

231. Jack Staub, *The Illustrated Book of Edible Plants* (Layton, UT: Gibbs Smith Publishing, 2017), 59.

and reduce wrinkles and cellulite. Rub a slice over problem areas. Cucumbers are associated with the moon and the element water and hold a refreshing energy to bolster beauty and healing rituals. Whiz some cucumber slices in a food processor and smear the paste over your face and neck for a refreshing beauty treatment that makes the skin glow. Use cucumber in bath magick to relax, refresh, and bolster beauty. Place a slice over each eye and rest to reduce eye fatigue. Press a piece of cucumber peel to your forehead to relieve headache pain and inspire fresh thought.

Eggplant

* *Solanum melongena*
* Grow in zones 5–12
* 65–85 days to harvest
* Health, prosperity, and youth

The eggplant is a common fall vegetable also known as the aubergine. Eggplants are a warm-weather crop. If you live in a region with a cool spring, you can grow eggplant by starting seeds indoors eight weeks before your last frost date. Harden off the seedlings by setting them outside for a few hours each day before planting out. Eggplants love the sun and thrive in warm, dry weather. In order to fruit, they need to be planted in an area with at least seven hours of direct sun exposure and rich, well-draining, evenly watered soil. Transplant the seedlings into the garden in late May or early June after soil has warmed. If you live in an area where the nights are cool, try adding mulch around each plant to help heat the soil or grow in black plastic pots to hold the heat in. If you are planting seeds directly into the garden, amend the soil well by mixing three inches of compost into the top six inches of soil. Boost production with a weekly feeding of liquid fertilizer.

The eggplant was cultivated from a spiny plant with bitter fruit native to India. Because of its bitter flavor, and the fact that the eggplant is a nightshade, early varieties were treated with suspicion and thought to cause madness.[232] The eggplant is associated with Jupiter and the earth. It is loaded with vitamins and antioxidants, including chlorogenic acid and nasunin, strong free-radical scavengers that protect

. . . .

232. Staub, *The Illustrated Book of Edible Plants*, 64.

cell membranes from damage and protect against age-related diseases. Eat eggplant to promote health and youth. Slice an eggplant into planks and drizzle them with olive oil. Cook them in a skillet until they begin to brown, then serve to attract health and prosperity. Serve eggplant at the height of summer to activate energy for abundance. Add dried eggplant flowers to prosperity charms to boost the workings. The leaves of the eggplant are toxic to eat but can be used as a poultice to treat abscesses, burns, and cold sores.

Peppers

* *Capsicum annuum* and *C. frutescens*
* Grow in zones 4–11
* 65–100 days to harvest
* Creativity, energy, hex removal, love, and passion

Peppers love the sun. Most peppers are warm-weather plants and are hardy only in zones 10 and 11. In all other zones they are grown as annuals. Sweet peppers take sixty-five to ninety days to harvest, depending on the variety. Hot peppers can take up to 100 days to mature. To extend your growing season, start seeds indoors eight to ten weeks before your last frost date. Plant them out into the garden a week or two after the last frost. Peppers require at least seven hours of direct sun and rich, well-draining soil. Amend the soil before planting by mixing three inches of compost into the top six inches of soil. In cooler regions grow peppers in the hottest part of your garden or plant them in black pots to hold in the heat. In hot areas sweet peppers require shade from the afternoon summer sun. Water pepper plants regularly to keep the soil evenly moist. Provide the plants support as they grow. Feed your peppers weekly while they are producing fruit.

There are hundreds of varieties of peppers. They come in a wide range of shapes and sizes. Whether hot or sweet, all varieties—from the sweet bell to the spicy ancho, jalapeño, pasilla, serrano, chili de arbol, New Mexico chili, and the hot cayenne—fall the under the same botanical name, *Capsicum*. The bell pepper is the largest and sweetest. Though often sold green, the green bell pepper is not ripe and would turn red, orange, yellow, or even purple, depending on variety, if left to mature. Peppers are high in vitamin C and carotenoids to boost immune health and improve eyesight. Magickally, sweet peppers hold positive energy to boost health and maintain energy. Green peppers foster growth and prosperity. Red peppers boost vitality and strength. Yellow peppers inspire creativity. Slice a sweet pepper and serve with a dipping sauce for a healthy snack with energy to refresh and inspire. Hot peppers are associated with Mars and hold a motivating energy to warm or get things moving. Mix up a batch of fresh salsa and serve it with a quesadilla to inspire affection. Grind a dried hot pepper and add it to rituals to inspire action. Roll an oiled candle in the ground powder to heat or activate a spell with fiery energy. Add cayenne as an impetus to get an action moving.

Alliums

The Allium family includes chives, garlic, leeks, onions, scallions, and shallots. They grow from seeds and bulbs. Inside each bulb is an embryo plant. As the daylight hours increase, the embryo wakes and begins to sprout. It sends up a green shoot, and as the weather warms, the bulbs begin to swell. Some alliums clump, while others form a single bulb. All are rich in sulfur, which gives them their characteristic flavor, smell, and eye-irritating qualities as well as their many health benefits.

Chives

* Allium schoenoprasum
* Grow in zones 3–11
* 60 days to harvest
* Health and protection

Chives are the smallest of the edible onions. They are cool-season, cold-tolerant perennials in zones 3 to 10 and will return year after year in the spot they are planted. Chives produce beautiful edible stems and flowers. Plant them in early spring for a late spring and early summer harvest. Plant seeds in a garden pot or sow directly into the soil as soon as it is workable. Chives thrive in rich, moist, well-draining soil in a location with full sun exposure. Water regularly to keep the soil evenly moist.

When chives sprout, the tops can be clipped off and used to flavor food. They have a strong, pleasing flavor and are loaded with potassium, calcium, beta-carotene, folic acid, and vitamin K. Add chives to meals to protect your health. Sprinkle chives over scrambled eggs or serve with sour cream and a baked potato to boost flavor and improve well-being. Mix chives into softened butter or goat cheese and serve with crackers to safeguard words. Plant chives around your home to shield it from unwanted attention. Tie chives in bunches and hang them to ward off negative energy. Chives can be used in knot magick. Take a bunch of chives and braid them together as you visualize the problem being tied up with the chives. Tie the braid into a knot and bury it where it will not be disturbed.

Garlic

* *Allium sativum*
* Grow in zones 3–10
* 120–150 days to harvest
* Evil eye protection, fertility, health, protection, purification, strength, and warding

There are all kinds of garlic grown around the world. Find one suited to your grow zone. Garlic plants form a bulb made up of sections called cloves. Each clove contains an embryo plant inside waiting to come to life. Tuck a clove into a pot with the pointed side up, or set garlic cloves into soil six to eight weeks before the first frost date. Though garlic will tolerate shade, it loves the sun and will develop more bulbs if planted in a sunny location.

Garlic has been used for so long its origin is unknown. Its use is recorded as far back as 3000 BCE.[233] Garlic has been used to cure everything from bites of venomous beasts to colds and fevers. It is highly nutritious and contains allicin and sulfur-containing compounds that work together to boost the immune system and create a curative effect.[234] Add garlic to foods to combat colds and flu. Garlic lowers the risk of heart disease by lowering high blood pressure and high cholesterol.

. . . .

233. Ben-Erik van Wyk, *Food Plants of the World: An Illustrated Guide* (Portland, OR: Timber Press, 2006), 50.

234. Michał Majewski, "Allium sativum: Facts and Myths Regarding Human Health," *Roczniki Pantswowego Zakladu Higieny* 65, no. 1 (2014): 1–8, https://pubmed.ncbi.nlm.nih.gov /24964572/.

And recent studies are showing that the antioxidants contained in garlic help prevent Alzheimer's disease and dementia by repressing free radicals that contribute to the aging process.[235]

Garlic is associated with Mars and fire and holds magickal energy for protection. Through the ages, people have carried garlic to ward against all sorts of evils. Heads of garlic were strung and worn to repel everything from illness to vampires. Even the smaller bloodsuckers, mosquitoes, and ticks will avoid you when it is worn. Use garlic to ward your home and body of negative energy. Hang braids of garlic to guard against evil and deter thieves. When you cook with garlic, save the paper skins. Put them aside to burn in rituals for exorcism, repulsion of energy suckers, and purification of spaces and objects. If your luck turns bad, your health fails, or you suspect you may have been cursed by the evil eye, make a garlic infusion with 9 cloves of garlic boiled for 9 minutes in spring water. Strain and add to bathwater and soak. Carry a clove with you to shield you from someone's negative energy when you have to go up against them. Or as you set out, take 3 cloves of garlic and grind them into a paste. Rub the paste on the soles of your shoes, and on the front step of your home to keep the negative energy from following you home. Crumble garlic skins with bay leaves and burn to rid yourself or your house of negative influences. Bake up a batch of garlic and eat before any challenge. If you come upon a clove too small to use, don't throw it away, instead tuck it into a pot, pointed side up. The tiny clove will reward you with a new batch of bulbs. Many think that only the cloves are edible, but garlic shoots, or scapes, can be clipped in the spring and early summer to add a delicate garlicky flavor to savory dishes.

. . . .

235. Carmia Borek, "Garlic Reduces Dementia and Heart-Disease Risk," *Journal of Nutrition* 136, suppl. 3 (March 2006): 810S–812S, doi:10.1093/jn/136.3.810S; B. C. Mathew and R. S. Biju, "Neuroprotective Effects of Garlic: A Review," *Libyan Journal of Medicine* 3, no 1. (2008): 23–33, doi:10.4176/071110.

Green Onion
* *Allium* spp.
* Grow in zones 3–10
* 60 days to harvest
* Clear thinking, healing, and protection

Green onions are non-bulbing perennials that produce edible, bright green, round, hollow stems that can be cut and used year after year. Like other onions, they flower in summer, producing an attractive round blossom that attracts pollinators. Choose an area with rich, well-draining soil and sow seeds directly in. Amend your soil with compost and then make a furrow that is two inches wide and a quarter inch deep. Make the next row a quarter inch apart. Drop the seeds into the furrows, planting thinly. Cover with soil and carefully water in the seeds. Green onions have thin, short roots that require constant moisture. Be sure to water regularly to keep the soil from drying out. Green onions thrive in full sun but will tolerate partial shade and can be grown in patio pots for convenient accessibility. Clip the tops as you need them, leaving the roots to grow again.

Green onions are a good source of healing energy. Chop and use them to top soup, chili, and noodle bowls to enrich the flavor and boost the nurturing energy. Sprinkle them over a sour cream baked potato for a simple, hot nourishing meal with nurturing energy to comfort and protect. Add a green onion to a bowl of ramen to increase flavor and feelings of well-being. Like other onions, green onions hold energy to ward and protect. Grow a pot of green onions outside your kitchen door to ward the home of negative energy and encourage stability. Cut onion flowers and add them to a vase to help the mood of a room stay cheerful. Chew on a green onion when you need help holding your personal space. During the holidays, add green onions to vegetable boards and party trays to keep conversations from turning malicious. When hosting a dinner party, place a green onion on each plate to help everyone stay positive and keep conversation light.

Leek

* *Allium porrum*
* Grow in zones 3–9
* 130 days to harvest
* Exorcism, health, love, and protection

The leek is an elegant onion. It has a tender texture and a sweeter, creamier, more delicate flavor than most onions. Leeks are biennial, which means they will not produce a flower stalk until their second year. Leeks thrive in full sun but will tolerate partial shade. Sow the seeds directly into the soil as soon as it is workable or start them indoors and transplant seedlings after the last frost. Leeks have short roots and need constant moisture. Water regularly to keep the soil from drying out. If your leeks begin to fall over, you can mound soil around them as they grow to give them support.

Leeks are native to Eurasia and North Africa. They were used by the Sumerians, Greeks, and Egyptians and later introduced by the Romans to the British Isles.[236] Leeks have healing properties and, when eaten, protect the physical body from illness. They are high in antioxidants that repair damaged DNA, support bone health, and protect the eyes against age-related disorders.[237] Cook leeks and drizzle with olive oil and lemon juice to protect against sickness. Eat in moderation. Leeks are associated with Mars and the element fire. They hold energy to draw good luck and boost positive energy, and like other alliums, leeks contain bold protective powers. Grow a pot of leeks near the entrance of your home to discourage negativity and thwart psychic attacks. Hang items decorated in leek motifs to stand guard and protect. Boil leeks and mash with boiled potatoes. Dress the dish with butter and serve to fortify health or comfort a wounded spirit. Leeks are high in fiber and can cause stomachache.

. . . .

236. Van Wyk, *Food Plants of the World an Illustrated Guide*, 47.

237. Brunlida Nazario, ed., "Health Benefits of Leeks," Nourish, last modified September 16, 2020, https://www.webmd.com/diet/health-benefits-leeks#1.

Onion

* ⁎ Allium cepa
* ⁎ Grow in zones 3–9
* ⁎ 80–150 days to harvest
* ⁎ Banishing, healing, lust, money, oaths, prophetic dreams, and protection

You may think of onions in terms of color, but there are more than twenty varieties that can be started from seed or from an onion set. An onion will grow a green top in cool weather, but it is dependent on the length of daylight to form a bulb. Because of this light requirement, onions are classified in three categories: short-day onions, day-neutral onions, and long-day onions.

Short-day onions form bulbs with ten to twelve hours of daylight. Day-neutral onions form bulbs with twelve to fourteen hours of daylight, while long-day onions form bulbs with fourteen to sixteen hours of daylight. Short-day onions begin to develop bulbs when the day increases to a length of ten to twelve hours. They need a mild winter climate (zone 7 or warmer) and are planted in fall to mature the following spring. Day-neutral onions are planted in early spring in colder regions and in fall in warm regions. For long-day onions, bulbing is triggered after the summer equinox. In cold regions (zone 5 and colder) they are planted in early spring as soon as the ground is workable for a summer harvest. When you are considering which type of onion to plant, choose an onion that will grow well in your region.

Onions were one of the first cultivated crops. In his book *Alluring Lettuces*, food writer Jack Staub writes, "This popular early vegetable was cultivated in the gardens of the ancient kings of both Ur and Babylon as early as 2100 B.C., and appears in tomb paintings of both the Old and New Kingdoms of Egypt."[238] In Greece onions were served and eaten as an aphrodisiac.[239] Onions are loaded with flavorful volatile oils and sautéing one in butter is the first step in many modern recipes. Onions can be used in magick by color. Use a purple onion to enchant or seduce. Use a red onion to "sweeten" or promote lust. Use a white onion to cleanse or clear.

. . . .

238. Jack Staub, *Alluring Lettuces: And Other Seductive Vegetables for Your Garden* (Layton, UT: Gibbs Smith Publishing, 2005), 84.

239. Delphine Hirasuna, *Vegetables* (San Francisco, CA: Chronicle Books, 1985), 60.

Use a yellow onion to enhance communication or soothe angry feelings when friends are quarreling.

Onions hold energy for protection. They are used in spells to banish harmful energies and ward against hexes and hauntings. When harvesting, leave the tops and braid them for a talisman to hang in your kitchen. Set out an onion to absorb the negative energy of a previous occupant. Use an onion to remove resentment after a roommate moves out. Slice it into quarters and set a section in each corner of the room to absorb negativity. Burn onion skins to get rid of a hostile atmosphere after an argument. Mix with garlic skins to deflect malevolent words and jealous eyes. Make an onion talisman to ward your home with 1 small white onion and 9 black-headed pins. Stick the pins in the onion and place it in a window to stand guard against evil trying to enter.

Shallot

* *Allium cepa* var. *aggregatum*
* Grow in zones 3–10.
* 70–90 days to harvest
* Health, protection, and purification

The shallot is a small, elegant onion with a mild flavor. Shallots require a spot with full sun exposure and fertile, well-draining soil. Like onions, shallots are day-length sensitive and need fourteen to sixteen hours of daylight to produce a bulb. In places with mild weather, some varieties can be grown from seeds sown in the spring when the soil becomes workable to produce a fall crop. In cold zones, shallots can be started indoors and planted out as seedlings when the weather warms. If you live in zone 5 or warmer, you can plant bulbs in fall in well-draining soil for next year's crop.

Cooks have valued the shallot since biblical times. Though shallots have a milder flavor than other members of the onion family, they contain more flavonoids and phenols, which make them both flavorful and nutritious. Shallots can be harvested as you need them. At the end of the growing season when the tops have died back, lift the remaining crop, and spread the shallots out to dry in the sun before storing. Once the shallots have thoroughly dried, knock the dirt off and braid the tops together. Hang the braid in a cool, dry place.

The energy of the shallot is both cleansing and protective. If you find yourself stuck in a rut or caught in a loop of misfortune, brew a shallot infusion and add it to your bathwater. Soak in the water to change your luck. Slice a shallot and add it to salad dressing to guard your words when you want to keep your point of view private. Add a chopped shallot to lemon juice and olive oil and use to dress a salad to brighten energy and keep conversations light. The shallot has a paper skin that can be burned to remove negativity from your home. Mix with other allium skins to break a curse or remedy the evil eye. Burn skins with garlic to remove a hex. Make a batch of protective moon oil with a minced shallot mixed with crushed mustard seeds. Sprinkle with salt and place in a small jar of olive oil. Set the jar out to soak up the light of a full moon. Retrieve the jar before first light. Use the oil to ward a room. Dip your finger into the oil and trace over a threshold or pour oil into your palm and press your hand to the door to ward the entrance.

Beans and Peas

Legumes have been a staple food for thousands of years. They are nutritious, and dried legumes have a long shelf life, which makes them easy to store and easy to pack. They were carried by sailors, soldiers, and settlers, who added them to cooking pots to bolster nutrition and add protein when meat was scarce.

There are many types of peas and beans, many of which are purely ornamental. Most varieties are heat-loving plants that require sturdy support. Legumes are nitrogen-fixing crops and should be rotated. Legumes collect nitrogen from the atmosphere and store it in nodules on their root structure. After the plant is harvested, the roots remaining in the soil break down, releasing the stored nitrogen into the soil.[240] Some seed packs come with a small package of inoculant. This is a powdered form of bacteria or fungus that works symbiotically with the plant to boost its ability to fix nitrogen to its roots. Before you plant the seeds, open the package of inoculant and sprinkle it over the seeds in the packet. Fold the seed packet closed and shake. Now the seeds are ready to plant.

. . . .

240. "Green Manures," Royal Horticultural Society, accessed December 21, 2021, https://www
    .rhs.org.uk/advice/profile?PID=373.

Most legumes are tender plants that love the sun (except for the sweet pea, the fava, and the garbanzo bean). Cold weather will slow growth and frost is deadly. When purchasing seeds, look for a variety that will thrive in your grow zone. Also provide support according to variety needs. Most peas do well with the support of a trellis, while climbing beans do well with the support of a teepee made of branches.

Bush Beans and Pole Beans
* Phaseolus spp.
* Grow in zones 3–10
* 50–65 days to harvest
* Energy, inspiration, luck, and spirits

Bean is the common name for many varieties in the family Fabaceae. They are classed according to their growth habits. Bush beans include snap beans (whose pods are eaten) and shelling beans. They require less support but take up lots of room in the garden. Pole beans grow tall, some varieties upward of fifteen feet. They yield up to three times more than bush beans and need sturdy support, but since they grow vertically, they can be managed in smaller gardens. Many varieties need a long season of warm weather, so consider your climate when choosing a variety. Most beans are quick to grow. Plant bush beans two inches apart in rows that are one to two feet apart. Plant pole beans in hills that are a foot apart. Mound up the soil and plant six to seven beans in each hill. Gently water the beans in. Harvest the pods when they are full and swollen.

Cultures around the world considered beans to be a food of the dead. Beans were found at burial sites from Egypt to Peru, shares ethnobotanist Storl. It was customary for the Germanic, Celtic, Baltic, and Slavic peoples to offer beans, among other foods, to feed the spirits.[241] Leave a handful on the hearth or throw some around the outside of the home to keep a troubled spirit from bothering you. Beans also hold energy for protection and can be used to thwart a ghost. Drop a handful into your pocket before you go somewhere scary. If you meet a spirit, you can deter it by tossing the beans in its direction. Keep a bowl of beans on your desk to distract the

....

241. Storl, *A Curious History of Vegetables*, 37.

attention of an energy vampire. Add beans to recipes to increase psychic vision. Eat bean dishes to renew energy or increase luck. Bean energy fuels creativity and stimulates communication. Eat a bowl of beans to encourage inspiration. Serve beans on threshold days, such as New Year's or the solstices, to inspire good fortune. Add them to soups to attract good fortune and encourage expansion.

Green Bean

* *Phaseolus vulgaris*
* Grow in zones 3–10
* 50–60 days to harvest
* Abundance, fertility, health, luck, and money

The green bean is a tender annual that produces a slender bean with an edible pod. The green bean is also known as the French bean, snap bean, and string bean. Green beans are one of my all-time garden favorites. They are easy to grow, and a single bush can produce pounds of beans throughout the season. Green bean plants come in bush varieties that grow as low bushes or pole varieties that grow into long vines. And they aren't just green but come in different colors, such as purple and yellow. There are even some varieties that are covered in flecks.

Green beans take up a lot of room to grow. The amount of room you need depends on the variety. Plant beans directly into soil after the last frost when the soil has become workable. Green beans do not like to have their roots disturbed, so if you are starting the seeds indoors, start them in a medium that can be buried. Plant them outside before they become unmanageable. Provide support as needed by each variety. Water regularly to keep the soil moist. Beans will not produce if the soil dries out. After about eight weeks the immature beans are ready to pick. Snip them off with scissors. Pick regularly to encourage the plant to produce more.

The green bean, unlike its European cousin the broad or fava bean (*Vicia faba*), is native to the Americas. It wasn't until the sixteenth century that green beans journeyed with Spanish explorers and were introduced to Europe.[242] Green beans are harvested when they are immature and still tender. They should have a firm texture

....

242. Staub, *The Illustrated Book of Edible Plants*, 20.

and snap when broken. While old-fashioned types have strings, most modern varieties are stringless pods that do not need to be pulled off before eating. Young, tender green beans are rich in vitamins A, C, and K. They are a good source of dietary fiber, folate, and silicon for healthy bones, skin, and hair. Add them to your diet to improve health and vigor. Grow green beans in your garden to draw prosperity to the home. Green beans hold life energy. Add them to meals to improve well-being. Serve green beans to friends and family to attract abundance and keep the feelings friendly. Add green beans to meals to open to a new way of doing things. Serve green beans at family gatherings to usher in abundance and cultivate a festive mood.

Pea

* *Pisum sativum*
* Zones 3–10
* 58–65 days to harvest
* Ancestors, divination, faery plant, love, and money

Peas are one of the first crops planted in spring. They grow up a support using tendrils to grab and climb. Plant pea seeds in an area with full sun exposure as soon as spring arrives. They like cool weather and need to be able to finish producing before it turns hot. In hot areas peas are grown in partial shade or planted as a winter crop. Amend the soil with lots of organic matter before planting so that the soil will retain moisture. Peas will stop producing if the soil dries out. Provide support for the vines to grow up. When planted in early spring, the pea offers one of the garden's first fruits ready for harvest.

Peas were one of the foods domesticated by Neolithic peoples.[243] They have been cultivated for at least 7,000 years. In the past they were eaten dried as a staple food and carried on ship voyages.[244] Today there are three common types of peas: shelling peas, snow peas, and sugar snaps. The shelling pea, also known as the English pea and

. . . .

243. "Neolithic Revolution," History.com, last modified August 23, 2019, https://www.history .com/topics/pre-history/neolithic-revolution.

244. Hirasuna, *Vegetables*, 61.

the garden pea, is harvested by splitting the pod and removing the pea. The inedible pods are discarded. Snow peas and sugar snaps have edible pods that are eaten whole.

The pea is a faery plant. It is always a good practice to leave the last pods on the plant for the devic energies. Pea porridge, a thick soup made with peas, onion, and bacon, is a traditional European dish left in offering to household spirits on Christmas Eve.[245] Peas hold energy for luck in love and finances and, like beans, aid in communication and inspire creativity. They can be eaten raw to encourage inspiration. Pick a pod and snap it open. Eat the peas one at a time while you muse the solution to a problem. Pick garden peas and shell by hand to increase financial opportunities. Give fresh unshelled peas to a neighbor to share your garden bounty and encourage a generous spirit.

Lettuce, Spinach, and Other Greens

Most greens are quick-growing cold-season annuals that are ready to harvest in just a few weeks. Growing your own salad greens for the family table is not only convenient, but it also gives the cook a source of fresh leaves that are far superior to the wilted supermarket variety to harvest whenever the need arises. Many loose-leaf varieties are cut-and-come-again crops, which means the leaves are snipped off as they are needed and the plant is left to grow.

Slugs and snails are the biggest threat to a healthy, edible lettuce crop. Pick them off as you spot them. Set out a shallow dish filled with beer to trap them in. Grow your lettuce crops in raised beds to help remedy the problem. If aphids and gnats pose a problem, make a soap shield. Fill a spray bottle with 2 tablespoons of dish soap and 2 cups of water. Spray your plants with the solution, which will dehydrate the insects.

In many regions a lettuce crop can be planted in spring and fall, allowing access to fresh lettuce throughout the growing season. For a spring crop sow seeds two weeks before the last frost. For a fall crop sow seeds eight weeks before the fall frost. Most lettuce varieties germinate when soil temperature reaches 55 degrees Fahrenheit, so if you have a cold frame, you can extend the growing season even longer.

. . . .
245. Storl, *A Curious History of Vegetables*, 194.

Lettuce

* *Lactuca sativa*
* Grow in zones 3–10
* 45 days to harvest
* Chastity, fertility, luck, money, peace, rest, and wealth

Lettuce is a common name for cultivars of *Lactuca sativa*. Today lettuce is divided into four categories: romaine, crisphead, butterhead, and loose-leaf. Iceberg is a popular crisphead lettuce. Bib and Boston are popular butterhead varieties. Loose-leaf lettuce is a favorite among gardeners because it's easy to grow and it has a mild, delicate flavor. Green leaf, oak leaf, and red leaf are popular loose-leaf varieties.

Lettuce is a cool-weather crop best grown as a spring or fall crop in most zones. The young lettuce plants need a sunny spot with rich, moist soil. Amend the soil well with compost before planting. Dig a furrow a quarter inch deep and plant seeds in a row. Cover and carefully water in the seeds. Keep the plants well watered, and as the weather warms, add mulch to help the soil retain moisture. Lettuce plants like the sun but will bolt in the heat, which means that if they get hot, they will stop producing leaves and send all their energy into producing a flower stock that will seed. When lettuce bolts it often turns bitter. One way to manage this problem is to plant lettuce crops north of a tall crop like peas or pole beans, then the young lettuce plants can have cool-season sun but will be shaded by the growing pea or bean plants as the weather warms.

Lettuce was first cultivated in 4000 BCE by ancient Sumerians, who grew it in irrigated beds.[246] The milky juice contains a mild sedative called lactucarium, which induces calm and sleep.[247] Eat lettuce before bed to treat anxiety and insomnia or aid in dreamwork. Lettuce is good for you. It possesses anti-inflammatory properties that help control inflammation and is a rich source of antioxidants that slow the aging process. Lettuce is associated with Jupiter, the element water, and the moon, and it holds a cooling energy to endow health, peace, and prosperity. Add lettuce to

. . . .

246. DK, *The Story of Food: An Illustrated History of Everything We Eat* (New York: DK Publishing, 2018), 50.

247. Hirasuna, *Vegetables*, 57.

meals to fortify health and inspire fresh ideas. Combine with watercress for a healthy serving of protection. Serve a salad of mixed greens at any meeting to stimulate positive energy for abundance. Serve salad at a friendly brunch to inspire calmness and instill a good mood.

Spinach

* *Spinacia oleracea*
* Grow in zones 3–10
* 45 days to harvest
* Clear sight, health, longevity, money, strength, and vitality

Spinach is an edible flowering plant in the Amaranthaceae family. It is a valuable cut-and-come-again crop and in many regions can be grown all year, except during the heat of summer, when the heat will cause it to bolt and go to seed. Spinach that has bolted becomes bitter. In the spring, choose a location with full sun exposure. Amend the soil well and sow seeds directly into the garden bed. Water well throughout the season and provide shade when the weather warms. Spinach is quick to grow and will grow continuously when planted in full sun where the nights are cool and water is plentiful. The leaves can be harvested in as little as six weeks. Cut the older, outer leaves and leave the young, small leaves to continue growing for a later harvest.

Spinach was one of the traditional "seven greens" gathered and eaten as a spring blood cleanser.[248] It is loaded with nutrients and, when included in a diet, improves health and vitality and sharpens the ability to think clearly. Spinach is loaded with vitamin K, B_9, lutein, and beta-carotene, which slows cognitive decline. A study by the Federation of American Societies for Experimental Biology suggested that eating a serving twice a day improves brain health and keeps brain function sharp.[249] Add spinach to your diet to help protect your brain from Alzheimer's disease, increase health, and boost physical strength. Magickally, spinach is associated with Jupiter and Mars, and like other greens, spinach has properties for money and growth.

....

248. Storl, *A Curious History of Vegetables*, 252.

249. Federation of American Societies for Experimental Biology, "Eating Green Leafy Vegetables Keeps Mental Abilities Sharp," Science Daily, March 32, 2015, https://www.sciencedaily.com/releases/2015/03/150330112227.htm.

Eat spinach to gain strength and courage. Add to meals when clear sight is needed. Sauté older leaves and add to an egg scramble to inspire creative thought. Whiz young leaves in a blender with ice and coconut water for a frosty drink with energy to open the mind.

Other Cole Crops

Cole crops are hardy cool-weather vegetables that include broccoli, brussels sprouts, cabbage, cauliflower, kale, mustard, Swiss chard, and turnips. These plants, also known as brassicas or cruciferous vegetables, are descendants of wild cabbages native to the Mediterranean and Asia Minor area. Cole crops do best when daytime temperatures are below 68 degrees Fahrenheit and the weather is damp. They can withstand light frosts without injury, and some even develop better flavor after a frost. In zones 7 through 11 broccoli, brussels sprouts, and kale can be planted in the late summer for a winter crop.

Cole crops are susceptible to mildew and other fungal diseases. Make sure the soil is amended to provide good drainage. Immediately remove any leaves that are affected and dispose of them. Do not contaminate your mulch or compost. Treat infected plants with an organic sulfur powder.

Broccoli

* *Brassica oleracea* var. *italica*
* Grow in zones 3–10
* 70–90 days to harvest
* Health, power, prosperity, and protection

Broccoli is a plant with a stalk and a large flowering head that is eaten as a vegetable. It is a cool-season crop planted in both spring and fall. Plant it when the weather will be cool as it matures. Plant seeds in rich soil that is well amended with organic matter. For a spring crop start seeds indoors five weeks before the last frost date and plant seedlings two weeks before the last frost. For a fall crop sow seeds at midsummer. Water well and do not allow the soil to dry out. Harvest the heads when the buds develop, before the flowers open.

Broccoli originated in the Mediterranean, where it has been grown for two thousand years. The Italians embraced it and named it "little sprouts," but it didn't become a mainstream vegetable until 1920 when the D'Arrigo brothers, California farmers, introduced the vegetable to the Boston market.[250] Broccoli holds energy to promote good health and protect against illness. Eat raw broccoli to protect your health and boost your mind powers. Make a comforting casserole out of steamed broccoli and cauliflower. Season with horseradish to revitalize energy and fortify health during flu and cold season. Add broccoli to a stir-fry to boost the food's ability to energize. Broccoli is associated with Jupiter, the moon, and the element water.

Brussels Sprout
* *Brassica oleracea* var. *gemmifera*
* Grow in zones 3–9
* 100 days to harvest
* Endurance, protection, and stability

Brussels sprouts look like small cabbages that grow along a stalk. They were cultivated from cabbage in Belgium in the thirteenth century.[251] Start seeds indoors in February or March. Plant seedlings out in April or May for a summer harvest. Brussels sprouts prefer cooler temperatures, so if your summers are hot, plant them with other summer crops that will partially shade them or grow them in an area with afternoon shade. Work compost into the top four inches to make the soil rich and water regularly throughout the season to keep the soil from drying out. If you live in a zone with mild winters, sow seeds in late summer or fall for a winter harvest. Brussels sprouts picked fresh from the garden have a mild, sweet, almost nutty flavor. Harvest as needed, leaving the rest on the stalk. A light frost will improve their flavor.

Drizzle the sprouts with olive oil and roast until tender for a treat with energy to awaken awareness and sharpen concentration. Top them with parmesan and serve to family members to instill health and harmony. Or roast them with carrots and

....

250. Hirasuna, *Vegetables*, 44.

251. DK, *The Story of Food*, 47.

potatoes and smash to make a delicious and hearty dish to enhance your health, endurance, and tenacity. Brussels sprouts are good for you. They are members of the cabbage family, and like the cabbage, they hold the power of protection. They contain glycosinolate glucobrassicin, a "compound that may help prevent damage to your DNA," and carotenoids to fortify eye health.[252] Add brussels sprouts to meals to fortify health. Shred raw brussels sprouts with carrots and cabbage to make a slaw that will power your day and wake your mind. Brussels sprouts are associated with the moon and the element water.

Cabbage

* Brassica oleracea
* Grow in zones 3–12
* 65 days to harvest
* Healing, health, luck, and protection

Cabbage is a cold-weather garden plant. It thrives in cool, moist northern climates and can become stressed when temperatures reach above 80 degrees Fahrenheit. Cabbage is easy to grow if you live in a region with a long, cool growing season. Cabbage is a heavy feeder. Amend the soil with lots of compost. Work it into the top seven to eight inches of soil. Sow seed outdoors in spring when the soil becomes workable, or start seeds indoors four to six weeks before the last frost date and transplants seedlings when they have grown to be three to four inches tall. In regions with cool summers cabbage can be planted in late spring for a fall harvest. Succession gardeners will plant cabbage for a winter harvest in the pea plot after the peas have finished producing and are cleared.

Cabbage is a food that sustained the peasant classes across Europe through the winter.[253] It is an excellent source of vitamin K, vitamin C, and fiber. In earlier times it was eaten fresh and made into sauerkraut to remedy scurvy during the winter.[254]

. . . .

252. Stephanie Booth, "Health Benefits of Brussels Sprouts," WebMD, last modified August 18, 2019, https://www.webmd.com/food-recipes/health-benefits-brussels-sprouts#1.

253. DK, *The Story of Food*, 46.

254. Storl, *A Curious History of Vegetables*, 59.

The American Cancer Society recommends eating cabbage for its glucosinolates, which stimulate the production of detoxifying enzymes that remove carcinogens.[255] Chop and add it to salads or soup to add healing energy. Fresh cabbage leaves were bruised with rolling pins and used to treat abscesses, abrasions, burns, gout, and tumors.[256] Today we know that cabbage contains antibacterial properties that help discourage infection.[257] Bruise a leaf and apply it to skin to stimulate the healing. Cabbage also holds energy for protection. Tuck a cabbage leaf under your hat to break a spell of bad luck. Tuck a cabbage leaf into your left pocket before facing a tricky situation. Cabbage is associated with the moon and the element water and holds energy to stimulate intuition. Eat it before bed to help fix your sleep cycle or gain protection from nightmares. Use green cabbage in money-drawing food magick.

Cauliflower

* *Brassica oleracea* var. *botrytis*
* Grow in zones 2–11
* 52–65 days to harvest
* Health, nurturing, and protection

Cauliflower is a close cousin to broccoli. It thrives when planted in an area with full sun exposure and rich, fertile soil. Amend the soil well with compost before planting. Plant out seedlings two inches apart. Spring crops should be planted in March or April. Overwintering crops should be planted in July or August. In the summer the heads are "blanched," or wrapped with outer leaves to keep them shaded while they are forming. This allows the best flavor and color to develop. To do this, tie the outer leaves up and around the forming heads or break off a few and lay them over top of the heads when they begin to form.

Cauliflower is an autumn food loaded with vitamins and antioxidants to nourish and repair your body at a cellular level. It has anti-inflammatory properties and

....

255. Hirasuna, *Vegetables*, 45.

256. Storl, *A Curious History of Vegetables*, 59.

257. DK, *The Story of Food*, 46.

contains glucosinolates, sulfur-rich compounds that may stop inflammation and boost immunity.[258] Cauliflower is a cultivar of the species *Brassica oleracea*. Members of the Brassicaceae family are also called cruciferous vegetables, from the Latin *cruciferae*, or "cross-bearing," as the shape of the four-petal flowers is thought to resemble a cross. The cauliflower has a protective, nurturing, feminine energy that will guard against illness when eaten. Toss it with olive oil and roast to bring out its creamy-sweet flavor. Roast cauliflower and puree with broth for a luxurious, creamy soup that will heighten intuition and balance emotions. Steam cauliflower and broccoli and top with a horseradish sauce to double the protective energy during the cold and flu season. Cauliflower is associated with the moon, Cancer, and water.

Kale

* *Brassica oleracea* var. *acephala*
* Grow in all zones
* 60 days to harvest
* Clear thought, energy, expansion, happiness, health, mood enhancer, and sight

Kale is a nutrient-dense green leafy cruciferous vegetable. It is easy to grow from seed. If you live in an area with a long growing season, you can sow seeds into the soil when the ground is workable. In areas with a short growing season, start seeds indoors in March. Harden off seedlings before planting by setting them outdoors for a few hours each day for a week to acclimate them to the change before planting. Transplant seedlings into the garden two weeks before the last frost date. For a fall crop sow seeds in July. Kale is heat sensitive, so be sure to provide shade or plant it in the shade of taller summer crops. Water regularly to keep the soil evenly moist throughout the growing season. Kale is a cut-and-come-again crop that will produce a continual harvest. Harvest the tender, young leaves while leaving the central portion to produce more. Keep the plant healthy by removing dead leaves. Like brussels sprouts, kale becomes sweeter after the first frost.

. . . .

258. Christine Mikstas, "Cauliflower: Your Kitchen Chameleon," WebMD, April 17, 2021, https://www.webmd.com/food-recipes/ss/slideshow-cauliflower-new-kale.

Exactly when people began to grow kale in their gardens is not known, but recipes that include kale, along with cabbage and turnips, were recorded in the oldest medieval Italian manuscripts dating back to the 1400s.[259] Kale is packed with vitamins, minerals, fiber, and protein. It is a source of easily digested calcium. It is loaded with phytonutrients, including powerful anti-inflammatory molecules that improve liver function and protect brain cells. Whiz kale in a blender with ice and coconut water for a refreshing green drink to enhance performance. Drink it whenever you need a mental boost. Eat young raw kale leaves to gain strength and courage. Add young kale leaves to salads with beets and feta to improve clear sight. Eat kale before any meeting for a quick wit and focused mind.

Swiss Chard

* *Beta vulgaris* var. *cicla*
* Grow in zones 2–10
* 60 days to harvest
* Anti-aging, beauty, health, and vitality

Swiss chard is a green known for its fleshy leaves and colorful stems that grow in shades of white, crimson, gold, and pink. Though chard is a cool-season crop, it is much more tolerant of heat than other greens, which makes it a wonderful plant for the home garden. Spring crops can be planted two to three weeks before the last spring frost date. In early spring sow seeds in a spot with full sun exposure as soon as the ground can be worked. For a fall crop sow seeds forty days before the first fall frost date. Water regularly. Chard likes water and needs a good soaking when the weather turns hot. Chard grows well in containers. It is one of the cut-and-come-again crops. Pick the leaves as you need them and leave the central portion of the plant to continue growing for a later harvest.

. . . .

259. Ariane Helou, trans., "An Anonymous Tuscan Cookery Book," *Ariane Nada Hedou* (blog), June 26, 2013, https://arianehelou.com/2013/06/26/an-anonymous-tuscan-cookery-book/. The *Anonimo Toscano* is a fourteenth-century manuscript written by an anonymous Tuscan. It contains 183 recipes from the Middle Ages. It was first published in Bologna in 1863 and is now kept in the Bologna University Library.

Swiss chard is also known as silver beet. Contrary to its name, Swiss chard is not native to Switzerland but originated in the Mediterranean. It was named by a Swiss botanist who named it after the artichoke, or *cardoon*, and added the name *Swiss* to honor his homeland and distinguish the vegetable from spinach.[260] The young leaves are eaten for salads, while mature leaves are steamed or sautéed. They are loaded with vitamin K. One cup contains three times your daily requirements. Chard is also packed with vitamins A, C, and E. It is high in fiber and contains riboflavin and B_6. It is a good source of manganese, magnesium, potassium, and iron. Add it to meals to prevent premature aging, anemia, and sickness. Chard is also high in beta-carotene to protect the skin. It fortifies eye health, helps reduce blood pressure, and helps prevent heart disease and cancer. Consuming chard can hasten recovery after a rigorous physical workout. Whiz it in a blender with ice and coconut water for a refreshing green drink to enhance athletic performance. Add young leaves to salads before job hunting to instill positive energy and revitalized mindset. Chop chard and add to stir-fries to boost nutrients and power to fortify and heal.

Melons

Seventeenth-century diarist and gardener John Evelyn praises melons in his book *Acetaria: A Discourse of Sallets*: "Melon, *Melo*; to have been reckon'd rather among *Fruits* and tho' an usual Ingredient in our *Sallet*, yet for its transcendent Delicacy and Flavour, cooling and exhilarating Nature, (if sweet, dry, weighty, and well-fed) not only superior to the *Gourd*-kind, but Paragon, with the noblest Productions of the Garden."[261] Melons with their sweet, bright flavor are a luscious summer treat. They reflect all the goodness of summer and inspire fondness and happiness. They add sweetness to any gathering.

There are many types of melons, but they are all warm-weather plants that require lots of sun and warm soil. If you live in a cool zone like I do, you should seek out a short-seasoned variety that will fruit in your garden. Melons require warmth

---

260. Staub, *Alluring Lettuces*, 56; Jaime McLeod, "What the Heck Is Chard?," *Farmer's Almanac*, last modified October 8, 2021, https://www.farmersalmanac.com/what-the-heck-is-chard-12445.

261. John Evelyn, *Acetaria: A Discourse of Sallets*, 2nd ed. (London, 1706), 155.

and should be planted in the hottest section of your garden. Provide lots of room, as they tend to sprawl and require a large area to grow. Seeds can be started indoors a month before the last frost date to extend the growing season. Amend your soil with compost. Melons need a continuous supply of water. Water regularly to keep the top four inches of the soil moist or the plants will wilt. Mulch well with a layer of compost to help retain soil moisture.

Cantaloupe

* *Cucumis melo* var. *cantalupo*
* Grow in zones 5–11
* 90 days to harvest
* Beauty, beginnings, healing, love, and refreshment

The cantaloupe is an orange-fleshed melon that grows on a vine. It is a popular summer fruit loved for its sweet, cool flavor. Cantaloupes need a long, warm summer to grow and fruit. If you live in a colder area, try starting seeds indoors three weeks before the last frost date. Melons do not like to have their roots disturbed, so be sure to use planting pots made out of cardboard or coir that can be planted directly into the ground. Wait until the soil warms to plant the seedlings. Do not plant outside too early. A cool night will cause a melon plant to become dormant, making it susceptible to fungal, slug, and insect attack. To sow seeds directly into the garden, choose a warm spot with full sun exposure. Amend the soil well with compost, then mound the earth up into a row of small hills. Plant several seeds or seedlings into each mound. Weed and water regularly to keep the soil from drying out.

Cantaloupes are native to Persia.[262] They belong to the muskmelon family, which includes casaba, crenshaw, and honeydew melons. Columbus brought them to the New World, and they were grown all along the Eastern coast by the seventeenth century.[263] Cantaloupes are associated with the sea, summer, the element water, and

. . . .

262. "Main Plant Entry for Cantaloupes (*Cucumis melo*)," Plants Database, National Gardening Association, accessed September 1, 2021, https://garden.org/plants/view/87175 /Cantaloupes-Cucumis-melo/.

263. D. Cameron Lawrence, "Savoring the Melon Season," NPR, June 18, 2008, https://www.npr .org/templates/story/story.php?storyId=91555071.

the moon. They contain vitamins and minerals to fortify health and beauty. Include cantaloupe chunks in summer fruit salads to boost nutrients and hydrate cells. Whiz cantaloupe in a blender with ice and coconut water for a quick pick-me-up that will restore energy and revitalize spirit. Whiz cantaloupe chunks with a spoonful of plain yogurt for a refreshing face mask that will help soften and hydrate skin cells. Spoon out cantaloupe and watermelon into balls to make a summer salad. Add mint leaves to infuse it with energy to open to new possibilities. Use cantaloupe in recipes to heal and grow.

Honeydew

- *Cucumis melo*
- Grow in zones 4–10
- 85 days to harvest
- Beauty, friendship, and love

The honeydew is a cultivar of the muskmelon, and like the other melons, honeydews love warm weather. They grow best in warmer growing zones but can be grown in colder climates with some planning. Honeydews need two to three months of heat to flower and fruit, which makes growing them a challenge in cool season areas. Unless you are in zones 9 or 10, you will want to plant them in the hottest part of your garden. Use a black plastic ground cover to keep the soil warm. Make a hole so that each seedling can grow through the plastic, or use mulch to hold in the heat and moisture.

Honeydew is a fruit of Venus associated with abundance, fertility, and love. It is used in food magick to kindle love and cultivate beauty. Its mild, sweet flavor can be used in dishes to encourage fidelity, friendship, and kindness. Serve a dish of honeydew, cantaloupe, and watermelon at the end of a friendly lunch to refresh and sweeten the energy. Eat melon to restore energy, lift mood, and open thought. Serve sliced honeydew with prosciutto and a drizzle of balsamic vinegar to encourage appreciation.

Watermelon

* *Citrullus lanatus*
* Grow in zones 3–11
* 80–96 days to harvest
* Abundance, cleansing, healing, love, refreshment, and wishes granted

Watermelon is a hot-weather, long-season crop. It takes at least eighty days of warm weather with soil temperatures above 70 degrees Fahrenheit for a watermelon plant to fruit. If you live in an area with a cold spring and cool nights like I do, growing watermelon can be a challenge. I've tried growing them for several years now with no luck, as my seedlings fail to grow very large and their fruits never get larger than a tennis ball. But as watermelon is my husband's favorite summer fruit, I'm going to keep searching for a short-season variety that will produce here. If you would like to try your hand at growing watermelon, try starting the seeds indoors four weeks before your last frost date. Harden the seedlings off for ten days before planting out. Choose a large area with full sun exposure. Watermelon vines need lots of room to creep over. Amend soil well with compost and mound it up into hills. Plant the seedlings out in groups of four or five into the hills and water in.

Watermelon is a vine-like flowering plant that likely originated in the Kalahari Desert.[264] They were cultivated by the ancient Egyptians as long ago as 2400 BCE. Watermelons were grown across Europe in the sixteenth century and traveled with Columbus to the New World, where they were planted in the area we now know as Florida and Mississippi.[265] The large, sweet, water-filled fruit is a summer favorite. It holds a refreshing, nurturing energy for good health, fond memories, and love. Eat cold watermelon on a hot day to revitalize and restore. Drink a glass of watermelon juice to clear mental blocks. Serve watermelon at family picnics and barbeques to brighten emotions and sweeten memories. Serve to a lover to kindle affection. Watermelons are associated with feminine energy, Cancer, Pisces, the moon, summer, the Fourth of July, and the element water.

. . . .

264. "All About Watermelons," Burpee, accessed September 1, 2021, https://www.burpee.com/blog/all-about-watermelons_article10022.html.

265. DK, *The Story of Food*, 134.

Use watermelon seeds in abundance spells. Save the seeds and plant one with a whispered wish to have the sprout energize its manifestation. Cut a watermelon into large slices and serve outdoors to children to sweeten their mood and foster fond memories. Have them call out a wish after spitting out a seed.

Root Vegetables

Root vegetables are the underground, starchy stores of carbohydrate energy the plant draws on during the colder seasons. They are loaded with health-boosting nutrients to power up meals and fortify energy. Root vegetables are the perfect cold-weather food. They add color, flavor, and texture to a meal and also make it hearty and satisfying.

Most roots are cool-season crops that are easy to grow if you provide good soil, regular water, and adequate room for them to grow in. Roots do equally well planted in the ground or grown in a raised bed. Amend the soil with compost. Root crops need phosphorus, which promotes abundant root growth. Bone meal, fish meal, rock phosphates and aged manure are good sources of garden phosphorus. Add these amendments to the soil at least two weeks before planting. If you are using manure, add it two months before planting.

Beet

* Beta vulgaris
* Grow in zones 2–10
* 60–70 days to harvest

* Aphrodisiac, beauty, clear sight, earth energy, healing, love, and youth

The beet is a vegetable plant with edible broad leaves and a large, sweet taproot and is known by the names garden beet, table beet, and beetroot. Beets are a cool-weather vegetable that can be planted throughout the year. Plant the first crop in the spring as soon as the ground is workable. Sow seeds directly into soil in an area with full sun exposure or partial shade. Beets thrive in rich soil that is slightly alkaline and take from forty-five to sixty-five days to harvest depending on the variety. Get the bed ready by digging the soil deeply and amending with compost. Beets will grow through the winter, but with age the root gets woody and becomes inedible.

Beets were first eaten for their leaves, and the root was used in medicines.[266] They have a long history as an aphrodisiac.[267] The deep red root is associated with Aphrodite, and a red ink made from beetroot juice will boost love magick. The root, as with all roots, can be used in spellwork to ground a relationship or bind a lover. The leafy greens have a higher nutritional value than the root and hold energy to heal past hurts and ease old wounds. Clip young leaves as you need them and add them to salads to patch up a relationship. They are packed with antioxidants and have more iron than spinach. All greens are associated with money and growth but these ultra-healthy greens can be cooked up and added to food magick to improve decision-making and aid clear-sightedness. Beets are imbued with earth energy, which gives both the root and leaves an earthy flavor, and when consumed, they can aid in grounding and balancing emotions.

Carrot

* *Daucus carota* var. *sativus*
* Grow in zones 4–10
* 70–80 days to harvest
* Beauty, clear sight, fertility, protection, strength, and youth

Carrots have been a favorite garden root vegetable down through the ages. They are so quick and easy to grow that they are often included in children's gardens. All they require is a sunny spot with sandy, well-draining soil. Choose an area with full sun exposure and prepare the soil by digging deeply. Carrots thrive in loose soil. Pick out all the rocks and amend with compost. Sow the seeds directly into the soil and water well. You can grow carrots in a container, provided it is deep enough to accommodate the long root. If your soil is workable in the early spring, you can plant your carrots three weeks before the last frost date.

Early carrots were white or purplish and were often confused with parsnips. It wasn't until the seventeenth century in Holland that sweet orange carrots were

....

266. Tori Avey, "Discover the History of Beets," PBS, October 8. 2014, https://www.pbs.org/food/the-history-kitchen/history-beets/.

267. Avey, "Discover the History of Beets."

cultivated.[268] Carrots were believed to be aphrodisiacs and were made into love potions.[269] They hold energy to increase beauty. Carrots are rich in beta-carotene, an antioxidant that fights free radicals, repairs skin tissue, protects against sun damage, helps smooth wrinkles, protects eye health, and slows aging. Eat a daily carrot to gain a youthful radiance. Eating a daily raw carrot will help to restore healthy hair and nails. A daily snack of raw carrots can help remedy night blindness. Shred raw carrots into a salad and eat it to enhance clear sight. Carrots are associated with Mars and masculine energy. Add them to meals to strengthen male virility or boost a woman's energies for courage, leadership, and strength.

Carrot seed oil comes from the wild carrot plant, Queen Anne's lace, and is used to aid in vision quests and clear-seeing exercises. It holds energy to balance emotions and stimulate the mind. Add a few drops of carrot seed oil to massage oil or a bath salt to open communication channels, boost awareness, or stimulate fertility.

Parsnip
* *Pastinaca sativa*
* Grow in zones 2–9
* 90–130 days to harvest
* Creation, earth, health, male, and sex magick

Even though the parsnip is a long-season crop, taking 130 days or longer, it is a root worthy of growing. All you need is a sunny spot with well-draining soil where it can be left to grow. Parsnips do not like to be transplanted. Sow seeds directly into the garden in early spring as soon as the soil is workable. They don't mind the cold and take a very long time to germinate. After about a month, your seeds should have sprouted. Just let them grow and water weekly through dry periods. Weed as needed to keep the bed clear. After about sixteen weeks, your parsnips should be ready for harvest. Pull them as you need them. Parsnips are biennial and can be left through the winter to be harvested the following spring. Spring parsnips are sweeter than fall parsnips but develop a woody core that should be carved out during meal prep.

. . . .

268. DK, *The Story of Food*, 54.

269. Storl, *A Curious History of Vegetables*, 73.

The parsnip was a wild root that grew across most of Europe. It was a popular vegetable with ancient Greeks and Romans. The Dutch gathered parsnips for soup, while the Irish made a beer out of them.[270] Though they look like a white carrot, they have a unique flavor that is part earthy, part woody, and slightly sweet. These delicious roots are most often roasted, mashed into potatoes, or made into chips. The parsnip was treasured as one of the earliest fresh harvests of the year because unlike the carrot, the parsnip can be left in the ground all winter. In fact, the chill of frosts improves the sweetness and flavor. Dig it up just before use when the ground is not frozen.

Potato

* *Solanum tuberosum*
* Grow in zones 1–8
* 80–90 days to harvest
* Compassion, protection, stored energy, and wishing

There is nothing quite like a new potato when it's been cooked up within an hour of being dug out of your garden. New potatoes have a melt-in-your-mouth quality that makes store potatoes seem bland. Potatoes are a undemanding crop. They are so easy to grow that I often grow them in large nursery pots because when planted in the ground inevitably a few are left behind and will determinedly grow and fill in the next year no matter what you've planted over them.

Potatoes love a sunny spot with deep sandy soil. They can tolerate partial shade and will grow easily in a deep container. Put soil in the bottom of the pot and place your seed potatoes on the soil. You can use seed potatoes or even old kitchen potatoes, whole or cut into sections. Cover over with soil and when the potatoes sprout, cover them again with more soil to encourage more potatoes to grow.

Though many think of the Irish when they think of the potato, it was first cultivated in South America, where it was a staple food. In the 1500s it traveled with the Spanish explorers to Europe and by 1600 had slowly spread from Spain to France and Italy, where it was treated with suspicion due to being a member of the nightshade

. . . .

270. Hirasuna, *Vegetables*, 61.

family. Potatoes are associated with Saturn, Pluto, the moon, Virgo, and the element earth. They hold a nurturing grounded energy to stabilize and secure life. Make up a meal to ground and comfort by serving a baked potato with butter and sour cream. Add chives, rosemary, parsley, or dill to add protection. Steam cauliflower with potatoes and mash to make a protective dish that will help your family avoid sickness. A potato can be carved into a figure and used as a poppet.

Radish

* * *Raphanus sativus*
* * Grow in zones 2–10
* * 30 days to harvest, depending on variety
* * Health, joy, protection, and stability

Radishes are one of the easiest crops to grow. They are quick to germinate, which means they are one of the first garden vegetables to sprout. They are also quick to mature. Some varieties are ready to harvest just three weeks after planting. Radishes require little space and will even tolerate partial shade. Sow seeds thinly in a row and cover lightly with soil. Keep evenly moist. The seeds should sprout in four to five days. Plant radish crops in succession to have a continuous harvest.

Long ago in Europe it was the radish, eaten grated and sprinkled with salt and served with beer, that "kept the country population healthy over the long winter months," writes ethnobotanist Wolf Storl.[271] Radishes are loaded with vitamins and glucosinolates. Though they are known for their spicy, edible root, the greens are chock full of vitamins and antioxidants and can be eaten raw or steamed to boost health and increase vitality. Radishes also hold energy for protection and, when eaten, can protect against the evil eye. Shred a radish and sprinkle it with salt. Spread whole grain mustard over a piece of toast and cover with radish slices for a wholesome treat with energy to boost health and fortify strength. Chop a radish and add it to a salad or sandwich to brighten energy.

. . . .

271. Storl, *A Curious History of Vegetables*, 225.

Sweet Potato

* *Ipomoea batatas*
* Grow in zones 3–11
* 120–150 days to harvest
* Ancestor veneration, beauty, comfort, harmony, health, and love

The sweet potato isn't actually a potato but a member of the genus *Ipomoea* along with the moonflower and the morning glory. The vine and the flower are both attractive and are sometimes sold as ornamentals that are perennial in zones 8 to 11. Sweet potatoes can be grown from slips that are ready to plant or from a kitchen sweet potato that has decided it wants to grow. Plant them in a large bed after all danger of frost has passed. Sweet potatoes come in bush and vine varieties, and both need a lot of room to grow. Dig the soil and remove any rocks before amending with compost. Water regularly to keep the soil evenly moist. If you are growing sweet potatoes as a food crop, remove the flowers so the plants will send their energy into the roots. Harvest your sweet potatoes when the plants start to die back. This happens three to four months after planting. Take a gardening fork and scoop them from the soil. Use them within a week or cure them to make them last longer.

Sweet potato tubers are the perfect comfort food, as they are both satisfying and nutritious. They protect the body against aging and have properties to help balance blood sugars. Serve sweet potatoes to help balance and center energy and bring comfort to the brokenhearted. Serve a sweet potato to the one you desire to encourage love and protect health. Sprinkle with ginger to turn an encounter lusty or drizzle with maple syrup to sweeten someone's thoughts toward you. Sweet potatoes are associated with Venus, love, and the earth. Magickally, sweet potatoes enhance the ability to give and to receive love. A sweet potato can be used as a poppet or carved as an effigy to use in love magick.

Turnip

* *Brassica rapa* var. *rapa*
* Grow in zones 3–9
* 50–60 days to harvest
* Banishing, ending relationships, money, protection, and warding

Turnips are a cool-season vegetable and grow easiest in cooler regions. They seem fuss-free compared to other vegetables. Sow seeds thinly directly into the ground as soon as you are able to work the soil. Keep an eye out for the sprouts. You should see them in about ten days. When you spot them, protect them by covering with a cloche to defend against slug attack. Water them regularly. For a fall crop, plant turnips in midsummer, about two months before first frost. Harvest them as needed.

Turnips are an old-fashioned vegetable. They were cultivated in China during the Chou dynasty in 200 BCE.[272] The entire plant is edible. Young turnips can be eaten leaves and all. As turnips could be stored for long periods and could survive the freezing winters, they became a staple food for much of northern Europe.[273] Turnips are less starchy than potatoes and have a sweeter, earthy flavor. The roots carry earth energy and were the original jack-o'-lanterns used to ward off unwanted spirits.[274] They are associated with both Lughnasadh/Lammas and Samhain. Incorporate them into spells for banishing negative energy and warding your home. To deter unwanted advances, serve turnips to the one you are trying to evade. Turnips have a mild, slightly peppery flavor, and when pulled from the garden and eaten raw, they taste similar to a radish. Peel, cube, and toss turnips with olive oil and roast in the oven for a healthy dish similar to roasted potatoes. Turnip greens are a good source of vitamins K, A, and C; manganese; and fiber. They are associated with money and growth. Add young leaves to salads and stir-fries to boost nutrition and protection power.

. . . .

272. Hirasuna, *Vegetables*, 70.

273. Hirasuna, *Vegetables*, 70.

274. History.com Editors, "How Jack O'Lanterns Originated in Irish Myth," *History*, October 25, 2019, https://www.history.com/news/history-of-the-jack-o-lantern-irish-origins.

Squash

There are many varieties of squash that are grown across the world. Some grow bushy and others are sprawlers that will creep across an entire lawn or garden bed. Squash are divided into summer and winter groups. Both are planted early in spring, but summer squash produces fruit right away that are harvested when the squash are immature and the skin is tender. Winter squash are harvested in the fall and winter months.

Summer squash tend to be bushy plants with broad leaves. They develop blossoms close to their base. Pollen from the male blossom pollinates the female blossom, and a few days later the immature squash is ready for harvest. Summer squash have tender skins and tender seeds scattered throughout the flesh. Popular varieties include patty pan, cousa, yellow squash (straightneck and crookneck), zephyr, and zucchini.

Winter squash requires a lot more room and a much longer growing time. Unlike the tender summer squash, the winter varieties are harvested when they are mature, and as they grow, they develop a thick rind that is not edible but greatly increases the squash's storage life. They can be harvested as you need them, and the surplus can stay on the vine until the stem turns brown. Winter squash develop their seeds in a cavity. The squash is split and the seeds scraped out when it is being prepared. Popular varieties include acorn squash, butternut squash, pumpkin, and spaghetti squash.

Squash are heavy feeders. Their soil should not be allowed to dry out once they begin to flower. Feed throughout the growing season with a solution of liquid seaweed or a tomato plant food dissolved in water. Spray the solution directly on the leaves as a foliar feed once a week. Fill a spray bottle with diluted liquid fertilizer and spray directly onto the leaves. Allow the droplets to dry before watering again. Once a month feed the plant by pouring a liquid fertilizer directly onto the soil. If the leaves turn yellow or the immature squash develop blossom-end rot, it is an indication that the soil is lacking minerals. Adding calcium to the soil usually fixes the problem. Remove the affected fruit and add ground eggshells to the soil or feed your plant a dose of calcium-rich liquid seaweed.

Butternut Squash

* *Cucurbita moschata*
* Grow in zones 3–10
* 85–90 days to harvest
* Beauty, deepening relationships, health, influence, and prosperity

Butternut is a winter squash with orange flesh that has a sweet, mild flavor similar to pumpkin. Plant seeds after all danger of frost has passed. Choose a location with a lot of room and full sun exposure. Dig the soil and amend the top six inches with compost before sowing seeds directly into soil. Seedlings will sprout in ten to twelve days. Squash plants have a shallow root system and need to be kept moist. Water regularly to help the soil retain even moisture. Mulch around each plant to help the soil retain moisture. When the plant flowers, you can help nature by hand pollinating the female blossoms. Simply take a small paintbrush and gather pollen from a male blossom, then dust it lightly over the female blossom's stigma. The fruit should set and begin to grow.

Butternut is a mellow-tasting squash that can be served up savory or sweet, much like pumpkin. Cut a butternut in half, scoop out the seeds, and roast it. Use the roasted flesh in recipes for soups, pasta, breads, cookies, and muffins. Butternut is loaded with dietary fiber, vitamin C, vitamin A, and beta-carotene to support eye health and fight macular degeneration. Beta-carotene is a carotenoid compound responsible for giving fruits and vegetables their orange pigment. It is a powerful antioxidant that protects cells against cancer and aging. Mash 1 cup of roasted butternut with 1 tablespoon of honey and rub it over your face, neck, and upper chest for a homemade beauty treatment. Rest for 10 minutes, then rinse for a radiant glow. Serve roasted butternut at mealtime to boost the immune system, support cellular health, and help maintain youthful-looking skin. Butternut holds a warming energy that can be used to deepen feelings and influence others to see your view of things. Add it to meals to support relationships.

Pumpkin

* *Cucurbita pepo, C. maxima, C. moschata*
* Grow in zones 3–9
* 90–120 days to harvest
* Banishing, divination, health, prosperity, and revealing the unseen

Pumpkins are a winter squash. They are one of my favorite crops to grow. A healthy pumpkin patch will reward a family with months of fruit that will last from Halloween to Christmas. Pumpkins are a long-season crop and require most of the growing season. Start seeds indoors three to four weeks before the last frost date. Pumpkins also require full sun exposure and lots of room to sprawl. If they don't get enough sunlight, they will not produce any fruit. To save on garden space, plant pumpkins at the edge of the garden and direct the vine to grow out across the lawn or walkway. Pumpkins are heavy feeders. Make sure to amend the soil well with compost before planting. Mix it into the soil, then form hills to sow the seeds into or transplant seedling plants and water well. The seeds should germinate in seven to ten days. Keep watered throughout the growing season. If you save seeds, be sure to plant your pumpkins away from other squash to avoid cross-pollination.

The pumpkin holds a stable, positive energy. Place a small pumpkin on your altar, hearth, or doorstep to draw abundance into the home. Pumpkin flesh holds energy to fortify health, cheer the spirit, and attract prosperity. The scent of baking pumpkin holds the power to cheer and comfort. Bake a loaf of pumpkin bread and share it with someone downhearted to lift their mood and improve their overall outlook. Make a batch of pumpkin cookies and give them to elicit fondness. Mix a cup of cooked pumpkin with cardamom, cinnamon, and maple syrup and serve it to compel a favor. Light a pumpkin-scented candle before guests arrive to make the gathering festive and fun. The scent will drive away negative energy and make your home warm and inviting.

Yellow Summer Squash

* *Cucurbita pepo*
* Grow in zones 3–10
* 58 days to harvest
* Awareness, fertility, health, and luck

Yellow summer squash is native to the Americas. Today there are a dozen varieties. Yellow summer squash is divided into two groups: crookneck and straightneck. Some varieties are more cold-sensitive than others, so be sure to buy a variety suited for your zone. If you live in a warm zone, sow seeds directly into amended garden soil. Summer squash seeds will not germinate if temperatures are below 60 degrees Fahrenheit. For cooler regions, start seeds indoors four weeks before the last frost date and plant the seedlings out a week after the last frost date. Choose an area with full sun exposure and amend the soil well with compost. Water consistently throughout the growing season. Squash are heavy feeders. Feed throughout the growing season with a solution of liquid seaweed or a tomato plant food dissolved in water.

Yellow summer squash is a favorite summer food grown in abundance in backyard gardens across the world. Squash is nutritious. It is high in antioxidants and magnesium for beautiful skin and hair.[275] Add squash to your summer diet to remain youthful. Squash is associated with wholeness of the spirit and activating the intuitive mind. Eat to increase awareness and spiritual enlightenment. Use squash in spells to increase fertility. Yellow summer squash is a food of Lammas.

. . . .

275. Corinne Keating, "7 Yellow Vegetables with Health Benefits," Healthline, last modified September 21, 2018, https://www.healthline.com/health/food-nutrition/yellow-vegetables.

Zucchini

* *Cucurbita pepo*
* Grow in zones 3–10
* 46 days to harvest
* Prosperity, protection, psychic awareness, sex, and spirituality

Zucchini is a stock garden plant known for its ease to grow and abundant production. Grow from seed or plant as seedlings. If you live in a warm region, sow seeds directly into soil after the last frost date. For cooler regions get a jump on the growing season by starting seeds indoors six weeks before the last frost date. Zucchini thrives in beds with full sun exposure and rich, well-draining soil. Dig the bed and amend it with compost before planting out. Keep your squash well watered throughout the season. Zucchini will stop producing if the soil is allowed to dry out.

Zucchini is an edible summer squash, meaning that, unlike winter squash, it is harvested while immature when its rind is still tender and edible although many a zucchini has been missed until it has grown enormous. Though squashes are native to the Americas, this Italian favorite traveled to Europe and was cultivated by the Italians who named it *zucchino*, or "immature squash." Zucchini gained favor and spread across Europe, where it became known as a courgette in France and a marrow in England and Africa. It returned to America during WWI to become a garden favorite.[276] Zucchini is easy to prepare. You can boil it, bake it, roast it, or shred it and add it to other recipes. You can use it in side dishes and main dishes and bake it into delectable cakes, breads, and muffins. It is low in calories and loaded with significant amounts of vitamins C, B_6, and K; riboflavin; folate; potassium; and manganese. Add it to meals to boost health and enhance vision. Add shredded zucchini to your scrambled eggs to fortify health and boost optimistic outlook. Eat zucchini to encourage spiritual enlightenment. Zucchini is a food of Lammas. Bake a loaf of zucchini bread and share with a friend to strengthen friendship and elicit feelings of gratitude. Zucchini is associated with wholeness of the spirit and fruitfulness of the intuitive mind. If you find a large zucchini, slice it in half longwise and scoop out

. . . .

276. Russ Parsons, "The Bloom Is Still On," *Los Angeles Times*, July 19, 2006, https://www.latimes
.com/archives/la-xpm-2006-jul-19-fo-calcook19-story.html.

the seeds. Fill the cavity with ricotta cheese and top with spaghetti sauce and shredded parmesan. Bake until the squash is tender and serve it to increase affection and boost fertility.

Other Favorite Large Edible Perennials

Some garden plants you only need to plant once to have them return a yield year after year. They thrive in the garden with little care, adding ornamental interest as well as providing food for the table. The most important requirement is location, location, location because this plant will become a fixture for years to come. Find a spot where your perennial can live and grow. Give it the room it requires and let it be.

Artichoke

* *Cynara scolymus*
* Hardy in zones 7–11
* Attraction, love, personal growth, and protection

Artichokes are often grown as a garden perennial. They produce large edible flower buds and grow well here in the Pacific Northwest. They thrive in cool, wet temperate regions and will live up to five years, often growing up to five feet in height. Globe artichokes are one of the common garden cultivars. They are easy to grow from seed. They have attractive foliage and produce large blue thistle-like flowers that attract bees and butterflies. The immature buds are edible. Sow seeds indoors in deep containers and keep moist and warm. Plant out when plants are eight to twelve weeks old. (These seedlings should have at least five true leaves.) Water when the weather turns dry. Mulch the plants in the fall to protect them from the harsh weather.

The artichoke is associated with Venus, Scorpio, and Zeus. It was cultivated by the ancient Greeks, Romans, and Egyptians for their large flowers.[277] The flower buds are cut before they bloom and are steamed or wrapped in foil and baked. Artichokes embody strength and courage. They are eaten to enhance personal growth. Use an artichoke as a meditation focus to see your way through a thorny issue. Artichokes also hold energy to inspire love. Drizzle an artichoke heart with olive oil and

. . . .

277. Amy Stewart, *The Drunken Botanist* (Chapel Hill, NC: Algonquin Books, 2013), 142.

balsamic vinegar and serve to heat passions and encourage affection. Dry artichoke leaves and brew an infusion to add to an attraction bath to increase sexual desire. Or stuff dried leaf bits into a mojo bag and carry it to increase ability to charm.

Asparagus

* *Asparagus officinalis*
* Hardy in zones 3–8
* Desire, health, love, and virility

This tasty vegetable is one of the "plant once and harvest for years to come" garden plants. Asparagus is native to the Mediterranean. It can be planted from seeds but is usually grown from crowns, or one-year-old plants, that are planted in the early spring. And while you might not get much of a harvest the first year or even second year, by spring of the third year, you should have finger-sized spears ready for harvest. The main requirement of asparagus is a place of its own to grow. Give it its own spot to take over. Once planted, it will multiply and grow. Choose an area with full or partial sun exposure and well-draining soil. Dig the soil to a depth of twelve inches and amend with compost. Asparagus are dioecious, meaning there are male and female asparagus plants. For a healthy productive bed, you should have a mix. After asparagus produce their edible spear, they keep growing until they eventually become a tall fern. If left to grow, the male and female plants will flower, and if the females are fertilized, they will produce small red berries providing seeds for more asparagus plants.

Asparagus holds a revitalizing energy and was once used as an aphrodisiac. Nicholas Culpeper, an English herbalist from the seventeenth century, wrote that asparagus "stirreth up bodily lust in man or woman."[278] It was a traditional food in France in the nineteenth century, served as an aphrodisiac to grooms at their wedding dinners.[279] To the Puritans, asparagus was a spring tonic added to meals to revitalize health and spirit. Asparagus is associated with vitality, Ostara, Zeus, Jupiter, and Mars.

....

278. Nicholas Culpeper, *The Complete Herbal* (Manchester, UK: J. Gleave and Son, 1826), 4.

279. Sean Poulter, "Now the Asparagus Crop Arrives a Month Early Because of Our Mild Winter Weather," *Daily Mail*, March 3, 2012, https://www.dailymail.co.uk/news/article-2109574/Now-Asparagus-crop-arrives-month-early-mild-winter-weather.html.

Rhubarb

* *Rheum rhabarbarum*
* Hardy in zones 3–8
* Celebration, clear sight, fidelity, health, inspiration, and love
* Warning: Do not ingest the leaves; they are toxic.

Rhubarb is a member of the buckwheat family. It is also known as garden rhubarb and the pie plant. Plant rhubarb from seeds or buy seedlings and plant in rich, fertile, well-draining soil. Rhubarb thrives when planted in an area with full sun exposure and humus-rich soil that can hold in the moisture. Keep it watered regularly to keep the soil evenly moist. Rhubarb likes to stay damp. For a strong, healthy plant resist harvesting until the third year and never take more than a third of the stalks. Rhubarb is a cool-weather plant. Give it a heavy mulch when the season turns hot and water regularly.

Rhubarb is native to Asia, where it was grown for its medicinal qualities.[280] Today, in traditional Chinese medicine, the dried root and rhizomes of the plant are used to treat diarrhea, constipation, liver, and gallbladder complaints, and headaches.[281] Rhubarb is a hardy garden plant that will yield a harvest from April to June. The bright pink stalks are the only edible part of the plant. Rhubarb leaves contain high levels of oxalic acid, a compound that is toxic when overconsumed, causing abdominal pain, convulsions, low blood pressure, shock, mouth and throat pain, and vomiting. Do not ingest the leaves. They can be used to make a natural insecticide.

Rhubarb is high in vitamins and minerals and contains anthocyanins, flavonoids that help fight cancer, lower blood pressure, reduce inflammation, and protect eye and brain health.[282] Rhubarb is associated with Venus and holds energy to sweeten and inspire affection. Use the sweet-tasting stocks to make a pie or chutney and serve to sweeten someone's thoughts about you. Or brew up a bright, stimulating rhubarb infusion to encourage friendships and inspire creative thought. Cut 2 cups of

. . . .

280. *Encyclopaedia Britannica Online*, s.v. "rhubarb," accessed December 30, 2021, https://www.britannica.com/plant/rhubarb.

281. Tenney, *Today's Herbal Health*, 136.

282. Christina Badaracco, "Health Benefits of Rhubarb," American Institute for Cancer Research, May 1, 2029, https://www.aicr.org/resources/blog/health-benefits-of-rhubarb/.

trimmed stalks into 1-inch pieces. Put the pieces into a saucepan and cover with water. Bring it to a boil and simmer for 40 minutes. Remove the pan from heat. Stir in sugar to taste. Let it cool. Strain and serve the infusion over ice with sliced strawberries. Serve a glass to a lover to encourage fidelity. Add the rhubarb infusion to a glass of iced tea and sip it to see into the heart of an issue.

CLASSIC CULINARY HERBS

A culinary herb garden is a plot of herbs grown for kitchen use. Having fresh herbs on hand makes you more likely to use them in your cooking and your practice. Having a culinary herb patch means fresh herbs are available as they are needed, and it furnishes a supply to explore and experiment with.

The kitchen herb plot should be close to the kitchen so that it is convenient to harvest when the herbs are needed. Most culinary herbs are inexpensive and easy to grow, and many are easily propagated by taking cuttings. Some can be grown in a bright kitchen window or in a patio pot on the back porch. For best success, group together herbs with the same requirements. Cumin, lavender, marjoram, oregano, rosemary, sage, savory, tarragon, and thyme are drought tolerant and don't do well if their feet stay wet, while basil, chervil, chives, cilantro, fennel, garlic, mint, and parley love moist soil.

Visit your local garden center to find out which herbs thrive in your climate zone.

Basil

* *Ocimum basilicum*
* Hardy in zones 10–11
* Cheer, creativity, exorcism, happiness, harmony, hospitality, love, luck, protection, and wealth

While I mostly grow sweet basil, there are dozens of varieties, most of which are tender leafy perennials with highly fragrant leaves. Basil plants are sensitive to the cold and are often grown as annuals, as they do not grow until soil temperature is consistently above 50 degrees Fahrenheit. In colder regions you will want to start seeds indoors, plant or grow seedlings in a greenhouse, and harden them off by setting them out to experience the uneven temperatures of wind and sunlight for a few hours each day before planting them in the garden. Basil likes the heat, so choose a sunny location with fertile, well-draining soil. Mist the leaves in hot weather to avoid wilt.

Basil is associated with Krishna, Lakshmi, Mars, and Scorpio. It holds an uplifting, peaceful energy to promote happiness, soothe anxiety, and end quarreling. The Greeks and Egyptians used basil as an herb of transition to "open the gates of heaven," and later it became a European tradition to wrap a bouquet of basil in the hands of the dead, writes Nancy Hajeski.[283] Basil holds energy to draw luck and banish negativity. Tuck a sprig into your pocket when you must deal with the hustle and bustle of crowds to avoid becoming anxious. The fragrant leaves hold a calming energy to heal strained relationships and aid communications. Brew an infusion of basil leaves and use it as a spritzer to improve mood and restore peace. Spritz a room to dispel anger after a hostile encounter. Bruise a basil leaf and rub it across your forehead before meditation to deepen intuition and communication with your higher self. Crumble dried basil over candles to empower spirit communication. Basil is also an herb of prosperity and can be carried to attract money or used to boost sales. Tuck a few basil leaves into your left pocket before any business venture to help things to go smoothly. Spritz a room with a basil infusion to draw opportunities or increase business. Give a basil plant as a housewarming gift to bring good luck to the new home and foster harmony to those within.

· · · · · · · · · · · · · · · ·

283. Hajeski, *National Geographic Complete Guide to Herbs and Spices*, 19.

Bay

* *Laurus nobilis*
* Hardy in zones 9–10
* Glory, luck, protection, psychic vision, strength, victory, vitality, wisdom, and wishes

The bay is a small aromatic evergreen tree native to the Mediterranean. The bay is also known as the laurel, bay laurel, sweet bay, and true laurel. Bay trees are slow-growing evergreen trees known for the distinctive flavor of their leaves, which are used to flavor soups and sauces. Their dark green leaves make them an attractive feature to add to any garden. Plant your bay in an area with full sun exposure, or grow one in a container and pot it up when it outgrows its pot. You can propagate bay trees from cuttings. I have a potted bay that has traveled with me through several address changes and now in my current zone must be brought inside for the cooler months, as it cannot tolerate temperatures lower than 20 degrees Fahrenheit.

The bay was used in celebration, worn for protection, carried as a luck charm, and used to enhance psychic abilities. Bay leaf tea can be useful in the treatment of migraines and contains enzymes that aid digestion.[284] Bring 2 cups of water to a boil and add 3 bay leaves. Boil for 3 minutes, then turn off the heat and steep for 4 more minutes. Remove the leaves. Sip the infusion after meals to calm the stomach, or drink it to alleviate stress. Add a stick of cinnamon to the leaves and boil for an infusion that, when sipped, calms and comforts and helps induce a restful sleep. Fill a spray bottle with a bay leaf infusion and spritz yourself to awaken creativity. Float bay leaves in a hot bath to ease muscle aches. The scent of bay clears away confusion to allow for clairvoyance and wisdom, and when burned, the smoke has a calm awakening effect. Burn a bay leaf to open the mind and stimulate psychic powers. Burn a dried bay leaf as incense to inspire creative thought. Write a wish on a bay leaf and burn it to send your desire out into the universe. Tuck a bay leaf into your left pocket before going into negotiations to gain the best outcome. Place a leaf under your pillow to inspire prophetic dreams. Use the evergreen leaves in Yule wreaths and garlands to bring in the green and embody hope for the coming year.

. . . .

284. Flushing Hospital, "The Benefits of Drinking Bay Leaf Tea," Flushing Hospital, April 1, 2015, https://www.flushinghospital.org/newsletter/the-benefits-of-drinking-bay-leaf-tea/.

Caraway

* *Carum carvi*
* Hardy in zones 4–10
* Anti-theft, banishing, clarity, communication, health, love, and protection

Caraway is an herbaceous biennial with feathery carrot-like leaves and umbels of white or pink June-blooming flowers. It is a relative of carrot and fennel, and all parts of the plant are edible. Caraway grows well in both full sun and part shade. Its one true requirement is that its soil stays evenly moist. Plant seeds in fall if you live in a temperate region. If you live in a cold zone, plant seeds in early spring as soon as the soil is workable. Choose an area with moisture-retentive soil. Sow the seeds directly into the soil and mulch well. Water regularly to keep soil moist or use a drip line.

Caraway is reputed to be one of the oldest culinary spices with a history that goes back 5,000 years.[285] It was grown primarily for its small but flavorful crescent-shaped seeds that were used as a culinary spice and as a charm against theft and curses. In Britain it was customary for farmers' wives to hand out seed cakes made with caraway seeds to workers at the end of wheat sowing.[286] Magickally, caraway has a reputation to keep things from being stolen. It was fed to pigeons, dropped into pockets, and fed to lovers to keep them from straying.[287] If ever your lover's eye starts to wander, drop a few seeds into their pocket or sew into the hem of their coat to keep their thoughts full of you. Serve caraway seed cake to strengthen a friendship when your best friend seems to favor another. Caraway seeds possess carminative properties to soothe. Brew an infusion of caraway seeds and chamomile to soothe frazzled nerves. Mix in a spoonful of honey and sip to calm a troubled spirit. Chew caraway seeds to freshen both insight and breath. Caraway is associated with Mercury and the harvest festivals. It holds energy for protection.

. . . .

285. Andi Clevely et al., *Cooking with Herbs and Spices* (Leicester, UK: Anness Publishing, 1997), 289.

286. Hugh Fearnley-Whittingstall, "Hugh Fearnley-Whittingstall's Caraway Recipes," *Guardian*, November 11, 2011, https://www.theguardian.com/lifeandstyle/2011/nov/11/caraway-recipes-hugh-fearnley-whittingstall.

287. Richard Craze, *The Spice Companion* (London: Quintet Publishing, 1997), 54.

Chervil
* *Anthriscus cerefolium*
* Creativity, happiness, inspiration, joy, luck, renewal, and youth

Chervil is a hardy cool-season annual. It is heat sensitive and grows best in regions where daytime temperatures are below 70 degrees Fahrenheit. It is an attractive plant with delicate fernlike foliage. Sow seeds directly into the soil two to three weeks before the last frost date. In warm regions plant chervil in fall after the heat of summer has passed. Chervil prefers partial shade and moist areas and is often grown in herb, cottage, and woodland gardens. It is quick to bolt when temperatures warm and will self-seed. Chervil is easily confused with poisonous hemlock, so never forage for it.

Chervil is one of the classic French herbs. It has a delicate anise-like flavor and is used to season omelets, fish, and sauces. It is an herb of comfort with energy to lift the spirit and lighten mood. Chervil is associated with Jupiter and holds a positive energy to encourage good spirits and stimulate creative thought. The young leaves have the best flavor. Snip a handful and use it to flavor eggs. Gather chervil leaves and brew them into an infusion. Drink it as a spring tonic to boost mood or increase vigor. Add a chervil infusion to bathwater or use it as a hair rinse to refresh creative energy or inspire a fresh outlook. Rinse your forehead to inspire psychic sight. Dip a cloth in the infusion and use it to clean a magick mirror or crystal ball to empower communications. Use a chervil infusion as a face wash to help diminish wrinkles and appear younger. Use it as a skin wash to ease the itch of insect bites.

Cilantro
* *Coriandrum sativum*
* Beauty, cleansing, enthusiasm, happiness, healing, longevity, and love

Cilantro is an annual that grows quickly from seed (known as the spice coriander). Plant it in spring after your last frost date. Sow seeds directly into fertile, well-draining soil in an area with full sun exposure. In warm regions, provide afternoon shade. Cilantro is fast growing and will bolt if temperatures get too warm. Plant it in a sunny border alongside flowers and harvest as needed. Or plant cilantro in a whisky barrel near the kitchen for easy access. Cilantro will self-seed, so plant the seeds where they can clump and come up year after year.

Cilantro is a cleansing herb with energy to banish negativity, calm emotions, and instill harmony. It is a natural detox used to help the body rid itself of heavy metals.[288] Whiz cilantro with ice and cucumber in a blender and drink to refresh and revitalize. Cilantro holds energy to cool and clear. Serve it in salsas or melon salads to quarreling parties to soothe ruffled feathers and inspire compromise. Chop the leaves and use them as a poultice to soothe insect bites. Add cilantro to bath spells and beauty regimes for radiant, youthful skin. Cilantro is associated with Mars, Aries, Saturn, Scorpio, and the element fire. It holds energy to boost love spells, stimulate attraction, provoke lust, and bind offenders.

After cilantro flowers, it produces a small seedpod known as the spice coriander. To harvest, wait until the stalk has dried. Then cut away the tops, hold over a bowl, and separate the seeds from the dry plant matter. Chew a handful of coriander to bolster your spirit and make your thoughts receptive when facing a new job or an interview. Add it to formulas to lift mood or inspire creativity. Use it in meditation to gain insight or when facing a transition to help ease the change. Brew an infusion of coriander and sip it to calm the psyche and concentrate thought.

Cumin
* *Cuminum cyminum*
* Anti-theft, exorcism, protection, and virility

Cumin is a tender flowering annual in the parsley family, Apiaceae. It is a tender, heat-loving plant that takes 120 days to mature. It is usually planted as seedlings but can be grown from seed if you live in a warm climate or start the seeds inside well before the last frost date. Cumin does not transplant well, so if you start seeds indoors, grow it in a medium that can be placed right into the soil when transplanting.

Cumin is a Middle Eastern spice with an ancient history. It was found in the pyramids of Egypt.[289] Spanish explorers transported cumin to India and South America,

....

288. Mark McClure, "Dosing with Chlorella/Cilantro for Neurotoxin Elimination," National Integrated Health Associates, accessed September 1, 2021, https://www.nihadc.com/library/detox-for-life-class-2-addit-resources/54-4-dosing-with-chlorella/file.html?accept_license=1.

289. Clevely, *Cooking with Herbs and Spices*, 292.

where it became part of the national cuisine.[290] Cumin seeds develop a pleasant nutty flavor after roasting. Tea made from cumin seeds is taken to aid digestion, fight colds, and help remedy sore throats and arthritis. Make an infusion with 2 teaspoons of cumin seeds and 2 cups of hot water. Let it steep for 5 minutes for a soothing tea that reduces muscle tension. Cumin is associated with Mars, Taurus, and the element fire. It holds a warm, earthy energy that will fuel protection magick. Burn it with frankincense to keep troubles away. Fill a small bag with cumin seed and hide it in an item to prevent its theft. Mix it with salt and add it to washwater to dispel negative energy. Add cumin to love spells to encourage fidelity.

Dill

* *Anethum graveolens*
* Concentration, love, luck, lust, money, and protection

Dill is a tender herb grown for its attractive feather-like foliage. It is sensitive to frosts. Sow seeds directly into the soil when the soil warms. Choose a place with full sun exposure and well-draining soil where it can clump and self-seed to return year after year. Dill does not transplant well. It is also heat-sensitive and will bolt when temperatures rise. Provide afternoon shade in warm regions.

Dill is native to northern Europe and Russia and grown for its pleasant-tasting leaves and seeds. To the medieval world, dill was a medicinal herb and a magickal one, added to wine to increase lust and used to counter hexes and curses.[291] Dill holds a protective energy and can help defuse a situation. Keep a handful of dill seeds in your pocket when you need to deal with someone who tries your patience. Pop a few into your mouth and chew them when you start to lose your cool. Carry dill seeds in a pouch to counter envy. Add some dill sprigs to a table vase of flowers to cheer dinner guests, inspire conversation, and discourage disagreements. Brew a dill infusion and use it to spritz across thresholds and ward the home from negative energies. Add it to bathwater to lift spirits or use it as a hair rinse to wash away a

. . . .

290. Barbara Santich and Geoff Bryant, eds., *The Illustrated Encyclopedia of Fruits, Vegetables, and Herbs* (London: Quarto, 2017), 283.

291. Folkard, *Plant Lore, Legends, and Lyrics*, 313.

negative outlook. Burn dill seeds to calm or pacify agitated spirits. Tuck a sprig into your pocket when you must venture into the unknown. Dill is associated with fire, Mercury, and Gemini. It holds energy to attract prosperity and good luck. Add to any money spell to activate and empower. Drop a few dill seeds into your pocket when you go job hunting to boost success. Chew on them to settle your nerves.

Marjoram

* *Origanum majorana*
* Hardy in zones 8–11
* Comfort, happiness, healing, joy, love, prosperity, and protection

Marjoram is one of the Mediterranean herbs and favors a place in the sun with sandy, well-draining soil. It is a tender perennial. Plant marjoram in an herb bed or patio pot in the spring after your last frost date. Sow marjoram seeds in a warm, sunny location with well-draining soil. Water evenly and keep the soil moist until seedlings sprout. Marjoram is low growing and makes an attractive ground cover. Grow it in a border, a planter, or even a kitchen window for an aromatic herb with a pine-citrusy flavor. Harvest marjoram by taking cuttings as needed.

Marjoram holds energy to foster joy and love and to draw prosperity. To the Greeks and Romans marjoram symbolized happiness. They wove it into garlands and crowned newlywed couples to wish them "marital bliss."[292] During the Middle Ages, marjoram was a sweet strewing herb stuffed into sachets and pomanders and used to scent washwaters.[293] The scent of marjoram is calming. Use it to restore joy to the grief-stricken. Add marjoram to foods to improve flavor and lift outlook. Drink a tea made from the leaves or flowers to lift your mood and foster joy. Add a marjoram infusion to bathwater and soak to calm the spirit and renew appreciation for life. Marjoram is associated with the moon, Aphrodite, Diana, Venus, Juno, Thor, Jove, Osiris, Mercury, and the element air. It holds energy for love, healing, protection, and prosperity. Use marjoram in love spells. Stuff a sachet with agrimony,

....

292. Hajeski, *National Geographic Complete Guide to Herbs and Spices*, 56.

293. Picton, *The Book of Magical Herbs*, 81.

woodruff, and marjoram. Tuck the sachet under your pillow to dream of love. Add an infusion of marjoram to your washwater and use it to wash thresholds, countertops, and floors to safeguard your home from hostility and bad luck.

Mint

* *Mentha* spp.
* Hardy in zones 3–8
* Communication, healing, inspiration, motivation, prosperity, protection, travels, and uplifting

There are at least eighteen species of mint and numerous hybrids that grow throughout the world. Most of these aromatic perennials are hardy, fast-growing, creeping herbs planted in areas to confine them. Mint will quickly take over a garden bed. It takes less maintenance when it is planted in a container, as a border, or as a ground cover. Mint is a woodland plant and will grow in partial shade. It thrives in moist, well-draining soil. Because mint grows by sending out runners, it is easily transplanted. Simply remove a segment with roots and plant it in the desired location.

Mint holds energy to restore vitality and clarity of mind. Stuff mint leaves into a mesh bag and drop it under running bathwater to revive and restore. Mint tea restores energy, encourages fresh thought, and enhances psychic abilities. Add a mint infusion to a footbath to relax the anxious and refresh the weary. Sip a mint infusion to lift mood and spirit. Use it as a hair rinse to renew your outlook or inspire a fresh way of thinking. Toss a handful of dried mint into a fire to enhance focus and induce calm clarity before rituals. Stuff mint leaves into your front left pocket when you must face something that makes you anxious. Touch the pocket and draw a deep breath to keep a level head. Crumble dried mint leaves and sprinkle around a room after an argument to restore feelings of peace. Make an incense to instill harmony and draw happiness by combining mint with meadowsweet and vervain. Mint also holds energy for protection. Grow along the front path to keep negative energy away. Tuck a sprig of mint into your left pocket to draw positive energy and avoid being cursed. Mint is associated with Hecate, Venus, Mercury, and the element air and is known for the adage "Grow mint in your garden to attract money to your purse."[294] Add mint leaves to your wallet to attract money. Place mint leaves under your pillow to evoke prophetic dreams. Mint has a refreshing, uplifting energy that can be used in health, motivation, and money spells. Like pepper, mint holds energy to heat things up: use it to stimulate business.

Parsley

* *Petroselinum crispum*
* Hardy in zones 3–9
* Beauty, death, love, protection, purification,
romance, victory, and wealth

Parsley is a garden biennial native to the Mediterranean. It thrives in rich, moist, well-draining soil and will grow in areas with full sun and partial sun exposure. Sow seeds directly into the soil four weeks before the last frost date or plant them in patio pots. Its attractive foliage looks nice when it is planted among flowers, and bees are attracted to its small flowers.

We often think of parsley as only a garnish on the side of the plate. Restaurants place it there because it freshens breath, aids in digestion, and stimulates the appetite. Parsley is a tonic herb and a blood builder with a cleansing nature. It helps fight cancer, cleanses glands, helps restore bladder health, and strengthens the immune system.[295] Parsley tea is prescribed to help with bladder problems, flatulence, and rheumatism.[296] Stir a spoonful of honey into a cup and sip to settle an upset stomach. Use a parsley poultice to soothe insect bites and stings. Add an infusion of parsley to bathwater to cleanse away negative energy or break a negative cycle. Parsley is associated with the element air, Mercury, Mars, Aphrodite, Persephone, Venus, and the liminal states in life. Magickally, it holds energy to promote fertility, encourage lust, boost luck, and cleanse away negative energy. It is used in purification baths, in meditations, and to cheer. Sip parsley tea to clear away negative thoughts.

. . . .

294. Picton, *The Book of Magical Herbs*, 41.

295. Victoria Zak, *The Magic Teaspoon: Transform Your Meals with the Power of Healing Herbs and Spices* (New York: Berkley Books, 2006), 59.

296. Kruger, *The Pocket Guide to Herbs*, 131.

Add parsley sprigs to a vase of flowers and use it as a centerpiece to keep dinner conversations light. Anoint candles in olive oil, roll them in dried parsley bits, and burn them to boost intuition and divination powers. Parsley holds energy to heal and protect. Plant parsley around ponds and fountains to help maintain a healthy environment. Plant parsley along walkways with rue to ward entry and keep negative energy from entering. Stuff parsley into your left pocket to calm and protect when going into a hostile encounter.

Rosemary

* *Salvia rosmarinus*
* Hardy in zones 8–11
* Beauty, communication, friendship, love,
protection, purification, remembrance, and rest

Rosemary is a fragrant evergreen perennial native to the Mediterranean. It is easy to grow as long as you don't overwater it. It thrives in full sun and well-draining soil. A rosemary plant can live for years. Plant it once and after it has established, you can easily propagate it by taking cuttings. If you live in areas where winter temperatures drop below 20 degrees Fahrenheit, plant as an annual or bring inside to overwinter. Rosemary grows well both in the ground and in patio pots.

Rosemary has been used for 2,000 years as medicine, a strewing herb, and as a culinary herb.[297] It was valued for its scent and flavor. The Romans hung sprigs of rosemary as a charm against evil.[298] The Greeks wore crowns made of rosemary and rubbed it on their foreheads to boost brain power and improve memory.[299] In the Middle Ages rosemary was carried to avert the evil eye.[300] Mourners carried rosemary to repel graveyard spirits.[301] The scent of rosemary eases headaches and calms the psyche. Pick a sprig, rub it between your fingers, lift it to your nose, and

. . . .

297. Burke, *The Modern Herbal Primer*, 123.

298. Clevely et al., *Cooking with Herbs and Spices*, 113.

299. Picton, *The Book of Magical Herbs*, 73.

300. Zak, *The Magic Teaspoon*, 68.

301. Burke, *The Modern Herbal Primer*, 123.

breathe in the scent to calm racing thoughts. Steep a sprig of rosemary in spring water and drink it to enhance mental ability or relieve tension. Pour an infusion into bathwater and soak to revive a weary spirit. Add it to meals or drink it as a tea to improve memory. Add rosemary to any meal you want to be remembered.

Rosemary is associated with the sun and Leo. It holds energy for protection. Burn a sprig of rosemary with juniper to purify a room. Make an infusion of chopped burdock root, a handful of rosemary, and some lemongrass. Let it steep for 9 minutes and strain. Add it to your washwater and scrub to cleanse a room of negative energy. Or combine a handful of rosemary with bachelor's button, basil, and lavender to make a floor wash that promotes peace. Stuff a pouch with hyssop, feverfew, and rosemary and wear it to gain safety while traveling. Plant a border with hyssop, lavender, and rosemary for an aromatic planting that will attract pollinators and draw positive energy.

Sage
* * Salvia officinalis*
* * Hardy in zones 5–9*
* * Cleansing, fertility, health, longevity,*
    protection, warding, wisdom, wish magick

There are more than 700 species of sage, many of which are not culinary herbs but still are nice in the garden with their interesting leaves and attractive flowers. *Salvia officinalis* is the hardy perennial cooking herb also known as garden sage, common sage, and culinary sage. Its soft, silvery-green leaves have a strong flavor that increases when dried. Garden sage blooms in purple-blue flower spikes that attract pollinators. Plant it as a small plant or sow seeds into pots or directly into garden soil. Sage favors a place in the sun with sandy, well-draining soil. Allow the soil to dry between waterings.

Sage was noted for its antidepressant, anti-inflammatory, antiseptic, and astringent properties, and it was used as medicine through the ages.[302] It is a component of the famous four thieves vinegar, a medieval remedy to ward off the plague, and

. . . .
302. Burke, *The Modern Herbal Primer*, 125.

since sage is a natural flea repellant, it helped keep the wearer healthy.[303] Sage is an herb of protection valued since ancient times to ward against evil. It was burned to drive away spirits and cleanse or clear away spiritual impurities and negative energy. Sage smoke is used to cleanse the body to rid it of negativity and unwanted influences, restore mood, or cleanse away the outside world before entering sacred space. Sage is associated with Venus, Jupiter, Leo, Zeus, and Consus, and though it is esteemed for its energy to cleanse, purify, and protect, it also holds power to enhance mystical qualities and open communications. Burn sage as an incense to enhance spirit communication. The smoke will act as a bridge to carry the messages. Burn sage while meditating on the name of someone you have lost touch with to occupy their thoughts and instigate contact. Crumble dried sage and rub it over your hands when meeting someone for the first time to ease communication, or tuck a leaf into your left pocket and touch it when your words falter. Sage also supports brain health and helps improve memory. [304] Brew a cup of sage leaf tea and drink it to sharpen concentration, improve attention, and enhance overall cognition.

Savory

* * Satureja hortensis and Satureja montana
* * Aphrodisiac, cheer, creativity, mental powers,
  passion, and psychic ability

Satureja is a genus of fourteen species of highly aromatic herbs, two of which are cherished as garden herbs, the annual summer savory, also called garden savory, (Satureja hortensis), and winter savory (Satureja montana), a perennial in zones 5 to 11. Both are lovely garden plants with small gray-green leaves and spikes of small white, pink, or pale lavender flowers. And both are widely cultivated as cooking herbs with warm energy and a minty-peppery flavor. Sow seeds just after the last frost date.

....

303. Carol J. Alexander, "How to Make the Legendary Four Thieves Vinegar Tonic," *Old Farmers' Almanac*, last modified March 25, 2021, https://www.farmersalmanac.com/four-thieves-vinegar-35968.

304. "Salvia Officinalis and Alzheimer's Disease," Alzheimer's Organization, accessed September 1, 2021, https://www.alzheimersorganization.org/sage-and-alzheimers.

Plant seeds in rich, well-draining soil in full sun. Water regularly until the plants have established; afterward, water deeply and allow the soil to dry out between waterings.

Savory herbs are very aromatic. They are associated with Venus, Mercury, Pan, and the element air and hold a helpful, soothing energy to boost mental powers, calm an upset stomach, or ease a cold. Dry savory and burn it as incense to inspire creative thought. Gather savory leaves and brew an infusion. Drink it to aid memory and heighten psychic senses. Sprinkle savory over food and serve it at dinner for wisdom to say the right thing or make the right decision. Sip a cup of savory tea to calm an upset stomach, or add the infusion to bathwater and soak to calm a worried mind. The leaves can be applied as a poultice to bites and stings for instant relief. Savory is often cooked in bean dishes to counteract flatulence.

Stevia

* *Stevia rebaudiana*
* Hardy in zones 9–10 (will overwinter in the ground when planted in zone 8 with protection)
* Compelling, friendship, healing, nurturing, and uplifting

Stevia is a tender perennial native to South America also known as sweetleaf and sugarleaf. Stevia seeds are notoriously hard to germinate. It is easy to grow if you purchase a seedling or are given cuttings. Stevia is a warm-weather herb that loves the sun. Plant it well after the last frost date in rich, well-draining soil with full sun exposure. If you garden in a hot region, provide afternoon shade through the hottest months. Mulch your stevia plant well in the fall for winter protection.

Stevia has been used for centuries as a sweetener and as a contraceptive. The leaf has a sweet flavor with a slightly bitter aftertaste, and though new to the West, stevia has been used for decades in many countries as an alternative to sugar. It contains chemicals that taste sweet but, unlike sugar, do not metabolize when ingested and do not cause a change in blood sugar; thus, it has become a guilt-free sweetener. Use it in place of sugar to improve health and instill a sense of well-being. Add a handful of leaves to a pitcher of iced tea to promote happiness and sweeten relationships. Stevia has energy to gently compel. Float a sprig of stevia in a glass of tea and serve it to gently persuade or influence opinion. Sprinkle dried stevia over the food to gain influence. Mix dried stevia with thyme and burn it as an incense to increase feelings of well-being. Mix stevia with coltsfoot to empower love magick.

Tarragon
* *Artemisia dracunculus*
* Hardy in zones 4–9
* Banishing, compassion, dragons, expansion, luck, rebuilding, and welcoming

Tarragon is a perennial herb in the daisy family also known as dragon's wort and little dragon. It is native to mild European regions and loves cool spring temperatures. Tarragon is difficult to grow from seed. It is usually planted as a seedling or propagated from cuttings. Plant it in a spot with full or partial sun exposure and rich, well-draining soil. While tarragon thrives in warm, somewhat dry conditions, it struggles in hot regions. In the fall add a layer of mulch to protect the roots through the winter.

Tarragon is an herb of hospitality. The scent is strongly inviting and encourages compassion for others. Use tarragon's grassy anise flavor to empower your cooking and make your guests feel special. Make an infusion of tarragon and add to a footbath to revive spirit after a troubling day. Tarragon holds a positive energy that can be used to expand or build. It has mild tranquilizing properties and can be brewed into a tea to promote calmness and encourage confidence. Tarragon also gives an excellent boost to spells for destiny and finding one's life path. It can be added to love charms and spells to instill peace, kindness, and good luck. Tarragon is known for its ability to banish negativity, and when grown on windowsills and near entries, it will protect the home from thieves and malevolent spirits.

Thyme

* *Thymus vulgaris*
* Hardy in zones 5–9
* Communication, courage, dreams, healing, love, luck, psychic powers, purification, sight, and success

Thyme is a low-growing, sometimes creeping, evergreen with small, fragrant leaves and thin, woody stems. There are 300 varieties of thyme, all valued for their scent and flavor. Thyme is easy to grow but the seeds are difficult to germinate. It is usually planted as a seedling or propagated from cuttings. Thyme is a sun-loving plant. You can grow it equally well in a patio pot, a sunny kitchen window, or a garden bed. To thrive thyme requires a spot with full sun exposure and well-draining soil. Water deeply when the soil has dried out. Thyme is one of the Mediterranean herbs and is susceptible to rot if its feet are kept wet.

Thyme has been used as medicine for over 2,000 years. Both the Romans and Greeks used it to treat indigestion, hangovers, insect bites, and melancholy.[305] Thyme holds energy to clear the mind, calm nerves, draw love, boost psychic abilities, and encourage courage, creativity, and intuition. It is associated with Mercury, Venus, water, Taurus, and Libra. Make a luck-drawing talisman by stuffing a pouch with bay leaves and thyme. Wear it to draw luck your way. Burn dried thyme and bay leaves as incense when you need to empower psychic sight. Wear a sprig of fresh thyme to aid in seeing faeries. Carry a sprig in your pocket to fortify confidence. Brew an infusion of thyme and marjoram. Add the infusion to your bathwater and soak to fortify attraction power. Fill a muslin bag with thyme, hops flowers, and rosemary and tuck it under your pillow to keep nightmares away.

. . . .
305. Burke, *The Modern Herbal Primer*, 127.

ACKNOWLEDGMENTS

I'd like to thank the amazing team at Llewellyn Worldwide.

A good editor is an absolute gift, and I have two marvelous women to thank, first and foremost the talented Heather Greene. Thank you for your keen insight, kind words, and personal support. It was your creative vision, expert advice, and gentle guidance that turned a troubled manuscript into a work fit to publish. Thank you for helping me turn content into the lovely book it now is.

The second is my amazing production editor, Lauryn Heineman. I am so lucky to have you on my team. Thank you for answering all my questions with explanations I could understand and for challenging statements and directing me to research content and citations that were questionable.

I'd also like to thank everyone in production who helped transform a manuscript into this beautiful book. Thank you to Kevin Brown for the gorgeous cover and Christine Ha for the wonderful design.

Thank you to the booksellers and librarians who support my efforts. A shout-out to the staff at Tigard Library. A big thank you to Barbara Peters and Patrick King from the Poisoned Pen Bookstore and Megan Love Smith from Crystal Lake Public Library. Thank you to my fabulous friend Britta Nicholson. Britta has a deep intuitive relationship with the earth and understands the seasonal cycles here. She has gifted me many of the plants in my garden. For my birthday, she presented me with two papa trees, and it was she who gave me my first dahlia and started an obsession. Thank you for sharing your love of gardening with me. Not only did your enthusiasm help keep this book going, but your insight and wisdom were inspiring.

Thank you to the ladies of my psychic circle. It was your friendship and exposure to your ideas and viewpoints that grew my spirituality and allowed my knowledge and awareness to expand. Thank you for making my world a fascinating and magickal place filled with limitless possibilities.

And last, thank you to my husband, who makes my writing possible.

RECOMMENDED READING

Books with Lovely, Inspiring Photographs

Kane, Dency, Lauri Brunton, and Erin Fournier. *Sanctuary: Gardening for the Soul.* New York: Friedman/Fairfax Publishers, 1999.

Mitchell, Keith. *The Garden Sanctuary: Creating Outdoor Space to Soothe the Soul.* London: Hamlyn, 2000.

Search, Gay. *The Healing Garden: Gardening for the Mind, Body and Soul.* Ontario, Canada: Winding Stair Press, 2002.

Streep, Peg. *Spiritual Gardening: Creating Sacred Space Outdoors.* Alexandria, VA: Time Life Books, 1999.

Some Helpful Informational Garden Guides

I recommend finding books by an author who lives in your area or at least your grow zone.

Bartley, Jennifer R. *The Kitchen Gardener's Handbook.* Portland, OR: Timber Press, 2010.

Colebrook, Binda. *Winter Gardening in the Maritime Northwest: Cool Season Crops for the Year-Round Gardener.* 5th ed. Gabriola Island, BC: New Society Publishers, 2012.

Deppe, Carol. *The Resilient Gardener: Food Production and Self-Reliance in Uncertain Times.* White River Junction, VT: Chelsea Green Publishing, 2010.

Don, Monty. *The Complete Gardener.* London: DK, 2021.

———. *Down to Earth: Gardening Wisdom.* London: DK, 2017.

Greer, Allison. *Companion Planting for the Kitchen Gardener.* New York: Skyhorse Publishing, 2014.

Hemenway, Toby. *Gaia's Garden: A Guide to Home-Scale Permaculture.* 2nd ed. White River Junction, VT: Chelsea Green Publishing, 2009.

Klein, Carol. *Grow Your Own Vegetables.* London: Mitchell Beazley, 2010.

Palmer, Nigel. *The Regenerative Grower's Guide to Garden Amendments.* White River Junction, VT: Chelsea Green Publishing, 2020.

Rees-Warren, Matt. *The Ecological Gardener.* White River Junction, VT: Chelsea Green Publishing, 2021.

Soler, Ivette. *The Edible Front Yard: The Mow-Less Grow-More Plan for a Beautiful Garden.* Portland, OR: Timber Press, 2008.

Wormser, Owen. *Lawns into Meadows: Growing a Regenerative Landscape.* San Francisco, CA: Stone Pier Press, 2020.

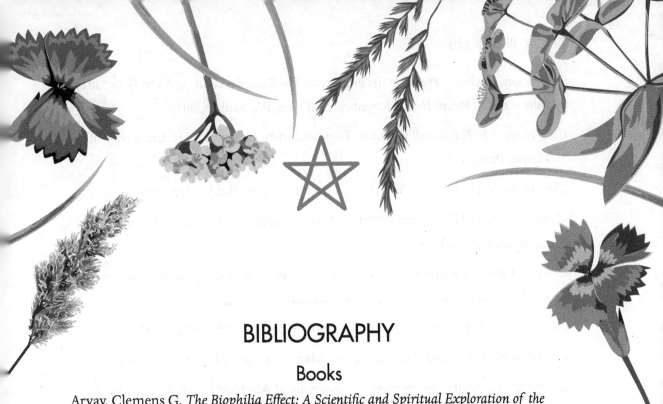

BIBLIOGRAPHY

Books

Arvay, Clemens G. *The Biophilia Effect: A Scientific and Spiritual Exploration of the Healing Bond Between Humans and Nature*. Boulder, CO: Sounds True, 2018.

Best, Michael R., and Frank H. Brightman, eds. *The Book of Secrets of Albertus Magnus*. Newburyport, MA: Weiser Books, 1999.

Blair, Katrina. *The Wild Wisdom of Weeds: 13 Essential Plants for Human Survival*. White River Junction, VT: Chelsea Green Publishing, 2014.

Burke, Nancy. *The Modern Herbal Primer: A Simple Guide to the Magic and Medicine of 100 Healing Herbs*. Dublin: Yankee Publishing, 2000.

Breverton, Terry. *Breverton's Complete Herbal*. New York: Random House, 2011.

Brondizio, Eduardo, Sandra Diaz, Josef Settele, and Hien T. Ngo, eds. "Global Assessment Report on Biodiversity and Ecosystem Services." Bonn, Germany: IPBES, 2019. https://ipbes.net/global-assessment.

Callery, Emma. *The Complete Book of Herbs: A Practical Guide to Cultivating, Drying, and Cooking with More Than 50 Herbs*. Philadelphia, PA: Courage Books, 1994.

Castleman, Michael. *The New Healing Herbs: The Essential Guide to More Than 130 of Nature's Most Potent Herbal Remedies.* Emmaus, PA: Rodale, 2010.

Clay, Horace F. *The Hawai'i Garden: Tropical Shrubs.* Honolulu, HI: University of Hawaii Press, 1987.

Clevely, Andi. *The New Guide to Herbs.* London: Anness Publishers, 1995.

Clevely, Andi, and Katherine Richmond. *The Complete Book of Herbs.* London: Smithmark Publishers, 1998.

Clevely, Andi, Katherine Richmond, Sallie Morris, and Lesley Mackley. *Cooking with Herbs and Spices.* Leicester, UK: Anness Publishing, 1997.

Craze, Richard. *The Spice Companion.* London: Quintet Publishing, 1997.

Culpeper, Nicholas. *The Complete Herbal.* Manchester, UK: J. Gleave and Son, 1826.

Cunningham, Scott. *Cunningham's Encyclopedia of Magickal Herbs.* St. Paul, MN: Llewellyn Publications, 1985.

Davidson, H. R. Ellis. *Myths and Symbols in Pagan Europe: Early Scandinavian and Celtic Religions.* Syracuse, NY: Syracuse University Press, 1988.

Deas, Lizzie. *Flower Favourites: Their Legends, Symbolism and Significance.* London: George Allen, 1898.

DK. *The Story of Food: A History of Everything We Eat.* New York: DK Publishing, 2018.

Dumezil, Georges. *Archaic Roman Religion.* Vol. 1. Baltimore, MD: Johns Hopkins University Press, 1996.

Emerson, Ralph Waldo. *The Fortune of the Republic and Other American Addresses.* Boston, MA: Houghton Mifflin Company, 1889.

Evelyn, John. *Acetaria: A Discourse of Sallets.* 2nd ed. London, 1706. https:// archive.org/details/acetariadiscours00evel/page/n13/mode/2up.

Fetrow, Charles W., and Juan R. Avila. *The Complete Guide to Herbal Medicines*. New York: Pocket Books, 2000.

Folkard, Richard. *Plant Lore, Legends, and Lyrics*. London: Sampson Low, Marston, Searle, and Rivington, 1884.

Foster, Steven, and Rebecca L. Johnson. *Desk Reference to Nature's Medicine*. Washington, DC: National Geographic, 2006.

Gerard, John. *The Herball: Or the Generall Historie of Plantes*. London: John Norton, 1597.

Gregg, Susan. *The Complete Illustrated Encyclopedia of Magical Plants*. Beverly, MA: Fair Winds Press, 2008.

Grieve, Maud. *A Modern Herbal*. Vols. 1 and 2. New York: Dover Publications, 1971.

Hajeski, Nancy J. *National Geographic Complete Guide to Herbs and Spices: Remedies, Seasonings, and Ingredients to Improve Your Health and Enhance Your Life*. Washington, DC: National Geographic, 2016.

Harrar, Sari, and Sara Altshul O'Donnell. *The Woman's Book of Healing Herbs: Healing Teas, Tonics, Supplements, and Formulas*. Emmaus, PA: Rodale Press, 1999.

Hatfield, Gabrielle. *Encyclopedia of Folk Medicine: Old World and New World Traditions*. Santa Barbara, CA: ABC-CLIO, 2004.

———. *Hatfield's Herbal: The Curious Stories of Britain's Wild Plants*. London, UK: Penguin Books, 2009.

Herb Society of America. "Calendula: An Herb Society of America Guide." Kirtland, OH: Herb Society of America, 2007.

Hirasuna, Delphine. *Vegetables*. San Francisco, CA: Chronicle Books, 1985.

Hoggard, Brian. *Magical House Protection*. New York: Berghahn Books, 2019.

Johnsen, Jan. *Heaven Is a Garden*. Pittsburgh, PA: St. Lynn's Press, 2014.

Johnson, Rebecca L., Steven Foster, Tieraona Low Dog, and David Kiefer. *National Geographic Guide to Medicinal Herbs*. Washington, DC: National Geographic, 2010.

Kaufer, Lanny. *Medicinal Herbs of California*. Guilford, CT: Falcon Guides, 2021.

Kruger, Anna. *The Pocket Guide to Herbs*. London: Parkgate Books, 1992.

Lecouteux, Claude. *Demons and Spirits of the Land: Ancestral Lore and Practices*. Rochester, VT: Inner Traditions, 1995.

Louv, Richard. *Last Child in the Woods: Saving Our Children from Nature-Deficit Disorder*. Chapel Hill, NC: Algonquin Books, 2008.

———. *The Nature Principle: Reconnecting with Life in a Virtual Age*. Chapel Hill, NC: Algonquin Books, 2011.

Mabey, Richard, Michael McIntyre, Pamela Michael, Gail Duff, and John Stevens. *The New Age Herbalist: How to Use Herbs for Healing, Nutrition, and Body Care*. New York: Fireside Books, 1988.

Martin, Laura C. *Garden Flower Folklore*. Guilford, CT: Globe Pequot Press, 2009.

McFarland, Ben. *World's Best Beers: One Thousand Craft Brews from Cask to Glass*. New York: Sterling, 2009.

McVicar, Jekka. *Jekka's Medicinal Herbs*. New York: William Morrow & Company, 1995.

Morgan, Diane. *Roots: The Definitive Compendium with More Than 225 Recipes*. San Francisco: Chronicle Books, 2012.

Murray, Michael T., Joseph E. Pizzorno, and Lara Pizzorno. *The Encyclopedia of Healing Foods*. New York: Atria Books, 2005.

Ody, Penelope. *The Complete Medicinal Herbal: A Practical Guide to the Healing Properties of Herbs, with More Than 250 Remedies for Common Ailments*. London: Dorling Kindersley, 1993.

Oster, Maggie. *Flowering Herbs*. New York: Longmeadow Press, 1991.

Palmer, Nigel. *The Regenerative Grower's Guide to Garden Amendments: Using Locally Sourced Materials to Make Mineral and Biological Extracts and Ferments*. White River Junction, VT: Chelsea Green Publishing, 2020.

Picton, Margaret. *The Book of Magical Herbs: Herbal History, Mystery, and Folklore*. London: Quarto, 2000.

Reader's Digest. *Magic and Medicine of Plants*. New York: Reader's Digest, 1986.

Rohde, Eleanour Sinclair. *A Garden of Herbs*. London: Medici Society, 1922.

Santich, Barbara, and Geoff Bryant, eds. *The Illustrated Encyclopedia of Fruits, Vegetables, and Herbs*. New York: Chartwell Books, 2017.

Small, Ernest. *North American Cornucopia*. Boca Raton, FL: Taylor & Francis, 2014.

Smith, Andrew. *Strangers in the Garden: The Secret Life of Our Favorite Flowers*. Toronto: McClelland & Stewart, 2004.

Starhawk. *The Earth Path: Grounding Your Spirit in the Rhythms of Nature*. San Francisco, CA: HarperCollins, 2004.

Staub, Jack. *Alluring Lettuces: And Other Seductive Vegetables for Your Garden*. Layton, UT: Gibbs Smith Publishing, 2005.

———. *The Illustrated Book of Edible Plants*. Layton, UT: Gibbs Smith Publishing, 2016.

Stewart, Amy. *The Drunken Botanist*. Chapel Hill, NC: Algonquin Books, 2013.

Storl, Wolf D. *A Curious History of Vegetables: Aphrodisiacal and Healing Properties, Folk Tales, Garden Tips, and Recipes*. Berkeley, CA: North Atlantic Books, 2016.

Tenney, Louise. *Today's Herbal Health*. Pleasant Grove, UT: Woodland Publishing, 1997.

Tusser, Thomas. *Five Hundred Points of Good Husbandrie.* London: Tuber & Co. 1573. Project Gutenberg, 2016. https://www.gutenberg.org/files/51764/51764-h/51764-h.htm.

United States School Garden Army. *Forty Lessons in Gardening for the Northeastern States.* Washington, DC: Bureau of Education, 1919.

Van Wyk, Ben-Erik. *Food Plants of the World: An Illustrated Guide.* Portland, OR: Timber Press, 2006.

Wentz, W. Y. Evans. *The Fairy-Faith in Celtic Countries.* Oxford, UK: Oxford University Press, 1911.

Wohlleben, Peter. *The Hidden Life of Trees: What They Feel, How They Communicate.* Vancouver: Greystone Books, 2016.

Zak, Victoria. *The Magic Teaspoon: Transform Your Meals with the Power of Healing Herbs and Spices.* New York: Berkley Books, 2006.

Journal Articles

Baluška, František, and Stefano Mancuso. "Plant Neurobiology: From Stimulus Perception to Adaptive Behavior of Plants, via Integrated Chemical and Electrical Signaling." *Plant Signaling and Behavior* 4, no. 6 (June 2009): 475–76. doi:10.4161/psb.4.6.8870.

Berger, Joel, Tshewang Wangchuk, Cristobal Briceño, Alejandro Vila, and Joanna E. Lambert. "Disassembled Food Webs and Messy Projections: Modern Ungulate Communities in the Face of Unabating Human Population Growth." *Frontiers in Ecology and Evolution* 8, no. 128 (2020). doi:10.3389/fevo.2020.00128.

Borek, Carmia. "Garlic Reduces Dementia and Heart-Disease Risk." *Journal of Nutrition* 136, suppl. 3 (March 2006): 810S–12S. doi:10.1093/jn/136.3.810S.

Braatz, Elizabeth Y., Zachariah J. Gezon, Kristin Rossetti, Lily T. Maynard, Jonathan S. Bremer, Geena M. Hill, Marissa A. Streifel, and Jaret C. Daniels. "Bloom Evenness Modulates the Influence of Bloom Abundance on Insect Community Structure in Suburban Gardens." *PeerJ* 9 (April 2021): e11132. doi:10.7717/peerj.11132.

Brenner, Eric D., Rainer Stahlberg, Stefano Mancuso, Jorge Vivanco, Frantisek Baluska, and Elizabeth Van Volkenburgh. "Plant Neurobiology: An Integrated View of Plant Signaling," *Trends in Plant Science* 11, no. 8 (August 2006): 413–19. doi:10.1016/j.tplants.2006.06.009.

Giulia, Pastorino, Laura Cornara, Sónia Soares, Francisca Rodrigues, and M. Beatriz P. P. Oliveira. "Liquorice (*Glycyrrhiza glabra*): A Phytochemical and Pharmacological Review." *Phytotherapy Research* 32, no. 12 (December 2018): 2323–39, doi: https://www.ncbi.nlm.nih.gov/pmc/articles/PMC7167772.

Hina Malhotra, Vandana, Sandeep Sharma, and Renu Pandey. "Phosphorus Nutrition: Plant Growth in Response to Deficiency and Excess." *Plant Nutrients and Abiotic Stress Tolerance* (2018): 171–90. doi:10.1007/978-981-10-9044-8_7.

Hirsch, Alan R., Maryann Schroder, Jason Gruss, Charlene Bermele, and Deborah Zagorski. "Scentsational Sex Olfactory Stimuli and Sexual Response in the Human Female." *International Journal of Aromatherapy* 9, no. 2 (1998–1999): 75–81. https://doi.org/10.1016/S0962-4562(98)80023-4.

Hudson, James, and Selvarani Vimalanathan, "Echinacea—A Source of Potent Antivirals for Respiratory Virus Infections," *Pharmaceuticals* 4, no. 7 (July 2001): 1019–31, doi:10.3390/ph4071019.

Jansen, Suze A., Iris Kleerekooper, Zonne L. M. Hofman, Isabelle F. P. M. Kappen, Anna Stary-Weinzinger, and Marcel A. G. van der Heyden. "Grayanotoxin Poisoning: 'Mad Honey Disease' and Beyond." *Cardiovascular Technology* 12, no. 3 (2012): 208–15. doi:10.1007/s12012-012-9162-2.

Kandeler, Riklef, and Wolfram R. Ullrich. "Symbolism of Plants: Examples from European-Mediterranean Culture Presented with Biology and History of Art: SEPTEMBER: Cornflower." *Journal of Experimental Botany* 60, no. 12 (2009): 3297–99. https://doi.org/10.1093/jxb/erp247.

Lowry, C. A., J. H. Hollis, A. de Vries, B. Pan, L. R. Brunet, J. R. F. Hunt, J. F. R. Paton, et al. "Identification of an Immune-Responsive Mesolimbocortical Serotonergic System: Potential Role in Regulation of Emotional Behavior." *Neuroscience* 146, no. 2 (May 2007): 756–72. doi:10.1016/j.neuroscience.2007.01.067.

Mathew, B. C., and R. S. Biju. "Neuroprotective Effects of Garlic: A Review." *Libyan Journal of Medicine* 3, no 1. (2008): 23–33. doi:10.4176/071110.

Majewski, Michał. "Allium sativum: Facts and Myths Regarding Human Health." *Roczniki Pantswowego Zakladu Higieny* 65, no. 1 (2014): 1–8. https://pubmed.ncbi.nlm.nih.gov/24964572/.

Noda, Y., T. Kneyuki, K. Igarashi, A. Mori, and L. Packer. "Antioxidant Activity of Nasunin, an Anthocyanin in Eggplant Peels." *Toxicology* 148, no. 2 (August 2000): 119–23. doi:10.1016/s0300-483x(00)00202-x.

Rafati-Rahimzadeh, Mehrdad, Mehravar Rafati-Rahimzadeh, Sohrab Kazemi, and Ali Akbar Moghadamnia. "Current Approaches of the Management of Mercury Poisoning: Need of the Hour." *DARU Journal of Pharmaceutical Sciences* 22, no. 1 (2014): 46. doi:10.1186/2008-2231-22-46.

Saki, Kourosh, Mahmoud Bahmani, Mahmoud Rafieian-Kopaei, Hassan Hassanzadazar, Kamran Dehghan, Fariba Bahmani, and Jafar Asadzadeh. "The Most Common Native Medicinal Plants Used for Psychiatric and Neurological Disorders in Urmia City, Northwest of Iran." *Asian Pacific Journal of Tropical Disease* 4, suppl. 2 (2014): S895–S901. doi:10.1016/S2222-1808(14)60754-4.

Yan, Wei, Ting-yu Wang, Qi-ming Fan, Lin Du, Jia-ke Xu, Zan-jing Zhai, Hao-wei Li, and Ting-ting Tang. "Plumbagin Attenuates Cancer Cell Growth and Osteoclast Formation in the Bone Microenvironment of Mice." *Acta Pharmacologica Sinica* 35 (January 2014): 124–34. doi:10.1038/aps.2013.152.

Zgair, Atheer, Jonathan C. M. Wong, Jong Bong Lee, Jatin Mistry, Olena Sivak, Kishor M. Wasan, Ivo M. Hennig, et. al. "Dietary Fats and Pharmaceutical Lipid Excipients Increase Systemic Exposure to Orally Administered Cannabis and Cannabis-Based Medicines." *American Journal of Translational Research* 8, no. 8 (August 2016): 3448–59. https://www.ncbi.nlm.nih.gov/pmc/articles/PMC5009397/.

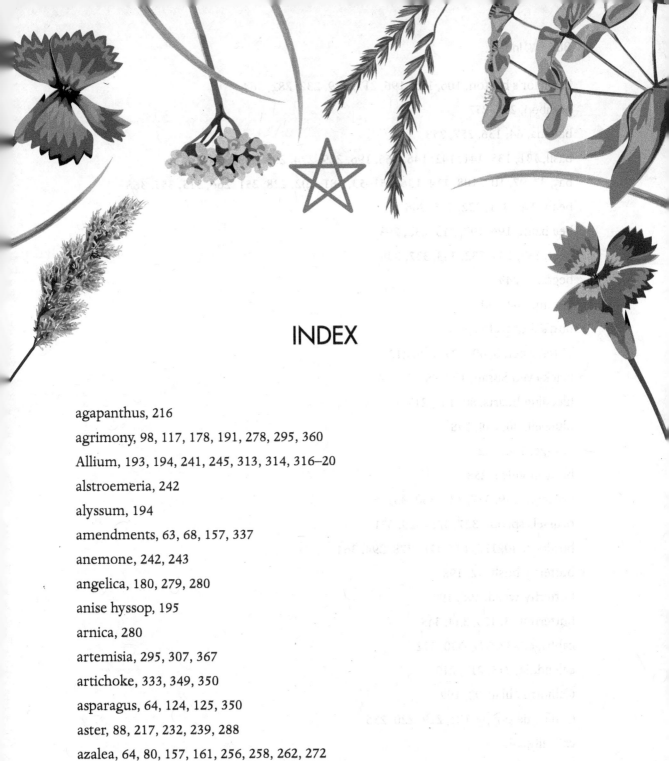

INDEX

To Write to the Author

If you wish to contact the author or would like more information about this book, please write to the author in care of Llewellyn Worldwide Ltd. and we will forward your request. Both the author and the publisher appreciate hearing from you and learning of your enjoyment of this book and how it has helped you. Llewellyn Worldwide Ltd. cannot guarantee that every letter written to the author can be answered, but all will be forwarded. Please write to:

Laurel Woodward
 Llewellyn Worldwide
2143 Wooddale Drive
Woodbury, MN 55125-2989
Please enclose a self-addressed stamped envelope for reply,
or $1.00 to cover costs. If outside the U.S.A., enclose
an international postal reply coupon.

Many of Llewellyn's authors have websites with additional information and resources. For more information, please visit our website at http://www.llewellyn.com.